"*Net Positive* is a must-read for business leaders. Paul's wisdom comes from years of authentic delivery of net positive and hugely successful businesses. Packed with practical and visionary stories, it will spark a movement of courageous action toward a better way of doing business for people and the planet. A wonderful rallying call to business leaders all over the world to step up to the greatest opportunity, and responsibility, of our time."

  —**SIR RICHARD BRANSON**, founder, Virgin Group

"*Net Positive* will be pure heresy to all those who still subscribe to the failed dogma of shareholder primacy—which is exactly why we need it. Paul Polman and Andrew Winston weave together the most profound corporate lessons of our time to give us a vastly more ambitious, and more hopeful, vision for the place of business in our shared future."

  —**ARIANNA HUFFINGTON**, founder and CEO, Thrive Global

"*Net Positive* makes a compelling and inspiring case that businesses can—and should—boost their bottom lines by contributing to their communities and protecting the environment."

  —**AL GORE**, 45th Vice President of the United States;
   Nobel Peace Prize winner; and
   Chairman, Generation Investment Management

"Polman and Winston have written a book for leaders that is carefully considered and deeply rooted in the real world of management. The authors are as obsessed as my company is with helping the world get better by transforming every business and every community. The financial success of an enterprise is both dependent upon and helps to advance connections to employees, communities, business partners, and the public sector."

  —**SATYA NADELLA**, Chairman and CEO, Microsoft

"Don't call it a 'business book.' *Net Positive* fundamentally rethinks the way human beings—CEOs, politicians, and activists—can together reset our planet's trajectory. The authors understand that we have the technology and science we need—it's the mindset revolution that now matters most."

  —**PAUL HAWKEN**, author, *Drawdown* and *Regeneration*

"Paul knows that when leading CEOs stand up for a more equitable world, governments are much more likely to do the same. Corporate courage unlocks political ambition and *Net Positive* shows us how."

—**NGOZI OKONJO-IWEALA**, Director-General, World Trade Organization; Finance Minister of Nigeria 2003–2006 and 2011–2015

"*Net Positive* turns courage and principled action into an electrifying strategy for business success. It's powerful, persuasive, and unlike any other book you've read."

—**KEN FRAZIER**, Executive Chairman, Merck

"It is in companies' own self-interest to bring their ingenuity and resources to a system that helps everyone succeed. *Net Positive* offers a new frame of mind, seeing not just the long-term benefits but also the immediate wins of getting profit and purpose to work for one another."

—**AJAY BANGA**, Executive Chairman, Mastercard

"*Net Positive* is an unassailable argument for embracing stakeholder capitalism. Every business leader should read this book."

—**MARC BENIOFF**, Chair and CEO, Salesforce

"*Net Positive* should be embedded across every business school curriculum. Its lessons bridge business, environmental, and social disciplines, using real and recent case studies to inspire the next generation of leaders. The clear message is: the net positive transformation can be done, and soon it will be our turn."

—**CELIA BRAVARD**, MBA/MS candidate, Erb Institute, University of Michigan

"This is an important book about the challenges facing business and the actions needed to transition to a net positive future. It is refreshingly direct in pointing out the courage needed as well as the respect for what it takes."

—**JESPER BRODIN**, CEO, IKEA, Ingka Group

"More than a CEO handbook, *Net Positive* plots a path to a new, more resilient social contract between C-suites and their employees. Paul and Andrew deliver the most compelling explanation yet of how to build a flourishing business by valuing your people and respecting our planet."

—**SHARAN BURROW**, General Secretary, International Trade Union Confederation

"Net positive companies are mission-critical in driving stable, inclusive, climate-protecting markets. This is as much a financial transformation story as a business how-to."

—**MARK CARNEY**, Governor of the Bank of England 2013–2020;
United Nations Special Envoy for Climate Action and Finance

"*Net Positive* is a must-read for anyone trying to build a successful company in growth markets. The principles explored in this book need to be built into the very foundations of the private sector, especially in this era of rapid change. Really, this is the future of business."

—**N. CHANDRASEKARAN**, Chairman, Tata Sons

"The tasty story of how mayo beat ketchup evolves into a master class on how CEOs and other leaders can lead the shift from degenerative to regenerative business models. A must-read."

—**JOHN ELKINGTON**, founder and Chief Pollinator, Volans;
author, *Green Swans*

"Polman and Winston don't shrink from the scale of our planetary challenges, and yet they leave you with much more hope than fear. The net positive train is leaving the station, and the bravest, smartest leaders are already on board."

—**CHRISTIANA FIGUERES**, cofounder, Global Optimism;
Executive Secretary of the UN Framework Convention on
Climate Change 2010–2016; and coauthor, *The Future We Choose*

"*Net Positive* doesn't just puncture—it totally annihilates—the myth that profitable business and a thriving society need somehow to be at odds. More than that, it sets out a compelling and hopeful vision, matched with a practical guide, on how business can unlock the keys to a fairer, more sustainable future. Paul's bias for impact and lessons from the front line of change at Unilever ring loudly."

—**ALAN JOPE**, CEO, Unilever

"For every business leader who understands that making a positive impact on the world is the only viable long-term strategy but doesn't know how to do it, here's your guide. No one is suggesting that going net positive is easy, but it is worth fighting for it. This is where our future lies."

—**ISABELLE KOCHER**, CEO of ENGIE Group, 2016–2020

"Investors are waking up to the fact that business can and should be profitable by serving societies, but many still don't know how to engage with companies in this direction. *Net Positive* hands these investors the insights they need to shape boardroom discussions and hold C-suites to account."

—**HIRO MIZUNO**, UN Special Envoy on Innovative Finance
and Sustainable Investments; Chief Investment Officer,
Government Pension Investment Fund of Japan, 2015–2020

"The beauty of *Net Positive* is its scale. Overhaul companies, shift industries, transform markets, put capitalism in greater service of the world."

—**JACQUELINE NOVOGRATZ**, founder and CEO, Acumen

"Paul Polman has been the world's most powerful business voice for the idea that business can thrive by paying attention to building societies that thrive. I was proud to serve alongside him on the UN panel that wrote the first draft of the Sustainable Development Goals. Now he has come forward with *Net Positive*, a radically different vision for the relationship between business, civil society, and government, replacing short-term self-interest with enlightened long-term partnership for our common goals. Business leaders would do well to listen to his bold and innovative ideas for the net positive advocacy that our societies desperately need."

—**JOHN PODESTA**, Chair, Center for American Progress;
White House Chief of Staff to President Bill Clinton
and counselor to President Barack Obama

"This book detonates the idea that net zero takes us far enough. It will be extremely uncomfortable reading for corporate laggards and the vested interests that support them."

—**MARY ROBINSON**, President of Ireland, 1990–1997;
UN High Commissioner for Human Rights 1997–2002;
Chair, The Elders

"The world faces a deep and interwoven set of global challenges, spanning health, growth, inequality, climate change, and biodiversity. They demand new and urgent collaborations from public authorities and the private sector. Polman and Winston both demonstrate the scale and urgency of these challenges and show business precisely how it must transform to embrace this new era of partnership and become a powerful force for economic and social renewal. It is an immensely important contribution."

—**NICK STERN**, Professor of Economics and Government and
Chair of the Grantham Research Institute on Climate Change
and the Environment, London School of Economics

"We don't just need net positive companies, we need a net positive movement. This book can start it."

—**PROFESSOR MUHAMMAD YUNUS**, Nobel Peace Prize winner;
founder, Grameen Bank

PAUL POLMAN + ANDREW WINSTON

net positive

HOW COURAGEOUS COMPANIES THRIVE BY GIVING MORE THAN THEY TAKE

Harvard Business Review Press

Boston, Massachusetts

HBR Press Quantity Sales Discounts

Harvard Business Review Press titles are available at significant quantity discounts. Special editions, including books with corporate logos, customized covers, and letters from the company or CEO printed in the front matter, as well as excerpts of existing books, can also be created in large quantities for special needs.

For details and discount information for both print and
ebook formats, contact booksales@harvardbusiness.org,
tel. 800-988-0886, or www.hbr.org/bulksales.

The web addresses referenced in this book were live and correct at the time of the book's publication but may be subject to change.

Editorial production by Christine Marra, *Marra*thon Production Services.
www.marrathoneditorial.org

Library of Congress Cataloging-in-Publication Data
Names: Polman, Paul, author. | Winston, Andrew S., author.
Title: Net positive : how courageous companies thrive by giving more than they take / Paul Polman and Andrew Winston
Description: Boston, MA : Harvard Business Review Press, [2021] | Includes index.
Identifiers: LCCN 2021021327 (print) | LCCN 2021021328 (ebook) | ISBN 9781647821302 (hardcover) | ISBN 9781647821319 (ebook)
Subjects: LCSH: Business ethics. | Values. | Sustainability. | International business enterprises—Moral and ethical aspects.
Classification: LCC HF5387 .P655 2021 (print) | LCC HF5387 (ebook) | DDC 658.4/08—dc23
LC record available at https://lccn.loc.gov/2021021327
LC ebook record available at https://lccn.loc.gov/2021021328

The paper used in this publication meets the requirements of the American National Standard for Permanence of Paper for Publications and Documents in Libraries and Archives Z39.48-1992

In printing this book, we have used natural inks and paper from responsibly managed forests for both the jacket and the text.

In service of the billions of people worldwide who are still left behind, and who deserve courageous leaders who will stand with them in building a better world

CONTENTS

PREFACE

From Paul

To tell you the truth, I have long hesitated to write a book as I have always felt that most of what I would say has been said or, as is the case for many CEOs, would be seen as an ill-conceived attempt to rewrite one's own history. That never appealed to me. However, Adi Ignatius, the editor in chief of Harvard Business Review, convinced me of the importance of sharing Unilever's and my own transformational story with a broader audience, as well as thoughts on where we need to go. The prospect of writing it with Andrew Winston made me finally decide to go ahead. I have long admired Andrew for his books *The Big Pivot* and *Green to Gold*, which I have leveraged extensively while running Unilever. Both books were ahead of their time. If only we would have listened then.

Thanks also goes to Jeff Seabright who is not only a dear friend but, as sustainability officer for Unilever, was also a great sparring partner in transforming our business model for the better and in helping us put this book together. His good memory, wise advice, and sense of humor are clearly better than mine.

I am writing this preface over Easter while in the Netherlands where my ninety-two-years-young, beautiful mother has just left us. I am glad I could spend the last few weeks with her. She has been a great inspiration and I owe much to her. As a schoolteacher who had to give up her beloved profession in the 1950s, simply because she was a woman raising a family, she taught us the importance of education.

Having lived through WWII, she knew the power of giving herself to the service of others, rebuilding destroyed communities, and working on a more peaceful and inclusive environment for all. Values like dignity and respect, equity and compassion came naturally to her and my father as they raised six children.

Easter for many Christians has traditionally been a time of new beginnings and that's how we are celebrating my mother's passing right now, but it is also a great metaphor for the need to create a better world where we can all live in harmony with each other and Mother Nature now and for generations to come. Covid-19 was perhaps a rude awakening, seeming to tell us that we cannot have healthy people on an unhealthy planet. The complex relationships between biodiversity loss, climate change, inequality, economic growth, and social cohesion have become increasingly transparent to many. So have the cracks in our economic system. We have come to realize that infinite growth on a finite planet is simply not possible. And anything we can't do forever is by definition unsustainable. Ultimately, we will reach a point where systems will collapse—indeed, this is happening.

I have also long believed that an economic system where still too many people feel they are not fully participating or are left behind will ultimately rebel against itself. We are seeing ample evidence of this, including in the political system where the strength of democracies and global cooperation are being tested in many ways. Of all the challenges, we need to single out climate change and inequality as the most pertinent ones we must all address. Not surprisingly, the two are closely related. In the absence of a full and robust multilateralism and in the face of increasing short termism, of politics especially, it is imperative for responsible businesses to step up and fill this void—not alone, but in new forms of partnership with governments and civil society.

This book is not only about some of the ways this can be done, but more important, why it's good for business itself. This is the idea of net positive. We did not want to debate capitalism here but instead, in a practical way, to argue for the changing role that business must play to continue to earn its license to operate. We say simply that profits should come not from creating the world's problems, but from solving them.

We wanted to make a book that is light on the "why," as most of us are convinced of the direction of travel needed, and instead focuses on the "how" where more of us struggle. The task is indeed difficult and complex, with many of the challenges outside our own control. Sometimes, it feels overwhelming. But for those of us in positions of responsibility, we know that denial, blaming others, or running away from it is not where the answers lie.

Above all, it requires a different kind of leadership, with courage being an important part of that. Courage to assume responsibility for your total societal impacts well beyond your own operations. Courage to set the higher ambitions you know are needed, even if you don't have all the answers. Courage to embrace the broader partnerships needed to drive the wider system changes. Courage comes from the French word *coeur*, which means "heart." Indeed in a business and policy world increasingly dictated by spreadsheets, computers, and fast trading, it's about bringing back the human element missing in so many places. As businesses will increasingly compete on trust, compassion and care will play an important role.

As Desmond Tutu said once when asked whether he was optimistic or pessimistic, "I am a prisoner of hope." While the moral case was made a long time ago, we simply cannot wait for the arc of history to bend the right way on its own. Fortunately, the economic case is increasingly attractive as well—as we point out in the book, we might be sitting on the biggest business opportunity ever. As we all try to avoid another pandemic or systems collapse, we are finding more and more that the cost of inaction is becoming significantly higher than the cost of action. Unlike when we started the Unilever journey based on conviction, we now have the economic evidence and incentive.

Although the Unilever model has shown its successes and shortcomings over the past ten years, as extensively discussed in the book, we all realize that we need to move faster and farther. A net positive approach not only prepares you to be competitive today, but more important, positions you well to be among the winning companies and industries of the future. Being a leader is a privileged position and there is nothing more gratifying than leveraging it to serve others and creating a better world for all. After all, the only impossible journey is the one you never begin.

—April 2021

From Andrew

At the start of the pandemic in 2020, as we dove into this book, I turned fifty and approached the twenty-year mark of working in corporate sustainability. I found myself looking back and assessing my progress in life. On the personal front, my wife and I raised two boys, an eighteen-year-old who was toddling around as I wrote my first book, *Green to Gold*, and the other born the day it came out fifteen years ago. They will judge how well we helped them become compassionate humans who care about the world.

On the professional side, it's harder to assess. My mission is to inspire companies to solve our biggest environmental and social challenges, not for philanthropy, but because it's good business. I think about progress at the macro level: in the struggle to move the business world away from short-term profit obsession—and toward purposeful, long-term value creation—are we winning?

Yes and no.

The number of companies addressing their environmental and social impacts has been rising fast. No large company seriously questions that sustainability is on the agenda. We won the first battle, but big problems remain. Our economic model, which overuses resources, encourages unfettered consumption, and pours wealth into a few hands, is hurtling us toward a cliff. The global challenges we're trying to solve (climate change in particular) are getting worse. We're not going fast enough.

We need companies to go far beyond just cutting some carbon emissions and being less bad; the work must move into positive impact territory. Unfortunately, the number of business leaders who have fully internalized this reality is insignificant. The world needs more courageous leaders willing to commit their organizations to deep change and serving the world.

A colleague once asked me, "Why are there so few Ray Andersons?" referring to the CEO of the carpet manufacturer Interface. In 1994, Ray had an epiphany: business as usual was a dead end for the planet. So, he focused his company on eliminating all negative impacts on the world. He was a pioneer and an inspiration—Ray's *Mid-Course Correction* was the first book I read in the field. Still, I said to my friend, shouldn't we also ask, "Why are there so few Paul Polmans?"

Why Paul? Early leaders like Ray, Patagonia's Yvon Chouinard, and entrepreneur Paul Hawken started the journey, but mostly led midsized, founder-owned businesses. Some large companies, like Walmart, were moving down the path, but nobody had tried to do what Paul was attempting: make sustainability the core mission of a world-straddling, public company with tens of billions in sales. Paul was all in. Like Ray, he spoke truth to CEO peers and world leaders, tirelessly making the case for a fundamentally different way of running a company and highlighting the failures of business as usual. Paul was mission-driven, but also focused on business success for the long term.

I loved it, and I haven't been alone. An annual survey asks experts to identify companies that are doing the best job of integrating sustainability into strategy. For ten straight years, Unilever has been the most frequently cited. That's a remarkable level of consistency in any dimension of company performance. Some will decry a consumer products company being named a sustainability leader, saying they produce a lot of stuff we don't need. That has an element of truth, but given the scale of our challenges, we can't build a thriving world without business.

We need more leaders willing to challenge the status quo, and we should celebrate those who do. I hope we stop lionizing CEOs such as GE's Jack Welch, who had great execution skills, but valued short-term shareholder profits above the planet and people—a style of business, dominant for decades, where firing employees makes a stock *rise*.

In the 2010s, I sat on Unilever's North American sustainability advisory board, so I'm not unbiased. But I had only met Paul a few times before he, and his top sustainability adviser Jeff Seabright, approached me about writing a book together. I wasn't sure I would publish another book on sustainability strategy, but this was a unique opportunity to explore how to build a company that serves the world. Part of Unilever's story has been well told, but not yet from the perspective of the person who led the charge. *Net Positive* is not solely about Unilever, but the company's experience is the motivating force. My job was to add an external point of view, synthesize, find the frameworks within the story, and make it accessible and easy to read.

In the end, "How do we create more Paul Polmans?" isn't the right question. No matter how much we celebrate (and overpay) CEOs, no leader can build a great company alone. If success came exclusively from the C-suite, then every MBA class and business book would focus only on leadership. Companies also need key principles, strategies, tactics, partners, and the intangible elements of culture, purpose, and inspiration. Every organization is unique, but there are ideas and lessons from the pioneers that can help all businesses do better. This book tries to provide a map and a compass, but not mark the trail precisely—we all need our own pathway.

My goal for *Net Positive* is to inspire the business community to step up, accelerate, and help lead us toward a thriving world. I hope this work, and the ripples from it, make my own life net positive.

—April 2021

Why Mayo Beat Ketchup

The Hostile Takeover Bid that Tells a Deeper Story

In early 2017, Unilever faced a near-death experience. The company was seven years into its ambitious strategy, the Unilever Sustainable Living Plan (USLP), which made purpose and enriching others' lives core to the business. It was making good progress on its aggressive goals, including doubling sales while cutting its environmental footprint in half, and helping a billion people improve their health and well-being. With a small handful of other corporate leaders, Unilever was helping redefine what being a good company means.

The strategy was working. After years of low or no growth, revenue was up 33 percent to $60 billion, and the company's stock had outperformed both its peers and the broader European FTSE index. Unilever is a sprawling, truly global company, connecting with 2.5 billion people every day through one of its three hundred–plus brands, including Axe, Ben & Jerry's, Clear, Dove, Hellmann's (mayo), Knorr, Lifebuoy, Omo, Rexona, and Suave. As part of its USLP strategy, the company acquired dozens of new brands, most of them mission-driven companies, and divested of slower-moving businesses that didn't fit the vision.

So, when Alexandre Behring, the chairman of rival Kraft Heinz (best known for its ketchup), came to visit Unilever's headquarters in London, CEO Paul Polman (coauthor) thought Behring might make an offer on one of the businesses for sale. But the meeting veered in a dramatically different direction. Behring offered to acquire *all* of Unilever for $143 billion, an 18 percent premium over the market price.[1] Hostile takeovers sometimes come with a smile. But they're still hostile, and they can destroy the soul of a business built up over a century.

Kraft Heinz had been acquired just two years earlier by Brazilian private equity firm 3G and Berkshire Hathaway, run by legendary investor Warren Buffett. The two investors were working together on this deal as well. 3G had never lost a takeover bid, but that would change over just nine intense days.

3G was well known for slashing expenses to increase short-term margins. A *Fortune* magazine article described 3G CEO Jorge Paulo Lemann as "the man who eats costs."[2] The consumer products industry was split between those racing alongside Kraft Heinz to leverage up, cut costs, increase margins, and pay little in taxes . . . and those who, as the *Financial Times* put it, "recoiled at what they view as a model that ultimately destroys businesses by starving them of investment."[3]

For companies selling similar products, Kraft Heinz and Unilever could not have had two more different business models. 3G was a perfect example of what shareholder primacy looks like in action. Unilever was intent on operating for the benefit of the many groups of people touched by the company (its stakeholders) in service of a better world. It has a 140-year history of purpose, going back to its original mission of improving hygiene in Victorian England.

Today, the USLP honors and expands on the company's roots, and represents one of the most comprehensive integrated business plans in the world. It clearly links sustainable and equitable operations to business performance and growth. The goal of the USLP is financial gain *because* of sustainability, not despite it—not profits with a side of purpose, but profits *through* purpose. Over many years, Unilever learned that whenever a focus on purpose was lacking, the company's performance suffered. So, being swallowed by an organization with an incompatible mission was potentially disastrous strategically and financially.

Unilever executives would have made a lot of money on the deal, but the chasm between 3G's and Unilever's strategies and values made the offer unacceptable. The business model was too important to put in the hands of people with no feel for long-term value creation. It was clear what had happened to companies that 3G bought. Organizations doing great work—such as beverage leader SABMiller, through its water and human rights projects in Africa—got squeezed in the 3G cost-cutting vise. A number of escapees from 3G acquisitions had come to Unilever seeking work with a purpose-driven company.

At this pivotal time, Unilever's leaders were not immune to the appeal of cost control and margin growth. They believed strongly in business performance and efficiency, but also knew that you can't cut your way to prosperity. Slashing people, R&D, or brand spending just to give investors a sugar rush of higher margins today was a recipe for disaster later. Unilever's leaders believed that by using the business model they knew best, they could unlock more value over the long term than 3G could. They would lean into purpose, continue to invest in the future, and improve the top *and* bottom lines (which they had done for seven straight years).

It was a stressful time with intense pressure to sell. Paul didn't want to be the one who handed over a century-old, responsible company to a firm like 3G, thinking, *Not on my watch.* To reject the bid, Unilever needed support from friends and needed to move quickly.

The Power of Unexpected Allies

For years, Unilever skeptics had been eager to see the company stumble. Many mainstream investors who preach shareholder primacy found the sustainability thing too hippie. But Unilever's model was working. At the time of the takeover bid, Unilever's operating margins were not at the top of the peer pack, but higher than those of competitors Nestlé, Danone, and Mondelez. Its revenue and bottom line were growing faster as well. Unilever consistently delivered 19 percent return on invested capital. It was creating long-term, reliable shareholder value, but as a result of its business model, not as the primary goal.

Still, the premium 3G offered sent a message: current leadership is leaving value on the table in the short term. That impression would normally be enough to ensure a successful bid, but 3G and Unilever's critics underestimated how strongly the leadership, the board, and unexpected allies cared about the company's approach to business. Critics had accused the company of spending too much time working with communities, governments, and the United Nations, and not enough on short-term profit-maximizing. But building those alliances paid off in a major way.

NGO and union leaders were among those who lined up in support. John Sauven, the head of Greenpeace UK—an organization that had scaled the headquarter buildings of Unilever, P&G, Nestlé, and many others to protest corporate misdeeds—had grown to trust the company, and he called to see whether he could help. Ron Oswald, the general secretary of the IUF—a federation of unions representing ten million workers in the agricultural and hospitality industries—went public opposing the bid. The IUF was fearful, he says, that Unilever's model "would be wiped from the face of the earth . . . Kraft Heinz was the epitome of what a company should not be: pure financial engineering."[4]

Public pressure mounted against the deal. Letters to Unilever's board urged it, as one investor wrote, "not to fall into the [short-term value] trap of Kraft Heinz."[5] Some high-profile Unilever supporters contacted Warren Buffett directly to express their displeasure. Still, Unilever execs were unsure that all the support would sway a majority of investors to side with them. The investors had strong incentives to cash in to meet their own quarterly targets (they also maximize short-term returns).

In the end, the substantial momentum opposing the takeover proved decisive. 3G lost support for the deal and had to back off. Unilever had dodged a bullet, thanks in part to the goodwill it had painstakingly earned by investing in partners and working with stakeholders on their net positive journey.

The Aftermath

The moment Kraft Heinz's Behring walked into Unilever HQ, investors faced a test: Which model of business will you invest in? The financial outcomes of that decision were substantial. The stock prices of the two consumer giants took off in different directions. Based on total shareholder returns, over the next few years, money put into Unilever yielded four times as much as the same amount invested in Kraft Heinz. Unilever's subsidiary, Hindustan Unilever, which trades separately on the Indian stock market, is now worth more than all of Kraft Heinz. Across Paul's full ten-year tenure, shareholders saw returns of nearly 300 percent.[6]

When the financial crisis that was tied to the 2020 pandemic hit, the relative strength of Unilever's model became clear. The company was in far better financial shape than 3G, with a stronger balance sheet. Unilever had the leeway to guarantee jobs for three months for both its direct and indirect employees.[7] It also allocated €500 million to support its partners, paying some suppliers early and extending credit to customers to help them stay afloat.[8] Meanwhile, in 2019, Kraft Heinz had to write down $15 billion and cut its dividend, and as its debt was reduced to a junk rating before the global pandemic lockdown—it then had to tap an emergency line of credit.[9]

The point here is not to revel in 3G's misfortune, but to highlight the differences in business models and outcomes. In a volatile, uncertain, complex, and ambiguous (VUCA) world, resilience is everything. Unilever's model yielded a strong financial position and deep connections to its employees, communities, business partners, and governments. Those relationships gave it speed. Within days of the lockdowns, Unilever reinvented supply chains to source and ship medical equipment, increasing the production of hand sanitizer, for example, by fourteen thousand times.[10] As billions of people changed their consumption habits overnight, Unilever moved quickly to shift employees between divisions and geographies. It assigned 300 of its 2,000 global procurement managers to focus on emergency supply chains in China. Unilever moved faster than its peers because of the trust it had built up with stakeholders over years.

Even in a grueling economic environment with so much disruption, Unilever did not sit still on its commitment to a long-term, multistakeholder business model. The company launched aggressive new goals, including carbon neutrality by 2039 and plans to label seventy thousand products with carbon footprint data.

While Unilever did not emerge from the failed takeover unchanged—the leadership team and board stepped up the company's short-term financial delivery—they remained firmly committed to the purpose-driven strategy. A long-term focus on serving stakeholders was too ingrained, and the value too clear, to retreat.

All businesses now face a profound choice: continue pursuing the shareholder-first model that forces shortsighted decisions, hurts business, and endangers our collective well-being . . . or build businesses that grow and prosper over the long haul by serving the world—that is, by giving more than they take.

A Better Model: The Net Positive Business

The Unilever versus Kraft Heinz standoff was not about which company makes better, more profitable condiments. Nor was it an academic exercise to debate in business school. It was a larger battle for the soul of business.

The companies represented two models at different ends of a spectrum. One serves a handful of owners of capital and funnels the gains to them. It maximizes shareholder returns and obsesses over cutting costs to raise profits *now*. It takes limited responsibility for externalities—or spillover impacts on others—of the business. The other model sees the purpose of business differently and aspires to thrive, over the long term, by serving all stakeholders. It helps the world tackle the biggest challenges, such as climate change, inequality and poverty, biodiversity loss, and racial divides. When people talk about the difference between shareholder and stakeholder capitalism, they're describing these two models.

The second model, which a small but growing number of companies pursue, is the only one fit for a thriving future and a stable society. But it needs to be pushed even further, so that businesses—through better operations, products, and services—create more value, attract more customers and partners, heal the planet, and increase the well-being of everyone they impact. Companies pursuing this model are better positioned for the future and ultimately more successful. Its time has come.

We're living in a unique era, with an incredible opportunity to reimagine the world and make business *net positive*.

What Is Net Positive?

The sustainable design gurus Bill McDonough and Michael Braungart suggest in their book, *The Upcycle*, that being "less bad" by reducing environmental impacts to zero leads us down the wrong path. We should instead create "more good." Take any business impact that you want to zero out, such as waste, accidents, or carbon. Normally, you would chart progress showing the metric going down. Instead, they say, flip the chart; draw the line rising from negative to zero, so that zero "becomes not a culminating point, but a crossing point," and then keep going into positive territory.[11] A safety metric rising into positive territory would indicate not only zero accidents but the creation of a "health-*producing* workplace." Going further, the organization might also make communities and customers healthier. Those positive impacts contribute to what many call the "handprint" of the business, distinct from the footprint that has more negative connotations.

A net positive business serves others. It follows the oldest moral guidepost we have, the Golden Rule, or "Do unto others as you would have them do unto you." This maxim, Kim Polman writes in her book *Imaginal Cells: Visions of Transformation*, has been "the bedrock of humanity, underlying our most successful religions and cultures."[12] To live by the Rule, a net positive business lives within natural boundaries or thresholds to respect the planet and its inhabitants. It observes moral boundaries for how we treat each other, and it tries to repair, restore, reinvigorate, and regenerate.

With that framing in mind, our vision of net positive is *a business that improves well-being for everyone it impacts and at all scales—every product, every operation, every region and country, and for every stakeholder, including employees, suppliers, communities, customers, and even future generations and the planet itself.*

This is a North Star. No company can achieve all these aims at once, but it's where we should be heading if we want a viable economy and planet. To exist as a relevant business today is to enrich the world.

The ultimate question is this: Is the world better off because your business is in it?

Core principles. In chapter 1, we'll explore five principles that underpin a net positive business: taking responsibility for the company's impacts on the wider world; focusing more on the long term (while seeking good results in all time frames); serving multiple stakeholders and putting their needs first; embracing collaboration and transformative change beyond the company; and, as a result of all this work, providing shareholders with solid returns. Some of this will sound familiar to sustainability advocates, but there's talk and there's action. Saying "we're responsible" and acting like it are wildly different things. Serving stakeholders ahead of shareholders goes against fifty years of economic orthodoxy, the Milton Friedman view that the purpose of business is shareholder value (see the box "Milton Friedman Is Dead").

MILTON FRIEDMAN IS DEAD

For fifty years, every business leader in market-based economies has been trained in one core ideology—the purpose of business is to serve only the shareholder. So sayeth the prophet Milton Friedman. In the church of neo-liberal economics, the only metrics of well-being are financial—profits for companies, stock markets for economies, and GDP for countries. A handful of companies have offered different visions for years, but most have been considered fringe. In big, public companies, Friedman's philosophy has gone mostly unquestioned. But cracks are showing. Friedman himself might have a different view in the modern world, where company success is based on much more than it used to be. Either way, given the scale and urgency of climate change, the moral imperative of tackling inequality, and the changing nature of financial markets, the quarterly-focused, shareholder-first mantra is wildly unfit for today's world and is ultimately self-defeating. We must kill the old philosophy if we want to survive and thrive. The sooner we understand that, the better.

What it's not. Companies most often use the phrase "net positive," if they use it at all, narrowly to talk about carbon footprint (you'll also hear both "carbon negative" and "carbon positive," which, confusingly, mean essentially the same thing). That approach avoids real responsibility: buy some carbon offsets and you can claim the business is net positive. We don't see offsetting as the goal in the long term. Are you cutting pollution in one location, but leaving another factory belching asthma-causing particulates near low-income communities? That doesn't cut it. Or maybe you're using 100 percent renewables in your operations, but allowing the supply chain factories to rely mostly on diesel? Nope. The standards here are high.

Net positive is also different from shared value, a concept introduced by impact investor Jed Emerson (he called it "blended value") and built on by thought leaders Michael Porter and Mark Kramer. The idea is important, but could hold us back nearly as much as our obsession with shareholder value. Shared value doesn't negate the negative things a company does, and the ambition may be too low. If all large companies pursued it, would they think big enough to truly tackle climate change, inequality, and racism at the scale and speed we need? Would we get the multiplier effect of collective action and courage?

Net positive is also *not* about being perfect. It's about fixing the problems that cause negative impacts and going beyond to create positive value for others.

What it looks like. The net positive company will operate differently from what's normal today. It will, for example, eliminate more carbon than it produces; use only renewable energy and renewably sourced materials; create no waste and build everything for full circularity; and replenish and make cleaner all the water it draws. As a people-driven company, it will ensure everyone working in the value chain has the dignity of earning a living wage. The company will offer extensive opportunities for inclusion of all races and abilities, and achieve gender balance in management and pay equity. Through its products, services, and purpose-led initiatives—not philanthropy—consumers and communities will be better off. NGOs will be treated as equals and collaborators, not antagonists. Government leaders will find they have demanding partners, not self-serving lobbyists, trying to develop a system of rules that benefits all. And investors who support long-term value creation will reap healthy financial rewards.

Picture how specific sectors might profit and grow by serving customers and the world through their work. Imagine what net positive could look like when companies solve the biggest challenges, not contribute to them:

- Food and agriculture companies embracing regenerative practices, making the soil richer, protecting biodiversity, and sequestering millions of tons of carbon

- Aluminum, cement, and steel manufacturers developing carbon-free products and taking carbon out of the air

- Consumer products companies increasing human and planetary well-being with everything they sell

- Natural resource and material companies giving back to the earth and improving lives in the indigenous communities they impact

- Social media companies helping people find truth and strengthening the democratic process

- Apparel companies decoupling their growth from further resource use, providing living wages, restoring dignity, and helping develop communities in their supply chains around the world

- Financial companies funding only clean technologies and serving the poor better than the rich, giving people a hand up and creating equal opportunities for all

These kinds of companies will regenerate the world. If being green is about doing less damage, and sustainability about reaching zero, net positive is about making things better.

A Reality Check

Does this all sound too perfect? Perhaps. There are practical tradeoffs along the way, and you can't advance on every front at once. For example, Unilever has built factories in remote areas of developing countries to build local economies. Those regions may not have access to clean technologies yet. Running on coal or oil means taking a step back on the company's global renewables goal, but it's in service of stakeholder well-being. While balancing multiple needs, the whole enterprise should move in the right direction. It's a challenge, a journey, and a complicated dance, and you can't get there in one leap. The goal is to be better tomorrow than yesterday.

Let's be honest. No company embraces the ambition that we propose here . . . yet. No organization, including Unilever, is far enough along the journey. But a growing number of companies are embracing elements of the net positive business model. The majority-family-owned or privately held leaders include IKEA, Interface, Mars, Patagonia, Tata, and Triodos. The publicly held leaders group has expanded to include such companies as Allianz, Danone, DSM, Fifco, Levi's, L'Oréal, Marks & Spencer, Mastercard, Microsoft, Natura, Ørsted, Olam, Salesforce, and Trane Technologies (and we certainly missed some). None are remotely perfect, and you could find problems with them all, but they are moving in the right direction. Most appear regularly in a GlobeScan annual survey that asks experts to name the most sustainable companies. Every year since 2011, Unilever has ranked number one.[13] That's not a good sign of broader progress. We hope to accelerate a healthy race to the top.

The journey is not easy. Unilever has plenty of war wounds and mistakes to point to. The pursuit of 100 percent sustainable sourcing covering thousands of ingredients has not yet fully materialized. For some critical issues, such as the impacts of the palm oil industry, the overall results for people and planet are, so far, mixed. The company should have moved faster to attack some burning issues at scale, like plastic packaging and waste, racial diversity, and consumerism (changing people's habits is tough). But Unilever is guided by doing the harder right thing versus choosing the easier wrong. Its ambitions push it beyond its comfort zone. We're asking you to join us in this uncomfortable ambition.

The opportunity here is profound, rewarding, and even fun. It's a new way of thinking about creating business value. A company giving more than it takes will not focus on profits with a side of philanthropy. Instead, it embraces purpose in the core of the business and creates *value from values.*

This is a revolutionary way of thinking in modern business. But true innovation is almost always driven by rebels who force disruption. We need a profound shift for business to help lead the way, become the trusted player it can be, and solve problems that matter. The future of capitalism, humanity, and the planet depend on it.

Business Has to Step Up

For many people in civil society and NGOs, the idea of business creating a thriving world is laughable. The skeptics say that profit-obsessed companies got us into this mess. It's a fair point. Industry overuses resources, externalizes costs, and uses corruption and political influence to put its own needs above the common good. Critics also say that the challenges facing us are societal, and thus government must solve them. They are right, to an extent—only governments can establish rules and enforce prices, like a carbon fee, on externalities. Governments also set the right policies to enable better business practices and outcomes.

On the other side, libertarians suggest that the private sector can solve any problem. Just privatize everything and the profit motive will take care of it. Neither of these views are right. Dominic Waughray, who runs the Centre for Global Public Goods at the World Economic Forum, says, "It's charming, but naive, to think either large companies *or* governments will solve it all." We need a partnership, he says, with the innovation, speed, and execution mindset of the private sector with the convening power and reach of governments.[14]

Business will take a big role based solely on the reality of its oversize share of the economy: in developing countries, the private sector accounts for 60 percent of GDP, 80 percent of capital flows, and 90 percent of jobs.[15] But there are two additional reasons business has to step up. First, global governance is failing us, right as problems that know no boundaries are growing. The multilateral institutions that, mainly, the United Nations created eighty years ago (after WWII) cannot manage today's sprawling, complex problems, including climate change, cybersecurity, and pandemics.

Second, transforming the world will require shifting a ton of capital to cleaner, more just pathways. Governments face financial constraints placed by economic neoliberals who have driven tax rates down for years and defunded public works. Corruption also siphons away money from the common good. Few governments have the necessary funds to do what's required. The UN estimates that the financing gap to achieve some of the world's sustainable development goals is between $3 trillion and $5 trillion per year (a fraction of the spending on the global Covid-19 response of $16 trillion and growing), or about twenty times the total of *all* international development aid today.[16] The bill sounds high until you realize that the global GDP is about $80 trillion, and banks have created a $600 trillion market in derivatives and other made-up financial instruments.[17]

People *want* business to step up. In a global survey by Edelman, three-quarters of respondents say they would like CEOs to take the lead on social change, not wait for governments to impose it. A similar percentage want their own CEO to speak out on climate, inequality, and other big issues.[18] Leaders are hearing this message. Walmart's CEO Doug McMillon has said, "It's time for businesses to take the lead, working with government and NGOs on serious issues like workforce opportunity, racial equity, climate, and sustainable, responsible supply chains."[19] McMillon also told *Time*, "We simply won't be here if we don't take care of the very things that allow us to exist."[20]

Given its outsized role in society and in creating the mess we're in, business has a fundamental responsibility to help clean it up by moving to net positive action. It's also irrational to think business could stay on the sidelines and watch environmental systems degrade and society sink. *Business cannot be a bystander in a system that gives it life.*

Some Bad News: Our Planetary and Moral Emergencies

It's fair to ask *why* business needs to step up—that is, what's the burning platform? Unfortunately there are multiple emergencies, and we don't have much time (but there's also incredibly good news).

We humans have created an amazing and ruthless contraption, capitalism, to trade goods and efficiently match supply and demand. The machine has produced exponential economic growth and lifted hundreds of millions of people out of poverty. But it has also brought about existential crises that threaten humanity. *Our current economic system has two fundamental weaknesses: it's based on unlimited growth on a finite planet, and it benefits a small number of people, not everyone.*

Humanity's consumption of resources can't continue at this pace, unless we find another planet. In recent years, we've hit Earth Overshoot Day—an estimate of when we've used more resources that year than the earth can regenerate—by about August 22.[21] Every day after that, we are stealing from future generations. This system can't continue. Economist Ken Boulding once quipped, "Anyone who thinks that you can have infinite growth in a finite environment is either a madman or an economist."[22]

Markets are the main tool of infinite capitalism, but as currently designed, they have fatal flaws (not logically fatal, just deadly to us). Unless we force them to, markets do not include the price of externalities, those negative impacts like pollution or reduced health, nor do they charge us for the shared natural resources we use up. Markets also leave billions of people behind and funnel money upward. They do not optimize for collective well-being, or even for our survival.

To talk about our existential crises, we'll use "climate and inequality" as a blunt shorthand for a range of intertwined challenges that affect planetary and human health. Climate is a proxy for environmental issues, such as air and water quality, or biodiversity degradation, its own existential crisis; and inequality is a stand-in for social challenges, such as unequal access, systemic racism, gender discrimination, and lack of inclusion. Some measures of societal health have improved, like the reduction in the percentage of people in dire poverty, but most of our challenges are large and growing.

The biophysical underpinnings of our economy and society—a stable climate, a web of life we are embedded in, natural resources like clean air and water, and more—are all threatened. In less than five decades, populations of mammals, birds, amphibians, and fish have dropped a shocking 68 percent.[23] As we increase production of material goods and continue tearing down the forests of Indonesia and the Amazon (we've lost half the world's rainforest), we create deadly air pollution (nearly nine million people prematurely killed every year) and accelerate climate change.[24] The links between biodiversity, climate, human health, societal development, and economic growth are getting clearer. *We can't have healthy people on an unhealthy planet.*[25]

As global warming advances, an estimated one to three billion people will become climate refugees when their communities become too hot or too flooded to live in.[26] If we don't tackle climate, everything else is moot. Apple CEO Tim Cook has said, "The stakes are high and failure is not an option . . . if you have not developed [a plan on climate], you've failed at your job."[27]

At the same time, inequality has soared. The economy is failing to build a just world where wealth, power, and well-being are available to all. Racial inequities are rampant, which Covid-19 made very clear; it will long be a stain on the US soul that people of color suffered hospitalization and death rates two to four times higher than whites did.[28] (Indigenous people in Brazil were also twice as likely to die.[29]) Opportunities for women still lag badly as well; at the current pace of change, it will take 257 years to close the gender pay gap.[30]

The massive income and wealth gains of the last thirty-plus years have all gone to the top 1, or even 0.1, percent. The people living middle-income lives have gained no ground. Even before the pandemic, roughly half of the world population still earned less than $5.50 a day, 260 million kids were not getting education, 820 million people were going hungry, and 5.2 million children died every year before their fifth birthday because of mostly preventable infectious diseases.[31] All of these are worse now. As the secretary general of the UN António Guterres put it, a tiny number of people are sailing around in "superyachts while others are clinging to drifting debris."[32]

Some ask why inequality, however morally unacceptable, is a business issue. The basic answer is that economies don't thrive without a growing number of people having disposable income. But a harsher reality is that it destabilizes society. Mellody Hobson, co-CEO of Ariel Investments and chair of the board of Starbucks, says inequality is a threat to growth because "civil unrest is bad for business . . . and civil unrest is based in economic inequality."[33]

Our existential challenges carry a heavy economic toll. A RAND Corporation study estimated that if the income distribution in the United States had held steady from the mid-1970s, the bottom 90 percent would have gained $50 *trillion* in wealth.[34] The median income would have doubled from $50,000 to about $100,000 today.[35]

On the environmental side, Swiss Re estimates that half of global GDP ($42 trillion) is at risk because it is "dependent on high-functioning biodiversity."[36] For climate change, it's easy to find estimates of loss to global GDP in the trillions of dollars. Swiss Re says we're on track to lose nearly one-fifth of global GDP by 2050.[37] Those are specific and scary numbers, but an existential threat has a different, more binary calculus. What's the "cost" to coastal cities such as Miami, Dhaka, or Manila if they become unlivable? It's infinite. It may be easier to get your head around the costs to a particular organization. Over five years, AT&T has spent $1 billion repairing damaged equipment and infrastructure from climate-related weather extremes.[38] The harsh reality of rising costs is flipping the script, challenging businesses to prove why they *wouldn't* pursue sustainability (see the box "From Why? to Why Not?").

On top of profound environmental and social challenges, nationalist or populist leaders have gained great power and democracy has weakened in more than eighty countries.[39] The United States took a turn back toward democracy in the 2020 election, but the focus on self-interest, both personal and at the country level, remains. Nationalist governments will not readily collaborate on shared challenges.

Given our nearly broken system, it's not surprising that, in the early months of the pandemic, only 9 percent of British citizens wanted to go back to the way things were. (This desire is a global phenomenon).[40] People want to "build back better" or institute a Green New Deal. As governments invest tens of trillions into economic stimulus, it would be a tremendous waste of lives and dollars to re-create the old, broken system. We missed an

FROM WHY? TO WHY NOT?

It's normal to ask employees to prove any investment is worth it, but with sustainability, the assumption has long been that it's a bad use of money. It must, CFOs think, come at the expense of profitability or growth. The question from worried executives is often, "Why would I do this?" But as the costs of our big challenges rise, and the actions that build a thriving world get easier, cheaper, and more valuable, the discussion shifts. The evidence is mounting that shareholder primacy is a failed doctrine that destroys our natural environment and social cohesion. We've hit the tipping point. As ADM's CEO, Juan Luciano, has said, "Until recently, it seemed risky to be a leader; now it's riskier to be a laggard."* The burden of proof has flipped. "Show us what you care about," employees are yelling. "Tell us," stakeholders demand, "why *aren't* you pursuing purpose and sustainability?" Yes, why *wouldn't* you take part in this epic and exciting journey?

*Juan Luciano (ADM), in conversation with authors, May 15, 2020.

opportunity during the financial crisis in 2008 when banks were too big to fail, but people too small to matter. We should focus now on job creation, enhancing social cohesion, and accelerating the clean economy.

Changing the way business and the economy function, while continuing to produce goods and services for eight billion people, has been compared to changing the engine on a plane while it's flying. It's a good analogy that puts the famous innovator's dilemma in concrete terms. Destroying the old to make way for the new without stopping is a feat of engineering. It's also terrifying for those who lose out in the new world. It's easy to fall toward despair, fear, or anxiety, but we'll accomplish more coming from a place of positivity and compassion.

The choices we make now about investments in a low-carbon world, and in the well-being of people everywhere, will determine what's possible and if humanity thrives . . . or even survives. The stakes could not be higher for business or the global economy, which is, as the economist Herman Daly once noted, "a wholly owned subsidiary of the planet." Early sustainability pioneer Ray Anderson from Interface used to ask pointedly, "What's the case for doing business on a dead planet?" Similarly, there's no business case for enduring poverty and, in fact, vast business opportunity in lifting billions up.

In short, *businesses cannot thrive in societies that fail.*

Go Big and Think in Systems

Given what we're facing, the speed and scale of sustainability efforts have been woefully inadequate—especially on the climate crisis, where winning slowly is the same as losing. Of the world's five hundred largest companies, almost all have set energy or carbon goals, but only 15 percent plan to reduce their emissions at the pace science demands (this percentage *is* growing).[41] We're at a dangerous moment. Because they're doing *something*, companies may think they're doing enough. The fashion and apparel business, for example, was an early leader, creating the Sustainable Apparel Coalition to develop supply chain standards. But at the same time, fast fashion dramatically increased sales of apparel . . . and the energy, water, and waste impacts that came with it.

We can avoid these disconnects if we embrace systems thinking. The international sustainable development nonprofit Forum for the Future describes systems as "parts connected by a web of relationships toward a purpose," and offers examples from natural ecosystems like the marine environment and socially created systems, such as education. A human body, a home, a neighborhood, an organization, a city, a planet—all are systems.

Consider our food system and its web of machinery manufacturers, natural capital like soil health, farmers, workers, wholesalers, food companies, retailers, and us, the eaters. Short-term, narrowly focused financial incentives drive the system to pay farmers very little, reduce the richness of soil, lower the health and nutritional quality of our crops, weaken labor rights, and much more. The food system sounds broken, but, Forum for the Future's CEO, Sally Uren, points out, it's actually doing exactly what it's designed to: "produce cheap food with little consideration of environmental and social impacts."[42] Changing a system means changing its purpose as well.

Our systems are devilishly complicated and intertwined, so pulling one string has unpredictable impacts on others. Things can spin out of control—we're entering a stage of reinforcing feedback loops on climate, where melting permafrost releases more greenhouse gases, and the dark ocean where arctic sea ice once floated absorbs more heat. Since we don't fully know where the tipping points are, we should feel more urgency, not less. Systems thinking also means understanding root causes. Only then, as Uren says, can we "identify where to focus our energy and interventions to solve for our big challenges."

The good news is that in complicated webs, some feedback loops work *for* us; a solution to one problem may solve many. Economic development that gives people living around rain forests more security, plus education on how to improve crop yields, reduces deforestation and carbon emissions, enhances biodiversity, and reduces pandemic risks. That's a lot of bang for the development buck. To use an apt metaphor, companies and governments must work *on* the forest, not in the forest.

As one of the leading thinkers in systems, the late Dana Meadows, once said, "We humans are smart enough to have created complex systems and amazing productivity; surely we are also smart enough to make sure that everyone shares our bounty and [we] sustainably steward the natural world upon which we all depend."[43]

The Great News: Tailwinds and Accelerators

If we only look at the challenges and system failings, it can be daunting. But a global effort to build a thriving world is worth it—it's the greatest business opportunity ever. The path to net positive is challenging, but great things are happening that are increasing buy-in, proving the value of sustainability, and making the shift easier.

Net positive pays off for business. Businesses that pursue a long-term, multistakeholder model create value in many ways. Not every step is automatically win-win, but over time the leaders save money, reduce risk, innovate more, build valuable corporate reputations and brands, attract and retain talent, and have higher employee engagement. Gallup's famous workplace studies show that engaged organizations see 17 percent more productivity, a 20 percent increase in sales, and 21 percent higher profitability.[44] Businesses that are more sustainable often find the holy grail of increasing revenues, as more consumers look for products that are good for them and the planet.

Unilever has reaped this reward. Its purpose-driven brands—the ones that connect to larger societal issues, such as sanitation and children's health, and work to help solve them—have grown 69 percent faster than the rest of the business and with higher margins.[45] By serving the needs of the countries it operates in, the company has built deep trust and gained unique access to new markets and growth opportunities. Unilever has also thrived in part by acquiring fast-growing, purpose-led businesses that would only sell to Unilever because of its track record.

The numbers back all of this up. An NYU meta-analysis of thousands of studies found a strong correlation between companies adopting sustainability practices and improved financial performance, especially over longer time periods.[46] JUST Capital ranks more than nine hundred public, US-based companies on their environmental and social performance and created a list of the highest ranking, the JUST 100. The leaders pay their workers 18 percent more, use 123 percent more green energy, and are six times more likely to have set diversity targets . . . and produce a 7.2 percent higher return on equity.[47]

Net positive pays off for investors. Doing right by stakeholders is good for shareholders. After years of guesswork, solid data now shows that companies focusing on environmental, social, and governance (ESG) performance get equal or higher returns in the market. In 2020, 81 percent of sustainable indexes outperformed their benchmarks, and over a four-year period, portfolios weighted toward higher ESG scores "outperformed their benchmarks by between 81 and 243 basis points."[48] And yet, investors still ask nervously whether ESG will outperform. That's an odd question—no asset class in history has had to prove that it *always* does better.

The money is moving fast in one direction. Global assets in sustainable investing have topped $40 trillion (and growing).[49] Moody's reports that the total sustainable bond market reached $491 billion in 2020.[50] With this much money in play, investors are pressing companies to explain their climate strategies and their approach to ESG issues. Shareholder activism on climate change is getting teeth. In 2021, ExxonMobil shareholders elected two board members (that management did not recommend) who were nominated by a hedge fund focused on long-term, stakeholder value.

No investor is asking tougher questions than Larry Fink, CEO of Black-Rock, the largest asset owner in the world. The man running a $9 trillion fund has a megaphone. For years, Fink's annual letters to CEOs and his clients have focused extensively on ESG. He has increased demands on company leadership to provide data on carbon footprint and climate risk. In 2021, Fink told CEOs that "there is no company whose business model won't be profoundly affected by the transition to a net zero economy . . . companies that are not quickly preparing themselves will see their businesses and valuations suffer."[51] The promise of higher valuations is a big tailwind for pursuing net positive.

Finance has begun to rewire itself to reward companies which put a premium on long-term value creation, but the sector is conservative about change. A net positive bank would move away from the derivatives madness and point capital at the *real* financial market. We need to finance an economy that operates in service of human values and life (not the other way around), delivering real goods and services to real people.

Business leaders are rethinking the purpose of business. In August 2019, the Business Roundtable (BRT), a group of more than 180 CEOs from America's largest companies, issued a statement on the purpose of business. We serve multiple stakeholders, not just shareholders, they said. A few months later, the World Economic Forum's (WEF) Davos Manifesto declared that "A company serves society . . . supports communities . . . pays its fair share of taxes . . . acts as a steward of the environment . . . consciously protects our biosphere and champions a circular, shared and regenerative economy." These are just statements, and the aftermath of the BRT pronouncement has been underwhelming—most of these companies haven't changed much. But rhetoric matters. These groups are saying clearly that business cannot solely maximize shareholder return anymore. A new consensus has arisen: just 7 percent of *Fortune* 500 CEOs believe their companies should "mainly focus on making profits and not be distracted by social goals."[52]

We have powerful frameworks to guide us. In 2015, 193 countries agreed to the United Nations Sustainable Development Goals (SDGs), also called the Global Goals. The SDGs are broken into seventeen interrelated focus areas and 169 individual targets, providing a road map and scorecard for what a thriving world could look like by 2030: no hunger, clean water, education for all, gender equality, reduced inequality and opportunity for decent work, clean energy, climate action, and more. No company or country prioritizes all the goals equally, but they provide a viable model for long-term growth, as long as businesses move towards them, at times, in partnership. The SDGs "give us a common language—it's a Rosetta stone," says Kathleen McLaughlin, EVP and chief sustainability officer of Walmart.[53]

Along with this blueprint, we now have brilliant ideas to provide a North Star. Frameworks like the Stockholm Resilience Centre's work on *planetary boundaries* (fifteen natural systems, such as climate and freshwater, with nine estimated to be nearing tipping points), economist Kate Raworth's *Doughnut Economics*, and Bob Willard's *Future Fit* all offer important perspectives. They deserve deeper exploration, and we recommend everyone internalize them. We won't do it justice, but these boil down to a big idea: the world is finite, with biophysical limits that we can't exceed without threatening our survival, and we have human and moral minimum standards that we don't want to live below—that is, providing a level of sufficiency for *everyone* to have enough to thrive. In between those minimum and maximum limits is what Raworth calls the "safe and socially just space in which humanity can thrive."[54] A net positive company operates in that space and helps others get there as well.

It pays off for the world. Achieving the Global Goals would create a world that is socially fair, environmentally secure, economically prosperous, globally inclusive, and more predictable and resilient. The *Better Business, Better World* report calculated that hitting the targets will open up at least $12 trillion in business opportunity and create 380 million jobs by 2030 (in just four sectors of the economy).[55] Beyond the SDGs, opportunities are everywhere. By spending 1 to 1.5 percent of GDP to get to net zero emissions, we can avoid $160 trillion of climate-related costs over thirty years.[56] An analysis of how the world handles resources, the *Circularity Gap* report, estimates that the global economy only recycles 8.6 percent of the material that flows through it.[57] That's an enormous failing, but it leaves trillions of dollars of value to extract through circular business models.

The cost of inaction is higher than action. The World Economic Forum's *Nature Risk Rising* report has identified more than half of global GDP as moderately or highly dependent on nature. All of the bad news items, including the record 22 weather disasters costing more than $1 billion each in the United States in 2020, will easily cost many trillions of dollars in the coming years.[58] Our whole economy is at risk. Combine that with the financial tailwinds and you get one inescapable, head-slapping conclusion: *It's going to cost us orders of magnitude more if we do nothing than if we take action on our biggest challenges.* Better still, much of the action is not expense, but investment in lower-cost, healthier businesses and economies.

Technology is (mostly) on our side.   In 2014, the International Energy Agency forecasted that solar would hit $0.05 per kilowatt-hour by 2050—a mark achieved thirty years faster, in 2020.[59] Over the last ten years, the costs of solar and wind power have plummeted 90 and 70 percent, respectively.[60] Renewables are now, on average, cheaper to build than all other forms of electricity.[61] Battery prices have also dropped as fast, accelerating the electric vehicle market. Most major automakers have committed to phase out gas and diesel and go all-electric (for example, GM by 2035 and Honda by 2022 in the EU market).[62] Daimler stopped all R&D in internal combustion engines.[63] Moving quickly to renewable energy and electric fleets is now a no-brainer. As the US national climate adviser Gina McCarthy said, "The question won't be whether the private sector is going to buy into it; the private sector is going to drive it."[64]

It's not just clean technology. Revolutions in big data processing, GPS modeling, drone-based aerial photography, robotics, computer vision, AI, and many more techs are powering what WEF calls "the fourth industrial revolution," an exponential change in how technology affects the world. These new tools can help solve our big problems. In our food system, "precision agriculture" is greatly reducing waste as seeds, water, fertilizer, and pesticides are placed exactly where they're needed and in precisely the right quantities. A modern Deere tractor is a rolling AI-driven computer. Companies such as Schneider Electric offer advanced building management systems that can slash energy waste. We have the technologies and know-how to build smarter homes, grids, cities, and food and transportation systems. And access to technology, specifically mobile, is also proving to reduce inequality and extreme poverty.

A big caveat here is technology's dark side: the information bubbles that social media creates are fomenting hate, misinformation, and the opposite of the solidarity we need to tackle shared challenges. These companies should

DON'T READ THIS BOOK

We could spend more time describing the planetary and moral emergencies we face, or keep making the business case. But it's time to stop trying to convince people and get moving. Some business leaders still doubt that climate change is an existential threat, or that inequality and racism are embedded in our institutions. They may not believe that their employees, customers, and communities will demand that they work to solve these challenges. They may doom themselves to be laggards who don't get it, and they will join the graveyard of businesses that did not see big shifts coming. They will be welcomed with open arms by the likes of Blockbuster, Sears, Enron, Lehman Brothers, and the fifty coal companies in the United States that have gone bankrupt in the last decade. They will miss the greatest business opportunity in history. If they doubt that business must help build a thriving world, or don't feel some personal responsibility to be part of the solution, then they shouldn't read this book. We need people who want to have an impact and care enough to make change happen at scale. As they say, go big or go home.

take a broader view of their impacts on the world and take responsibility for them—that ownership is a core attribute of net positive businesses.

Young people want to see change. Young millennials and Gen Zers care much more about sustainability and climate change than their elders, and also believe strongly that business needs to do something. Nine in ten Gen Zers think companies have an obligation to solve environmental and social problems.[65] The McKinsey *True Gen* report concluded that "In a transparent world, younger consumers don't distinguish between the ethics of a brand . . . and its network of partners and suppliers . . . actions must match its ideals, and those ideals must permeate the entire stakeholder system."[66] Younger generations choose who they work for and buy from differently. They also act on their beliefs—look no further than global climate campaigner and teenager Greta Thunberg. Companies soon will find they have more than one Greta inside the organization.

So, the pressure is on, and that's a good thing. We have to fight through some persistent myths and preconceived notions, such as: renewables are too expense, diversity and inclusion targets are impossible because there are not enough qualified people of color, or we can't operate with no waste. All wrong. Humanity has many of the technologies and solutions it needs, it is filled with problem-solvers and entrepreneurs to figure out the rest, and there's a lot of capital out there. What holds us back then, if anything, is a lack of willpower, moral leadership, and imagination—things that net positive companies embrace.

We have a choice . . . between less prosperity, slower growth, widening inequality, and rigid borders . . . or a burst of innovation and productivity, inclusive growth, more resilient industries, and the emergence of a reconnected world. The courageous crowd of leaders moving in the right direction is growing. Business is ready to tackle the hardest issues, and the wind is at our back.

We can do this.

A Map of *Net Positive*, the Book

Because we can offer an insider perspective, this book draws heavily on the experience of Unilever, a company that's traveled a path toward net positive for years. But others are leading, too, and we'll learn from some of those stories as well.

This book is not a detailed how-to on achieving operational goals, such as slashing carbon emissions. Instead, our purpose is to help organizations transform themselves so they achieve those big goals as a natural course of doing business. We hope to provide core principles and strategies for building a new kind of organization that serves the world. While much will need to happen at once, we recommend a rough order of battle, which the book follows.

Here's a short summary of each chapter.

In chapter 1, *You Break the World, You Own It (Core Principles of a Net Positive Company)*, we lay out five foundations of a new, long-term, multistakeholder model. A core story in this chapter is how Unilever pushed back on investors to stop quarterly reporting, unleashing the organization to think longer-term. It's an important example that will pop up multiple times.

We then move into the strategies, starting with three areas that make up an inner core of change and action. The first step is looking inward to your own purpose (and we mean *you*). Chapter 2, *How Much Do You Care? (Becoming a Courageous, Net Positive Leader)*, starts with the traits leaders need to run a net positive business—a mix of purpose, humanity, humility, positivity, inspiration, collaboration, and courage above all. A purpose-driven leader understands that they are here for something bigger than themselves. They serve today's world and future generations.

In chapter 3, *Unlock the Company's Soul (Discovering Organizational and Employee Purpose and Passion)*, we move from self to organization. Using Unilever's history as a jumping off point, we explore the Unilever Sustainable Living Plan (USLP), the core tool of the company's decade of success. But, as we'll discuss, an organization can only find its soul if it has its own house in order—that is, the business is running well—and the leadership is sending the right signals to drive net positive behavior. It's also critical for employees to find their purpose and connect it to the organization's mission.

In chapter 4, *Blow Up Boundaries (Thinking Big and Setting Aggressive, Net Positive Goals)*, we start to unpack a fundamental and important tension. The transformation starts inside, with self and organization, yet an outside-in perspective will guide us. The world's biggest challenges and thresholds inform the goals the company sets; a company pursues net zero emissions in large part because of the planet-wide emergency of climate change. This chapter provides guidance on goal-setting, with "science-based" targets—commitments to move at the pace facts and science demand—as a critical bare minimum. The bigger goals meet the world's needs, but also remove mental constraints from the organization and help it prepare for larger, systemic change.

Chapter 5, *Be an Open Book (Building Trust and Transparency)*, describes the importance of opening up as a bridge between the inner work and the necessary partnerships with external stakeholders. With trust in decline, but transparency on the rise, it's a tricky time for business. Putting the needs of others ahead of yours and serving all stakeholders, including those who normally serve you (suppliers), builds deep trust. Those who earn that trust experience unique access to markets and partnerships.

The outer core work comes with three fundamental strategies. At the start of chapter 6, *1+1=11 (Creating Partnerships with Synergies and Multiplier Effects)*, we offer a model for thinking about partnerships in two large categories. First up, collaborations that work on issues that your sector may share, both risks an opportunities, or things that you and key suppliers may productively manage together. These partnerships can be very fruitful, but don't change the wider system.

Chapter 7, *It Takes Three to Tango (Systems-Level Reset and Net Positive Advocacy)*, moves on to partnerships that do work to change full systems. These require the three prongs of society—business, government, and civil society—to work together in new ways, change the rules of the game, and build policy frameworks that are more just and help us live within planetary boundaries. It's the end of traditional, self-serving lobbying, and the exploration of net positive advocacy that moves a sector or region down a better path. The work at this scale also aims to help entire economies and countries develop so that business and people thrive.

The last pillar of the outer core brings up issues that companies work hard to evade. Chapter 8, *Embrace the Elephants (Managing Issues Nobody Wants to Talk About . . . but We Can't Avoid)*, dives into tough topics like excessive executive compensation, tax avoidance, corruption, human rights, money in politics, and diversity and inclusion. These issues are contributing to our largest problems, in particular inequality and power imbalances. A company cannot be truly net positive if it doesn't address these thorny issues.

Finally, we end the strategies and action ideas with chapter 9, *Culture Is the Glue (Putting Values into Action, Deep in the Organization and Brands)*. Culture runs through all the strategies, but we see it as a culmination of the work. Embedding culture into the business at the brand level, like Unilever's well-known work with Lifebuoy on hand washing and Dove on self-esteem, is next-level work. We look also at how a strong net positive culture comes through diversity and inclusion, changing reward systems, bringing new entrepreneurial businesses and leaders into the company, and challenging cultural norms of intolerance.

We end the book with chapter 10, *Net Positive World (Looking Around the Corner to Greater Challenges and Opportunities)*. We explore what is coming at business in the near future and making the net positive agenda bigger, tougher, and more rewarding. Companies will need to help rethink capitalism, economic metrics like GDP, the nature of well-being, the purpose of a consumption-based economy, and the role of business in defending pillars of society like democracy and freedom. This is a call to action to join all of those who want to build a thriving world together.

We live at a critical time in human history, with ever-rising expectations on all businesses and humans to be better. As former secretary general of the UN Ban Ki-moon has said, "Ours can be the first generation to end poverty—and the last generation to address climate change before it is too late."[67] Time is very short, but the opportunities are vast.

With the right leadership, working together on our hardest issues, we can heal the world. We can be net positive.

So, let's get going.

1

You Break the World, You Own It

Core Principles of a Net Positive Company

It is not your responsibility to finish the work [of perfecting the world], but you are not free to desist from it either.

—Rabbi Tarfon, first century CE

Stores that sell fragile items like pottery or glassware may post a sign, "You break it, you own it." It's a warning to be careful with valuable things and think about your actions.

Over the last fifty years, the world's economists and the private sector dove headfirst into a global experiment, without really thinking about what might break. With remarkable self-confidence in the outcomes, they embraced an obsession with short-term profits and shareholder primacy. It seemed efficient, but there was little consideration of what would happen when *everyone* focuses on a single metric. The results, both good and bad, have been extreme.

As we've noted, in just a few decades, a billion people moved out of dire poverty, mainly through economic growth.[1] But the downsides now threaten to destroy those improvements and undermine the collective well-being of all people. In short, we in business—with a strong assist from governments and all of us as consumers—have cracked the world.

The existential threats of climate and inequality have gotten exponentially worse. Left unchecked, the cracks will become chasms that swallow business and humanity. Nobody is coming to save us. We broke it, we own it. That means we're now responsible not just to our own companies, partners, employees, and investors, but to all of society. With that view of a company, running Unilever was, at times, like leading the world's biggest NGO (but one with a profit motive).

Responsibility is a core divider between a typical business and a net positive one. After all, the current model of shareholder capitalism generates tremendous financial value for business by pointedly *not* taking ownership and treating issues such as pollution or inequity as "someone else's problem." So, taking responsibility is the first step. As former Patagonia CEO Rose Marcario says, it's obvious that "business does environmental harm . . . the problem is when businesses don't take responsibility . . . and when they're not curious about how to curb that harm."[2]

Five core principles that center on responsibility will take company performance to a new level. They help corporate leaders expand their horizons, rethink their jobs, and reshape the role of their business in society. These attributes, fully embraced, separate the net positive companies from the merely well-run and well-meaning businesses:

- Ownership of all impacts and consequences, intended or not

- Operating for the long-term benefit of business and society

- Creating positive returns for all stakeholders

- Driving shareholder value as a *result*, not a goal

- Partnering to drive systemic change

Adopting these five tenets as core operating principles is radical and difficult, but they reinforce one another, making it easier to create a high-performance company that gives more than it takes.

1. Ownership of All Impacts and Consequences, Intended or Not

While you might outsource your supply chain, your logistics, or your investments, you do *not* outsource your responsibility for them. It's getting harder every day to externalize environmental and social costs that your business imposes on society. Planetary boundaries enforced by nature (such as extreme weather or water shortages) are now costing companies real money. Stakeholder pressure is forcing businesses to internalize their social impacts as well. It's time to proactively say "we own" everything that happens with our suppliers, with our customers, and at the end of life of our products. It can seem like a big leap, but that's what it takes to become net positive.

Are you producing energy or manufacturing something cheaply with fossil fuels? Then, you're more profitable because you've avoided the costs that carbon and air pollution impose on society, from reduced health downwind to global climate change. Do you make a food product that's profitable? Its high margins could depend on slave labor and deforestation in the supply chain. Maybe you offer low-cost investment opportunities for the wealthy, while providing high-interest financial products to the poor? No problem, if you avoid thinking about how you've increased inequality.

All of these are predictable consequences. Unintended outcomes can be even more damaging. Tech companies set out to give everyone access to all information, with an ideal of enhancing knowledge and human connection. Unfortunately, without intending to, they also created misinformation bubbles that spread vile, hate-filled ideologies which undermine society. Some bad outcomes were hard to see coming, but that does not get leaders off the hook.

In this new world, you own the impacts of your business from deep in the supply chain to the end of a product's life, and stakeholders will make sure you know it. When home goods company Wayfair sold mattresses to the US government, the company's leaders apparently didn't know or worry that their products were going to detention camps for migrant children—until customers started a boycott and five hundred employees walked out in protest. That was a lot of trouble and brand damage for a $200,000 sale.[3]

When Coca-Cola used antimony in bottles (which doesn't affect the drinks), it didn't think about the health problems it created when people living on landfills burn the bottles. And when Tide designed a colorful detergent pod, the brand didn't think through how appetizing the candylike package would be to little kids (or that teens would start a deadly viral challenge to eat the pods). The list goes on.

Unilever has faced pointed attacks over skin-whitening products in India. Many Indian women defend the use of these products, saying it's their choice to pursue an "ideal" of lighter skin. But for Unilever, it was a major mismatch between the message of whitening, and the purpose of a brand such as Dove that helps women build self-esteem and appreciate their own unique beauty. The company took the whitening ingredients out of those face creams a couple of years ago and has rebranded the products "Glow & Lovely" instead of "Fair & Lovely." But the brand damage was done.

A major lesson from these errors is that it's better to be proactive and look holistically at how your company treats everyone along multiple dimensions of well-being, even if it leads to some rude awakenings. For example, while Unilever was building millions of toilets in India and bringing electricity to communities to power cooking stoves, the company discovered that some people working on Unilever-run tea plantations didn't have consistent access to plumbing and power in their homes. You have to get your own house in order before you can tell anyone else what to do.

Owning all of the company's impacts on people and planet isn't just about discovering downside risks and problems. There are important upsides to taking a harder look at the business across all impacts: opportunities for efficiency and savings, innovation for growth, and deeper connections with people. Owning everything changes the culture and focus of the business, making it more human. It can spur executives and employees to think about broader impacts, increase the well-being of everyone they affect, and move toward net positive.

2. Operating for the Long-Term Benefit of Business and Society

Short-term thinking is enticing. It's simpler to focus solely on maximizing profit today than worry about complicated, systemic issues that take years to solve. Many investors want profits now, and the short-term focus is lucrative for executives with vested stock or nearing retirement.

Even CEOs who talk about their legacy may still go for quick wins, since tenures are getting shorter all the time—more than one-third of the largest public companies in the world had at least three CEOs in just ten years.[4] It's a long process to build a net positive company that serves society. Much of the benefit could come after the current execs leave. The companies themselves are not lasting as long either. A combination of short-term earnings focus and technology has cut the lifespan of S&P 500 companies from sixty-one years in 1958 to eighteen years (and dropping) today.[5] The number of public companies has fallen by half since the mid-1990s.[6]

Two other factors, both stemming from company boards, are also driving CEO's to focus on the short term. The average duration of executive compensation plans globally is a shockingly low 1.7 years.[7] And in a survey of senior executives, boards were the top source of pressure for short-term results—above investors.[8] It's not surprising that in this environment, business leaders focus on the near term.

We're not saying a company should *ignore* short-term needs for profitability or put off profits to a later date as a sacrifice to serve society now. But leaders need the freedom and opportunity to solve big challenges, which will take many quarters of hard work. You cannot tackle climate change or inequality running the rat race of quarterly reporting. The systemic thinking and deep collaboration that we need will not emerge from short-term thinking.

Creating long-term value means not shooting for the moon in a given year, but investing every year to get the compounding effects and benefits of consistency over time. During Paul's decade as CEO, Unilever achieved ten consecutive years of top- and bottom-line growth. If you can invest in factories or intellectual property that way, why not invest in collaborations and the future of humanity. A short-term focus kills value-creating opportunities. So, if you need every choice to prove out financially within a quarter, this may not be the story for you.

The Unilever Sustainable Living Plan (USLP), launched in 2010 with a ten-year horizon, has forced long-term thinking at the company. It's a tool for converting a long-term philosophy on how to run a business into action, and a road map to shift the business toward serving others.

Some executives say long-term planning is useless in a fast-changing world with sudden shocks (such as pandemics). But companies should stretch their thinking, using tools like scenario planning. The point of doing this kind of work is not to develop a detailed strategy for *what* the company does for ten or twenty years. Instead, think about *who* you are. What are your personal and corporate values that won't change? Why do you exist and how do you help build a thriving world? In short, what is your purpose?

There's growing evidence that a long-term focus pays off. A study from McKinsey Global Institute and FCLTGlobal calculated that at companies operating with a true long-term mindset, "average revenue and earnings growth were 47% and 36% higher, respectively, and market capitalization grew faster as well." The long-term companies also increased R&D spending and rode out stressful times better.[9]

We believe that more companies have failed because of short-termism than have tripped up because they were too visionary. The pressure to constantly outpace competitors on short-term financial metrics has driven companies to stray from what's clearly right. Well-known examples include Boeing losing its focus on safety, and Wells Fargo putting sales metrics ahead of ethics. These actions destroy trust. Companies can come back from disaster and rediscover who they are, but the brand damage is real.

Some might justify a short-term focus, ironically, because the problems seem so large. The more urgent or bigger the need becomes, the more reactive and short-term we behave. It's the fight-or-flight instinct. But as safe as it seems to stay focused on the now, it's better to run the business with a long-term perspective and a clear moral compass. It will help the company be proactive and lead the shifts that are coming instead of being victimized by them. The company will be more resilient, riding out the storm or profiting from it . . . for the long haul.

3. Creating Positive Returns for All Stakeholders

Early corporate responsibility efforts focused on public relations and community affairs. The goal was to keep NGOs or other stakeholders at bay and avoid conflict. Today, most large companies work in good faith with outside groups, but still start mainly by asking, "What's in it for us?" A net positive business puts stakeholder needs *first*. This shouldn't feel strange. The core reason any company exists is to satisfy customer needs and make their lives better. So, extend that logic, and think also of employees or communities not as groups to appease, but as people you can help thrive.

This principle is at the core of becoming net positive, since the "positive" means better outcomes for stakeholders. In practice, it's about innovating and offering new products and services that improve lives and heal the planet. Or about helping employees find their purpose and improve their health and well-being, while building a diverse, inclusive company. Or helping suppliers make their businesses more efficient and sustainable, which builds tighter relationships and spurs joint innovation. Or helping communities thrive, going beyond the old argument that companies do enough by providing jobs and paying taxes (global communities may need much more than that, including support for local schools or building water and energy infrastructure).

At the national level, most companies only talk to politicians to lobby for what they think is good for the business. Most commonly, that translates into fighting all regulation. It's not a good strategy anymore, if it ever was. The focus should be on helping the countries they operate in to develop—creating industries to attract capital, helping reduce corruption, fixing broken tax systems to increase revenues and build a level playing field for business, and so on. A more functional country and economy will be better for all.

It's not wrong to seek advantage, profit, or growth from these enhanced relationships—net positive applies to business as well. Partners in civil society may expect a company to act like a nonprofit in its efforts to serve the world. One of Paul's earliest external meetings as CEO was with the executive director of UNICEF. She asked Unilever to donate bars of soap for neonatal kits being distributed to reduce the rate of death in childbirth. Paul said, Look, I don't have "soap," I have Lifebuoy—I'll give you all the Lifebuoy you want. At first, the director was shocked and said it was self-serving to brand the effort. Over time, the NGO got comfortable with including Lifebuoy, and today, UNICEF and Unilever have a long-lasting global partnership on sanitation and helping communities thrive.

Providing branded products as part of a larger program that improves well-being is win-win, and there's nothing wrong with that. If the work to serve a need in the world is done authentically and genuinely, why shouldn't the brand get credit? If Apple or Dell provides technology to a community as part of a development program, they're sure going to use their own computers. Positive outcomes for all should be profitable. But, more important, it has to be to remain viable for the long term. It's a good thing if the core business is engaged in programs like this. Marketing and brand budgets are *much* larger than corporate foundation funds. The more your company grows through these efforts, the more good work you can do. Bigger business, bigger impact.

We also need to find win-win solutions for the critical stakeholders that normally do not have a seat at the table, such as future generations and the planet itself. We should be handing our kids and grandkids fewer problems, not more. Using up resources and creating an unlivable climate is a horrible thing to do to them. We're also leaving them a world with hundreds of millions of people in poverty because we're not investing in sufficiency for all. The planet, with all its species and ecosystems, is the biggest stakeholder of all. It can't speak, but it does communicate. Today's extreme weather is a warning about what's to come. As many say, Mother Nature always wins.

There's an important nuance and strategy to all of this. *Creating positive returns for stakeholders does not mean satisfying all of them at the same time, or focusing equal attention and resources on each. You can't prioritize everyone at once.* Some years, you may spend more to develop employees. Other times, you invest in brands and products that serve consumers well, so they grow in the coming years. Or you may hold back some short-term returns from shareholders to invest in communities or in rapid carbon reduction and renewable energy. *But the long-term outcomes for each group need to be positive, and that includes shareholders.*

The idea here is to optimize outcomes for multiple stakeholders versus trying to maximize for just one. It's the obsession with value creation for any single group that knocks things out of balance.

4. Driving Shareholder Value as a Result, Not a Goal

The great Peter Drucker reportedly once said, "Profit for a company is like oxygen for a person. If you don't have enough of it, you are out of the game. But if you think your life is about breathing you're really missing something."[10] Years earlier, Henry Ford also commented that a business run solely for profit must die, because it has no reason to exist and, he said, "the best way to make money in business is not to think too much about making it."[11]

It's time to wake up from our fifty-year zombielike obsession with profits. Shareholder value should be a result, not an objective. The single biggest hurdle to building a long-term company that serves the world is the relentless pressure for quarterly performance. It warps companies and the economy. Some institutional investors, such as pension funds and national sovereign funds, take a long-term view and worry about systemic risks like climate change. But the dominant influence on public companies—which ripples through every business—remains the equity investors and analysts.

These shareholders want smooth, rising earnings, and companies play games to satisfy them. With the rise of stock options as incentives for senior executives, it became even more tempting to manipulate earnings in ways both legal and shady. Stock buybacks, for example, are mostly a gimmick to boost short-term earnings and distract from the fact that you're not investing in things that will make the business more valuable.

Many investors are not your long-term friend. The average holding period of stocks has plummeted from eight years in the middle of the twentieth century to about five months in 2020.[12] If we keep shareholders in the driver's seat, we cannot build a system that optimizes for well-being for all, which requires long-term thinking. Unfortunately, even in the face of existential long-term challenges like climate change, global companies are getting more short-term focused, not less. One major study concluded that if businesses adopted more long-term thinking, they "could earn an additional $1.5 trillion per year in returns on invested capital."[13] That's an awful lot of shareholder value.

There's a philosophical reason to hit pause on the shareholder obsession: the markets are often completely disconnected from economic reality. During the pandemic of 2020, after a short crash, the big indexes quickly returned to all-time highs, even as the world's economy shed the equivalent of roughly 400 million full-time jobs.[14] So, if you believe that a stock's value eventually ties to the value of future cash flows—which it's supposed to— then you don't need to pitch shareholders to buy the stock. Increase those long-term flows, and the buyers will come. And if the stock market is *not* connected to actual corporate performance and cash flows, then it's a casino, and why bother speaking to short-term shareholders at all.

We still have some distance to go before most companies see that shareholder return should be a result, not the sole objective. Investors still hold a dominant position in the psyche of CEOs, says Andrew Liveris, the former CEO of Dow.[15] Unfortunately, the data backs him up. A 2019 Stanford survey of CEOs and CFOs showed that while 89 percent believe it's important to incorporate stakeholder interests in their business planning (the good news), only 5 percent said that stakeholder interests were more important than shareholder interests.[16]

CEOs and CFOs clearly see the short-term way as the path of least resistance, but eventually it catches up with you. As Ecolab executive chairman Doug Baker told us, short-term pressure has its place in running the business, but if you focus solely on the short-term, you get what he calls "easy meetings, hard life"—that is, the investor calls are great, but you end up with bigger problems down the road.

Stopping Quarterly Reporting

The best way to step away from the short-term whirlpool is to stop talking to investors so much. Say directly, and publicly, to investors, "We're not going to report quarterly earnings or provide guidance anymore."

Paul took this big step about three weeks into his job as CEO, figuring the board couldn't fire him that quickly if it went badly. Dropping quarterly reporting was (and is) highly unusual. Most CEOs take hundreds of meetings a year with investors—that's a lot of time *not* managing strategy, growth, innovation, customer focus, and so on. If you don't step away from the earnings treadmill, you're a hostage to the financial market. Profit is not a purpose, but an end product. And after ten years at the helm, Paul's end product was strong, with total shareholder return of 292 percent, far outrunning the 131 percent for the FTSE index.

That performance came from pursuing the goals of the USLP, not talking to investors every ninety days. This idea did not always seem radical. Nearly forty years before Milton Friedman's profits-first manifesto, Robert Wood Johnson, the chair of Johnson & Johnson, committed to a different approach. He penned *Our Credo* that said his family's company should serve patients, doctors, and nurses first. Then came employees, followed by communities (in which he included protecting the environment). Last were stockholders, who would "realize a fair return."[17] Not a maximum return right away, but a fair one.

Regretfully, few companies have followed Unilever's lead in abolishing guidance and reporting, but a net positive company will. Some CEOs, while not going quite as far as Unilever, have pushed back on investors just the same. Back in 2014, Apple announced new climate change and energy goals. When investors challenged CEO Tim Cook to commit to only do climate projects that were clearly profitable, he told them if they didn't believe in climate change, then they should sell their Apple shares (which have gone up 500 percent since that meeting). Pointing out how many choices they make at Apple for reasons beyond short-term pay off, he said, "If you want me to do things only for ROI [return on investment] reasons, you should get out of this stock."[18]

There is another path to changing this whole dynamic. We wouldn't have to work so hard to put shareholders at the back of the line if the owners of capital saw the worth in long-term value creation. The organization FCLT-Global, or Focusing Capital on the Long Term, is working to make this shift happen. FCLT brings together multinationals such as Bloomberg, Cisco, Dow, DSM, Tata, Unilever, and Walmart . . . with major-asset owners and investors such as Barclays, BlackRock, the Carlyle Group, Fidelity, Goldman Sachs, State Street, and TPG. The organization is generating analyses that show how a longer-term focus outperforms and developing road maps and tools to help companies adopt better practices. Investors are moving in the right direction, but until most of them refocus on the long term, the best thing you can do is walk away from the quarterly profits insanity.

5. Partnering to Drive Systemic Changes

You can't improve outcomes for all stakeholders if you don't identify, understand, and take ownership of those outcomes. But this does *not* mean taking sole responsibility or going it alone. You'll need partners in the journey to fix those cracks in the world.

All companies—and especially multinationals—touch more of the planet and many more people than they realize. For most, their main impacts fall outside of their direct control. So, tackling a company's footprint, let alone solving the systemic issues threatening our well-being, requires cooperation. A single company working alone on big issues like human rights or decarbonization may be able to solve 30 or 40 percent of the problem in its own operations. But getting to a 100 percent solution requires changing the underlying system.

For example, in some parts of the world, such as regions of India, China, or Africa, getting to zero carbon is nearly impossible. They're still dependent on coal and diesel, or maybe just starting to ramp up renewables. You're not going to move your factory, so the logical step is to develop a broader coalition to change what energy options are available to all.

Plastic waste is another thorny problem that connects multiple sectors of the economy and billions of consumers. Going it alone won't do much. A company can collect ocean plastic for a single product and get some marketing bang out of it, but that doesn't solve the larger issue. Likewise, ensuring a living wage and eliminating child labor in the supply chain will not happen without extensive collaboration across a sector and deep changes in cultures and governmental policies.

Some sectors have an increased need for collaboration. The food business is filled with complicated challenges which are increasingly laid at the door of consumer-facing companies. A CEO of a food and beverage giant once told Andrew that a good product used to be one that tasted good and was safe. That was it. Today, he said, a good product also has to be responsibly sourced, manufactured, and distributed. This expanded view of responsibility is now table stakes. The next level of taking ownership in the food sector is tackling larger societal problems, including immense food waste and poor nutrition and health around the world. There are now a growing number of partnerships to address these problems.

We don't eat 40 percent of the food we produce, which is an incredible waste of resources, especially since the food system contributes up to 30 percent of global greenhouse gas emissions and uses 70 percent of the world's fresh water. In response, the Champions 12.3 coalition, which includes Nestlé, Kellogg, Tesco, and Unilever, aims to meet the Sustainable Development Goal 12.3 target of cutting food waste in half by 2030. The battle starts with the right people at the table.

Similarly, we can't solve nutrition and health challenges without a broad mix of players. Our world has two problems that are, oddly, at either end of a spectrum—more than 650 million people are obese, while 460 million are underweight, and two billion have micronutrient deficiencies.[19] More than fifty million kids under five suffer from "wasting," meaning they are below typical height and weight.[20] Many countries struggle with "stunting," the damage to mental abilities from lack of nutrition in the first thousand days of life.[21] To deal with the deficiencies, Unilever helped create the Scaling Up Nutrition initiative, a collective effort of multiple stakeholders to end malnutrition. Unilever has fortified sixty billion servings of their food products (with a goal of 200 billion by 2022) with vitamins, iron, and iodine. Goals like this can help solve numerous problems at once.

The larger systems changes can only happen in partnership with groups outside of a company's control—peers, community members, NGOs, governments, consumers, suppliers, and more. Done right, a network of stakeholders creates multiplier effects that help build something bigger and faster. An effective network needs trust, which you earn by being transparent about your challenges and failures. Building that trust and launching successful partnerships also requires fulfilling the first four principles of a net positive business. If you don't take ownership, think long-term, work for the benefit of others, and put shareholders in proper perspective, how big will the thinking be? Why would stakeholders trust you?

Collaborations addressing the biggest systems also need the right legislation to succeed. Policies can create perverse effects or be ineffective if there's not a binding framework to stop free riders. Companies need to take a productive seat at the table on policies such as climate targets, human rights standards, child labor laws, tax laws, and subsidy regimes that create a level playing field.

The inspiration and framework for tying all of these elements together should be the Sustainable Development Goals. We can use them to reframe the social contract, rethink the role of business in society, and redesign the policies we need. The SDGs push us to go deeper and seek a planet and society in balance.

Organizational "A Game"

In combination, the five principles are the core of the net positive model. Making these principles nonnegotiable will mean the difference between solid sustainability players doing some good work, and world-class companies that create much more value for humanity. Our problems are big, so we need businesses and their leaders to play at a different level and bring their "A Game."

The top-notch companies will also need to nail the basics. Underlying the five net positive principles is a more fundamental one supporting them all: nothing about the new model undermines the need to properly run a business. Your products have to taste good or work well or make customers look good. They need to be affordable for the quality and service they provide. Hiring the best people is a must. The business will need the discipline to build efficient supply chains and manufacturing, smart distribution channels, innovative R&D, effective marketing, and so on. Pursuing net positive is only possible if it's built on top of a strong foundation and an uncompromising culture of performance.

People at companies like Unilever often feel the burden or challenge of keeping the high standards of the sustainability vision. But instead of thinking of the net positive principles as additional work on top of the basics, consider it the model that everything flows through. A company can ruthlessly focus on costs at times, but only *within* this better model, not as the core strategy. To help build communities, for example, you need to make careful choices about where to spend your budget, but the idea of improving the well-being of those communities remains unquestioned. Finally, investments in the business, in product quality, and in innovation are necessary as well, but they should focus on delivering long-term benefit for many stakeholders. There may need to be occasional, short-term compromises—you can't do everything at once—but the vision is to be better in nearly every way, using regular check-ins on progress. Done right, you'll see a compounding, growing advantage from a better business model.

Net positive is the big leagues. We have to be pioneers, create new territory, and continuously reinvent the company and the future. Without this level of thinking, you can easily get left behind. It also requires true dedication to building a better business, but "better" can mean many things. For a net positive business, it includes delivering profits *and* transformative change beyond its own direct, short-term interest. A better company creates well-being for people and planet.

What Net Positive Companies Do to Develop More Responsible Core Principles

- Develop a deep understanding of and take responsibility for how the business affects the world, from operations to value chains, and from communities to the planet.

- Broaden the meaning of a business in a number of dimensions:

  - **Value chain.** Work to optimize not just their own businesses, but suppliers' operations and customers' lives as well.

- **Time.** Seek compounding benefits over the long term, for the business and the world.

- **Stakeholders.** Look beyond the obvious employees and customers to a full array of those connected to the business.

- **Money.** Rethink how to invest capital and reduce the focus on investors and their rewards.

- **Independence.** Move away from a go-it-alone or "it wasn't invented here" mentality to be open to real partnership.

2

How Much Do You Care?

Becoming a Courageous, Net Positive Leader

Yesterday I was clever, so I wanted to change the world.
Today I am wise, so I am changing myself.

—Rumi, thirteenth-century Iranian poet

The Western economic system is largely based on two tragic misunderstandings—one about the world of nature, the other about human nature. Two of the most important thinkers of the last three hundred years, Adam Smith and Charles Darwin, didn't say what everyone thinks they did.

Charles Darwin did not coin the phrase "survival of the fittest." As biologist Janine Benyus points out, Darwin wrote about being adaptable and fit to survive, not being the fitt-*est*. Many species thrive in natural niches not by destroying others, but through cooperation. Entire ecosystems collaborate for general health and resilience. Nature, it turns out, is not the cage-match-to-the-death we were led to believe.

In the human realm, the obsession with "free" markets is largely based on a misreading of Adam Smith's *The Wealth of Nations,* published in 1776. Libertarians and neoliberals rely on Smith's famous "invisible hand" to demand zero constraints on capitalism. Unfettered markets will yield the best outcomes—or so they say. But that understanding of Smith is wrong.

The invisible hand was a minor point in Smith's work, mentioned only a few times. He introduced it seventeen years before *The Wealth of Nations,* in his lesser-known essay *The Theory of Moral Sentiments*. While Smith suggested that self-interest would yield the common good, his emphasis was on the latter part of that equation. Those who do well in the markets (that is, the rich), he wrote, are "led by an invisible hand to make nearly the same distribution of the necessaries of life which would have been made had the earth been divided into equal portions among all its inhabitants."[1] Who knew that Adam Smith was such a socialist?

He based his belief in spreading the wealth on a more optimistic view of human nature than what modern dogma holds as true. Smith believed that self-interest aligned with sympathy and justice.[2] The opening line of *The Theory of Moral Sentiments* declares, "How selfish soever man may be supposed, there are evidently some principles in his nature, which *interest him in the fortune of others*, and render their happiness necessary to him, though *he derives nothing from it except the pleasure of seeing it* [emphasis added]."[3]

In short, we are happy if we see others happy. We have innate compassion, and empathy feels good. In this sense, the caring that leads to the happiness of others *is* selfish.

The one-two punch of misusing Smith and Darwin has beaten the humanity out of business and the economy. Twentieth-century economics developed models where people and organizations coldly maximize utility. It took the *people* out of the equation, turning markets into machines of mindless cogs. Even worse, in company financial statements, people are not even considered assets; employees appear as a liability on the balance sheet.

It doesn't have to be this way. We can pursue success and wealth, but also fairness, justice, and equity. The fields of behavioral economics and psychology are blowing up the coldly rational view of people, and instead recognizing how humans act in real life, with caring, biases, faults, and emotions.

CEOs and other executives should bring their full selves to work, but the constant demand for short-term results presents a challenge. Even the NGOs pressuring companies to do better recognize the problem. Kumi Naidoo, the former executive director of Greenpeace and Amnesty International, says that "even the most enlightened executives are captured in a system, a tyranny of quarterly reporting cycles, that makes it nearly impossible to push things forward."[4] Pushing back on the system requires, above all, courage.

Of course some people prefer the system they're trapped in. We shouldn't pretend that everyone in business cares about the state of the world. While visiting the Zaatari refugee camp in Jordan, Paul met other CEOs who seemed to be there under duress. One billionaire hedge fund manager even complained about how the "bloody refugee boat people situation" ruined his holidays on his megayacht in the Mediterranean. Stories like this confirm the worst fears of business haters and, sadly, it's not an unusual interaction in the halls of power.

But most CEOs and executives are human. They have kids and grandkids who challenge them about their actions. They care about what's happening and want a world that's healthier, safer, and more just. They may believe it's their job to be willfully blind, but few want more pollution, climate change, or human suffering. Many seem to think that they can't act in line with their beliefs, either individually or collectively. But they can care, and to truly lead, they must.

Net Positive Leaders: Finding the Willpower

Countless books, classes, and business school cases have explored leadership. We've long tried to distill what makes someone worthy of being followed. And that applies to all people, not just CEOs. Many people sit atop some kind of pyramid in an organization, managing or influencing others to work toward a goal. People can lead and inspire from many places.

No matter the level, there are evergreen leadership skills that were important fifty years ago, and will be fifty years from now. Effective leaders share traits, such as discipline, toughness and holding people to high standards, strategic thinking, intelligence, curiosity, and a desire to understand key drivers of a business like technology. In today's volatile, uncertain, complex, ambiguous world, other traits, in particular adaptability and resilience, become critical as well.

But leading a net positive business takes more than the basics. The best leaders, the ones people will want to follow into this new territory, are first and foremost good human beings. They are at ease with themselves, have integrity, and what they say and what they do are in sync. Net positive leadership is also about putting others' interests ahead of your own. It helps to know your own strengths and passions as well. The sweet spot is leading in the overlap of what you're good at, what you like, and what the world needs. Getting there might require developing new skills and leaving your comfort zone.

We see five critical traits that help create a net positive leader, which we'll explore in this chapter:

- A sense of purpose, duty, and service

- Empathy: a high level of compassion, humility, and humanity

- More courage

- The ability to inspire and show moral leadership

- Seeking transformative partnerships

The world needs leaders who are the opposite of the old "company man" who coldly maximizes profits, and who instead embrace being more vulnerable, open, caring, empathetic, and human. Organizations should strive for those traits as well. The obsession with shareholder value has turned businesses into soulless money machines. It's all numbers, statistics, and profits. Companies have become robotic, valuing only contractual relationships instead of open, trusting partnerships (neither of us are big fans of contracts— we're writing this book together on a handshake).

Businesses rejected the balance of ethics that Adam Smith talked about in favor of pure efficiency. As Oxford business professor Colin Mayer says in his book *Prosperity*, the humans in the equation have been replaced with "anonymous markets and shareholders over whom we have no control."[5] We've all done a good job of divorcing our personal selves from work life, but at a high cost. We believe that a business is and should be human, with real people serving the needs of other real people. If we start with people as the core of business—not with the pursuit of short-term profits—then the first step in building a more human business is to look inward to find the strength to change how business works.

A company can only head toward net positive if it has leaders courageous enough to challenge business as usual—leaders who understand that *profit should come not from creating the world's problems, but from solving them.* How can we keep earning when the world is burning? The solutions to many of our challenges are available, and there's plenty of capital to invest. What's stopping us? Part of the answer is that resistance is high, from both inertia and vested interests. So, finally, leaders need determination to fight through the roadblocks. Willpower comes from cultivating net positive leadership principles, such as purpose, humility, and courage. Underlying those traits, basic human values can be our guide and foundation of a new kind of leadership: justice, compassion, dignity, and respect—it's the Golden Rule again. When you know what the right thing to do is, you'll find the courage to take a stand.

Getting Off the Sidelines

The world lacks enough moral leadership. Business executives have been playing it too safe and avoiding conflict on tough social and environmental issues. But it's not acceptable anymore to stay quiet. We've heard CEOs say that politics is none of their business. But it's wrong, strategically and morally.

If you're quiet, you're complicit. If you stand back and watch leaders in government or business undermine democracy, science, and civil rights, you're helping autocracy and ignorance take over. To paraphrase a number of philosophers, the only thing necessary for evil to triumph is for good people to do nothing.

Things are changing. Companies have begun to speak out more, wading into thorny debates about LGBTQ rights, guns, immigration, climate policy, and more. When the state of North Carolina passed a bill banning transgender people from using the bathroom of their choice, CEOs spoke up. Leaders with a large presence in the state, such as then-CEO Mike Lamach from Trane Technologies[6] and Brian Moynihan from Bank of America,[7] sent a stern letter to the governor, joined by dozens of other CEOs (including Paul). The law, they said, did not fit their values.

When the Black Lives Matter movement gained steam, organizations of all kinds issued statements about their commitment to racial equity. Businesses set new policies, such as concrete targets for diversity in management, or commitments to spend more money with Black-owned businesses in the supply chain. The Oscars even said that films would only be considered for Best Picture if they met inclusivity and representation standards.[8]

It's sometimes hard for leaders to know when to say something. But it may not be completely in their control—employees and other key stakeholders may demand that the company take a position. Some issues, such as protecting democracy or defending science, need to be universal, with all companies engaging. Many US companies publicly supported voting and democracy before the 2020 election, and then spoke out again in reaction to the insurrection of 2021. Every organization also should advocate for pro–climate action, such as a price on carbon, since it's life and death for the economy and society. But on some issues, such as plastic waste, for example, your company may not have a stake, so let others take the lead. A CEO can't be everywhere.

Stepping into the advocacy game is not optional, but it's not risk-free. There can be blowback. Coca-Cola ran a feel-good ad during the 2014 Super Bowl, with a group of young women singing "America the Beautiful" in multiple languages. On social media, a horde of haters came out to complain. A few years later, Nike featured football player Colin Kaepernick—who had been protesting racial and police violence by kneeling during the national anthem—in its thirtieth-anniversary Just Do It campaign. The company stepped into a firestorm of debate, and videos quickly surfaced of people burning their Nike shoes. But there were also good outcomes. Coca-Cola watched as a second wave of positive reactions swamped the negative voices, and Nike's online sales jumped 31 percent in the days after the ads ran (brand value also increased by $6 billion).[9] At both companies, pride among employees was high.

Getting off the sidelines can be a moment of truth and inspiration. After (another) tragic school shooting in Florida, the CEO of Dick's Sporting Goods, Ed Stack, was distraught, especially since his stores sold assault weapons. In his book, *It's How We Play the Game*, Stack says he kept thinking that day, *"Somebody has to do something. This has to stop."* But suddenly, he writes, *"I realized that somebody had to be me."*[10]

1. A Sense of Purpose, Duty, and Service

In the early 2000s, John Replogle was flying high in business and life. He was president of the Guinness brand for Diageo and living in a lovely house in a nice town with his young family. But one day, after he spoke with a mentor about his personal mission statement, he got into the car with his two young girls, looked at them, and broke down. He realized he wasn't doing something that he felt had real purpose.

There was nothing wrong with selling beer, and Diageo has generally been a good actor in the industry, but Replogle wanted more. He decided to work only for sustainability-minded companies from then on. "I went

PERSONAL PURPOSE

Who are you and why are you here? These are questions that philosophers have been trying to answer for millennia. But it doesn't have to be daunting to find your purpose. For many the answers will flow naturally. Some frame it as finding your personal superpower—the thing you do best. Oprah Winfrey has said that her purpose is "to be a teacher and inspir[e] my students to be more than they thought they could be."* The core question for finding your purpose as an agent of net positivity is this: What do you uniquely do to make this a better world?

*Stephanie Vozza, "Personal Mission Statements of 5 Famous CEOs (and Why You Should Write One Too)," *Fast Company*, February 25, 2014, https://www.fastcompany.com/3026791.

from living in black and white to living in color," he says. He had great success in this phase of his career, becoming the CEO of two well-known purpose-driven companies, Burt's Bees and Seventh Generation, which he sold to Unilever.

As many have noted, *passion is about finding yourself, but purpose is about losing yourself in something bigger than you.* We can follow our interests into hobbies or do work that we love. Many of us find passion and build successful careers that we enjoy. But not everyone finds purpose at work. True fulfillment comes not only from doing what you enjoy, but also serving a bigger mission and touching the lives of others in meaningful ways (see the box "Personal Purpose"). It's about wanting to make a difference—to help, to give, to serve. A sense of personal duty is the path to unlocking more potential and being bigger than yourself. It lays the foundation for building purposeful brands and net positive companies.

For those who understand their purpose, it's easy to feel cognitive dissonance in a workplace focused only on profit. It's an empty shell of a mission—if all you care about is profits and your salary, literally *anything* that makes money would be fine to sell. But most of us have deeper aspirations for ourselves and our families. Those who have done the work to identify their purpose have an inner lighthouse guiding them to the right path, helping them become moral leaders. Bringing your values to work and living your purpose will make you feel alive, and you'll bring out the best in everyone around you.

There's no better example of building a company successfully around meaning than the story and life of Patagonia's founder, Yvon Chouinard. Chouinard grew up in Maine with a love of the outdoors. He became one of the world's preeminent mountain climbers, and he launched Patagonia to sell equipment. The company evolved into a beloved brand, offering high quality clothing for the outdoors and, for the last decade, healthy and ethically sourced food for active people. The company's values are simply stated: build the best products, cause no unnecessary harm, and use business to protect nature.

But Chouinard was never comfortable being a business leader. As he says in his book, *Let My People Go Surfing,* it's as hard for him to admit being in business for sixty years "as it is for someone to admit being an alcoholic or a lawyer." Yet Chouinard understands the power of business, which "can produce food, cure disease, employ people, and generally enrich our lives . . . and do these good things and make a profit without losing its soul."[11]

The company exists both to help people enjoy the outdoors and also to protect the environment—for thirty-five years, Patagonia has donated 1 percent of revenue to grassroots environmental groups. The company has performed incredibly well. It never sought growth but has still expanded quickly, passing $1 billion in sales (and it easily could've been much larger). Patagonia grew by exciting customers and demonstrating better ways of operating—lower resource use, recycled content, a lifetime guarantee to repair products to reduce material use, and incredible benefits and quality of life for employees. Patagonia has inspired many much larger organizations, such as Walmart, that have asked Chouinard to advise them.

Chouinard and the company's CEOs, including Rose Marcario, who led Patagonia through a rapid growth phase from 2014 to 2020, have stayed true to the core purpose and duty to the planet. When the United States passed tax cuts for corporations in 2018, Marcario donated the $10 million they saved directly to environmental causes. They're also not afraid to take a hit in sales to do what they know is right. The company has consistently challenged how people think about consumption, promoting the idea that you shouldn't buy stuff if you don't need it. When the US government reduced the size of some national monuments and parks, Patagonia converted its entire home page from selling its products to just blare, "The president stole your land."

Chouinard has always aligned his personal and business values. He nurtured the core mission while adapting. "In every long-lasting business," he writes, "the methods of conducting business may constantly change, but the values, culture, and philosophies remain constant." A core of purpose and values will give you the courage to convert caring into action, to build net positive companies that give more than they take.

Purpose-driven companies run by purpose-driven leaders are better for society, outperform their peers, and attract the best people like moths to a flame—both Patagonia and Unilever are among the most in-demand employers in the world. Work is not always fun, but it's much easier when you feel that you have meaning. John Replogle said that ever since he made the switch, "even when I have a tough day, I know there's a reason why it's worth struggling." And there will be many struggles. Fighting against climate change, or for justice and equality while doing business well, is not easy.

Purpose can lead you through even the worst that life can throw at you. Victor Frankl was a psychiatrist who spent 1942 to 1945 in the concentration camps in Auschwitz and Dachau. He lost his parents, wife, and brother in the Holocaust, and yet miraculously maintained hope. In Frankl's *Man's Search for Meaning,* one of the twentieth century's most important books, he explains: "Life is never made unbearable by circumstances, but only by lack of meaning and purpose."[12] If he could use meaning to survive the worst imaginable, there is hope for all of us to fight the hard battles against our existential threats, together.

2. Empathy: A High Level of Compassion, Humility, and Humanity

"There but for the grace of God go I." Like many proverbs, it's an idea that has percolated through society and religions for centuries. It recognizes that there's a lot of luck in life. We don't diminish the hard work that gets any CEO or leader to the top. But many people start with a tremendous advantage. The two of us are white males, born in wealthy countries, who had supportive parents committed to helping us thrive. We were handed a winning lottery ticket in life.

Acknowledging the luck and putting yourself in others' shoes to be more empathetic is hard work for many. It's also not as common in business as it should be; just 45 percent of employees believe their CEOs have empathy.[13] Sadly, men in particular have been taught that being compassionate is a weakness.

Leaders today need to see others as human beings, not "human doings," and value what everyone brings to the table. They should cultivate empathy and compassion, even if it's uncomfortable. As the former CEO of Ben & Jerry's, Jostein Solheim, says, "If you don't feel the pain that we're inflicting on Mother Nature, or empathize with the deep anxiety and fear that a Black person feels in America . . . you can't run a sustainable business."[14]

One tool that can help develop empathy is the "veil of ignorance" thought exercise, popularized by twentieth-century philosopher John Rawls. Imagine you are setting up a political and economic system, but you don't know your "place in society, class position or social status . . . [or] fortune in the distribution of natural assets and abilities, intelligence and strength . . ." What kind of system would you design if you didn't know whether you would be born a white male in a wealthy country, or a Syrian girl in a refugee camp? What kind of policies would you want in place, and how would you want companies to behave?

The answer is obvious. Respect, equity, compassion, humanity, and justice would be at the core. The system would provide a basic foundation of well-being and dignity for all, with people at the center, not money. Executives, work toward that vision proactively—we can't wait for the world to magically get healthier and more just.

Ajay Banga, chairman and former CEO of Mastercard, says what makes you stand out now is not just older measures like intelligence (IQ) or emotional skills (EQ). "I say you need DQ—decency quotient—when you come to work every day," he says, "and care about the people who work with you, for you, above you, around you."[15]

There are many executives who are leading with their humanity. The chairman of Indian software giant Wipro, Azim Premji, has made humanity core to his life. He put large portions of his company shares into his $21 billion foundation, which focuses on transforming the lives of the poorest and most vulnerable. Premji has said that "to live with integrity . . . becomes easier if we retain the core quality of humility."[16]

In 2021, Nigerian Ngozi Okonjo-Iweala was named director-general of the World Trade Organization—the first woman and the first African to lead the global organization.[17] She also chaired the Global Alliance for Vaccines and Immunization (GAVI), and sat on the boards of Standard Charter Bank and Twitter. In short, she's impressive. Yet she puts the mission of her work ahead of herself, saying, "when it comes to doing my job, I keep my ego in my handbag."[18] Similarly, IKEA's CEO Jesper Brodin, runs a thriving business, but remains unpretentious. He has been one of the most active and effective leaders in driving business and society toward sustainability, but he maintains a low-key, Swedish style and shows respect for others. "Believe in yourself and your strengths," he says, "but don't forget to rely on other people's strengths, too. Because we're truly stronger together."[19]

Humility does not, however, rule out doing big things. Jacqueline Novogratz, chief executive of Acumen Fund, talks about paired values, working in tension. "You've got to have the humility to see the world as it is," she says, "but have the audacity . . . to imagine the way it could be."[20]

We face many challenges with no easy answers: How do you shift Indonesia's approach to producing palm oil? How can we ensure that all workers in the apparel or electronic supply chains make a living wage? What needs to happen for renewable energy and storage to fully power a factory or datacenter? The only way to solve tough questions like these is to say, humbly, to the world, "I don't have all the answers and I need help." As Wipro's Premji says, "Leadership is the self-confidence of working with people smarter than you."

3. More Courage

All five attributes of net positive leaders are important and reinforce one another, but courage rules them all. Poet Maya Angelou captured it best: "Courage is the most important of all the virtues, because without courage you can't practice any other virtue consistently."[21]

The word *courage* comes from Latin and an Old French word *corage*, meaning "heart." Taking a hard stand requires both the head—the logic and the "why"—and heart. Empathy and a sense of purpose give you courage to make decisions you wouldn't otherwise, to go the extra mile, and to push through the discomfort. If you're not uneasy, you're not going far enough. Jeff Hollender, Seventh Generation cofounder and chair of the American Sustainable Business Council, told us that sustainability goals and public statements should be aggressive enough to make everyone nervous: "When you publish your sustainability report, if you don't give your lawyer a heart attack, you're not doing it right."

It takes courage to go out of your comfort zone and think ten times bigger than you or your peers normally would—to set absurd goals that nobody could possibly do alone. Executives often want to have things under control and predictable, so they shrink the scale of goals—they play not to lose instead of playing to win. That inherently reduces the potential for the business, and for the world.

Net positive leaders go after the biggest challenges. The cement sector, for example, is one of the largest sources of greenhouse gases, producing around eight percent of global carbon emissions.[22] India's Dalmia Cement is putting a stake in the ground and shooting for carbon negative by 2040. There are some more aggressive corporate carbon goals in the world, but for this sector, which makes something so energy intensive, it's a sizeable leap. CEO Mahendra Singh is investing in a big experiment, building the largest carbon capture and sequestration facility in the industry. It's an attempt to make carbon neutral cement by capturing CO_2 in the production process and repurposing it for fuels, chemicals, or materials.[23] Dalmia's 2040 goal, he says, "is difficult to understand, difficult to visualize, but easy to dream."[24] It takes fortitude to dream big.

All of our biggest challenges are daunting and need courageous people to tackle them. Christiana Figueres was the executive secretary of the UN Framework Convention on Climate Change (UNFCCC) from 2010 to 2016. She is largely credited with making the historic 2015 Paris Agreement a reality. A *New Yorker* article about Figueres described how hard her assignment was: "Of all the jobs in the world, Figueres's may possess the very highest ratio of responsibility (preventing global collapse) to authority (practically none)."[25] Somehow, Figueres managed to herd the leaders of some 190 countries toward an acceptable climate agreement. Speaking about how business needs to approach the climate challenge, she has said, "It takes leadership, it takes a cold cost-benefit analysis [in the long term], and frankly, it takes moral courage."[26] She has demonstrated all of those skills.

With courage and a moral compass, leaders can do what they know is right, even at risk of great cost . . . or of angering people who are armed. When Ed Stack made his decision to get off the sidelines on guns, it was a highly contentious issue in the United States (and still is). He watched high school students who had survived a Florida massacre start a global movement on gun safety (which inspired Sweden's Greta Thunberg to launch her school climate strike). Stack thought, "If those kids could muster up the courage to take their fight to the country, we have to be brave enough to make this move."[27]

Stack was running the business his father started, but he had expanded it greatly to more than $8 billion in sales, with 850 stores and thirty thousand employees. The hunting segment—guns, equipment, and gear—delivered about $1 billion in revenues. One of its store brands, Field & Stream, sold the kinds of assault weapons being used to slaughter kids in schools. After he told the leadership team he wanted to get out of the gun business, they estimated they would lose many longtime customers and at least $250 million in sales.[28] Stack said he didn't care about the impact on the bottom line. His decision got national attention and he received hundreds of invitations for interviews. Stack took just two on major networks and then decided he had said enough, which showed a great level of humility as well.

The aftermath was worse—and better—than expected. Dozens of employees quit, and sales did take a big hit, at first. Stack got death threats and needed security. But then a wave of positive responses and "buycotts" gave Dick's more business, and competitive pressure diminished as Walmart, Kroger, REI, and others restricted gun sales as well.[29] The company found ways to innovate around its offerings in the stores that had lost hunting business.[30] Dick's quickly rebounded financially.[31]

Stack's efforts demonstrated one key aspect of courage, speaking truth to power—in his case it was powerful gun lobbyists, politicians, and passionate customers. Similarly, when Paul told Unilever investors that the company would not provide quarterly earnings guidance anymore, it took chutzpah to rebuff the all-powerful investors. It wasn't as if other CEOs felt differently. A CEO of a $15 billion industrial company once told Andrew, "Nobody wants to run their company the way a twenty-eight-year-old stock analyst would want you to." But that CEO wouldn't go public. GE's famous leader from the 1980s and '90s, the late Jack Welch, also admitted, "Shareholder value is the dumbest idea in the world."[32] Unfortunately he said it after retiring. It seems many CEOs and political leaders are more courageous once they leave office.

Perhaps if a CEO can't face investors who don't care about the company's future, they may not be the right person to lead. Bill George, the leadership expert, author of *True North*, and former CEO of Medtronic, says that some leaders lack courage because they "focus too much on managing to hit their numbers . . . they avoid making risky decisions and fear failure."[33] He cites the example of Indra Nooyi, former CEO of PepsiCo, sticking to her guns after developing a strategy, Performance with Purpose, to diversify the company's offerings away from just sugar water. Activist investors almost ran her out of the company, but she balanced short-term wins with invest-ments in transformation. That's courage.

Far too many companies sit back and wait on critical issues, saying, "We're a fast follower." Or executives will say something to us like, "We want to do more, but we're not Unilever." We've heard similar things about innovation and not being like Apple, one of the most creative and impactful companies in history. How sad. Why wouldn't you want to build a vibrant, exciting business that outperforms peers and attracts talent? Great compa-nies don't follow, they lead.

Taking on investors is hard, but imagine publicly rebuking a powerful world leader. Ken Frazier, the CEO of Merck, showed tremendous moral fortitude when he resigned his position on the president of the United States' American Manufacturing Council. His decision came on the heels of the infamous neo-Nazi rally in Charlottesville, Virginia. Speaking about the clash of white supremacists with counter protestors, Trump said that there were "very fine people on both sides."[34] Frazier could not in good conscience work with the president after that. He left the council, saying, "America's leaders must . . . clearly reject expressions of hatred, bigotry and group su-premacy, which run counter to the American ideal that all people are created equal."[35] After the George Floyd murder, Frazier spoke out again, saying that Floyd "could be me or any other African American man."[36] He called out the business community, saying it should "take leadership when it comes to . . . police reform and access to capital. The business community can uni-laterally make an impact on joblessness and issues of opportunity."[37]

Frazier's story should not be news. That it sticks out as rare is a tragedy. Why do leaders find it hard to advocate for the world we want? Why should it feel risky to fight for human rights and the end of slave labor; or for a diverse organization that gives people with different sexual orientations, skin colors, or abilities the same chance; or to actively avoid the destruction of the planet? It may not be easy to figure out how to get there, but let's make it easier for people to say what they know is right. Be courageous and others will follow.

4. The Ability to Inspire and Show Moral Leadership

A leaders' responsibility is ultimately about inspiring and uniting people behind a common purpose. It's not just about giving energy, but unleashing it. It's the ability to motivate and mentor others to higher levels of performance, and helping them both find their own clear sense of direction and figure out how to express that purpose. Or as Bill George (one of Paul's mentors) said, help people find their true north so they can become "genuine and authentic" leaders. George also worked to show employees the good their work did in the world. When he was CEO of Medtronic, he would regularly invite in people to talk to employees about how a Medtronic pacemaker saved their life.

Leaders in business (or life) will be more trustworthy, inspirational, and follow-worthy if their words and actions match. Employees sniff out hypocrisy. Every executive shows their level of commitment through a mix of what they say, do, and prioritize. They create the "shadow of a leader," which helps define the culture of the organization. With today's level of transparency, it's not just about how people act at work, but also what they do in their private lives. With the exponential rise of telework and video meetings, our colleagues now literally see into our homes. Social media puts all our actions on display—we're always in public, especially senior leaders with high profiles.

Why hide your values, or assume they don't apply at work? We know people who sit on boards of conservation organizations, but doing less than nothing to help preserve the environment through their companies. There's no acting in the dark anymore, or being passive. Inaction is action. In 2020, when Facebook CEO Mark Zuckerberg did not take down posts that inflamed violence, workers staged a walkout.[38]

Demonstrating your values matters. Employees see when their leaders do *not* live up to the stated values, and that disengages them. Leaders should find ways to show what they prioritize at work and at home. For example, you can demonstrate life balance and a commitment to well-being through your actions. Inspire people to be healthy and find balance. *Exhausted people don't serve anyone well. We end up with burned out people on a burned-out planet.* Be a mentor to others and help them bring their full selves to work. That's how we get a multiplier effect.

Paul made personal connections central to his style of leadership. When he traveled the world to experience different markets, before going to the local office, he visited homes to talk to real people and understand their lives. At Unilever's annual leadership conference, he gave every one of the hundreds of executives a book to drive new thinking, and took the time to write a personal note to each one. He also tried to connect with people in Unilever's ecosystem, even when it was difficult—like a visit to the widow of a man who died on the job while working at a Unilever facility. Taking personal responsibility for safety, even for people outside of the company's direct control, shows caring and commitment, and people notice. It's also the right thing to do.

Big events and stressors bring out the best and worst in leaders. As Covid-19 hit the world, some companies canceled contracts on customers and diverted business to the highest bidder when markets got tight. Or they kept no promises to employees and furloughed or laid them off with no help. Others honored their commitments and handled the hard choices with humanity. AirBnB's CEO Brian Chesky won praise during the crisis for his "empathetic, transparent messaging about layoffs."[39] Some leaders walked the talk. Dr. Ed Kuffner, the chief medical officer of Johnson & Johnson's Consumer Companies, volunteered in New York City hospitals during the worst days of the early pandemic.[40] He called it "a relatively easy decision," but it was dangerous, and we're sure employees knew it.

The insurrection in the United States in January 2021 was also a profound test of corporate values. Many companies stayed quiet, which was a moral failing. But a number of courageous CEOs, such as Marriott's Arne Sorenson—a good man and leader who recently lost his battle with cancer too young—quickly came forward and took a stand, pausing all donations to the politicians who supported an attempted coup. It was risky—many employees and potential customers could be offended. But it was the right thing to do.

Inspiration comes from actions matching values, showing you care, and connecting to purpose.

5. Seeking Transformative Partnerships

We've been talking about the inner traits that make for net positive leadership. For a long time, corporate strategy has also focused on the inside of companies—what capabilities you have, and how to build strategies and tactics out from there. But that inside-out view of a business is only one part of the equation. The most critical element of the net positive mindset is understanding the world's needs—that is, an outside-in perspective. Don't ask only what you're good at and what you can offer the world. Ask instead, What are the world's limits and constraints? Where are we failing humanity?

We will move beyond incremental solutions to our big problems only if we bring all of these outside needs and perspectives into the business. That starts with leaders who are open to listening (humility) and seek to work with stakeholders toward a larger goal. It's a new mindset to see that learning from NGOs or critics, trying to influence consumer behavior, supporting pro-sustainability government policies, and embracing the latest science should all be part of the normal operation of the business.

The early stages of building a more sustainable company are filled with lower-hanging fruit that are mostly internal. The easy efficiencies can come swiftly, and you may continue finding them for years to help pay for more ambitious measures. But you will quickly discover how many things you cannot do alone. Transformative change requires broad partnerships. Leaders have to demonstrate that they're open to working with others, not just commanding from behind a desk. And not just open to others, but seeking them out and hungering to solve bigger challenges with them. The regular bias for action that any good leader has needs to become a bias for *transformative, collaborative* action.

A net positive company treats everyone as worthy of respect and partnership. Shifting entire value chains means not just pressuring suppliers to do better, but innovating with suppliers to rethink how products and services are delivered. Finally, the system won't shift without the right policy changes, which means creating open, productive partnerships with governments.

Working well with these diverse groups is a new leadership skill. Nobody in this chain of stakeholders works for you or the company. Putting yourself on par with all partners, or even being in service to them, requires humility, and being acutely aware of and shedding any disdain you might have (such as assuming NGOs have no business acumen). For NGO leaders, it's also unhelpful to think business people have no soul. Don't judge or put people in boxes.

Coalitions will only be transformative if everyone at the table is open to working in true, equal partnership. The partners also need to see the benefits of the work. It sounds trite, but finding the quick win-win-wins, where there is value shared by all, is how you build common ground, bridge the gaps between everyone, and build trust.

Many companies and CEOs are deeply committed to transformative work. François-Henri Pinault leads Kering, the $19 billion luxury conglomerate with high-end brands such as Gucci, Yves Saint Laurent, and Balenciaga. For years, Pinault has been vocal and innovative about how to value and protect nature. Kering's Puma brand was the first major company to estimate the financial value of what nature provides the business. Its "environmental P&L" was groundbreaking and raised awareness about how much value companies extract from natural systems without paying for it.

Pinault and his company work with stakeholders to shift the fashion industry, which has an enormous land, water, and carbon footprint. Kering has partnered with the University of Cambridge to study how fashion companies can transform biodiversity strategies, and is working with Conservation International to convert one million hectares of farmland to regenerative agriculture by 2025. It's all part of its commitment to heal six times the land area used by its entire supply chain.[41] That's net positive work.

After French president Emmanuel Macron gave Pinault a mission to lead his sector on environmental protection, he launched the Fashion Pact, with the help of Paul's organization IMAGINE. The Pact brings together dozens of the biggest fashion brands to address climate change, biodiversity, and protecting the oceans.

How much impact can a group of two dozen big players in the sector have? How many hectares of regenerative agriculture can they create? How many people can they inspire through their brands? The answers are unknown, yet, but it's exciting to explore the potential for real change when everyone is working together.

Talking to the Grandkids

This Bible verse is telling: "The harvest is plentiful, but the workers are few" (Matthew 9:37). There's so much need in the world, and much good work to do, but there are not enough people on board.

We need more leaders who are decent, empathetic, kind, and feel an obligation to improve society for everybody. A net positive company thrives by caring and putting people first. Companies may seem like unlikely leaders of a movement to bring more humanity to the world, but why not? We can shift from faceless and robotic organizations and economies and recognize each other's humanity.

The first step is caring about what's going on in the world. Do you care that hundreds of millions of people go to bed hungry, not knowing if they'll wake up the next day? Or that two and a half billion people still do not have access to clean drinking water and sanitation? Or that in most countries women still do not have the same rights as men? And on and on.

Without getting overwhelmed, we can work toward solutions and feed our own souls. As Adam Smith said, putting yourself in service of others will make you better off also. So, the answer to the question "Do you care?" is actually another question: Who do you serve? (How rewarding is it if the answer is "my shareholders"?)

Paul gave a radio interview years ago in the United States. The host asked why he was doing all this sustainability work—was it because it was good for the business, or was it for his grandchildren? Without taking a beat, he said, "My grandkids, of course." Andrew was listening to that interview and, at first, thought it was a missed opportunity to say how good sustainability is for business. But when you get down to it, "For my loved ones" is the right answer. Why else are we working if not to serve others, even if it's just for our inner circles.

How do we heal the world? The solution, perhaps, is as simple as love. In the end, finding our humanity at work is about knowing who we work for, and what we'd want our loved ones to say about the way we've spent our lives. The CEO of a large European automaker recently gave her board homework for a strategy session—write a letter to your grandkids about what you did on this board.

What would your letter say?

What Net Positive Companies Do to Foster Courageous, Caring Leadership

- Ask, "What kind of world would we want if we did not know in what circumstances we were born into?" (The "veil of ignorance")

- Cultivate a sense of responsibility and duty to serve the world, and encourage people to bring their values to work

- Help people in the business find what they do uniquely for the world (their purpose)

- Embrace empathy, compassion, and humility, and openly seek help and partnership from others

- Reward courage, speak truth to power, and do what's right even if there are costs

3

Unlock the Company's Soul

Discovering Organizational and Employee Purpose and Passion

Nothing can be greater than a business, however small, that is governed
by conscience, and nothing can be meaner or more petty than a
business, however large, governed without honesty and brotherhood.

—Lord William Lever, founder of Unilever

What motivates people? What makes them happy? After millennia of philosophers trying to answer that question, twentieth-century economists, mostly led by the Chicago School of economics, decided the answer was simple: we just want more money and stuff.

When Andrew got his economics degree, the models all assumed that people only seek to maximize utility and outcompete others. Newer fields of study, including behavioral economics, came to different, much more realistic conclusions: people are *not* always rational and have dozens of cognitive biases that affect decision making. We look for information that confirms what we already believe, for example, or we rely too much on the first (or last) piece of information we heard.

Another line of research sought to develop a better view on what really drives us. Two Harvard business professors, Nitin Nohria (who became dean of the business school) and Paul Lawrence, dug into this issue in their book *Driven: How Human Nature Shapes Our Choices*. Their work concedes that there are two fundamental human drives that fit the dog-eat-dog economic model: we want to *acquire* and to *defend*.[1]

But they add two fundamental drives to the equation: to *bond* with others and to *comprehend* our world. We need connection, meaning, and purpose. Is there any doubt that this is true? Fordham University professor Michael Pirson builds on Nohria and Lawrence's work in his book *Humanistic Management*. Pirson asks us to imagine a company that works to satisfy all four drives. That company would be built around performance and growth, like any profit-maximizing firm, but critically, would also pursue connection and purpose.

Finding personal and organizational meaning is not a soft-hearted, anti-business strategy. In fact, satisfying basic human needs is a powerful path to business success. A net positive company will work to satisfy all four drives for its employees. It will improve their lives by giving them good paying jobs, of course, but mainly by helping to discover and unlock their purpose—letting them connect heart and brain.

That work begins by finding the organization's purpose.

Reviving Unilever's Heart

In 2000, Unilever bought Bestfoods for $24.3 billion.[2] It was Unilever's largest acquisition ever, and the biggest in the history of the food business. The company was optimistic and on a buying spree. Expectations were high, but by 2008, a different picture emerged.

The share price had not moved in a decade. Some brands were slowing down and, after selling some big businesses, such as US detergents, revenues were down from a peak of €55 billion to €38 billion. Unilever had lagged its biggest competitors in margins and annual growth for twenty years; it was the only one that had shrunk significantly during the 2000s. The company lost its status as the world's largest consumer goods company, becoming a distant number three, far smaller in revenues and valuation than its main rivals, Nestlé and P&G.

What happened is an old story. In expectation of synergies and growth, acquisitions commanded a high price, but then failed to deliver. Shareholders demanded a return, so executives focused on delivering unrealistic, short-term profit targets. This led to drastic reductions in investment and innovation, the lifeblood of a consumer goods company. For years, Unilever didn't build a factory, launch a significant new brand, or engage in meaningful M&A other than selling "underperforming" business. (There's some truth to the saying that there are no underperforming businesses, just underperforming organizations.) Core brands were starved of advertising and promotional support, which accelerated the decline. The words "marketing" and "innovation" were replaced by "finance" and "restructuring." It's a death spiral that many companies can relate to.

Unilever had fallen victim to shareholder primacy.

The organization seemed to be accepting its decline. Market shares in key strongholds were dropping rapidly, but alarm bells didn't seem to be going off. In Germany, total sales shrunk by more than half in twenty years, and the plan was to sell the shrinking business and exit the market. But why avoid a battle? Don't run away from the hardest issues, run toward them. If you can win in the toughest places, you can win everywhere. And you can't win if you don't try.

The overall decline affected the culture and made the organization more internally focused. Despite attempts to create a "one Unilever," the company was highly decentralized, and people had more allegiance to their own wallets, brands, functions, and regions than to the overall company. Pride and cohesion seemed to be lacking—company bathrooms used competitors' soaps, and cafeterias stocked competitors' teas and offered butter but none of Unilever's margarines.

Paul arrived at Unilever after a career in consumer goods, the three most recent years as Nestlé's CFO and head of the Americas business. He was the first CEO Unilever had ever hired from outside the company. The litany of issues facing Unilever may sound dire now, but the possibility of what the company could offer was captivating. Unilever was filled with fantastic people selling beloved products. The heart of an exciting organization with purpose was still there, even if it was beating slowly.

It was time to reinvent Unilever, keeping what was valuable—core values, capabilities, and a long history of leadership—but giving a shock to the system and jolting the business back to vigor and success. They needed to nurture the core while stimulating progress (to paraphrase Jim Collins's *Good to Great*). If the basics aren't there—growth, investment, innovation, pride, unity, and openness to new ideas—the rest falls apart, and you can't do anything big. Even a simple sounding goal like "zero waste" will seem impossible.

Unilever needed to get its mojo back and fight. It's no fun to work in a declining business. The first priorities were the basics: get the house in order, put the right people on the bus, sharpen the strategy, bring back a growth mindset and culture, and get moving.

Getting the House in Order

If you don't have the foundations of a healthy business in place, any attempt at a mission-driven strategy or net positive model will likely fail. You won't have the resources, energy, and focus on purpose that you need. Getting the house in order at Unilever centered on a few areas:

Focus on basics and reinvest in the business. Paul increased investments in people, brands, R&D, and manufacturing to improve quality, ensure competitiveness, and reestablish the vibrancy and growth of the core businesses. He introduced new tools and practices to identify growth areas, drive out costs, and free up capital for reinvestment—no different from most companies, but it was hard work.

In the first year, the 9 for '09 program gave everyone solid, but achievable, growth and cost-cutting goals to prove what they could accomplish by working together and leveraging global scale. The slogan "We are Unilever" resonated—the former chief sustainability officer, Jeff Seabright, says they were finding the "Uni" in Unilever. Another initiative, Max the Mix, focused on developing innovative products that delivered more value for consumers and higher margins for the business. To drive R&D effectiveness up, they set a target that 75 percent of innovations had to add to margins and achieve minimum scale—on average, new initiatives were adding only £2.5 million to turnover, a rounding error for a £38 billion revenue company.

Restarting growth, eliminating non-value-added costs, and rigorous working of capital management (from positive to negative) freed up funds to reinvest in long-term, purposeful business priorities and to accelerate M&A. As the business came back, so did confidence and enthusiasm about the company's potential, which led to more investment. It was the start of a positive virtuous circle, the proverbial flywheel gaining momentum.

Create a compelling vision based on core values. The growth message was clear, but the language from the top changed in other important ways. Consistently using words such as *purpose, multistakeholder,* and *long-term*—and then acting on those ideas—started shifting the culture. Unilever also created a new strategy framework, the Compass, a simple two-page document laying out the basics of winning in consumer goods. The Compass made clear why the company existed and provided discipline, a common set of values, a bias for action, and clear standards of leadership—things like maintaining a growth mindset, investing in people, and taking responsibility. A company run by principles, within a framework, is far more effective than one run on rules.

With the launch of the Unilever Sustainable Living Plan (USLP) a year later, the core "why" in the Compass shifted to match the new mission. This brought the strategy and sustainability roadmaps into alignment. In a small language shift to build pride, Paul said the new strategy should always be referred to as the *Unilever* Sustainable Living Plan (not some generic sustainable living plan). It's important to play your own game—you'll always be a distant second trying to be someone else.

Simplify structure for speed. Unilever reorganized to reduce decentralization and complexity. Being close to different geographies and markets to understand them was vital, but so was solidarity and common purpose. Leadership wanted Unilever to feel like a single company with powerful brands, not a conglomerate of independent silos, but remain agile enough to win in highly competitive markets. It was a balance. The company moved to leaner structures to get faster feedback from markets and minimize the "lost in translation" syndrome companies often suffer from. The center of gravity had to switch from internal focus on self-serving interests to an "outside-in" view, centered on the citizens the company served. To break up those product and country fiefdoms, Unilever reorganized around major product categories—food and refreshments, health and beauty care, and home and personal care.

Bring the board along. No organization can succeed over the long term without the support of the board of directors. Yet, as we mentioned, senior executives rank boards as the number one source of pressure for short-term performance.[3] The gap comes, in part, because board members struggle to understand what ESG (environmental, social, and governance) means, how it's tied to strategy, how to provide active oversight on it, and how to prepare for higher external expectations. In a survey of EU companies, only 34 percent of board members said they had the knowledge they needed on climate change (versus 91 percent on finance).[4] Most board members grew up in another era and find a focus on purpose unsettling. They often express concerns that addressing ESG issues will expose the board to more risk, but it's the reverse—understanding and managing sustainability issues reduces risk and increases opportunity. Our grand challenges, such as climate change and pandemics, are exposing these board shortcomings and raising more questions about how to improve corporate governance.

Unilever changed the board to support a long-term, multistakeholder model. It increased racial diversity, and sadly it's still the only major board in the United Kingdom that's gender balanced. Unilever has been blessed to bring in people with significant knowledge in areas ranging from climate change to the future of food. Unilever leadership also exposed the board to the company's many partnerships and mission-driven activities, which greatly increased buy-in. When the board is in sync, sustainability goes deeper into the DNA of the company. During the aborted Kraft Heinz takeover attempt, the board was tested, but united in not only sticking with the USLP, but strengthening it.

Connect employees to the mission. The structural changes were easier to make than shifting beliefs. With a new CEO, turnover in the executive ranks, and a new, intense mission, many employees were skeptical—especially after many previous attempts to revitalize the company had failed. For some, the USLP looked too ambitious. Unilever leveraged the Compass to get everyone engaged. To drive performance, the organization borrowed a page from the book *Execution* by Larry Bossidy, and asked all 170,000 employees to write a "3+1" plan for themselves: three business goals tied to the Compass, and one personal area to work on. Sandy Ogg, the SVP of HR at the time, says that senior leadership looked at samples of employee plans and called some people to say, "You're awesome and what you're working on is cool." Or, in harsher moments, they might "call some guy sitting in the middle of Sweden and say, 'I looked at your three-plus-one and it's not great—step it up, dude.'"[5]

Sending the Right Signals to Create the Right Environment

Getting back to basics laid the groundwork for profiting from purpose, but those elements were not enough. Paul and the management team also had to send clear signals about the new direction. Leaders should demonstrate complete consistency in message, commitment, actions, and behavior to avoid the "say/do" gap. People will remember what you do more than what you say. If you don't walk the talk, why would anybody take you seriously?

When Paul told investors he would not provide quarterly guidance anymore, the move was a powerful signal to investors. But it had an even greater impact on the organization. It told managers they could think bigger, make investments in innovation and in stagnant brands, and make decisions for the long-term. This is in stark contrast to the common bad habit of manipulating earnings to hit quarterly targets.

Unilever sent signals across the business to align the organization around the revitalized mission and long-term focus. For example, while exiting the quarterly earnings game, Unilever also examined how its *own* $26 billion pension fund was being managed. Like any fund, it had money in the whole market, including fossil fuels. It wasn't consistent to talk about long-term thinking and climate change while investing the pension for short-run returns, and putting money into coal companies. Take the systems view: Unilever's business will be severely damaged by climate change, so the company was partly financing its own demise.

Unilever committed its pension fund to align with the UN's Principles for Responsible Investing, which commits the money managers to consider ESG performance (they had no guidelines prior). The incentives for the fund managers shifted to reward performance over the longer term, not the quarter. The fund started to perform better. The company was also consistent and creative in financing. It issued the first corporate sustainability bond, for £250 million, to build more sustainable factories in South Africa, China, Turkey, and the United States.[6] These fiscal moves gave the company credibility and a seat at the table to push financial markets to think longer-term.

Unilever also revamped executive compensation. Even with slowing sales in the 2000s, bonuses remained high. That disconnect created a disincentive to grow and evolve. For consistency, the pay system was harmonized so people at the same level got the same pay structure globally, after tax, no matter where they lived (which took self-serving salary discussions out of the equation). Unilever sent organizational signals in a range of ways that we'll touch on throughout the book, such as revamping the supplier code to reflect USLP goals and priorities; issuing one of the earliest integrated annual reports (that is, financials and ESG performance in one document); releasing human rights and modern day slavery reports; publishing a tax code; changing recruiting policies; improving gender parity in management and pay (the company hit 50/50 in gender in 2019); and adding gender and racial diversity to the board. Combined, these efforts created a multiplier effect and accelerated change. Consistency built trust and more action.

The right Key Performance Indicators (KPIs) also sent clear signals to support the longer-term, multistakeholder vision. The original USLP provided many publicly stated metrics, but there were other important internal targets to help track the move toward net positive: metrics on diversity, the pay gap, and how in-demand the company was as an employer of choice, for example.

Sending the right signals took focus, commitment, and courage. But you know what most of them did not need? Money. Sure, how you allocate capital and prioritize budgets sends powerful signals, and those shifts happened in Unilever as well. But it doesn't cost anything to send important signals about what a company cares about or harmonize your values across operations. So, why not do it?

Starting at the Top

As the former Unilever marketing head and architect of driving purpose back into brands Marc Mathieu says, "If you want to change a brand in the consumers' minds, you have to change it in employees' minds first, especially the leaders."[7]

Change efforts can be like rebuilding an engine while the car is moving and accelerating. The biggest area of work to get the house in order was in HR. For a change agenda this big, the company needed to get the "right people on the bus," which meant executives who cared about the world and its challenges and had enthusiasm for purpose. Unilever had an outside firm interview the senior leadership team and map skills to jobs. The project exposed some disturbing insights about the culture and capabilities: a low level of curiosity, lack of diversity of thinking, and low awareness of key trends in the world. Doug Baille, a senior operational exec who took over HR in 2011, says the assessments showed "we were weak in thinking systematically."

In those early months, the personnel changes were dramatic. It's okay to have productive skeptics around, but cynics are harmful. No company has the luxury to spend time trying to convert people. Some execs self-identified as uninterested in the whole purpose thing, including the then–marketing director. About 70 of the top 100 executives were "refreshed" along with substantial changes to the board.

In parallel, the HR systems needed reworking to make the new strategy come alive. They tied job descriptions and requirements to the USLP, for example, to help create a purpose-driven performance culture. If you choose a purpose-driven path and the business results look lousy, skeptical shareholders will say, "I told you so." The whole experiment to show how business can be a force for good is ruined. As Unilever pursued purpose, the organization felt *more* pressure to do well financially, not less.

As the top executive ranks shifted, the best people were matched not with the biggest jobs, but with the roles most critical for future success. Unilever combined communications, marketing, and sustainability into one job, chief marketing officer, tasked with embedding the USLP into the company. It was a central role, not some special sustainability group on the fringes of the organization. Keith Weed, the first person to hold the combined job, says the position aligned internal and external communications and clarified how the company talked about purpose. In creating this position, he says, Unilever built "an organizational machine to help deliver the USLP and its big ambitions."[8]

Unilever also needed the right capabilities and buy-in in key departments—R&D, sales and customer development, marketing, supply chain, finance—to integrate the strategy and build consistency. Getting these areas on board is a hard lift. For most companies, finance is the most difficult area to change, and it was no different at Unilever. Finance execs feel the analysts and investors breathing down their necks more than any other company leaders. They also tend to be risk avoidant, which is not the way net positive companies play the game.

To build more knowledge and commitment, Paul encouraged the CFO, Graeme Pikethly, to represent Unilever on key global sustainability partnerships, such as the World Business Council on Sustainable Development's Redefining Value project. Pikethly also served as vice chair of the Task Force on Climate-Related Financial Disclosures (TCFD), a protocol that every CFO now needs to understand.

The HR moves helped ensure that people truly got the mission, and that their souls were in it. All of this work to get the house in order, send the right signals, and align the organization got Unilever's heart beating stronger. But these were basics—hard work, but frankly nothing new. Getting to the next level required more—it took purpose.

Seek Purpose

There's nothing more powerful for an organization than getting to the heart of why it exists, and then making that purpose come alive. It ripples through the company and builds trust with consumers, suppliers, communities, and other stakeholders. Having a clear North Star is the hidden ingredient that builds resilience and decides success over failure, engagement over indifference, and respect over disdain.

But what is corporate purpose? Colin Mayer, the head of The Future of the Corporation program at Oxford's Said Business School, argues that "the purpose of business is to solve problems profitably, and not to profit from causing or exploiting problems."[9] That's a good, tactical way of saying "giving more than you take." At a deeper level, purpose should express an enduring and meaningful reason for the organization to exist. Everything about the business should orient around delivering this purpose, profitably, and in the long term (see the box "Five Questions to Ask").

There are many inspiring purpose statements like Unilever's (to make sustainable living commonplace), such as:

- Bayer: *Health for all, hunger for none*

- LinkedIn: *Create economic opportunity for every member of the global workforce*

- Tesla: *Accelerate the world's transition to sustainable energy*

- Timberland: *Equip people to make a difference in the world*

FIVE QUESTIONS TO ASK

The work of living your purpose must start at the corporate level. Mission-driven commitments, such as zero deforestation or respect for human rights, must apply to the whole company or there's no credibility. You'll know that purpose is core to strategy if you can answer yes to these five questions. Does the purpose . . .

1. Contribute to increasing your company's growth and profitability today?

2. Significantly influence your strategic decisions and investment choices?

3. Shape your core value proposition?

4. Affect how you build and manage your team and organizational capabilities?

5. Take up part of the agenda of your leadership and board meetings, every time?

- IKEA: *Create a better everyday life for the many people*

- Schneider Electric: *Empower all to make the most of our energy and resources*

With a solid commitment in place at the corporate level, embedding it deeper in the organization means developing purpose statements for individual product lines. Food and candy giant Mars also runs the world's largest pet care business (Iams, Pedigree, Whiskas), with a purpose *to create a better world for pets*. Unilever's Dove brand seeks to *help girls raise their self-esteem*, and Knorr wants to *ensure that wholesome, nutritious food is accessible and affordable to all*. Bringing purpose to brands is black-belt level net positive work (more on this in chapter 9).

Brands use missions as beacons to guide them toward the right initiatives to pursue with stakeholders. Purpose also helps them focus acquisitions and strategic expansions—Unilever has acquired dozens of purpose-led businesses. The company used purpose as a powerful way to drive a turnaround, but it is not alone in this approach. When Hubert Joly took the helm of the troubled electronics retailer Best Buy in 2012, he needed to get revenues going and trim costs. The leadership soon asked, Joly says, "What do we want to look like when we grow up?" The answer was to go beyond selling devices and pursue a purpose of enriching lives through technology.[10] In an era of declining retail, Best Buy's mission drove innovation in product and service offerings. The company is now worth four times what it was in 2012.

Purpose is a core pillar underpinning a strong organization, like pylons of a skyscraper, allowing it to grow tall. But some companies do not bury the pylons very deep. They slap a purpose sticker on the company and talk a good game, even if there's a fundamental disconnect. You can tell when purpose statements are trying to cover the damage they do, or distract from the true obsession, maximizing profit any way they can.

Some of the most famous corporate implosions, like Enron's bankruptcy or Boeing's 737 Max safety issues, came from organizations with seemingly strong mission statements. Purpose alone doesn't guarantee that you serve the world. You need a basic overlay of service, shared values, and behaviors that help the world thrive. Philip Morris has a clear purpose around the right to smoke, and fossil fuel companies talk about serving the world by providing energy. But if your core product kills or makes the planet unlivable, how much is your purpose worth?

Many banks talk about purpose, but if they aren't making their investment portfolios sustainable, then their money is still flowing to businesses that deplete the world. French insurance leader AXA started divesting from coal in 2015, an early move that delivers on its stated purpose, to "act for human progress by protecting what matters."

Purpose should drive consistency in all behaviors, not just picking from an à la carte menu of actions.

Making it legal. Companies that want to make clear that they are a multi-stakeholder business can seek certification from B Labs and become B Corps. In contrast to the profit-maximization focus of traditional businesses, B Corps sign a Declaration of Interdependence to be purpose-driven and use business as a force for good. If a B Corp lives its principles, it will be on the path to net positive, for sure. This isn't just for small companies. French food giant Danone certified a large portion of its business with B Labs, making it the largest B Corp in the world (passing Brazil's Natura, the first large public company to get certified).[11] The number of B Corps is growing fast, with more 3,500 (as of this writing) in seventy-four countries.

Companies can go a step further and build purpose into their legal structure by becoming a benefit corporation (available in some US states). In Europe, Danone became the first listed company in France to be named an Entreprise à Mission, which officially embeds purpose and ESG objectives into its articles of association.[12] An amazing 99 percent of shareholders supported the move. Unilever was fortunate to acquire several B Corps, with Ben & Jerry's being a true pioneer of the movement. These businesses have outperformed the rest of Unilever and helped change the culture for the better.

Purpose pays off. An eight-year study of high-growth companies was looking for traditional drivers behind success, such as innovation. But the authors found that purpose, a factor they hadn't been seeking, created "more unified organizations, more-motivated stakeholders, and more profitable growth."[13] Purpose also attracts talent, engages employees, and provides psychological well-being. Having a clear "why" creates a sense of excitement that's hard to match.

The JUST Capital 100—a list of companies ranked highly on purpose and serving society—produced 56 percent higher total shareholder returns over five years.[14] Research by Deloitte showed that mission-driven companies have 30 percent higher levels of innovation and 40 percent higher levels of employee retention.[15] In the United Kingdom, over a three-year period, B Corps grew twenty-eight times faster than the economy.[16]

Purpose attracts customers as well. Two-thirds of consumers say they are willing to switch to an unknown purpose-driven brand, and 70 percent say they pay premiums for more sustainable products.[17] When people have searched for a product online, Google has reported, they used the keyword "sustainable" ten times more in 2020 than in 2015.[18] Purpose-led companies can tap into a growing, multitrillion-dollar market for sustainable and ethical products.[19]

There are many paths to finding purpose. Unilever, over time, came at the issue in a few ways, including rediscovering the original mission of the company; helping top executives—and then all employees—find their individual purpose; and seeking outside-in perspectives on what the world needs (the UN's SDGs gave the company a full list of areas to tackle).

Purpose is a great way to create business value, but it's a lot easier to act on if the business is running well to begin with. Companies need purpose and performance. Unilever had a history of both to draw on.

Retrospective Purpose—A History of Serving

To make the drastic changes the company needed, it was not enough for Paul to stand on a soapbox and decree it. Unilever needed to go back to its roots, the undeniable heart of the company. So, in the weeks before assuming the CEO role, Paul researched Unilever's rich history. He visited Port Sunlight, the small village in northwest England where, in 1878, the founding Lever brothers built a community for workers from their nearby soap factory. Before the factory was fully running, they built houses, a school, a health-care facility, and theater and art houses.

About 131 years later, Paul deliberately held the first meeting with his senior team in the place where it all started. The discussion focused on the values that had made the company great and lasting. The Lever brothers created the company's first brands, Sunlight detergent and Lifebuoy soap, to improve health in Victorian Britain. Lord William Lever, even in the nineteenth century, spoke in terms of shared prosperity and serving society. His early aim was "to make cleanliness commonplace and to lessen work for women" and he pitched a form of moral capitalism.[20]

It wasn't all smooth sailing. An attempt to build a community like Port Sunlight in the Congo, with the Belgian government, failed. It led to forced labor plantations, a not uncommon but deeply troubling problem at the time.[21] But at home, Lever Brothers was highly innovative and socially progressive. It was the first company in the United Kingdom to offer pensions and a guaranteed six-day workweek. As workers left to fight in WWI, the company held their jobs open and paid the men's wages to their families. It was highly unusual. So, a century later, when Paul's chosen successor, Alan Jope, guaranteed jobs for months after the pandemic started, he was following in the founders' footsteps.

Not every company has 140 years of history to draw purpose from, but most have a founder with a story. They have a reason for being, and it pays to find it. In India, Mahindra Finance's leader, Anand Mahindra, looked back to why his grandfather founded the business, and refocused the company on a mission of helping rural communities "rise." Through fair lending rates on homes and small agribusinesses, the company grew to serve 50 percent of Indian villages and six million customers.[22]

At Unilever, the purpose work never stopped. It was an early leader in modern corporate sustainability. In the 1990s and 2000s, the company created the Marine Stewardship Council (MSC) with World Wildlife Fund to protect fisheries, cofounded the Round Table for Sustainable Palm Oil, developed a code of practice for sustainable agriculture, and ran many community programs in emerging markets. Some brands had started to integrate purpose. The two biggest initiatives were Lifebuoy's hand-washing program and Dove's global self-esteem campaign. These efforts were all good models of corporate social responsibility. But they were disjointed, not tied into the core of the business, and looked more like typical corporate social responsibility (CSR) work.

The history was there. Lord Lever had implanted meaning and "doing good" in the company's DNA, and other Unilever CEOs had championed similar themes. But they were never central to the company's strategy and, too often, they faded into the background like a recessive gene.

Many Unilever managers took the company's heritage for granted. The company needed a way to bring the history into the foreground again. It needed a framework, focus, consistency, and an ambition to seek transformative efforts—the systems changes that are the hallmark of a net positive company.

A new direction would take some effort and time—and a big, new plan to rally around.

Purpose Going Forward: The Unilever Sustainable Living Plan

After two years of refocusing on Unilever's history of service and prepping the organization by getting it growing again, it was time to launch a more formal, unified strategy around purpose. It was time to look forward and understand the landscape. You need both, or you get stuck in nostalgia for the past.

In 2010, the company launched the Unilever Sustainable Living Plan (USLP). The need to stop the decline of the business and rediscover purpose and identity was core to the launch. It moved purpose from a nice-to-have to an explicit driver of success by significantly increasing ambition and embedding it throughout the company. As former Unilever sustainability executive Gavin Neath says, Paul's framework made the company's history and purpose "central to the company's strategy, and [we] managed it like other business activities, setting targets and metrics and rewarding good performance."[23]

Beyond the business reasons, the USLP also came from a deeper, elemental, and moral place. The leadership knew it was no longer good enough for companies to be less bad. With climate change and inequality, big business needed to be good; they needed to be net positive.

The USLP translated the company's purpose of making sustainable living commonplace into a core aim: double the size of the business through strong performance, while decoupling environmental impact from that growth, and optimizing Unilever's positive social impact. At launch that translated into three audacious goals to achieve in a decade:

- Improve the health and well-being of more than one billion people

- Reduce environmental impact by half

- Enhance millions of livelihoods through the growth of the business

The environmental impact goal had a broader meaning, committing to "decouple" the business from material use. Unilever would aim to grow without using more resources. In practice, some goals went further—aiming to use only green energy, for example. Other goals sought to reduce impacts by improving standards, such as a 100 percent sustainable sourcing target. Back in 2010, these were highly aggressive goals, especially for a $40 billion revenue company. With the other two statements focused on social impact, the total intention of the plan was to move toward net positive.

Beneath the three overarching goals sat seven subcategories, each with specific targets for the business: health and hygiene, nutrition, greenhouse gases, water, waste, sustainable sourcing, and better livelihoods. That last category covered the entire social agenda. At the urging of Marcela Manubens, Unilever's global VP of integrated social sustainability, it was later expanded into three social agenda items: fairness in the workplace, opportunities for women, and inclusive business (see figure 3-1). As the company continued to learn by doing, there were other adjustments along the way, but the three big goals remained in place for a decade.

FIGURE 3-1

Unilever Sustainable Living Plan

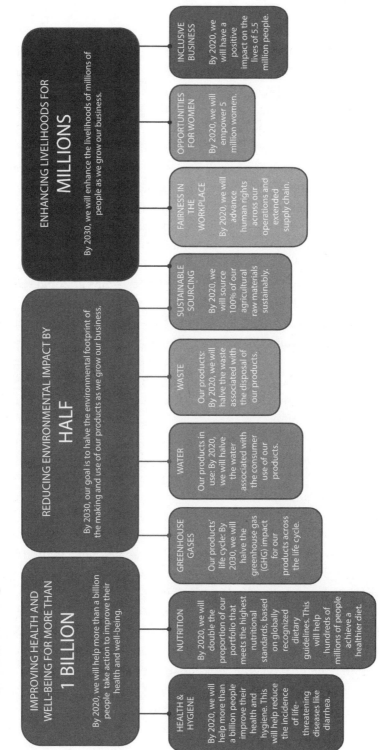

Before the USLP, a small handful of mission-led, privately held business leaders had developed aggressive plans to build net positive businesses—Patagonia, IKEA, Mars, and Interface with its Mission Zero. But for big, public companies, extensive sustainability goals were nearly nonexistent. In 2007, British retailer Marks & Spencer launched Plan A (because there is no plan B) with about one hundred targets for operational footprint, sourcing, customers and products, health and well-being, and more. It was detailed and leading-edge, and it inspired others, including Unilever.

The USLP broke new ground. It set more audacious targets and aspirations at the scale of one billion people, extended the time frame to a ten-year horizon, introduced the idea of decoupling, and covered all brands and the full value chain. It also set a few goals for entire systems, not just the company. The plan was more than just strategy or tactics—the "P" could stand for philosophy as well. It was an aspiration and a way to prepare for a world that was evolving quickly. The USLP needed to be seen as a way of doing business.

The plan accomplished much in terms of measurable outcomes (see the box "The Success of the USLP"), and Unilever learned a great deal through creating and implementing something so broad and deep. Let's look at what worked, what they needed for it to succeed, and what they would do differently in hindsight.

What worked. When it launched, the USLP did two important things. It said to the world, "We don't have all the answers," making the company accessible and human, and it said, "We can't do it alone," which forged crucial partnerships.

The USLP was meant as a guiding star, but flexible enough to evolve as the business and the world changed. The plan was not a CSR-style add-on, sitting to the side of the core business. It was, and is, the strategy, and it's hard-wired into the growth agenda. Because it wasn't separate, the company could not excel if the USLP was not successful, and vice versa. From early on, the USLP was independently verified by PwC and used as a tool of transparency, accountability, honesty, and trust. The plan included more than fifty public targets, a choice that was heavily debated. Some saw it as a risk if they missed some. But with trust in business so low, being more transparent was the best way to restore it.

The USLP was also hard-nosed. Managers had to provide facts, testing, and proof that the purpose-driven initiatives to help society—such as reach-

THE SUCCESS OF THE USLP

At the ten year mark in 2020, the USLP had hit or exceeded most of its goals, achieving, for example:

- Over €1.2 billion costs avoided

- Helped 1.3 billion people improve health and hygiene

- 100 percent renewables for electricity in manufacturing

- 65 percent reduction in CO_2 from energy in manufacturing

- Global gender parity in management: women are 51 percent

- 67 percent of agricultural raw materials sustainability sourced, up from 14 percent; 99.6 percent of palm oil and 88 percent of twelve key crops

- Water use down 49 percent per ton of production

- Zero waste to landfill at all factories*

*For extensive statistics on the USLP, see *Unilever Sustainable Living Plan 2010 to 2020 Summary of 10 Years' Progress*, Unilever, March 2021.

ing 1.3 billion people (as of today) with health and hygiene programs—were effective in their mission *and* helped the business. As former HR exec Sandy Ogg says now, "There was nothing soft about the USLP (or about Paul)."

What it needs to succeed. Buy-in from employees and major stakeholders is a must. If the goals in a plan like the USLP are big enough, then it's clear you can't do it alone, and partnership becomes essential. A company also needs credibility as a whole before driving it into the brands or divisions. And that comes in large part from consistency. Both the individual leaders and the businesses need the courage to walk the talk and follow through on their promises. When you know what's right, find the strength to fight for it.

Key learnings. Unilever made mistakes that others can learn from. It underestimated the level and regularity of communications needed to sell the plan to stakeholders. The board was a particularly important internal stakeholder, and continuing to educate them about the world's thresholds and the company's approach took more work than expected. To focus efforts and attention, Unilever set up a separate board committee on sustainability and corporate reputation; it was a better option than just adding the agenda to the audit or compensation committees. (Today as reporting requirements increase, board audit committees should also be competent in nonfinancial reporting. Things are moving fast.)

Externally, Unilever should have engaged shareholders more in the value creation discussions. By not reporting earnings quarterly and abolishing guidance, Paul had many fewer conversations with investors. The ones that did happen were more strategic, but they needed to make the case for tying purpose and ESG performance to strategy and financial outcomes. The general low level of understanding of ESG materiality, and lack of metrics to measure or compare performance, made these discussions harder. We have better data now, but at that time, the proof of the link between ESG and value creation was grossly absent. When you're promoting a model that treats profit as a result, not an objective, investors need to be enrolled and educated; otherwise, they will make life difficult. Unilever lost some initial investors and it took more time than expected to attract investors who would embrace the long-term model. Most companies still cater to their existing shareholder base rather than seek out better partners.

Looking back, it's also clear that the first plan had too much of the "E" in ESG, and not enough of the social agenda or governance. It wasn't complete. The company strengthened those areas over time, and more recent events, such as Covid-19, have further increased awareness of a weak social contract and the need to address racial and income disparities.

When you go public with a big plan, NGOs and others will hold you to a higher standard and demand more. Taking the lead makes you a target. It's mostly a good thing, because you attract partners, but if you miss some of the goals that require help—for example, shifting the supply chain—NGOs will be critical when you don't quite get there. At times, Unilever ran ahead of NGOs and was almost a bigger advocate on an issue. You want NGOs who are willing to join the journey and support each other. The company learned also that it takes a long time to set up broad partnerships to tackle big challenges.

Cynics and skeptics abounded when Unilever launched the USLP. Back in 2010, the bottom-line benefits of sustainability had yet to be proven. And after years of financial underperformance, many felt Unilever could ill-afford cuddly experiments with "purpose." But time has vindicated the USLP, and it accomplished a great deal for the company. It brought much-needed oxygen to a business that was stagnant. It has been a purpose-driven roadmap that inspires, encourages consistency, provides a lens to help make better choices, and drives the business. Unilever is more successful and re-silient today, and the plan has directly paid off in many ways, both financial and intangible.

The only real regret is that, given the state of the world, the USLP wasn't *more* aggressive, as the world is still falling far short of what's needed. Many of the original goals are table stakes or not good enough anymore. They're not fully net positive.

We'll talk more about the USLP in the next couple of chapters, diving into how the targets helped expand thinking and how the plan created trust and transparency with stakeholders.

Create Authentic, Purposeful Leaders

The USLP would not succeed without strong leaders throughout the or-ganization. Early on, Paul asked leadership guru Bill George to create an executive training program with Unilever's Jonathan Donner, the VP of leadership and development. They brought in a number of other experts on leadership and together, they created the Unilever Leadership Development Program (ULDP), a week-long exercise, and launched it with the top 100 executives.

The program explored what type of leader businesses would need in a decade, assuming a volatile, uncertain, complex, and ambiguous (VUCA) world. A core element of the program was guiding executives to find their own individual purpose. Donner describes the program as a journey, "tak-ing a long, hard look at who you are, what you want to do with your life, and how you convert it into something that can be bigger than yourself."[24] He was fascinated by one of George's key ideas, the "crucible," a transfor-mational event that affected one's life path and leadership style. They asked attendees to share deeply personal moments that made them who they are.

It was important to start with the CEO. Vulnerability was part of being honest and authentic, and it closed the distance between people. Paul shared his personal crucible moments, including his father working himself to death by holding two jobs to ensure a better life for his children; climbing Mt. Kilimanjaro with eight blind people from all over the world (it started his foundation, which now supports more than twenty-five thousand visually impaired children in Africa); and surviving a terrifying experience during a terrorist attack in Mumbai. With the CEO opening up, people got more comfortable and told their personal stories.

They embraced transparency. An HBR case study notes that in one session, "two people competing for the same position publicly shared their development plans."[25] That's a powerful way to instill transparency and trust as core values. Donner credits the program with jump-starting the organization's path to purpose and promoting the trust and risk-taking required to make it happen.

Unilever also hired a top search firm, MWM, to conduct in-depth interviews with every executive and provide thorough feedback on their professional profile and aspirations. As the execs worked through the program and began self-reflection, they drew on these brutally blunt assessments to build detailed personal development plans. They considered what they wanted in their careers, and whether they had the skills or experience to get there. Paul eventually read hundreds of these plans and provided each with a personal response. It helped him get to know the talent better, and learn what his extended team wanted for their work and personal development.

Unilever extended the week-long program to the top 1,800 people in the company. The next wave of development was to translate that organizational energy into more tangible action. Unilever worked with leading thinkers in systems (Peter Senge), leadership (Bob Thomas), and business sustainability (Rebecca Henderson) to help the executives take their purposes from mission to action. They also drew on the work of adviser C.K. Prahalad, who taught executives about "bottom of the pyramid" markets in the developing world.

Over time, Unilever offered a one-and-a-half day version of purpose training to *all* employees; to date, more than sixty thousand have completed the program. The chief HR officer, Leena Nair, says attendees uncover their own purpose and passion, their skill gaps, and how they want to manage their physical, mental, emotional, and spiritual well-being. This information gets integrated into a personal "future-fit plan."

Purpose is the best way to inspire and unlock the potential of the whole organization, and it all begins with looking inward and finding individual purpose. *Unlocking the company's soul has to start with baring your own.*

Create Inspired and Demanding Employees

No matter how many executive purpose retreats you do, a plan as broad as the USLP goes nowhere without buy-in across the organization. As Nair says, "the USLP becomes real because of employees—people bring this to life." The goal was always to get the entire organization rowing in the same direction, while meeting employees' needs for personal meaning. This approach has become even more important as younger workers take over the global workforce.

Grant Reid, the CEO of Mars, has talked about how Gen Zers are already reshaping the workplace and demanding transparency. They want a holistic view of the world, and confidence in the sustainability of the products.[26] They're innovative and demanding, and they will soon be an economic force. By 2030, millennials are set to inherit more than $68 trillion from their baby boomer parents.[27]

Deloitte's 2020 global survey of the two younger generations revealed that their top concerns—out of all possible issues—are climate change and protecting the environment.[28] As consumers and employees, Ms and Zs make clear that they care deeply about values and sustainability. Two-thirds say they won't take a job with a company with poor CSR practices.[29] A Gallup study concluded that "a deeply felt sense of purpose ties millennials to their jobs." If younger workers know what their organization stands for, the study found, 71 percent plan to stay there. If they don't know the purpose, only 30 percent say they will stick around a few years.[30] It's not as big, but there's a purpose gap among older workers as well.

Unilever's training helps connect personal purpose with the larger goals of the company. Employees should understand their company's approach and its strengths and weaknesses as it travels toward net positive. Think of it as prepping them for a dinner-table conversation with friends and family who may have tough questions: Why do you use so much plastic in packaging? Are there kids or slaves working in your supply chain? Why don't you pay farmers enough? Why are you still using fossil fuels?

For employees to have deeper knowledge and buy-in, a two-day program won't do it. There have to be consistent and extensive communications. Paul wrote a regular blog for ten years, repeatedly reinforcing themes around purpose, partnership, and performance. He regularly held CEO calls with groups of new employees and all-company town halls that around ten thousand employees attend. Country and local leaders run another eighty regional town halls every week. Executives try hard to seize opportunities to celebrate those doing good work, or talk about the USLP to celebrate its progress and reinforce its ambitions.

Giving employees the chance to live their values creates a talent magnet. Unilever gets two million applications annually for fifteen thousand positions, and a million students apply for roughly six hundred graduate intern roles. *Three-quarters of new hires say they came to Unilever because of the mission.* Over the last decade, Unilever's standing as an in-demand employer rose dramatically. On LinkedIn, Unilever is one of the most followed organizations in the world, right behind highly desirable tech giants like Apple and Google. In fifty-two of the fifty-four countries where Unilever recruits from universities, it's the employer of choice within the consumer goods sector. It's the most in-demand employer overall in twenty countries. At the beginning of the 2010s, Unilever wasn't even in the top 10 in its category in such core markets such as the United Kingdom and India.

The benefits of finding personal purpose are hard to describe. As Mark Twain (possibly) said, "The two most important days of your life are the day you were born and the day you find out why." When we feel that we're becoming who we really are, it gives us a sense of belonging, and life becomes infused with meaning. With purpose, a job can serve deep human needs.

The Rewards and Risks of Deep Engagement

Beyond employee attraction, the purpose work has also paid off in rising employee engagement. Unilever HR leader Nair says that her department has data going back decades, showing that the percentage of employees happy to be working there continues to rise every year. More than 90 percent say they have pride in the company, an impressive number in a world where engagement scores average just 15 percent.[31]

Sunny Verghese, who founded the $24 billion agribusiness company Olam, based in Singapore, has a strong view on employee engagement. At a basic level, he says, you satisfy people with training, providing a safe working environment, and fair goals. Up a level from that is "engaged," where people have more autonomy and a chance to master skills as part of a winning team. But making people "inspired," Verghese says, is a different animal: "They need to see a purpose . . . and that all the effort is going to make a difference." It's not about more profit or growing more cocoa, but finding meaning, especially for the younger workers.

Olam's purpose is *to re-imagine global agriculture and food systems.* To invite workers into that mission, his company ran an exercise asking employees to reimagine the global agriculture system so it could feed nine or ten billion people—and do it with a fraction of the resources used today. More than eighteen thousand employees answered the call. In a different part of the food chain, Trane Technologies—one of the world's largest producers of climate solutions for buildings, homes, and refrigerated transport of food—invited its thirty-five thousand employees to join a worldwide innovation brainstorm dubbed Operation Possible. The goal was to identify "absurdities standing in the way of a better future" and rank the favorites. The employees picked as their top choice "the coexistence of hunger and food waste," a serious challenge that they can help with. In the early days of the USLP, Unilever also wanted to engage everyone in the journey. Miguel Veiga-Pestana, the global head of external affairs and sustainability when it launched, helped organize a 24-hour online global brainstorm. It brought together twenty thousand people inside and outside the company to pose questions and seek answers about how to reach the USLP goals. It was a powerful way to enroll people in the vision. Again, years later, when designing the post-2020 USLP, Unilever opened up the discussion and fifty-five thousand employees chimed in. That's a huge number of people feeling that they have a stake in the future of the company.

There's an interesting problem (and opportunity) that arises with so much engagement: it drives internal expectations through the roof. Employees who come there to change the world can sometimes find it a letdown to have a regular, nonsustainability job to do. But every job needs people thinking in systems, in net positive terms, and about how to help the world thrive. These inspired new hires pressure the company to go faster.

Employee demands on business to do more, especially on climate, is a growing force to be reckoned with. Before 2020, when Amazon started to take leadership positions on climate change, the company had been quiet on sustainability. Things changed when nearly nine thousand employees signed an open letter to CEO Jeff Bezos with a list of demands, such as a zero emissions goal and cutting political donations to climate deniers.[32] Other workers launched Amazon Employees for Climate Justice to continue the pressure.[33] Employees are calling out their companies on social media, and even at press conferences, if actions don't meet the ethics or stated values. There is little chance this trend will slow down. So, embrace your younger employees and let them pull you into the future.

If you're heading in the right direction, employee pressure is not a problem, but an advantage. For a company trying to accelerate toward net positive, it's a powerful asset to have aggressive allies all over the organization. Take advantage of it and help create internal social activists and entrepreneurs who will demand much of the company and themselves in service of the world.

Serve Employees and Enable Their Humanity

Much of the discussion on employee engagement focuses on the benefits to the company, such as higher productivity. But what if companies operated in service of those employees? They would work to improve employee well-being, a net positive result, and enable them to bring their full selves to work. They would help them with big life moments by, for example, providing extensive leave for new parents or others providing caregiving.

The Covid-19 crisis was a big test—and opportunity—for companies. How did they handle employee needs? Did they treat them like numbers and assets, or like people deserving respect? Employees, communities, and governments were watching companies closely to see if they would keep paying their vendors, or how they handled layoffs—did they provide help with mental health, loans, retraining, and more? Some companies failed their Covid-19 test miserably, which is a good way to destroy engagement. Some put staff at direct risk by not giving them enough protective gear—meatpacking plants were particularly negligent. The companies that succeeded in the crisis took care of direct and indirect staff, ensuring some financial stability for suppliers and customers. It's not expensive to do this right. Unilever was watchful of employee mental health as people shifted to at-home work, to ensure that nobody felt isolated or left behind.

Outside of moments of crisis, companies can help their people live more sustainable lives—like a Goldman Sachs program offering all US employees access to clean energy for their home or subsidies for employees to purchase electric vehicles.[34] Organizations are also encouraging employees to be active citizens. Hundreds of companies, including HP, L'Oréal, PVH, SAP, and Walmart, joined the Time to Vote initiative, giving employees election day off to go do their civic duty. In 2020, Old Navy (owned by Gap, Inc.) paid employees for eight hours if they worked at the polls.[35]

As more people want their voices to be heard, and protests in the streets are common, companies will face more moments of choice. How supportive are they? In early 2021, consulting giant McKinsey made the wrong choice. As protests grew in Russia in support of opposition leader Alexei Navalny, McKinsey's Moscow office sent an email to staff saying that demonstrations "will not be authorized . . . employees should stay away from public areas . . . and please refrain entirely from making related posts in any media . . . this line of conduct is mandatory." Even for Russia, that's Siberia-level cold. And it had to be enervating for employees.

In contrast, during global climate marches, Patagonia and Canadian retailer Lush shut down stores to let their people join the movement. The Australian enterprise software company Atlassian goes even further to encourage employees to become climate activists. Cofounder Mike Cannon-Brookes wrote a blunt blog, *Don't @#$% the planet*, announcing that employees could take a paid week every year for charity, marches, and strikes.

Companies are now realizing that they also need to address systemic problems (such as racism) that their employees face—in one survey, 87 percent of employers "plan to take steps to overcome barriers and build a culture of dignity over the next three years." That's up from 59 percent just a few years ago.[36]

Treat people the way *they* want and need, or what some call the Platinum Rule (a twist on the Golden Rule, where you treat people the way *you* want to be treated). Ask employees how they want to serve society, and help them make a net positive impact.

The Magic of the Unlock

Every organization has an origin story. Not all are as clear as Lord Lever's focus on health and well-being. But there is always a reason the company came to be. Every person has a purpose or two, even if they haven't thought about it in that way.

It is true, though, that timing is everything. Companies can do the right thing, but at the wrong time. The classic case is BP's Beyond Petroleum campaign in the late 1990s, an attempt to pitch the oil giant as an energy company of the future. The company's investments remained almost entirely focused on fossil fuels, and the culture got stuck in a cost-cutting mode. The intention was good, but the execution lacked. Our friend David Crane led energy company NRG for years, pushing his board to start the transition away from coal. He was right, and was thinking about the long-term, but the culture of the organization was not ready, nor were the shareholders. So, the board pushed back, hard.

If the organization is ready and has the necessary elements in place, then identifying company and personal purpose, and finding the links between them, creates a virtuous circle. It's how you unlock the company's potential. Academic data proving this case is getting stronger. A study on corporate purpose and financial performance found clear correlations between what they defined as "purpose-clarity" and financial and stock market performance.[37] The companies rated highest on purpose also saw an increase of 4 percent in return on assets. One of the authors of the paper, Harvard Business School professor George Serafeim, has issued a string of analyses showing that firms that manage their material sustainability issues well outperform their peers.

Putting the hard data aside, listen to Best Buy's CEO Hubert Joly, who says, "If you can connect the search for meaning of the individual with the purpose of the company, then magical things happen." Whether magical or practical, the connections between personal, brand, and company purpose create a stronger, more successful business that's more resilient—a business prepared for the tough work ahead.

Building a net positive company requires courage, big thinking, and working on systems in deep collaboration. With purpose, the company and its leaders will be ready to stretch their thinking and redefine what's possible. As Paul was leaving Unilever, the company conducted important purpose work with the incoming executive team, led by adviser Valerie Keller. One outcome was a new mantra around the company's Compass strategy tool: *People with purpose thrive, brands with purpose grow, and companies with purpose last.*

What Net Positive Companies Do to Find Purpose and Unlock Higher Performance

- Go back to their roots to understand the original purpose of the company and its reason for being, and to leverage the company's DNA to serve stakeholders better

- Look forward to understand how the world's needs will evolve and where the company's purpose can best serve the world

- Get their house in order and invest in people, brands, and innovation to speed the pursuit of net positive

- Send the right signals and set policies that drive net positive thinking and behavior

- Help top executives become authentic leaders, and be consistent in word and deed to live the company's purpose

- Enable all employees to find their own purpose and connect it to the company's

4

Blow Up Boundaries

Thinking Big and Setting Aggressive, Net Positive Goals

The person who says it cannot be done
should not interrupt the person doing it.

—Chinese proverb

Breaking the sound barrier, running a four-minute mile, surviving in space. Each of these seemed impossible . . . and then they became commonplace. In 1947, a test pilot died when his plane disintegrated as it approached supersonic speed (760 miles per hour). Some scientists worried that a plane would not hold together at that speed. But just a few months later, Chuck Yeager passed Mach 1.0 in his Bell X-1.[1] When British runner Roger Bannister ran a mile in 3 minutes 59.4 seconds, he proved the human body could do it. Within a year, three people ran four-minute miles in a single race.

It takes courage and perseverance to go beyond the boundaries of what was done before. But once limits are revealed to be largely invented, the mindset shifts, and many repeat the feat, or go beyond it.

Consider the goals of a net positive company to be the four-minute barrier for business. It seems almost impossible, but the chase is exciting, and when the barrier breaks, the floodgates will open. Once you see it done, it's doable. A zero-waste factory seemed ridiculous, but now it's fairly commonplace. Green energy was too expensive, but now it's cheaper than fossil fuels in most of the world. An electric car that could go hundreds of miles was science fiction, but now it's on its way to obsoleting the combustion engine. Eliminating the scourge of polio was a dream, but cases are now down 99.9 percent. Some executives claim there isn't enough talent to get to gender parity in large companies, but a few, like Unilever, have already gotten there.

Going further and finding ways to not just cut negative impacts, but create a positive handprint, can seem daunting. But unlike breaking the speed of sound, which was not required for humanity to thrive, attaining net positive goals is essential for our economy and society to flourish over the long term. We have hard tasks ahead, like building a circular or even regenerative economy, decarbonizing industry and transportation, ending dire poverty, and building an inclusive and just society. They're not impossible. But we need courage to believe that a single company or person could make progress on such lofty ideals.

We turn now to blowing up the boundaries in our thinking and organizations that hold us back from net positive outcomes. Think of it this way: if we stick to the proverbial "four walls" of business, then the most we can possibly achieve for many impacts is zero—no waste, carbon, or accidents in operations, for example. That's great, but to cross into net positive territory, we have to expand our horizons.

Broaden Your Thinking

We can't make token commitments on something as large as climate change. Our goals need to match the moment. Whether they seem doable or not is not relevant, and we're running against time. However, before a company can work toward the systemic change we need, it has to transform itself. It must find the silos getting in the way of larger thinking and break them up. No more playing it safe or falling back into incremental and linear thinking. While it's tempting to play not to lose, or to avoid committing to a goal before having all the answers, we have to think about how to win—we can't think small.

The bottleneck in achieving systems change is as much ourselves as it is actual barriers. A big enough goal will be tough to swallow, but it will drive new thinking. When Unilever's Lifebuoy soap set a goal to teach one billion people healthy hand-washing habits, the global head of the brand at the time, Samir Singh, thought the number was impossibly large. But, he says, "it pushed us to think more creatively about everything": building partnerships with public health bodies and NGOs, figuring out how to reach poor and rural areas more effectively, finding impactful innovations in behavior change, and exploring how best to teach kids and mothers about hygiene in a way that sustains changes in habits.

If a goal is not making you uncomfortable, it's not aggressive enough, and someone else will likely disrupt you. We have an innovator's dilemma. It's not in the traditional sense from Clayton Christensen's work about how entrenched companies can't shift to new, disruptive technologies because they have so much invested in the status quo. Instead, we have an *emotional* innovator's dilemma. We know that, say, human rights violations in the supply chain are not acceptable. But we don't move because of fear, or because we don't see others moving, or because we don't know how it will affect shareholder value.

The bigger goals—usually ones that start with "zero" or "all"—expand horizons and force that all-important systems thinking. You need to be more holistic to understand all the additional benefits, or consequences, of hitting these targets. Zero waste factories generally have better safety records and run better, and the people are more engaged. When you break down old thinking, you see that you can manage a factory to zero waste *and* save money. The most sustainable buildings save money on energy (or make more than they need), but they also make people more productive and happy to work there or, in a hospital, help them heal faster. Sometimes the cause and effect can seem counterintuitive. *The magic word here is "and," not "or."*

It's a form of intellectual laziness, or dated thinking, to only see tradeoffs. The first boundary to challenge sits between your ears. Many of these big targets are not tradeoffs at all, as technology has improved or new processes become commonplace. The boundaries you put around people determine their thinking and behavior—if it's too narrow, behavior will be different than if you open up what's possible. But you'll need two things in place to help the organization set net positive goals: an understanding of what the world needs (an outside-in view) and more freedom to think big (the space to succeed).

Outside-In

It's not always clear to executives why the company has to go as far as *zero* impact, let alone going into net positive territory. After all, the decision on how much or how fast to cut costs in a single area of business would normally be driven by when the payoff is right or when there's capital available. Why go much faster?

It's clearly not just an internal calculus—you take on bigger goals because they are the right scale to help solve *global* problems around resource use, waste, climate change, and more. The difference is bringing the outside realities into the business. The key idea is to think about the thresholds that the planet can't overstep without serious ramifications, such as 1.5 or 2 degrees Celsius of warming.

The Stockholm Resilience Centre developed a model of planetary boundaries that would be bad to breach. The original list of nine include climate change, biodiversity loss and species extinction, ocean acidification, freshwater use, and introduction into the environment of toxic pollution, micro-plastics, and other "novel entities." One of the main authors, Johann Rockström, talks today about fifteen global natural systems and how many are near tipping points. He says that three—loss of arctic sea ice, glaciers in west Antarctica sliding into the ocean, and coral reef death—have likely already passed a point of no return.[2]

It's ironic that the best way to blow up mental boundaries in a company is to understand the physical boundaries in the world. But limits do exist. As with all good science, the debates on these thresholds rage on. The exact numbers, or even if you can measure some accurately, are up for discussion. But the basic idea of limits on a finite planet, in these categories, is unassailable. It should guide thinking in all organizations globally.

That's the "outside-in" on science. But there's also a need to understand better the range of systems (natural and human-made) that the business is interacting with. Executives should hear unvarnished views from stakeholders on their priorities. Unilever has used external advisory boards to get blunt advice and provide an early warning system so leaders can prepare responses and strategies. There are different kinds of councils, with some focusing on the NGOs' or critics' perspectives, others on more strategic help, and some on a specific topic where deep knowledge is important. For instance, in addition to the global sustainability advisory board, Unilever created a specialized sustainable agriculture advisory board in 2000, which later expanded to focus on all sustainable sourcing.

Andrew has served on many of these strategic advisory groups, including for Caesars Entertainment, HP, Kimberly-Clark, Trane Technologies, and Unilever (in North America). The good ones give the advisers regular access to the C-suite and board. The best ones are clearly led by the top executive. Kees Kruythoff, the head of Unilever North America at the time, led the council meetings—it was *his* meeting, not the sustainability officer's.

Longtime advisers on Unilever's global board, such as sustainability expert Jonathan Porritt, spent significant time visiting operations around the world and reporting back to Paul. Listen to these boards with humility. Let them talk about what's going on in the outside world and expand your thinking. Killing them with PowerPoints about how great you're doing won't help you.

It's also good to reach out to NGOs, critics and supporters alike. They may raise an issue that you should address and need their help on. If you're coming from the shareholder-primacy view, an NGO's concern would only matter if it affects costs or the public image. But if you approach the NGO with a genuine desire to understand an issue and help solve it, you may innovate more with a knowledgeable partner. Or you'll get tough love to help avoid mistakes.

When Unilever found a technology to make oil from used "sachets," the small-format packaging that creates so much waste in India and elsewhere, it reached out to an NGO partner to discuss the innovation. The NGO was not enthusiastic about such technology, saying, "We have no interest in capital investment in a broken paradigm." Harsh, but fair—recycling plastics was viewed as a nonsolution, one that makes things a little less bad, but avoids the real issue, the entire packaging and product distribution system.

The NGO pointed out that the industry needed more radical change in materials and business models (such as package-free stores). You only hear these honest appraisals if you start from humility and a desire to learn. Unilever's former chief sustainability officer Jeff Seabright says that NGOs help you go far beyond getting your house in order. "Let the NGOs in and create a constructive tension . . . the 'house' at Unilever is much bigger now with more people flowing in and out, working together, reshaping the business," he says.

All of this is at odds with a more traditional and prevailing mindset of operations and strategy that's "inside-out," where products or innovations are shoved at customers, regardless of whether they address real needs or solve broader challenges. In a volatile world, looking inward and serving yourself (and shareholders) is a recipe for quickly becoming irrelevant. The beauty of an "outside-in" perspective is that it puts people and solving shared challenges at the core. It was a key driver of the Unilever Sustainable Living Plan (USLP).

The Space to Succeed

How people behave in a company and what they prioritize are driven by values, but equally controlled by rules, norms, and boundaries. If you put people in a little box, narrowly defining their role or what the company can take on, you stifle creativity. You won't innovate at the scale we need. Reward people for the wrong things and you get the wrong outcomes.

Sometimes the organizational design boxes people in or creates roadblocks. Different parts of the company need to be coherently connected so goals don't work against one another. Manufacturing could have a goal, for example, of operating at the lowest cost, but that could conflict with targets for responsiveness, speed, or customization. Or in a multinational, the profits for a brand may be measured globally, so growth goals would apply evenly across the world. But that doesn't align with goals to invest in new markets or in brands that need more time to establish themselves.

The solution is to give people space to think about the long term. When Paul abolished quarterly earnings guidance, it gave the organization breathing room and distance from relentless pressure to perform in ninety days. If you know management is not going to ask for justification for every choice you make within the quarter, you can set bigger goals. People still needed to deliver and hit performance targets, and that forced hard choices about priorities, but they ended up being better choices. It's a fine balance. Ask everyone to think big, but also acknowledge that financial and human capital are finite; you should make plans to shoot for the stars, but you can't do it all at once.

Focusing on a common set of values and purpose helps managers prioritize. The two core and closely related strategy documents at Unilever—the

USLP and the Compass—were the guideposts. A factory manager might choose to invest in converting operations to achieve zero waste, and focus less on producing at the lowest possible cost per unit that quarter. Brand executives can choose how best to invest in purpose-driven social change. Unilever established that tough social issues—race, diversity and inclusion, LGBTQ rights, public health, and so on—were part of the business's priorities. Investing some of the marketing budget in community projects like hand-washing programs then becomes a *business* decision, not one based on philanthropic or corporate social responsibility priorities.

With fewer boundaries, everyone has more flexibility in thinking about where the business can go. Unilever became much more inclined to buy mission-driven B Corps when leadership thought in a larger way about what they wanted the company to achieve.

Breaking Boundaries with the USLP

The USLP not only helped revitalize Unilever, but it also refocused the company, which was too insular, on the outside world. The inspiration came from the realities of planetary challenges and the needs of people everywhere. When the UN's Sustainable Development Goals (SDGs) launched in 2015, Unilever's plan became even more centered on global targets.

The creation of the USLP was not inside-out and did not rely on a process of consensus. Paul sat down with precisely two people, the sustainability leads at the time, Karen Hamilton and Gavin Neath. They gathered perspectives from external advisers and NGOs, such as Greenpeace and World Wildlife Fund (WWF). They also drew on internal expertise on sustainable agriculture, life cycle analysis, nutrition, and hygiene. But in large part, the three of them wrote it. They knew that some people in management would not see the plan as either immediately practical or desirable. Internal buy-in would take time, and many in the organization only began to pay attention when, Neath says, "they realized Paul was deadly serious about it."[3]

The three big USLP goals—help a billion people improve their health and well-being, halve the environmental footprint while doubling sales, and enhance the livelihoods of hundreds of thousands of people—were boundary breaking. The company's existing purpose-driven programs, such as the Lifebuoy hand-washing training, had reached several million people—a great accomplishment, but ridiculously far from a billion. The hundredfold increase in the goal extended people's thinking. Many subgoals went further than ever before, such as the target for *all* sourcing to be sustainable. It was more holistic, versus doing well-intentioned, but disjointed, work in a few parts of the company under the banner of corporate social responsibility.

The words "zero" and "all" appear frequently in the USLP. Zero goals may not get you to net positive alone, but they sure break boundaries. It's unlikely you can hit a target like that without partners, or without working on more systematic design issues. For example, to hit a long-term zero emissions goal, Unilever looked at all sources of carbon, bringing focus to issues like the refrigerants used in ice cream cabinets. Working with industry partners to develop natural refrigerants with much lower global warming impact has been a multiyear project—the time frame that forces partners to break the boundary of quarterly thinking.

The organization used interim goals and quick dopamine hits of success to give confidence, generate positive motion, and change behavior and the culture. Unilever created or modified other tools to help embed the USLP in the organization; an internal price on carbon, for example, sends a signal to employees to get serious about emissions reductions. The company also owes a lot to the former marketing head Marc Mathieu, who added "brand purpose" to the design of its "brand love key," which marketers use to lay out the core focus of a product and the main benefits it provides to consumers (more in chapter 9).

Net positive companies put purpose at the core of a brand, which is a powerful way to unlock innovation. The USLP mission "to make sustainable living commonplace" drove R&D and brand teams to break boundaries on what their products could do for the world—not just functional benefits, but greater impacts on systemic challenges. The Domestos cleaning brand, for example, moved from making marginal improvements in cleaning efficacy, which barely kept the business alive, to focusing the brand partly on the health issue of open defecation. It unlocked a whole new horizon.

The USLP was never meant to be a static ten-year plan; it was a living document. Net positive companies need goals that evolve as the understanding of thresholds and the world matures. Once Unilever had halved greenhouse gas emissions, the next level targets got more aggressive. The bar needs to be continuously set higher. As the understanding of boundaries and systems expands, so can the vision of the sustainability plan.

Unilever's Energy Work

In addition to going through a materiality analysis, one of the first things a company does to understand its impacts on the world is to run a life cycle assessment of the whole business. It's eye-opening to discover where a company's impacts really are, and it helps blow up boundaries. For most sectors, the vast majority of the carbon footprint, in particular, is outside of the company's direct control. Unilever's data looks like that of most consumer products companies, with only 4 percent of the greenhouse gas footprint in manufacturing or distribution.[4] The lion's share is in supply chains and in the consumer use phase of products (mostly heating water to wash clothes, dishes, or people).

Fighting deforestation is a high-leverage activity for upstream emissions, and efforts to change consumer energy use are the best way to tackle downstream emissions (through innovation to develop products that can wash in cold water, for example). But while that full value chain work is the ultimate target, the thresholds view of the world still forces the company to manage its *own* footprint. It was good business, but if Unilever was going to advocate for climate action more broadly, it had to walk the talk and dramatically reduce its own direct emissions first.

The original USLP aimed for a 40 percent reduction per ton of production in both Unilever's on-site emissions and also emissions related to purchased electricity from the grid. That goal would allow the company to hit its 2020 target of doubling sales without adding a gram more of carbon per year—it would decouple emissions from expected business growth.

Over time, Unilever increased the aggressiveness of the goals and moved the energy targets to absolute reductions, not per ton. By the Paris climate meeting in 2015, Unilever was aiming for carbon positive in its operational communities, one of the first companies to set such a goal. For example, it bought renewable energy to cover electricity emissions for its Port Sunlight plant, but also covered the emissions of another firm, a bottle blower, on site. The company extended its goals to become carbon positive across the business by 2030, sourcing 100 percent of all energy (electric and thermal) from renewables, and eliminating any electricity from coal by 2020. But a tough challenge for decarbonization, as many companies find, is how to manage industrial heat, where it's still common to use coal and diesel.

In some developed markets like the United Kingdom, there was access to biogas. In India and China, however, the company had to help create local businesses to turn agricultural residue—from fields they were buying food from—into pellets or briquettes for biomass. Unilever also installed solar thermal in places with lots of sunshine, such as Kenya, and switched off diesel generators. In 2016, the company opened a state-of-the-art personal care factory in Dubai, with solar providing 25 percent of the facility's energy needs.[5]

Over the decade, Unilever got much more efficient, reducing absolute energy demand by 29 percent by 2019 (while growing). Total savings have reached €733 million since 2008, showing that you can set absolute goals and do even better. The company has hit its target for 100 percent renewables for electricity and is about half way to using renewables for all energy use.

Decarbonizing operations is important, but it's now the most basic of table stakes, and Unilever's most recently set goals reflect that reality. The target is to reach carbon neutrality for all products, from supply chain through sale, by 2039. To make this kind of progress, you need goals that change behavior.

Courageous and Uncomfortable Goals

In the years since the USLP was launched, its format has been endlessly emulated. Similar structures—three big overarching missions (like improving the lives of a billion people) and multiple subgoals beneath—popped up at Mars, Olam, 3M, DuPont, and many other companies.

Mars's impressive plan, Sustainable in a Generation, has three areas of focus: healthy planet, thriving people, and nourishing well-being.[6] The candy and pet food giant set aside $1 billion for fighting climate change, a number Unilever's next-gen USLP matched a couple of years later. The race to the top, with sharing of best practices, has increased the number of these big-picture plans.

Not every company needs the same plan structure, but they need something to establish robust, sometimes scary goals using a range of approaches and styles. We look here at five key dimensions of effective sustainability goals that will point the organization toward net positive: make them "SMART," focus both on the "what" and the "how," make sure they are in keeping with science (or go even faster), apply them to the full value chain, and target a positive "handprint" (a positive impact, as opposed to a "footprint," which is used mainly as a negative).

In every category, we'll give a number of examples in quick succession. Every organization is a bit different, but there are some goals that almost everyone should have. Remember, if some of your targets don't make you uncomfortable, you're not pushing hard enough. The chairman of Indian IT giant Wipro, Azim Premji, says, "If people are not laughing at your goals, your goals are too small."[7]

SMART 2.0

In the world of motivational speakers, there's a nice acronym people use to help set good goals. Make them SMART, we're advised: **S**pecific, **M**easurable, **A**chievable, **R**ealistic, and **T**ime-bound. We agree entirely with specific, measurable (which generally means quantitative), and time-bound (there's a deadline). But the other two are problematic. What is realistic, besides what you already know how to do? But you can't really know what's plausible until you apply some ingenuity. If you step back and look at a whole system, large shifts may be more possible than you realize.[8]

The goals should be big and heavily influenced from the outside-in anyway. The climate doesn't care whether it's realistic to eliminate carbon emissions by 2040 or 2050. As Apple's CEO Tim Cook said, "Something magical happens when you set a goal that's a bit crazy . . . the results are always better."[9] So, let's use *results-oriented* for the "R."

We also don't love *achievable*. If you know it's feasible, it can't be big enough. Corporate goals have long been set from the bottom up (and inside out); ask everyone what they think they can do, and then set a slight stretch target. You can cut energy 10 percent of this year? Okay, let's call it 12 percent. *But a goal with a clear glide path isn't really a goal—it's an action plan.*

We prefer *aspirational, ambitious,* or *audacious* for the "A." Go for carbon neutral by 2030, or try to improve a billion lives. *If you shoot for the moon and miss by 10 percent, so what? You'll go much further than if you target an incremental improvement and beat it.* It's also more inspiring.

We also recommend another "A"—mostly *absolute* goals versus relative. They provide better clarity to the organization about where you're headed.

Rather than recalculating impacts taking growth into account, just set a total goal in reduction and let the organization figure out where to best find the cuts. One more "A" is critical: *accountability*. Who owns the goal and who has a stake in it?

One quick thought on the "M" in SMART, whether it's *measurable*: sometimes qualitative targets make sense, but quantitative metrics for measuring environmental, social, and governance (ESG) performance are improving. In Andrew's database of the ESG goals of the two hundred largest companies, www.pivotgoals.com (run jointly with sustainability consultants Jeff Gowdy and Sustainserv), virtually no companies had set quantitative social or governance goals a decade ago. Many had vague statements of intent, but they lacked numbers.

Today, more than 25 percent of the largest companies have specific numeric social goals, such as zero human rights violations or a target percentage of women in management. Many new goals are coming. In the wake of the Black Lives Matter movement, cosmetics and beauty product chain Sephora committed to buy 15 percent of the products it sells from Black-owned businesses.[10] To help it reach the goal, the retailer also relaunched its incubator program to accelerate small beauty companies with BIPOC (Black, indigenous, people of color) founders.[11] Unilever also set a goal to spend €2 billion annually with suppliers owned by people from underrepresented groups.[12]

The goal database has also shown a big increase in goals with "all," "zero," or "100%" in them. As the goals get bigger, there are clearly more of the proverbial BHAGs (big, hairy, audacious goals) that take leaders out of their comfort zone. But try to see zero goals as more than just uncomfortable—they're opportunity goals. They send the organization out to understand the problem more clearly, find partners to work with, and build better systems that eventually move past zero into net positive territory.

What and How

Most ESG goals have a specific outcome, or a "what," which makes them easy to picture. Reducing emissions 30 percent, for example, is a classic "E" goal—it's clear and drives action. A great example of an "S" goal is Woolworths' commitment to income parity: "No salary wage gap between male and female employees of equivalent positions on a per-hour rate at all levels of the company." There is no wiggle room for interpretation in that one.

The outcome goals can sound simple, but still force companies to break boundaries. They unlock the organization, changing how it operates and who it works with. After the USLP launched, Unilever's former manufacturing sustainability manager, Tony Dunnage, was assigned the goal of moving the global manufacturing organization to zero waste. He quickly reached out to others for help, talking with academics, suppliers, and outside companies to come up with plans for what to do with multiple waste streams. An Indonesian plant had some nontoxic sludge to deal with, and no place to put it in the regular waste system. The zero waste goal forced the company to find a willing receiver—it became feedstock for cement plants owned by LafargeHolcim (which conveniently had facilities in all the same areas as Unilever). As an energy source for manufacturing, it offset fossil fuels, reducing Holcim's carbon footprint.

Unilever moved all 242 factories to zero nonhazardous waste to landfill in 2014, six years early, which saved about €223 million in material and disposal costs over the remaining years. That freed up the company to think about reducing waste along the whole value chain, so it held meetings with peers and suppliers to address industry-level waste issues. These knock-on benefits came from setting a bold outcome goal from the start.

For many goals, however, stating the outcome will not be enough. The organization may need a boost in thinking about *how* to get there. In these situations, process goals help, and the difference is important. Let's say you have a personal goal to improve your health. That's too broad, so you set a more specific target: "In the next six months, I'll lose ten pounds." But putting that "what" goal on the wall without a plan won't get you far. A process goal could focus on exercise, with a target to go running three times each week. That's fairly specific, but even better would be something like, "Every Sunday night, I will schedule three runs on my calendar that week."

When Marriott became the largest hotel company in the world, it created a new, detailed set of sustainability goals (Andrew advised the firm throughout the more-than-one-year process). The "Serve 360" goals included specific process targets in each major category. In operations, the company committed to having 650 hotels pursue LEED building certification. A smaller goal was to have every property put impact metrics on its website, forcing owners to measure these things, which usually drives improvement in outcomes.

Another significant issue for hospitality is human trafficking, which often runs through hotels. An outcome goal on this topic is hard to guarantee, so Marriott set a goal to train 100 percent of its employees on human rights and awareness of trafficking. It also committed to embed human rights criteria in recruitment and sourcing policies.

Having good process goals on top of big outcome goals improves the odds of success and makes sure you're consistent across the organization.

Science-Based: The Bare Minimum

If your doctor says you have cancer and you need six months of chemotherapy to beat it, you don't say, "I'll shoot for four months, and maybe do six months as a stretch target." Nor do you say, "My political party does not support chemo." Science is being politicized with climate change and even with pandemics. But truth and fact matter. The planetary diagnosis is in, and on carbon, it's clear. The world needs to cut emissions in half by 2030 and eliminate them by 2050 (or earlier). Setting a carbon goal for anything less than that pace is taking part in a suicide pact.

A goal that puts a company on the path of reduction that science demands is, logically, called a science-based target (SBT). These goals are about doing what we must, not what we think we can or what would look like enough effort to stakeholders. And they're driven by outside-in knowledge: look at the world's boundaries and set your goal accordingly. But the words "science-based" don't fully cover the range of boundary-breaking targets we need. A broader term, "context-based," covers goals grounded in more than just the thresholds science provides. Human limits of acceptability—that is, ethics and fairness—come into play, as well as more nuance on geographic, social, and economic dimensions. A water goal, for example, should be set by watershed, with an eye toward both the total available and also the fair allocation for the business in the community. Full context includes moral limits, such as not accepting modern slavery in supply chains. When we talk about SBTs, we're using the term as a proxy for a larger science *and* moral context.

When seen through the lens of thresholds, an SBT is not a stretch goal; it's the bare minimum both biophysically and morally. In the mid-2010s, an SBT on carbon was rare. Today, 1,300 companies have signed up to the World Resources Institute's Science Based Target Initiative (SBTi), and a few hundred have committed to RE100 (100 percent renewables).[13] These goals clearly drive performance: between 2015 and 2020, the companies with an approved target from SBTi cut emissions 25 percent, far outstripping the 3.4 percent global *increase* in energy and industrial emissions over the same period.[14]

While the number of businesses setting a climate SBT is growing, it's still not common enough. Just 30 percent of the *Fortune* Global 500 have a goal that's all renewable, carbon neutral, or science based.[15] But the leaders are pushing the bar higher every day. In early 2020, Microsoft set the most aggressive climate goal in the world. Not only would the company, by 2030, be carbon negative (i.e., net positive), but by 2050 it would remove from the world the carbon it had emitted since it was founded.[16] Microsoft's commitment to wipe out historic emissions was the first retroactive neutrality goal.

To help get there, Microsoft has become one of the largest investors in carbon sequestration projects; it's the first buyer of carbon credits that Land O'Lakes is helping farmers generate through smart soil management.[17] This is the real deal. Carbon reductions like these, from regenerative agriculture, are *real* carbon reductions, not just carbon or renewable energy offsets, which vary greatly in their legitimacy and value.

At one of Unilever's regular USLP stakeholder events, the current CEO, Alan Jope, commented enthusiastically about the trail Microsoft was helping to blaze on carbon and the difference it would make.[18] It's great when companies surprise and spur one another on. Google took Microsoft's cue and went further, saying it was offsetting its historic emissions, not by 2050, but effective immediately.[19] Google accomplished this with power purchasing agreements and less-than-perfect renewable energy certificates (RECs), which allow you to buy the clean energy attributes of production somewhere else, so you, not the power generator, can claim the carbon reduction. But Google also committed to use *only* renewable power (and battery storage) on-site for all its data centers worldwide by 2030—that is, no renewable energy credits or offsets of any kind. The company is clear that it doesn't yet know how it'll do it, but don't bet against Google. (IBM is also looking to reach 90 to 100 percent renewables, without offsets or sequestration, by 2030.[20])

The race to carbon neutrality has accelerated. While few have done it yet, the World Economic Forum asked all members to set a 2050 net-zero emissions target.[21] Leaders are already going faster. Amazon has gathered more than one hundred large companies to sign the Climate Pledge to be net zero carbon by 2040. Unilever is targeting 2039, just to juice the competition a bit. IKEA wants to be climate positive by 2030, and it has decoupled growth from greenhouse gas emissions (revenues are up 14 percent in five years, while emissions fell 14 percent). IKEA already generates 32 percent more electricity from wind and solar than it needs for its operations.[22] Walmart is also targeting zero carbon by 2040 and has declared that it wants to be a regenerative company. The $600 billion revenue retailer committed to, by 2030, "manage or restore" one million square miles of ocean and fifty million acres of land, which will include adopting regenerative agriculture practices.[23]

In areas like biodiversity, target-setting is still in its infancy, but some organizations and companies have picked up the measurement challenge. The Science Based Targets Network (SBTN) is working with companies such as Natura, Unilever, and LafargeHolcim to develop a method for setting SBTs for nature, based on the best data on the Earth's limits. While the science is still being worked out, a shortcut goal on biodiversity could be to support biologist E. O. Wilson's Half-Earth Project, which seeks to conserve half of the planet's land and ocean. Or look to the Business for Nature coalition, with nine hundred big companies and major NGOs urging governments to adopt policies to reverse nature loss this decade.

Leaders such as Microsoft and Natura are going beyond their own neutrality to remove *more* carbon than they emit, or helping set new standards to create a multiplier effect. These net positive actions go beyond the science, and beyond the boundaries of four walls.

If the science isn't always clear, or you don't know if you're comfortable with an aggressive goal, consider reversing it and seeing how it makes you feel (see the box "The Reverse Goal Challenge").

Four Walls . . . No Walls . . .

Operational goals, even ones with "zero," help walk the talk, but are limited to the boundaries of the business. To have a bigger and possibly net positive impact, you have to set targets for the larger life-cycle footprint. Choices you make in product design and service delivery create ripple effects across

THE REVERSE GOAL CHALLENGE

To understand why science-based goals are the minimum and why "zero" or "all" goals make the most sense, just reverse any goal you're considering and say it out loud. If you set a target to get to 60 percent renewables, you're also committing to a goal that says, "40 percent of our energy will produce climate changing gases and will cost us more." A goal that half your product portfolio will have sustainability attributes by 2025 means your target is also "half our products will make no improvements in environmental or social impact, and perhaps make things worse." If you committed some percentage of your investment portfolio to responsible investing funds, does that mean the rest is committed to irresponsible investing?

the value chain. For example, Apple has committed to carbon neutrality in its full value chain, but it also set an unusual goal on material use. Lamenting the linear systems of metals going into electronics and becoming e-waste, the company said it wanted to build a closed-loop supply chain and "challenge ourselves to one day end our reliance on mining altogether."[24]

Net positive companies need aggressive goals for suppliers and for customers, but which one to focus on differs by sector. Companies that make energy-using products look downstream for opportunities. Trane Technologies, the large ($44 billion marked cap) manufacturer of climate-control equipment, committed to cut one gigaton (one billion metric tons) of carbon emissions from customers' footprints by 2030. Tech companies also tend to set downstream targets, arguing that their products enable emissions reductions—in customer operations or in the world in general—greater than what they produce directly. They point to how virtual meetings negate the need for carbon-intensive travel, or how big data and analytics make transportation or buildings much more efficient. BT and Dell were early adopters of these "enablement" targets, and more recently Telefonica set a target to reduce customers' emissions by ten times its own by 2025.

Financial firms have a different challenge and opportunity. The physical impacts from their offices and employee travel are trivial compared to the footprint from the businesses they fund (picture a portfolio of energy projects that a bank provided project finance or loans to). These so-called "financed emissions" are *seven hundred times* larger than the banks' own direct emissions. Some banks have finally pulled financing from coal and, in a rush of recent announcements, most big banks have set goals for their investment portfolios. Morgan Stanley and Bank of America committed to net-zero financed emissions by 2050—as has Citigroup, which CEO Jane Fraser announced on her first day on the job (that's showing your priorities).[25] A large coalition of investors called the Asset Owners Alliance, initiated in part by Allianz and its CEO Oliver Bäte, have committed their $5.5 trillion in investment portfolios to transition to net-zero by 2050.

This is good, but from a threshold perspective, it's way too late. If you're financing infrastructure until 2049, you're still building carbon-spewing facilities that last decades past the global drop-dead date of 2050. A better example is Australian insurer Suncorp, which stopped underwriting new investment in oil and gas, pledged to end insurance of existing projects by 2025, and vowed to cease investing in the sector entirely by 2040.[26] Thirty large investors with $5 trillion in assets agreed to portfolio decarbonization targets by 2025. Goals like these will accelerate the shift to the clean economy.

Supply chain goals are more common, and multinationals are increasingly imposing their science-based targets on their suppliers. Food giants were early adopters, since industrial agriculture dominated their life-cycle footprint. General Mills, Kellogg, and Campbell's Soup all set SBTs on carbon for the farms and agri-businesses they buy from. Other companies from across a range of sectors—GSK in pharma, H&M in retail, Schneider Electric, and Walmart with its Gigaton Challenge, to name a few—set carbon neutral goals for their full value chain. Alternatively, instead of setting a goal for them, you can push suppliers to take ownership. The retailer Target set a goal that 80 percent of its suppliers would set their own SBT.[27]

The leading companies are using both carrots and sticks in innovative ways to ramp up productive pressure on suppliers, particularly on climate. Grocery retailer Tesco partnered with the bank Santander to offer preferential financing terms to suppliers who demonstrate strong overall performance on climate issues, including setting aggressive targets.[28] And on the stick side, Salesforce gave suppliers strict standards on their climate action in what looks exactly like a contract (they call it a Sustainability Exhibit). Suppliers must measure their total value chain emissions and provide their products and services on a "carbon neutral basis."[29] If they don't deliver, it's a "climate breach" and Salesforce will charge them a nontrivial, first-of-its-kind (as far as we know) "remediation fee." That sounds more like a cudgel than a stick, but good for them.

A net positive value chain goal can also shift a company entirely away from one supply chain to different, more sustainable options. Unilever has committed to source 100 percent of the carbon ingredients in its cleaning and laundry products from sources that are not fossil fuel based. The company is pursuing what it's calling a Carbon Rainbow of diverse sources of carbon from captured CO_2, plants, algae, and waste.[30]

Starbucks is also working to shift some of the supply chain for its coffee drinks to new, more sustainable sources. An in-depth assessment of the company's footprint revealed that, even with thirty-one thousand stores using energy, the biggest portion of its life-cycle carbon emissions come from the supply chain—more specifically, from milk producers.[31] Industrial dairy and its greenhouse gas–producing cows make up 21 percent of the company's carbon footprint. Until dairy from farms using regenerative agriculture practices is available at scale, Starbucks' best path to cutting supply chain emissions is to reduce use of cows in the supply chain.

The CEO, Kevin Johnson, said that "alternative milks will be a big part of the solution." Starbucks has to get coffee drinkers to order nondairy items, which will not be easy. Only a few companies have effectively shifted consumer behavior. For years, Swedish food chain Max Burgers has increased nonmeat options on its menus and successfully communicated data on the carbon footprint of meat from the typical industrial system. Meat orders went down substantially. Healthy food chain Panera is heading in a similar direction, committing to make half of its menu plant-based.[32]

Setting targets for your supplier and customer impacts is a powerful and effective way to break down boundaries in how the organization sees itself. Of course, the more of the life cycle that your goals cover, the less control you have, which makes them more uncomfortable. That's a good thing. They take you into new territory. Starbucks probably didn't imagine it would need to take a stand on cow burps, but here we are.

Broader Positive Impact

There's a logical progression for thinking about goals. Start by addressing your immediate footprint and walking the talk. Then, expand your sights to the value chain and possibly the industry. With those foundations in place, you can set targets for creating a positive impact on the broader world, or increasing your "handprint" in measureable ways.

The USLP utilized goals at all levels, from its operational footprint reduction targets to the big handprint goal of improving the lives of a billion people. It also included a highly unusual goal at the time: a target on recycling rates, not for itself, but for some of the countries it operated in. The company was trying to improve recycling rates in the entire system. That kind of target certainly blows up boundaries and forces collaboration. As the USLP continues to evolve, it adds more net positive goals that tackle systems.

Handprint goals that go well beyond SBTs are becoming more of a fixture in company purpose and sustainability statements. A few examples in the environmental realm:

- Timberland: *Create a net positive impact on the environment by 2030.* The CEO has also talked about "giving more than they take." Clearly, we're on the same page.

- Kroger: *Zero Hunger|Zero Waste in its communities.* With more than 2,750 supermarkets, Kroger is donating three billion meals by 2025 and creating a $10 million innovation fund to accelerate novel ideas that reduce food waste.[33]

- Kering: *Have a net positive impact on biodiversity* by regenerating six times the total land area used by its supply chain.[34]

Looking beyond the community lens to shared, systemic problems, a group of major environmental NGOs under the banner of Nature Positive created a "global goal for nature," calling for net zero loss of natural habitat now, an increase in total habitat by 2030, and recovery of thriving ecosystems by 2050.

On the social side, companies have gotten more specifics with commitments in money and outcomes in terms of human thriving. For example:

- Henry Ford Health System: *Eliminate suicide among its patients.* Instead of treating disease and illness only, the health provider proactively worked to improve community health and outcomes (in Detroit). Instead of only treating disease and illness, the health-care system used technology to give people quicker access to care and stay in touch with them. In two years, suicides were down 75 percent and some years hit zero.[35] Other health systems have followed Ford's lead, and with the rise of deaths of despair, programs like this can have important ripple effects.

- Citigroup: *Break down barriers of systemic racism and increase economic mobility in communities of color,* committing more than $1 billion to the effort[36]

- Mastercard *Bring one billion people, and fifty million micro and small businesses, into the digital economy.* It will also help twenty-five million female entrepreneurs build their businesses. The executive chairman, Ajay Banga, sees this effort as a way to build back after Covid and increase resilience in the world. "If we're going to recover in any sort of long-term, sustainable way," he says, "we have to make sure everyone is included . . . This is an opportunity to . . . help society-at-large thrive."[37]

Goals can also be aspirational for the whole world. Dow pledged to "redefine the role of business in society and facilitate the world's transition to a circular economy," and Toyota has talked about "establishing a recycling-based society." There need to be specifics and metrics on these statements, but they can be inspiring if they are backed up by action.

Pivot Yourself, Pivot Others

In a world as disruptive as this one, change is mandatory. For some companies, an honest examination of what planetary boundaries mean for them could shake them to the core. They may need to make a deep pivot and change the business they're in to avoid irrelevance. But the shift could also represent an enormous opportunity to take part in large new markets.

In 2006, when the leadership of Danish Oil & Natural Gas (DONG) examined their business with an outside-in view, and projected its likely future, they must not have liked what they saw. DONG set aggressive new goals that didn't just bend or blow up boundaries; it rethought the company entirely and made a big pivot from an old business to a new one, fit for a low-carbon future. DONG came to the 2009 global climate conference with a fresh vision to shift from 85 percent fossil fuels to 85 percent green energy. Over the next decade, the company sold off assets, changed its name to Ørsted, and built the world's largest offshore wind business (with 29 percent of global installed capacity).[38] It hit the 85 percent target and then set new ones. Carbon emissions will drop 98 percent (from 2006) by 2025, with a complete phase-out of coal by 2023, a 50 percent cut in supply chain emissions by 2032, and complete value chain neutrality by 2040.[39]

The market is valuing Ørsted's future a great deal higher than the oil giants'. For example, BP's revenue ($279 billion) is thirty-three times higher than Ørsted's ($8.4 billion), but its market cap of $92 billion is just 1.4 times higher than Orsted's $65 billion (as of this writing).[40]

Any fossil fuel company without a plan like Ørsted's is not serious. Fossil fuel companies face an existential threat in the global need to eliminate carbon emissions, but you don't need a burning platform that dramatic to shift models toward net positive. In 2014, the health-care giant CVS Health took cigarettes off the shelves of its roughly eight thousand stores (now ten thousand). The move wiped out about $2 billion in sales. It was a smart strategic play to reposition from drugstores to health more broadly, but it was also courageous. Similarly, when the heating and cooling business division of Ingersoll Rand spun out as an independent business, it renamed itself Trane Technologies and became a "climate company" (a nice double meaning). Both the scale of its industry's climate impact—cooling creates roughly 5 percent of global emissions—and the opportunity to do something about it were irresistible.

At a smaller level, midsize company Clarke Environmental had produced pesticides to kill mosquitoes for decades before the founder's grandson, Lyell Clarke, took the company to a new place. The company developed organic repellants, which won a US Green Chemistry Award, and changed its mission to protecting public health and "making communities around the world more livable, safe and comfortable."

These moves were brave, tough pivots, and they put pressure on others, or inspired them, to pivot as well. Finland's Neste has gone down a parallel path to Ørsted, moving from oil-refining to become the world's largest producer of renewable diesel and jet fuel, made from waste. A whopping 94 percent of Neste's 2020 profits came from renewables.[41] Ørsted's and Neste's ten- to fifteen-year head start should worry other energy companies. Italian energy giant Enel has now set a science-based target, committing to phase out coal by 2030 (or sooner) and decarbonize by 2050.[42]

It doesn't require a complete business model redesign to force change on others. Leaders can drive the industry to face tough issues head on, something Unilever has done repeatedly. In 2014, Unilever stopped using microbead plastics, a year before any voluntary or mandatory bans were discussed. In 2018, the company started pressing Facebook and Google to manage illegal and extremist content better. It paused social media advertising in 2020, joined by a few other large advertisers, including Coca-Cola and Levi's.[43] These actions and more—producing a human rights report, disclosing fragrance ingredients, issuing green bonds—put pressure on competitors to pivot in fundamental ways.

All of this work pushes the pace of change. The first companies to open up their thinking and blow up boundaries will do more, do it bigger, and lead, which is a lot better than following. *It's better to make dust than to eat dust.*

The longest-lasting companies have often shifted their core focus at least once. IBM made only computing machines for decades, but then evolved to mainly provide tech and consulting services. The Wallenberg family in Sweden, long-term owners of multiple companies, has a credo dating back to 1946: "To move from the old to what is about to come is the only tradition worth keeping."

What Net Positive Companies Do to Blow Up Boundaries

- Understand the thresholds shaping the world, both biophysical and societal or moral, and assess how their business will fare in a world that lives within those limits

- Question what business they're really in and whether the current model is fit for the future

- Remove rigid constraints on what the company can work on, and give people space to think big, work for the long-term, and invest in the future

- Set aggressive goals that move a company toward net positive and are, at *minimum*, science-based; cover the suppliers and consumers; and inspire the company to improve its handprint, not only reduce its footprint

- Use the reverse goal challenge and reconsider every goal by asking, What are we *not* committing to do?—and seeing whether they're proud of that target

5

Be an Open Book

Building Trust and Transparency

For nothing is hidden, that will not be revealed;
nor anything secret, that will not be known and come to light.

—Luke 8:17

In September 2015, the United States Environmental Protection Agency announced that Volkswagen (VW) had violated the Clean Air Act and cheated on emissions tests by programming its diesel cars to look as if they produced less pollution than California law allowed—much less. In real-world driving conditions, the cars emit up to *forty times* the legal limit of NO_x,[1] a major pollutant that damages people's health and contributes to millions of deaths from air pollution annually.[2] VW sold half a million of these fraudulent cars in the United States and eleven million worldwide.[3]

The day the news of "dieselgate" hit, VW lost a quarter of its market value. It then lost its perch as the largest automaker in the world.[4] VW had lower sales for a few years and paid fines of more than $33 billion.[5] Abusing society's trust is a bad idea, as Wells Fargo or Boeing can attest to as well. A study from Accenture, "The Bottom Line on Trust," put numbers on how damaging it can be.[6] It rated seven thousand companies on three drivers of "competitive agility": growth, profitability, and sustainability and trust. The trust component alone, Accenture was surprised to find, "disproportionately affects a company's competitiveness and bottom line."

Every "trust incident" that reduced the competitiveness score also hit revenue and earnings hard—up to a 20 percent loss in some sectors. These numbers should worry any leader, since trust takes time to build, and just seconds to lose.

If a company does something wrong, it will come out. The VW scandal is surprising because the automaker got away with it for seven years. In the modern age of radical transparency, with employees carrying cameras everywhere and posting on social media, it's unlikely a company could hide something that big ever again.

Trust in Decline, Transparency Rising

High-profile scandals happen often enough to keep trust in business low. But trust in *all* institutions has been dropping for decades. While 73 percent of global respondents to the *2021 Edelman Trust Barometer* say they trust scientists, only 48 percent trust CEOs, and 41 percent trust government leaders.[7] Lack of trust costs everyone money; low trust, more lawyers' fees. It impedes collaboration and reduces efficiency. Lower trust takes a toll on employees, but the reverse is also true. People working in high-trust organizations are 76 percent more engaged, 50 percent more productive, and much more loyal. They experience 40 percent less burnout and take 13 percent fewer sick days.[8]

Trust becomes even more critical in times of crisis. After the pandemic started, trusting a brand to do what's right was a deal breaker for 81 percent of consumers.[9] Having the trust of major stakeholders, Edelman summarized, gives companies more license to operate. And remember the NGO support that Unilever got during the hostile takeover attempt—that was based on trust.

Microsoft CEO Satya Nadella has said that "our business model depends on one thing, and one thing alone—the world having trust in technology."[10] Since trust provides the foundation to build the deeper collaborations we need to solve the world's biggest challenges, it's the lifeblood of a net positive company. It's the most valuable asset a company can have.

From all this data, some larger truths emerge. Living with trust makes us happier; stewing in mistrust leads to fear, anger, and alienation. Modern life is built on social cohesion and a sense of "we," not "me." No society thrives long without trust as the basis of prosperity. But what truly drives trust? Being open.

Transparency on the Rise

There's an old saying that Warren Buffett likes: "Only when the tide goes out do you discover who's been swimming naked."[11] In a world demanding openness about everything, the tide is always going out. If you have a good handle on the problems in your (or your partners') operations—and you're working toward solutions in a genuine, consistent way—then you are in great shape, and transparency isn't threatening. But if something is out of line with your stated values and goals, such as human rights violations in the supply chain, the tide going out will be embarrassing.

Trust and transparency are the grease of a multistakeholder model. If you're hunkered down in a boardroom, viewing NGOs as the enemy and all businesses as competitors, you stay quiet. You don't risk getting penalized, or losing any advantage you have, by sharing too much. CEOs have generally worried about being too open—their legal, PR, or communications departments have scared them with tales of declining reputations or legal liability (a bigger fear in the United States). That's an excuse. Being secretive is not a good strategy. It makes it harder to build trust. It also misses out on the opportunities for connection and learning that come from openly sharing your challenges.

Transparency will find you anyway. Employees, customers, communities, and investors are challenging companies, asking tough questions about what they stand for and who they serve. Two-thirds of shareholder resolutions are now tied to environmental, social, and governance (ESG) issues.[12] ESG performance is getting more transparent: in 2021, S&P Global released its ESG scores on 9,200 companies—the scores it uses to select companies for the Dow Jones Sustainability Indices (DJSI).[13] Investing giant Black-Rock has also said that it expects companies to disclose carbon emissions and greenhouse gas (GHG) reduction targets.[14]

In the food and consumer products sectors, questions fall under the banner of the "clean label" movement. Consumers want to know much more about what they're buying, and its ingredients—nothing artificial or unnecessary, no long chemical names. This is part of what's driving the rapid growth of organic foods. But a "clean label" philosophy can go beyond food, especially for younger workers and consumers (millennials and Gen Zers). They want more information on everything they buy or use. The younger clients of private wealth bankers, for example, are now effectively asking for "clean" portfolios that have a positive impact on the world.

Transparency is enhanced by a leapfrog in technology—camera phones in everyone's hands, and new tools, such as block chain, that track everything. All bad actions can go viral. When a Starbucks store manager called the police on two people of color for loitering—which half of us do in Starbucks—a video of the incident was viewed eight million times in a few days. Everyone with a mobile phone is an auditor.

Trust, backed by transparency, is a powerful combination. They are enablers of net positive work, and they create goodwill and intangible value. Forty years ago, more than 80 percent of the value of companies in the S&P 500 was wrapped up in tangible, hard assets—factories, buildings, inventories, and so on. Today, it's the reverse: intangible assets make up more than 80 percent of the total.[15]

Intangibles have been hard to measure, but business is getting better at it, including putting numbers on the value of the brand, customer loyalty, employee engagement, and trust. Companies, especially ones on the net positive path, should constantly communicate this value to financial markets, and clearly link intangibles to the company's value creation model.

Building Trust

An old Dutch proverb translates roughly as "Trust comes on foot and leaves on horseback." It takes time, consistency, and humility to build it. A company can't compartmentalize and be trustworthy only in the public aspects of its business. What's happening under the waterline matters even more. You can't just talk trust; you have to demonstrate and earn it. Have the humility to say, "I don't know how to do this. Can you help me?" Have the vulnerability to share what isn't working. Remain open-minded about what you may be doing wrong, try to serve others and put their needs ahead of yours, and do the best you can to do the right thing. People will appreciate it and trust you. As with purpose, trust is often built bottom up, project by project, choice by choice. Let's look at five paths we believe companies should embrace to build trust.

Share Your Plans, Your Successes, and Your Failures

The Unilever Sustainable Living Plan (USLP) was a blueprint for reviving Unilever and putting it on a path to net positivity. But it was also a powerful transparency tool. From the first day, the detailed plan—with its three big goals, seven subcategories (later nine), and more than fifty individual targets—was open to public critique, warts and all. Going public with specific numbers creates accountability, which is critical. It puts a fire under the organization; once a target is out there, it's not voluntary anymore.

One of the most challenging goals was Unilever's commitment to 100 percent sustainable sourcing of agricultural inputs by 2020. With hundreds of ingredients across thousands of products, that's a tall order. Most inputs had no accepted definition for what "sustainable" meant. Putting the target out there allowed Unilever to ask for help and gave it credibility in the pursuit of answers.

Jan Kees Vis, Unilever's global director of sustainable sourcing development, has worked for years to build standards and codes for sustainable agriculture. He has needed the trust of peers, communities, and NGOs on thorny issues. The company's commitments, he says, helped hold everyone's feet to the fire. "I could point to the USLP," Vis says, "and tell suppliers and partners, 'This isn't just me talking . . . it's one of my goals, and my policy calls for fair treatment of workers and better land management practices . . . if you doubt we're serious, I'll bring in my CEO to say the same thing.'"[16] By developing standards openly, you hold yourself (and partners) accountable for better performance, before NGOs do it for you.

The scale of the goals also built relationships. When you say, "We want one billion people to improve their hygiene habits," you're clearly thinking big and can't possibly do it on your own. You're saying, "We don't have all the answers," which gives you credibility. This combination of hubris and humility draws NGOs, entrepreneurs with new technologies, and willing governmental leaders to work with you. Pier Luigi Sigismondi, the former chief supply chain officer for Unilever, says, "When you go public and say you need help, you start getting a lot of emails and requests to join the movement."

To keep the transparency and trust going, Unilever released USLP progress reports audited by PwC. The report gave every target a green, yellow, or red mark, along with explanations about what was not working. The hardest goals to hit, for example, have consistently been reducing the carbon footprint of products during consumer use. The energy needed for hot water for soaps and shampoos makes up roughly two-thirds of the company's value chain carbon footprint. Even with product innovation, Unilever has never solved this human behavioral problem (things like long showers). It's important to be positive. Be honest, but offer hope and optimism. The best way forward is to talk openly about such challenges and share the knowledge about what's worked.

USLP-level transparency is more normal now, but it was not a decade ago. Outside of the early leaders, such as Interface, IKEA, and Marks & Spencer, almost no companies had published concrete and aggressive targets—most hadn't even estimated their footprint yet. This level of openness is still uncomfortable for many leaders. A strong current of old-school thinking remains, an interior voice that says, "Don't tell the market too much because you'll be held accountable or they'll come after you."

And yet the opposite is true. Being open often turns those who are standing on the side throwing darts at you into partners.

Tell People What They Want to Know (and Don't Hold Back)

It's not up to you what your customers or communities want to know about your business or products. It's a safe bet that their demands will keep rising. So, embracing transparency is a process of letting go. Net positive companies adopt a mindset that the company doesn't actually belong to them, but to all stakeholders.

Unilever has worked to be proactive and share things that others do not. It was early in posting its tax principles online (based on a belief in supporting society through fair taxation), for example, and in publishing operational data that normally stays private. Unilever publicly shared its list of the 1,800 palm oil mills in its supply chain—latitude, longitude, and the name of the business. When Jeff Seabright was the chief sustainability officer, that transparency created a memorable moment.

He was meeting with an indigenous peoples group when a woman from Colombia spoke up, saying a palm oil company was destroying her community. Seabright pulled up a list of mill locations. The woman's jaw dropped and she said, "There. Near Cartagena. That's my community, and that company is the one poisoning and killing my people." The company could now look into what was happening with that specific supplier. Seabright says, "It was poignant and human, and it showed the power of transparency." It also identified a supplier the company needed to help change or distance itself from.

Operational transparency is just one kind of openness. Think about what your major stakeholders want to know, or will want to know soon. Prospective and current employees may want information about how fair the pay is, for example. They can search Glassdoor for salary data, which then makes it harder for a company to maintain a gender or racial salary gap.

For their part, investors are increasingly asking for ESG metrics and disclosure of material sustainability risks. Larry Fink, CEO of the world's largest asset owner, BlackRock, has asked all companies "to report in alignment with the recommendations of the Task Force on Climate-related Financial Disclosures (TCFD) and the Sustainability Accounting Standards Board (SASB), which covers a broader set of material sustainability factors."[17] He pointed out in 2021 that they had seen a 363 percent increase in SASB disclosures in one year.

Consumers are also demanding more, and they want to know what's in everything. Unilever broke new ground on sharing information on what's listed on product labels as "fragrance," which is not a single thing—it can contain dozens of chemicals. The subingredients have always been hidden from consumers. Unilever looked at more than one thousand of its products and posted online every chemical that makes up more than one hundred parts per million of a fragrance (with an explanation of what that ingredient does). Consumers can find the details online, or use a phone app, SmartLabel, to scan a bar code and get the full list while shopping.[18]

The Environmental Working Group, an NGO that advocates aggressively for protecting human health and reducing exposure to chemicals, publicly praised Unilever. Founder Ken Cook applauded the company for raising the bar on transparency and "breaking open the black box of fragrance chemicals."[19] At first, the major fragrance suppliers—longtime partners such as IFF, Givaudan, Firmenich, and Symrise—were wary. They have significant intellectual property wrapped up in their flavors and fragrances. But Unilever's former chief R&D officer, David Blanchard, says that they did understand where consumers were headed on transparency, and that it was smart to be proactive. The train was leaving, and once you start giving consumers information, Blanchard says, "transparency becomes almost unstoppable."

One of the fastest-growing food chains, Panera Bread, has made openness core to its brand. The company's "food promises" focus on the words "transparent," "raised responsibly," and "clean." Panera defines the latter as "no artificial preservatives, sweeteners, or flavors and colors." The company publishes a unique "No No List" of ingredients it says "will never be in our pantry." Panera says that its commitments are "all about trust."[20] Similarly, in 2020, Unilever announced a new goal to "communicate the carbon footprint of every product we sell" on the packaging, a nontrivial task when you sell seventy thousand products.[21]

Business customers are also demanding more information about their supply chain footprint, and it can be a competitive advantage to give it to them. Singapore-based agricultural supplier Olam launched a data product, AtSource, which gives customers information on ninety sustainability indicators—carbon footprint, waste, number of farmers, diversity, and so on—for all the raw materials and ingredients it sells. With AtSource, Olam is helping food companies develop a data-based, honest story they can tell their consumers.

If you can't give customers the data, they may go around you. To track deforestation, Global Forest Watch collects reams of satellite images of forests and palm oil plantations. Unilever brought in a small firm with expertise in AI, Descartes Labs, to get better at using satellite images to identify problem areas.[22] The company is moving toward a real-time picture of deforestation in its supply chain, with or without palm suppliers' help.

Data-driven transparency is revolutionizing business. Along with better information, having independent parties assess a company's operations enables trusted labels, which assure customers that the story is true. For many years, Unilever sold tea that was certified by the respected NGO, the Rainforest Alliance. Certifications are not perfect, but they give consumers a backstory, and a somewhat transparent look at how a product is made. People can buy a product with more confidence that it's good.

Put the Needs of Communities ahead of Your Own

A license to operate is not a literal piece of paper, but it can feel real. If communities don't trust you, doing business there will be difficult, if you're allowed in at all. Being a good steward means showing people your commitment to their well-being. Helping communities in moments of crisis, such as hurricanes and pandemics, is important for letting them know you're there for them. But it's the longer-term work that builds lasting trust.

By pursuing profits through purpose, companies and brands can approach communities and help them thrive as a normal part of doing business. It starts with the question, "How can we best help you with our products and skills?" and *not* by asking, "How can we make money off these people?" Communities can tell the difference when there's a genuine desire to invest in the country and build long-term relationships and lasting business.

Across the world, many of Unilever's brands have run programs to help communities develop and thrive. Lysoform and Klinex hygiene brands in Europe provide cleaning products to schools, along with educational materials on staying safe and healthy. In Greece and Italy, they hit a target of reaching ten million people in a couple of years. Unilever Indonesia also runs hygiene programs reaching millions of kids every year, and the Ethiopian division's hand-washing program is fighting deadly diarrhea and the scourge of trachoma, a disease that comes from rubbing dirty hands on your eyes and can lead to blindness. Unilever brands work on a range of challenges: Sunlight detergent runs a program to build water stations in Nigerian villages, and multiple brands work on rural programs that help smallholder farmers thrive. Net positive companies, wherever they operate, lift up communities.

These initiatives all contribute to the overarching USLP goal of improving the lives of one billion people. But communities know that it's also good for Unilever's business—more focus on hygiene and nutrition, for example, bring higher sales of Pepsodent toothpaste and Knorr's flavor mixes. These programs are almost always branded, using Unilever cleaning or water purification products. It's important to be authentic. As one executive working in Vietnam says, "They see the sincerity of what we try to do." You build trust by being genuine in your desire to help *and* being honest about the benefits to your business.

Those benefits are most definitely real. As part of the USLP's growth goals, the Living Hygiene platform had aggressive targets to take one sleepy cleaning brand and double its size globally. Doina Cocoveanu, who led that work, said they did more than double sales, but it wasn't from any one thing. New markets and innovations (some purpose-driven, but not all) unlocked growth.[23] By not relying on the purpose programs as the single driver, they freed up the business to serve the community honestly. Being net positive does not require *only* focusing on mission-driven initiatives—they're an important part of the normal mix of business, but not the whole thing.

Years of working with governments, investing in countries, and helping people improve health and hygiene (among other goals) has built trust. It's a philosophy of doing business, not a series of one-off programs.

Be Transparent with Trustworthy Critics

Find knowledgeable critics and invite them in. It builds trust that will grow in value, and it's the best way to learn what you need to improve. The leading companies do this systematically. VBDO, a Dutch association working to make capital markets more sustainable, benchmarks pension funds on their performance as responsible investors. When asked what makes the leaders better, VBDO executive director, Angélique Laskewitz, says they open up. The ones they rank the highest invite in critical stakeholders, including VBDO and unions, and ask openly, "What do you think of our sustainable investments policy?"[24]

It can be painful, but companies should invite productive critics in to discuss the hardest issues, including the human rights travesties of modern slavery and child labor. In 2011, Unilever asked the international NGO Oxfam to review labor conditions in its operations and supply chain, giving it free reign to explore. The company was an open book. Oxfam chose Vietnam as a good case study to assess four major issues: freedom of association and collective bargaining, living wages, working hours, and contract labor.

Unilever lawyers worried about exposing the company to legal liability, and the board was uncomfortable about giving outsiders ammunition for attacks. But Unilever leadership felt it was worth the risk. Being up front and more open makes NGOs less likely to pull you down; they need you to keep setting the pace if you're doing good things. Transparency is not about being right about everything, but being willing to be open and make the journey toward improvement.

Oxfam concluded that Unilever had adequate policies, in theory, but significant problems in reality, such as paying wages that were higher than the minimum, but still below a living wage. The report helped NGOs understand the situation better—if Unilever had challenges in dealing with the complexity of subcontractors, most likely everyone did. It also made it safer for other companies to open up.

Since that time, Unilever set a goal that none of its 169,000 direct employees would be paid below a living wage by 2020. After effectively meeting that target, Unilever made a supply chain commitment in 2021. The company will require any organization "that provides us goods or services" to pay a living wage by 2030.[25] These efforts were kick-started by the original transparency work years earlier.

The Vietnam report came out in 2013, the same year as one of the biggest tragedies in the history of business, the collapse of the Rana Plaza garment factory in Bangladesh. The shocking deaths of 1,100 workers woke up the world to the outrageous working conditions for the people making our clothes and electronics. Companies started looking more closely at the issue, and Unilever increased its focus on the social side of the USLP.

With the Oxfam report as the basis of its thinking, Unilever issued a company-wide human rights report in 2015, the first of its kind. The company was transparent about its operations in 190 countries, all with different norms, laws, and views on human rights. It was honest, which it needed to be. As Sharan Burrow, the general secretary of the International Trade Union Confederation, told us, a company is for real when it's truthful about these issues. "We've seen human rights reports that tell you it's all good news," Burrow says, "which tells you they're lying." The ones who get it "know they're not perfect, do their due diligence on human rights and labor issues, and then, instead of covering it up, ask the rest of us to help them resolve it."[26]

Marcela Manubens, Unilever's global VP of integrated social sustainability, has led Unilever's social sustainability and human rights agenda since 2013. She believes that the first report was critical to make any progress. She says, "Transparency was the key element and it's an enabler . . . it allows me to talk." It gives her and Unilever credibility to work with NGOs and communities on tough issues. If the company hadn't done the hard work, with help from the author of the highly respected Ruggie principles on human rights, John Ruggie, how seriously would they have been taken?

The report also increased the comfort talking about the issues inside Unilever. Manubens didn't want the report to speak only to a few experts in human rights—she wanted everyone in the company (or any stakeholder) to read it, get it, and ask, "What's my role in this?" As the organization got more familiar with the issues, it took action, such as improving working conditions, strengthening the right to association, and refining the complaint procedure to better capture abuses. In most places, the workers did not have an easy mechanism to communicate, such as an anonymous complaint line or regular interviews with auditors. Unilever also urged the Consumer Goods Forum to look closely at labor and human rights in the palm oil supply chain and in the shrimp industry. It trained more than one thousand companies in the extended supply chain on how to eradicate forced labor.

Multinationals have a big target on their back, and companies touting their good works get even more attention. When the criticism comes, it's important to figure out who you're dealing with (see the box "Know Your Critics"). You want helpful organizations, even if they're unhappy with you, but not pure cynics who won't work in good faith. Some people want to solve problems; others just come to knock you down. Find the right partners, build trust with them, and work on big things together.

When in Doubt, Do the Right Thing

During the pandemic, some companies made bad choices. Supermarkets in the United Kingdom, including Sainsbury's, Tesco, and Walmart's Asda, came under fire for taking pandemic tax relief while paying out nice dividends to shareholders (they're all paying back the taxes).[27] Governments offered loans to businesses to help keep them afloat. A program in the United States intended for small businesses was oversubscribed. Dozens of large, publicly held companies, many with lots of cash on hand, grabbed millions from the pot.[28] In a number of companies, executives paid themselves big bonuses while furloughing thousands of workers.

Now, compare those actions to how IKEA handled things. Some governments offered funding to cover 80 percent or more of salaries for furloughed workers. When IKEA's business recovered faster than it expected,

KNOW YOUR CRITICS

Many stakeholders seek progress on issues they believe you're not moving fast enough on, such as plastics in the ocean, climate change, renewable energy, or inclusion. But criticism varies greatly in its usefulness. When your company faces some judgment, first figure out who you're talking to:

- *The concerned and knowledgeable* raise issues of genuine concern and point out what you may have missed, such as better ways to improve standards for agricultural products or working conditions for farm-workers. Listen to these people.

- *Skeptics* challenge you, calling out greenwashing or pushing back when a company says something can't be done. They may come to the table with solutions that deal with the complexity of systems and unintended consequences. If you don't get defensive, they make you better.

- *Absolutists* are a vocal minority with a single-issue focus and, at times, overly simple answers—they may want companies to stop using palm oil entirely, for example, which could drive millions of people into poverty. Or some demand zero animal testing, but consumer packaged goods (CPG) companies are legally required to test on animals in China and Russia. Business can do more to tackle problems like that and change the laws from *within* these markets. If absolutists can be pragmatic about the paths to their goal, they can help.

- *Cynics* believe business is always the problem, assume you're lying, and judge companies only by their mistakes. They generally abdicate responsibility to help find workable solutions. Their minds are closed and they are unhelpful, so don't spend time trying to please them. Just head toward net positive, and you'll make it hard for them to sustain their objections.

it announced it would repay the United States and eight governments in Europe.[29] It was the right thing to do. Thankfully, IKEA was not alone during the crisis, and most companies tried to contribute to the greater good.

French luxury giant LVMH produced hand sanitizer, Apple made face masks. Ford, GE, and 3M made ventilators. To help those companies manufacture something they never had before, health-care and biomedical company Medtronic released the design specs and software code for one of its portable ventilators.[30] For its part, in addition to shifting production to medical equipment, Unilever converted buildings at Kenyan and Tanzanian tea plantations from schools into temporary hospitals. These companies made moral choices, putting the immediate needs of people ahead of business objectives for the moment, and showing communities who they are.

Companies are increasingly asked to make choices about how they operate in the world and what they stand for. Stakeholders are watching, and opportunities for companies to do the right—or the wrong—thing are increasingly common. As protests about racial equality and police brutality raged in the United States in mid-2020, IBM's CEO Arvind Krishna called on governments to combat systemic racism. The company stopped selling facial recognition software—which has inherent racial bias and misidentifies people of color much more often—to police or other security agencies. The software has inherent racial bias and misidentifies people of color much more often.[31] Microsoft and Amazon quickly joined IBM. Again, the right thing to do.

The more companies do what's right, the higher expectations become. With a plan as public as the USLP, stakeholders often expect Unilever to solve every environmental or social problem that touches their business in any way, including the darker corners of the supply chain that need attention. That's a high bar, but at the same time, it's not hard to at least identify the problems. Many NGOs and unions know what's going on.

Even before Unilever's human rights report unearthed issues, stakeholders were clearly telling them about problems in the supply chain. Ron Oswald is the general secretary of the IUF, a federation of unions representing ten million workers in agriculture and hospitality. In the late 2000s, IUF ran a campaign against Unilever over a tea factory in Pakistan with eight hundred employees, yet only twenty-two full-time jobs. The rest were contingent labor, daily contractors with low wages and no job security. IUF called the campaign, cleverly, Casual-T.

As part of a larger effort to reduce contingent labor across the business, Paul worked with Oswald in Pakistan to craft a solution. The plan was to create a few hundred permanent jobs, with benefits. Before launching it, however, they went to the community and asked people what they wanted—fewer, but better jobs, or more contract positions. The workers chose the stability. On the first day, the newly hired workers brought their families with them to celebrate.

As it does so often, it turned out that this net positive solution was better for Unilever. When you put people on the payroll, you have better economics. You don't have to constantly hire contract workers. Employees also are more engaged; they feel like part of the company. Unilever also saved money by *not* needing high-priced employees in London to manage labor cases against the company—money that could go to hiring more workers at the factory.

Because of years of working in good faith, and the trust that built, unions now help Unilever identify problems and fix them before they implode. Oswald raised awareness about a problem in logistics. Large trucking fleets in western Europe are often registered in eastern European countries such as Lithuania, Bulgaria, and Poland, where there are poor working standards and lower wages. The drivers live in more expensive western countries, but make $300 to $400 a month for excessively long shifts. When stories like these pop up, executives should probe, ponder their own humanity, and think, "What if I had gone down a different path and this was my life?"

But empathy is only a start. In this case, there is no easy solution. They can't just fire the bad actors since, Oswald says, the problem is rampant across the continent. He has seen a lot in his work, but says, "I never thought I'd deal with systematic human rights issues in western Europe." Unilever and IUF are building a coalition with beverage and CPG companies to make these truckers' lives better. It's a work in progress, but a good example of addressing a situation companies have long ignored. It's hard to maintain trust with society if you don't do the right thing when buried problems come to light.

And they always will.

In the Room Where It Happens

If you're trusted, you'll get a seat at the table for important conversations. When the United Nations began working on the Sustainable Development Goals (SDGs) in 2013—an update to the Millennium Development Goals (MDGs) set in 2000—the private sector did not have a prominent voice in the process. Representatives from national governments and the UN did not trust multinationals. But a few governments knew they had to bring business to the table, since the world was unlikely to achieve the SDGs without everyone involved.[32]

The UK and Dutch governments put forward Paul as a candidate because they trusted him. The company had worked on the MDGs, partnered with UNICEF's World Food Programme, and engaged with UN secretary-generals Kofi Annan and Ban Ki-moon in the past. Unilever built credibility that it would put the larger needs of the world first, not only pursue its own self-interest. Paul became the sole business representative from the private sector on the SDG working group. Those first meetings were somewhat tense, as all eyes turned to the businessman, wanting him to answer for the sins of capitalism. But the working relationship improved and Unilever kept its front row seat to the development of the world's dashboard. It was a defining moment for Paul and for Unilever.

The company had access to the latest thinking about the global development field, plus regular engagement with heads of state. Unilever got a head start on seeing the SDGs, understanding their vision and power, and starting to internalize them. It was the first company to talk about them in an annual report. But the influence went both ways. One of the company's largest purpose-led initiatives has been its hand-washing program for kids to help them avoid deadly diseases. With some nudging, a hand-washing target made it into the final list of SDGs. That was good for both public health and Unilever's business.

Over those two and a half years of work on the SDGs, the company created enormous goodwill. What had begun with trust, built even more. As with the UN, many countries have trusted Unilever and given it unique access. When the UK government created a committee to improve human rights in its supply chain, the members included the Red Cross, Oxfam, Amnesty International, academics . . . and Marcela Manubens, the Unilever exec leading the company's human rights efforts. She had been working with the UK government on the creation of the Modern Slavery Act. Manubens was the only private sector representative on the team. Similarly, when Ethiopia created its National Forum on how to fight Covid-19, Unilever was the only business invited.

Unilever has had trusting relationships with governments for a long time. In the 1950s, after India secured its independence from the United Kingdom, it did not allow foreign companies to own a majority of an Indian subsidiary. Unilever, with its long-established presence in the country and local senior staff, got a special exemption and maintains majority control of Hindustan Unilever to this day.[33]

But at times, it can be a mixed blessing to be in the room where the bigger conversations are happening. Governments and NGOs may expect you to do much more than your peers. Getting ahead is good, but not so far ahead that you're disadvantaged. There is an interesting twist to these meetings, however—it becomes clearer to stakeholders who is *not* in the room. The critics can target others in the sector and ask why they're not doing more, holding up the leaders as examples. It levels the playing field and gets the laggards moving.

As trust builds, longtime critics may come to you for assistance. Over many years, Unilever built a solid relationship with Greenpeace, even though the NGO has campaigned against the company many times. Greenpeace's former executive director, Kumi Naidoo, once faced an awful situation and needed help. When dozens of Greenpeace activists attempted to board a Russian oil platform, they were arrested, charged with piracy, and faced fifteen years of hard time.[34] Naidoo pulled every string he could to free them, and he talked to Paul often during the ordeal. Paul spoke with Russian leaders directly and drew on deep relationships in the country to help get the activists released. Naidoo says that he doesn't see how Unilever got any direct benefit from putting its neck out. The company was taking a risk in alienating political leaders in a growing market.

Even with intense appreciation for Unilever's help in Russia, Greenpeace simultaneously pressured the company on issues it saw a problem with, such as the use of pesticides in tea in India. It helps that they have a productive and respectful relationship. Naidoo comments that the trust built from the Russia experience helps Greenpeace and Unilever "work on things they agree on and dialogue on things they disagree on."[35] Relationships between the private sector and civil society are clearly challenging, and there's a constant tension. But they are also rewarding, productive, and necessary. Nothing important that needs to change can be changed alone. Humility, honesty, and putting others first will build trust. Be an open book, and the potential for successful partnerships grows exponentially.

What Net Positive Companies Do to Build Trust

- Start always with transparency and being open about what they're trying to accomplish

- Work with society by proactively inviting them in instead of waiting for them to bang on—or knock down—the door

- Develop shared goals for society, working with stakeholders

- Publish reports on their progress and start open discussions about successes and failures—they ask for help

- When entering into new markets or partnerships, start with what they can do for stakeholders, not themselves

- Stand up and speak out to support their values, especially when it's hard; they are courageous about using their voice

6

Make 1+1=11

Creating Partnerships with Synergies and Multiplier Effects

If you want to go quickly, go alone.
If you want to go far, go together.

—African proverb

In an emergency, when people need to get pails of water to a fire or sandbags to stop a flood, they may create "bucket brigades," lines of people passing heavy items. It's much faster than everyone hauling a single bucket, and it's a classic example of partnership yielding nonlinear returns. Our shorthand for the multiplier effects from collaboration is "one plus one equals eleven."

To fight the battle against our environmental and social challenges, we need the rapid expansion of productivity that comes from partnership. No company can make a serious dent in the problems that a whole industry, or the world, faces. Only together can a sector or region shift the standard practices or cost structure of, for example, building efficiency technologies, renewable energy, or sustainable palm oil. Some of a net positive company's goals will be impossible to reach without help. Making facilities zero waste, for instance, could be difficult for some materials. You may get to half the solution on your own, but then need to find companies that can use the material, or value chain partners to share the burden of building recycling infrastructure.

When Unilever's former manufacturing sustainability director, Tony Dunnage, was tasked with moving the company's two hundred–plus factories to zero waste, his boss asked him, "What budget do you need? How many people and how many consultants?" Dunnage says he shocked his boss when he answered, "I don't need any people or budget . . . what I need is partnerships."[1]

Nowhere is this need for collaboration more urgent than in battling climate change. Large companies are almost all working to cut their direct and indirect (from the electric grid) carbon emissions—called Scope 1 and Scope 2 by the Greenhouse Gas Protocol. But the real breakthroughs come from assuming responsibility for, and teaming up to tackle, supplier and customer emissions, called Scope 3. In most industries, Scope 3 makes up the large majority of value chain emissions.

A net positive company, because it uses a multistakeholder model, will inherently look for alliances within an ecosystem of players that share interests. This network should grow to include peers, suppliers, NGOs, and governments. It's not just that some issues are hard to solve alone; it's that our challenges are so intertwined, it's impossible to work on one problem at a time. Partnerships will inevitably overlap, forcing systems thinking. The Sustainable Development Goals (SDGs), with their seventeen areas for action, are deliberately designed to interact, in systems, and reinforce one another. Without partnering, which is the seventeenth SDG, achieving the other sixteen goals will be impossible.

The SDGs are a partnership for humanity; they're multigenerational, with purpose at the core, and aim to ensure that nobody is left behind. The companies that embrace the opportunity from meeting the SDGs—an estimated $12 trillion and 380 million jobs globally, by 2030, in only four sectors—will thrive.[2] It's the biggest business opportunity in history, waiting to be unlocked.

As someone wise once said (likely Einstein), we can't solve our problems with the same level of thinking that created them. The time for higher-level, transformative partnerships has arrived.

Two Core Types of Partnerships

This chapter and the next explore collaborations in two big categories (see table 6-1). We draw a distinction between problems that can be solved with a subset of stakeholders, and optimize results *within* our current system, and

TABLE 6-1

Two scales of partnership

Chapter 6: 1+1=11 Creating Partnerships with Synergies and Multiplier Effects	Chapter 7: It Takes Three to Tango Systems-Level Reset and Net Positive Advocacy
Scaling with the system	Changing the system
May need competitors to get more done	Need more players (policy, finance)
Solving shared industry risk	Building the greater common good
Localized regions or supply chains	Full systems
Some civil society partners	All participants in the system
Action (More "do")	Action and advocacy (More "say")

those that require *all* the players (and in particular governments) to *change* systems.

Think of competitors working with their shared suppliers to innovate around new materials for recyclable packaging. The effort would benefit everyone in the sector. That's the first category, and what we're calling a *1+1=11* partnership, since it creates multiplier effects. Companies can make progress on issues like this without much government support, but it doesn't mean *only* business coming together; you may need technical perspective from academia or NGOs. These partnerships often address opportunities or risks that competitors share—for example, a human rights issue in the sector's supply chain is everyone's problem. Broadly speaking, this kind of collaboration is focused on action to scale up solutions.

In contrast, a systemic partnership works to change underlying dynamics. Taking the issue of packaging again, a net positive company would go beyond working with peers on new materials. It would advocate for, and help design with governments, better policies to create a circular economy, change consumer habits, eliminate plastics from certain uses, and support public-private financing to fund new recycling infrastructure. These are the kinds of structural and business model changes that address the packaging issue in the longer term. A systems-level partnership needs all three societal players at the table: the private sector, governments, and civil society. We call that It Takes Three to Tango. Efforts to reset systems fall more into advocacy—not entirely, as sometimes action demonstrates what's needed in terms of policy, but mainly.

Making the "tango" partnerships happen depends on first showing success with 1+1=11 alliances. Until you demonstrate positive, measurable change for the sector or value chain, it's hard to be taken seriously in larger conversations with all stakeholders.

No categorization is perfectly clean. The real world is messy, and approaches can blur into each other. You can start with a sector project and expand it to work on a bigger system. But before diving into partnerships, we want to explore quickly the mix of initiatives a company embarks on and provide a sense of what a net positive company's portfolio of efforts will look like.

The Mix of Initiatives Today and Tomorrow

Consider the programs or initiatives a company works on under the banner of sustainability. In total, those initiatives will create some impact—a reduction in negative outcomes or an improvement in positive ones. Think of the total effect you have across initiatives as a pyramid (see figure 6-1).

The first efforts, shown at the bottom, generally start internally, working on one's own footprint within the four walls of the business. You may cut carbon emissions through reductions in energy use, for example. Even with targets such as zero waste, which force you to think bigger and blow up boundaries (chapter 4), the impact is limited by the company's own footprint. This is critical work, and net positive companies understand that the problem starts at home. You have to earn a seat at the table by getting your own house in order.

Above that base we show partnerships that extend the work beyond the company, starting with the value chain. For most sectors, the environmental and social impacts of the business fall largely in those Scope 3 emissions, so the potential for impact is bigger. Moving up the pyramid, the work ventures further out to sector-level projects, and potential positive impact grows. The reality of these sector partnerships, however, can fall short of expectations. Too many companies are unwilling to assume responsibility beyond their own operations. Or the value chain partnerships remain transactional and focused on extracting the lowest cost for everyone. Net positive companies

FIGURE 6-1

Mix and impact of initiatives (today)

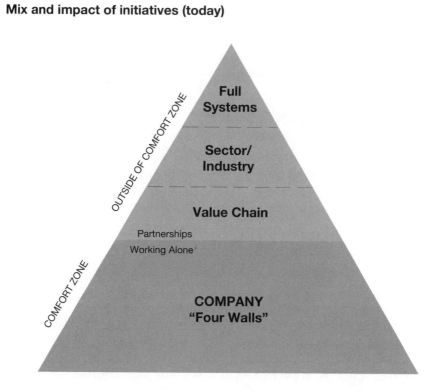

take broader ownership and look for greater wins—they understand the vast power of partnership.

The top of the pyramid is where the full systems change collaborations come in (those we take up in chapter 7). We draw the pyramid with this shape to indicate, directionally, that most of the work today is at the bottom, with internal efforts. A single, well-run sector partnership to reduce impacts across the industry could dwarf the individual work, but there are still few of those broader collaborations. Companies are also somewhat wary of venturing out of their comfort zone into these partnerships. The mix of initiatives today, then, is weighted to the easier-to-manage, smaller-impact ideas—the pyramid is bottom heavy.

A net positive company's mix, however, will look radically different (see figure 6-2). Driven by purpose and an understanding of the imperative, the company's efforts will shift dramatically upward. They will unlock bigger value by building strong alliances that involve the value chain, sector, or

FIGURE 6-2

Mix and impact of initiatives (tomorrow)

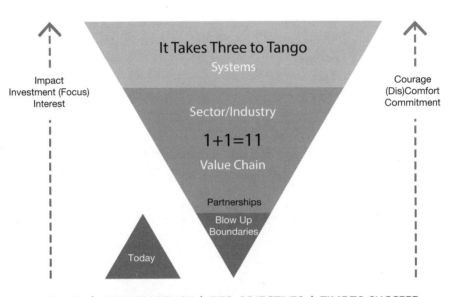

TRUST | TRANSPARENCY | TIED OBJECTIVES | TIME TO SUCCEED

full systems. In this future scenario, today's four walls efforts (shown in the small shaded triangle next to the big pyramid) are still science-based and comprehensive—such as going to 100 percent renewable energy—but the total impact is tiny in comparison to what value chain, sector, and systems partnerships achieve.

As you move up the scale, there's more impact and interest from all stakeholders, but it takes more courage, commitment, and investment of energy and focus. Success breeds success, and the bigger thinking comes from having solid 1+1=11 partnerships operating successfully.

Partnership Challenges

The potential for net positive outcomes is large and worth the effort, but partnerships are challenging, especially as the mix of players expands. The larger the scope, the more complicated it is and the more points of failure you can run into. The number of corporate alliances grows every year, but an estimated 60 to 70 percent fail.[3] A prodigious collaborator like Unilever has seen many fall short. Partnerships can underperform for many reasons.

Misaligned vision and objectives. Even with consensus that there's a problem, organizations have different motives for being in the room. Steve Miles, the former global brand EVP for Dove, says, "You need an intersection of interests, but don't expect the Venn diagram to perfectly overlap—that can't happen with an NGO."[4] Unilever may focus on sustainable sourcing for a commodity, covering multiple environmental and social dimensions, whereas an NGO, such as Oxfam, might zero in on livelihoods and decent wages. It's not incompatible, but it's not exactly the same either.

No clear understanding or agreement on what each brings to the table. In the United States, a promising partnership that Unilever had with energy company NRG didn't go as planned. The goal was to set up a new kind of business relationship to provide a strategic portfolio of clean energy projects across multiple facilities in North America. But neither company was organized to execute on that goal, and each thought the other party had capabilities it didn't. So they fell back into one-off renewable energy projects, negotiated at each site separately. Similarly, in another partnership, Unilever and the NGO Acumen were aligned in principle, but found that their scales were not in sync. Acumen worked with smallholder farmers and co-ops, while Unilever needed to find solutions for sustainable sourcing an order of magnitude larger.

Ill-defined or lacking metrics on business value. Partnerships, especially the full systems ones, are hard to put a value on (in the traditional, short-term, shareholder maximization mindset). A food company might spend money today to meet healthier food guidelines by reducing salt, fat, and sugar. A short-term view would say it's not worth it. But the investment can pay off in growing markets for healthier food. There's a "greater good" argument as well—unhealthy societies don't thrive. Also, without good metrics, collaborations can lack the frequent feedback loops they need to adjust course.

Cultural challenges. Business executives can find it difficult to deal with competitors, NGOs, and governments around the same table. Leaders need new skills—listening, finding common ground, and convincing people to commit time and resources. Chief sustainability officers are often well prepared for this work, having had to "matrix" in their companies to get anything done.

Unilever, even with all its successes, has had failures that demonstrate all of these hurdles. In one large collaboration, Unilever, Mondelez, DSM, the Global Alliance for Improved Nutrition, and the World Food Programme came together for a five-year initiative to tackle child undernutrition. The program, part of a larger multistakeholder platform called Project Laser Beam, was well funded—$25 million each from the companies—and the partners were experienced. But it didn't result in long-lasting improvements. The project was designed top down and globally without enough focus and coordination at the local community level. There weren't solid metrics and output measures, so they lacked a feedback loop. But mostly, a misalignment of objectives weakened the effort.

Partnerships can become talk-fests, lacking scale and impact. A net positive company, however, unlocks the power of these partnerships; it does fewer, but bigger ones to increase impact. Less is more, if done well. Robust and lasting partnerships also have a long-term commitment—they are embedded in the company, and not subject to support from individual executives.

With hurdles out of the way, let's move to the pathways to greater performance. We can jump these hurdles, and there are excellent examples to learn from—not as many as we need yet, but real successes.

Making 1+1=11

We won't focus here on the general elements of a good partnership, which are, in theory, not too hard to figure out (they're the flip side of the challenges). The difference in these collaborations, then, is not how to manage them, but the overall purpose and approach. They are intended to serve the larger good as much as help the partners themselves, and have impact, scale, and staying power.

We will run through examples from six approaches to net positive partnerships with varying and expanding partners:

- Within your value chain

- Within your industry

- Across sectors

- With civil society

- With governments (nonsystems)

- In multistakeholder groups (nonsystems)

The lines here aren't set in stone, and a given partnership can run through multiple approaches in its lifetime. But it's helpful to start by identifying the shared problem you're trying to solve and who needs to be at the table. The goals here are working at a deeper level than just "cut emissions" or "reduce human rights problems with my suppliers."

We try to use examples with a track record and outcomes to point to, which shows commitment and consistency over time. Let's look at the six approaches.

Partnering within Your Value Chain

The first step out of the safety of your own operations is to reach out, in genuine partnership, to your direct value chain. It's the start of expanding your sense of ownership—net positive companies don't outsource their life-cycle responsibilities. This is the biggest immediate unlock in value, given the much larger total footprint in the value chain. There are often enormous savings or higher revenues if you work better, in trust and cooperation, with suppliers and customers.

If you take the short-term, profit-maximizing view on business, you see suppliers in purely functional terms—they're just companies that serve you at the lowest possible cost (so you can keep margins high and please investors). This is a somewhat exaggerated description, and few companies are that coldly removed from suppliers they've been doing business with for years. But it is the prevailing model in many sectors—fashion companies, for example, will change suppliers on a dime for a penny in savings. For a long time, Unilever suppliers felt like the relationship was purely transactional, which was true—the company's buyers had a traditional cost-cutting mindset. Unilever saved money, but lost out on greater value.

Flipping the script and serving suppliers will help you both, ultimately, serve the customers or citizens at the end of the value chain. That's the real change needed to create a net positive effect. You build the pie together instead of splitting the pie differently. Early in the development of the USLP, Unilever set uncomfortable goals and made it clear that it could not reach them alone. It made partnership a deliberate cornerstone and launched a new program called Partner to Win to create a stronger bond with suppliers.

Marc Engel, Unilever's chief supply chain officer, says, "We wanted suppliers to be excited about the journey and join us."[5] Unilever also needed significant product innovation to shrink its footprint and hit the USLP targets. Like all CPG companies, Unilever takes credit for innovations, but most of time, suppliers create new ingredients and invent new product benefits. Unilever can implement and scale those new ideas, but it gets the bulk of its innovation from supplier R&D.

Before the USLP launched, Unilever's suppliers did not view the company as a place for innovation. The suppliers were not bringing them new ideas. It was a huge lost opportunity. When you're a big customer, Engel says, "you're partly paying for the supplier's R&D, so the question is, are you getting the benefit, or is someone else?"[6]

The goal of Partner to Win was to become the trusted customer of choice and the preferred innovation partner for major suppliers. Engel admits it was an odd fit for him at first. But Paul took Engel on a trip to meet four major suppliers and experience how nonstrategic the relationships were. The new program asked the top 100 suppliers, which provided a significant percentage of the company's inputs, to develop joint business plans with a five-year horizon. Unilever gave accountability for key supplier relationships to each of the top 50 executives in the company—*all* executives, not just buyers. Paul was responsible for two relationships (including top supplier BASF); the chief R&D officer owned two; the head of deodorants, three; and so on.

Through Partner to Win, Unilever built strong bridges, which paid off as suppliers increasingly brought them new ideas. The list of joint innovations that use suppliers' best technologies to solve a societal need is now long. In just one category, products that help people in water-stressed regions, Unilever launched soaps that kill bacteria faster, one-rinse softeners, and waterless shampoo. The company also worked with sustainability leader

Novozymes to replace some chemicals in detergents with enzymes. The new formulations cleaned clothes as well, but at lower temperatures, a major win for reducing carbon emissions in the use phase of the product.

Deeper relationships pay off in paradoxical ways: if you only look at price, you won't get the lowest price. It sounds ridiculous, but it's only when you work with suppliers to coordinate innovation investments and improve overall cost structures—without obsessing about the price per unit—that you really get better prices. So, don't focus on the number, but on joint value creation. Don't focus on the transaction, but on the customer you both serve. As always, there's no way to work this closely, and share savings, without a deep well of trust.

Marc Benioff, the CEO of Salesforce, tells a story about meaningful connections between customers and suppliers. In his book *Trailblazer*, he describes a visit with David MacLennan, the CEO of Cargill, the largest privately held company in the United States and a big Salesforce customer. They walked out of Benioff's office and saw a dozen people wearing Salesforce "trailblazer" T-shirts. MacLennan asked him, "Are those your employees?" Benioff said, "No, they are *your* employees . . . but they use our technology so they have become part of our family."[7]

Net positive companies partner with innovative suppliers to develop and test new technologies that slash footprint or improve lives. While Apple was becoming essentially carbon-free in its own operations, it also looked for carbon-reduction solutions across its value chain. In a fascinating move, the company partnered with mining giants Alcoa and Rio Tinto to cut emissions in aluminum smelting. The metal is one of the most recycled materials in the world, but new aluminum production is incredibly energy intensive, creating about 1 percent of total global carbon emissions (and one-quarter of Apple's product manufacturing footprint).[8]

The joint venture the three companies created, ELYSIS, developed a carbon-free smelting technology that emits only oxygen. At scale, they expect it to reduce operating costs by 15 percent with higher productivity. Apple invested $13 million in the venture, provided technical support, and then bought the first batch of ELYSIS aluminum at the end of 2019.[9] Apple's VP of environment, policy, and social initiatives, Lisa Jackson, said that "for more than 130 years, aluminum has been produced the same way . . . that's about to change."[10] Apple doesn't make a dent in global aluminum use (think: cars, cans, and construction). But it's plenty big enough to lend its brand and demonstrate proof of concept, which helps attract other aluminum buyers. That's already happened—Audi is using ELYSIS zero-carbon aluminum in the wheels of its new electric sports car.[11] With more momentum, the joint venture can shift the industry toward massive carbon reductions, making it a large net positive play for Apple, and a tipping point for the world.

As you take on more responsibility for impacts and find ways to increase your handprint along the value chain, you'll need more of these relationships. They unlock tremendous value, build resilience, and increase transparency, traceability, and trust. Unilever invested in trust during the initial Covid lockdowns by, as we said earlier, setting aside €500 million to support its suppliers and extend credit to customers.[12] That's net positive financing.

What Net Positive Companies Do to Maximize Value Chain Impact

- Take responsibility for their total value chain impacts and assess areas with the biggest potential for collaboration

- Treat suppliers as partners and family, not as low-cost providers of commodities, and look for joint value creation versus value transfer

- Build trust and transparency with their suppliers and customers through aligned objectives and incentives and, in some cases, open books

- Identify large challenges holding back the industry, and large opportunities to improve lives, or test new technologies together

- Start and end with the citizens they serve in mind

Partnering within Your Industry

As you expand your horizon and your view of responsibility, it becomes clear that you and your peers share many challenges that would benefit from cooperation. These issues may be impossible to solve alone, too costly, or need to be attacked at an industry level because they drag everybody down. With issues such as slave labor in apparel or e-waste for tech, for example, if one competitor looks bad, they all look bad (and the reverse holds as well). Net positive companies work actively with peers to change industry norms, reduce combined impacts, and greatly improve outcomes and the sector's image.

Companies shouldn't be one-upping their competitors on shared challenges and opportunities. What good does it do if, say, only one food company tackles child labor problems in West African cocoa production? The issue is better solved collectively, in a "precompetitive" way. Likewise, when Merck helped J&J produce its Covid-19 vaccine to speed access, it put the world and its sector ahead of itself, helping a much-criticized industry garner praise.[13] Net positive companies understand that despite the pressures to perform, *we should not compete on the future of humanity.*

Bringing major peers together reduces risks and costs of the whole endeavor (it's not completely new for sectors to work on general cost-cutting, so why not on sustainability programs also?). The expense will end up less per company, and the system will be more robust. A net positive company is happy to take the lead and invest in better solutions if peers quickly follow. But it helps to create a sense of urgency and movement, and an understanding that it's not optional. Get enough companies in one room and, as Dow's former CEO Andrew Liveris says, "you gain speed and mass."

The number of industry collaborations is picking up, and they have diverse aims. Let's look at a few of the goals that sector-wide collaborations can pursue. These efforts can have broad impact and prepare companies for larger systems and net positive work down the road:

Implementing industry-wide operational improvements. Industry alliances can find ways to greatly improve how the sector operates at a tactical level—there are plenty of opportunities down in the trenches. The Consumer Goods Forum (CGF), which Paul helped found in 2009, brings together four hundred consumer goods retailers and manufacturers with $4 trillion in combined revenue. The industry worked together at times before CGF, but in a less focused way. They continue to collaborate on issues such as food waste, human rights and forced labor, health and wellness, packaging, and avoided deforestation. The group hasn't always lived up to its potential, as some members play it too safe or stall on tough issues—with an unwieldy fifty-five-member board, talking about human rights or other complex issues can feel like pulling teeth.

But when there's a clear connection to efficiency and cost savings, the conversation goes more smoothly. The sector has had a number of solid successes in improving operations across companies. For example, the partners standardized the size of shipping pallets globally. For context, there are more pallets in the world, about ten billion, than people.[14] When billions of stacks of products move in and out of trucks, warehouses, and stores, inefficiencies add up. With a small number of standard pallet sizes, fulfillment is quicker and companies can pack trucks up to 58 percent tighter, saving significant fuel and carbon emissions.[15] CGF members developed, agreed to, and implemented these standards, together. The benefits accrue to both individual companies and the collective.

Tackling the highest impact sectors. The Mission Possible Partnership, led by the Energy Transitions Commission, RMI, We Mean Business, and the World Economic Forum, is assembling companies from high-energy-intensity sectors: aluminum, aviation, cement and concrete, chemicals, shipping, steel, and trucking. The goal is technological disruption and developing sector roadmaps for the transition to a low-carbon world.

Sharing best practices. The food and agriculture sector covers 40 percent of the world's land surface, uses 70 percent of freshwater, and produces up to one-third of greenhouse gas emissions.[16] CGF launched a coalition to tackle food waste, which Denis Machuel, CEO of Sodexo, calls "the food sectors' single most important climate action."[17] Our future depends on this sector—which will have to feed many more people—getting it right. The World Business Council on Sustainable Development (WBCSD) and its chairman, Sunny Verghese, CEO of the Singapore based agribusiness Olam International, created the Global Agribusiness Alliance (GAA) for food suppliers. Their goal is to share best practices for reducing operational impacts, managing soil and land use (which could lead to carbon sequestration), enhancing livelihoods, protecting water resources, and cutting out food waste. The focus is on developing more specific action pathways because what business does well, Verghese says, is not theorizing and modeling, but executing.

The big players are on board because the motivation is both carrot (collective work is more effective) and stick; they avoid, as Verghese says, "the rap of big, bad agribusiness . . . just like big, bad pharma or big, bad energy." Verghese is clear-eyed on the challenges. "We are an intensely competitive industry, so we will never come together unless the world is literally burning down," which he points out is happening. (It gives new meaning to the phrase "burning platform for change.")

Getting to tipping points. To catalyze more sector partnerships, Paul co-founded IMAGINE, a foundation and for-benefit company, with former Unilever execs Jeff Seabright and Kees Kruythoff, and with transformational leadership expert Valerie Keller. They focus on transforming sectors by bringing together a critical mass—at least 25 percent of the total value chain—to reach tipping points. One initial target is the fashion sector, a $2.5 trillion behemoth with an enormous environmental footprint in water and material waste (73 percent of clothes end up in landfills or incinerators), and a serious problem with over-consumption (the growth of fast fashion).[18]

IMAGINE has helped the Fashion Pact, led by Kering CEO François-Henri Pinault, design a pathway to manage their shared impacts on three major challenges: climate, biodiversity, and oceans. The members agreed to science-based carbon reductions in keeping with the global 1.5°C goals (cut emissions in half by 2030 and to net zero by 2050), including a move to 100 percent renewable energy by 2030. The biodiversity plan includes commitments to regenerative approaches for cotton, and the oceans work focuses on eliminating single-use plastics and microfiber pollution. None of these companies could do this work alone.

Committing to codes of conduct and standards of practice. Standards are not sexy, but better standards and data can greatly improve environmental and social outcomes. A decade ago, the Sustainable Apparel Coalition created the Higg Index, a tool to help brands and retailers consistently measure a company or product's sustainability performance. Similarly, the information and communication technology (ICT) industry's Responsible Business Coalition commits members to imposing a shared code of conduct (tied to multiple standards, including the Universal Declaration of Human Rights) on themselves and tier one suppliers.[19] A coalition of large mobile providers has also committed to joint science-based targets for greenhouse gas reductions.[20] These commitments can drive a sector toward net positive. Obviously, intentions and standards are not outcomes. But when standards drive substantial changes in company operations, they result in sizeable reductions in footprint across a sector. Most standards are not targeting net positive outcomes, yet, but they engage sectors and open companies up for bigger thinking later.

Solving new problems before they get big. As the use of clean technologies grows exponentially, these industries are getting larger, with their own environmental or social problems. For example, as wind power advances, older turbines get retired. There are few solutions for the end of life of these football field–length blades—they're not easily recycled. Owens Corning, which makes materials that allow the blades to grow longer and stronger, estimates there will be a quarter million metric tons of blades needing a waste solution within two years. The company is taking responsibility for the life cycle and collaborating with peers in the American Composite Manufacturers Association to find solutions such as extending the life of the blades or stripping metals and turning them into pellets for packaging and other uses. They're working together to find solutions they can scale.

Testing or accelerating new business models. In an innovative test that's challenging norms, the Loop program, led by TerraCycle, is working with CPG giants, including Body Shop, Honest Company, Nestlé, P&G, RB, and Unilever, as well as retailers Carrefour, Kroger, and Walgreens. The program gives consumers their favorite brands in reusable containers. When people are done with the shampoo, ice cream, or other products, Loop picks up the box, cleans the empty bottles and cans, and refills them. It may or may not work, but it's worth the experiment.

What Net Positive Companies Do to Shift Their Own Industry

- Lead sector partnerships to address the biggest shared hurdles and opportunities to help the world thrive

- Gather a critical mass, roughly 25 percent of sector production or more, to work together and create tipping points

- Worry less about who gets the credit, or how to compete on issues, and focus on broader solutions

- Identify operational shifts that save everyone money, resources, and footprint

- Develop joint standards, such as how to best measure sustainability performance, or science-based goals that members individually, and the whole sector, can shoot for

Partnership across Sectors

Once sector players are comfortable working together, they can expand their efforts and work with other sectors that face similar issues—they may share parts of a supply chain, for example. These are some of the largest and most impactful 1+1=11 partnerships. They help companies get past inefficiencies of scale.

The stresses of a volatile world are bringing strange bedfellows together. The pandemic drove companies across sectors to jointly solve problems. During the initial rise of the virus, it was clear the world needed more medical equipment, and fast. Unilever joined the Ventilator Challenge UK consortium to combine resources and quickly make more ventilators. Partners included Airbus, Ford, multiple Formula 1 race teams, Rolls-Royce, and Siemens (and Microsoft for IT support). This was a short-term partnership, but others like it may work out over many years.

One of the longest-standing and successful joint efforts brings cross-sector peers together with suppliers (with a critical assist from an NGO convener) to work on new cooling technologies. The refrigerants that have dominated the industry for more than a century, chemicals in the fluorocarbon class (CFCs and HFCs), do enormous damage to the climate. They have high global warming potential, meaning they trap more heat than a similar amount of carbon dioxide—up to eleven thousand times more over a twenty-year period. Some damage the ozone layer as well.[21]

In the 1990s, a few companies started working on better solutions. The group, Refrigerants, Naturally!, was founded in 2004 by Greenpeace with

Coca-Cola, McDonald's, and Unilever (PepsiCo and Red Bull are now core partners as well). The group has focused largely on refrigerated cases and vending machines, working with chemical suppliers to create sufficient market demand for substitutes. The new options include, ironically, hydrocarbons and CO_2 itself, which has zero impact on ozone and, by definition, a global warming potential of 1.[22] After scaling up for a decade (these things take time), the partners stopped procuring machines with fluorocarbons in 2017. Coca-Cola hit its one-millionth unit with new technology in 2014, and in total, the group has put more than seven million units into service.[23]

Looking back on what has made this partnership effective, Amy Larkin, formerly of Greenpeace, comments that her global NGO worked with a few leadership companies first. They moved the technology forward, "and then, together, we moved a multitrillion dollar industry" (they also had the clout to pressure governments to change global regulatory standards, venturing into Three to Tango territory).[24] This multiplier effect is what makes 1+1=11, and together, Larkin says, they will cut an impressive 1.5 percent of global greenhouse gas emissions over twenty years. The progression from an NGO with an idea to implementing a new technology at scale came from having the right cross-sector mix in the room.

This successful example of a multiplayer partnership helped define what precompetitive looks like (see the box "Don't Worry about What's Precompetitive"). At the time, nobody was pitching soda or ice cream on how it was refrigerated. Consumers are much more aware of the environmental and social aspects of what they buy now, so there's more pressure to solve shared challenges. In particular, packaging and plastic are pressing issues. A couple of innovative partnerships are searching for new models.

Spirits giant Diageo recently created a new beverage sector partnership, along with a small sustainable packaging company, Pulpex Limited.[25] They invited PepsiCo and Unilever to test out a nonplastic, paper-based container. It's a smart collaboration since the companies mostly operate in different spaces—alcoholic beverages, nonalcoholic drinks, and consumer packaged goods. It allows some scale without direct competition.

Retailers and CPG companies are experimenting with ways to greatly reduce packaging, or even eliminate it. British retailers Asda (owned by Walmart), Morrison, and thirty others teamed up to offer packaging-free

DON'T WORRY ABOUT WHAT'S PRECOMPETITIVE

To solve problems at scale, competitors need to work together. But it's hard to say which issues are precompetitive and which could give you an advantage. When the refrigerants coalition came together, nobody was competing on how they cooled their machines. But times have changed. Some consumers may, in fact, buy something based on the complete story of how it's manufactured or distributed. But either way, working together should be the default option. Step back and ask yourself, is this a problem that makes everyone in the sector look bad? Is it something that we can't solve alone? Or on social issues, like racial equality, consider how unhelpful it is for just one brand to be a champion. Embrace transparency. You should rarely hold back proprietary information about a shared challenge. If you do, you may see some short-term advantage, but you'll never get the 1+1=11 benefits that solve the problem for all. Start with trust, do what's right for the community and the sector, and *then* worry about how to take advantage of it. Once you've reduced shared hurdles, you'll find that companies are not equally prepared to act quickly. If you've built a net positive business that's aligned around purpose, with people who have a mission, your company will move quicker and reap the benefits faster.

options in stores.[26] Consumers fill their own bags and jars from bins holding grains and nuts, detergent, shampoo, and many other products. In Indonesia, Unilever partnered with a packaging-free store to offer eleven brands from what look like soda machines, but dispense TRESemmé shampoo, or Lifebuoy and Dove soaps, instead.[27] The shape and look of packaging has long been part of a brand's image, but in the end, it's not the purpose of the product. And, unique packaging that can't be reused creates pollution, a net negative.

It's possible that all of these efforts will be failures, or they may not reduce total impacts as hoped. Is it better to ship reusable bottles and then clean them, or would a more robust recycling infrastructure with 100 percent recyclable packaging achieve lower impact? There's only one real way to find out: real-world testing, measurement, and sharing of outcomes. These partnerships are invaluable learning experiences, even if they stumble, as long as we fail fast, fail forward, and move on.

What Net Positive Companies Do to Solve Problems across Sectors

- Identify key challenges that cross industries and form broader coalitions to solve them—issues such as education, joint energy buying, human rights, labor laws, and climate change are some of the many that offer fertile ground

- Develop new business models by putting unlikely industries together

- View their responsibility to stakeholders extending beyond their own industry footprint

Partnering with Civil Society

Most large companies have some basic partnerships with civil society organizations—an annual United Way fundraising effort, or supporting a cause in developing markets, or a pet project from the CEO. Many are CSR-style initiatives—essentially cause-related marketing. They are little more than donations, and not real collaborations. A company can sprinkle some money around with limited effort, since it doesn't require much in the way of people resources or planning. At best, the program is linked to a brand, but far removed from the overall company strategy.

Companies often shy away from deeper partnerships with stakeholders outside the private sector, such as academics, NGOs, or philanthropies. But net positive companies seek out civil society partners to make their businesses more effective and resilient. They embrace partners for their knowledge, passion, ability to solve problems, and close relationships with communities. In these richer collaborations, the stakeholders are more than just places to donate money to, or conveners of meetings; they are major actors in executing a program.

Unilever, like all companies, started with more standard, somewhat shallower CSR-style work. The company had a history of a "100,000 flowers blooming" approach to NGO engagement. They were spreading the philanthropy fertilizer around, with little coordination. All of it was well intended, but not necessarily impactful. Around the time Paul arrived at Unilever, Rebecca Marmot (now the chief sustainability officer) came to the company to take a global role working on advocacy, policy, and partnerships. She collected information on Unilever's philanthropic and brand-related partnerships and was shocked at the volume. "We lost count when we got to *four thousand different partnerships*," she says.[28]

Part of her job, with Paul's urging, was to make sense of it all. They quickly centralized efforts from all over the world and across hundreds of brands, focusing on key themes, such as health and hygiene, food and nutrition, and livelihoods. Then, they moved into deeper, more strategic relationships with only five global NGOs: Oxfam, PSI, Save the Children, UNICEF, and the World Food Programme. Once there was centralization, *then* they could decentralize, but do it strategically, letting local markets customize and leverage the larger relationships. The big efforts were handled globally for maximum impact, but they reserved 25 percent of the partnerships budget for local initiatives.

This focused partnership model helped Unilever work on larger, more coordinated efforts, which ensured that the global and local efforts reinforced one another and tied into the business. One program, dubbed Perfect Villages, worked with NGOs to help local communities develop more holistically. They partnered with schools to improve education, helped local businesses get microfinance, worked to improve local infrastructure, and more.

Unilever and UNICEF have collaborated productively for a decade, on WASH (water, sanitation, and hygiene) issues and through multiple major initiatives with key brands, such as Lifebuoy's hand-washing campaign and Domestos's efforts to provide safe sanitation (which has brought access to toilets to thirty million people). Charlie Beevor, now Unilever's VP of homecare, worked on the Domestos brand early in the collaboration with UNICEF. The program, he says, was directly tied to the brand's purpose, connecting it "to an intractable societal problem affecting 2.3 billion people."[29] The story of fighting for improved sanitation has been integral to the product; Beevor says the mission has been proudly and prominently displayed on roughly 270 million Domestos packages. Marmot also makes it clear how important this connection is, saying, "If you really want to change the way business operates, then surely you need to mainstream this way of thinking into the absolute core of the business, not keep [partnerships] as a separate thing."[30]

When NGOs and companies have respect for one another as teammates, they can up one another's game. NGOs often go to shareholder meetings to apply pressure on management on issues of concern. When NGOs came to Unilever's annual meetings, Paul liked to show, when he could, that the company was already planning to go further on an issue than the NGO was advocating for. The game was to push the NGO to then use its leverage over *other* companies in the sector, making everyone go faster. Having good relationships with NGOs is critical. In ten years at the helm, no NGO seriously attacked Paul or Unilever—not Greenpeace, Amnesty International, or Transparency International. It wasn't because Unilever was perfect; it was about relationships, partnerships, trust, and a desire to continuously push the boundaries.

NGOs give a business credibility on the ground, but a net positive company has to build deeper, direct community relationships as well. That often means working with the true power holders in most developing country communities, the women. Unilever Vietnam ran a local program to teach kids about dental hygiene. They partnered with the ministries of education and health, bringing dental trucks to schools for free checkups. But to get kids and families to participate, they also needed the support of local women's associations, the largest of which had *one million* members. With their support, the initiative was wildly successful. Over ten years, the program reached seven million children. The incidence of tooth decay in kids under age ten plummeted from 60 to 12 percent.

The Shakti initiative is another of Unilever's successful programs that enhance communities by working with women. The program operates in many countries (under multiple names), but it is largest in India. In more rural communities, Unilever partners with local women, focusing on those in disadvantaged situations. The company teaches them how to set up shop and sell small amounts of Unilever products. The program obviously has commercial benefits as well—it's a distribution channel to remote villages. Shakti has gotten to scale—tripling in a decade—and is now part of the mainstream business, making a sizeable contribution to Hindustan Unilever's revenues. But the economic and social impact for the 136,000 Indian women in the program is even more significant. As Hindustan Unilever chairman Sanjiv Mehta says, "Their status in the village and family rises, and they increase their family income by about 25 percent."[31] It's hard to imagine a better net positive win-win than that.

Even without a direct connection to sales, Unilever helps enrich the communities it operates in. In Assam, India, where it had plantations (it has since sold them), the company ran the only school in the region for the disabled, placing it right by the factory. Most companies would feature that story in an annual report as a big deal. Net positive companies think it's just a normal way of doing business.

What Net Positive Companies Do to Build Successful Partnerships with Civil Society

- Work with NGOs and communities strategically, not solely in philanthropic CSR initiatives, and make these partnerships an integral part of their longer-term strategy

- Embed these efforts in their businesses by focusing their NGO and community work where they can best improve well-being through their business and brands

- Treat civil society organizations as equal partners and cherish their advocacy for the voice of the people

Partnering with Government (Nonsystems)

The most challenging partnerships are often the ones with governments, but given their reach and scale, these collaborations can have the highest impact. We're not talking yet about real systems-level change (see chapter 7), but focusing for now on opportunities to help communities develop and make the business operating environment better for all.

Companies bring a range of skills and capacities that help governments be more effective, especially in developing countries. Adopting a collaborative attitude toward government, instead of the normal adversarial tone, can lead a net positive company to work on surprising issues. Unilever helped the Vietnamese government develop pension systems and stock ownership plans so the company could offer employees the same benefits everywhere. Unilever has helped many governments build capacity and knowledge to fight the blight of counterfeit products (which sucks revenue away from businesses and communities). The company has even trained tax inspectors in Colombia, Nigeria, Vietnam, Bangladesh, Pakistan, and elsewhere. They help these countries create, enforce, and mechanize a better tax system—one that is efficient, broadens the tax base, collects more of what's owed (so the country can invest in development), and creates a level, predictable playing field for multinationals.

People from other companies often ask Unilever why it does this kind of nitty-gritty government work. The benefits are many. Being a good partner on taxes builds trust with authorities, which makes all government partnerships more productive. It opens up discussions around other regulatory issues, such as building recycling systems to help with packaging and waste goals, or creating incentives for nutrition and micronutrient programs. Unilever found it could work effectively with these governments on many strategic issues because of their ongoing relationships on tactical issues, such as taxes.

Net positive companies bring their best practices from other countries to solve shared problems. For example, multinationals in the consumer products industry have largely abandoned the practice of animal testing, with the painful exception of products sold in China and Russia where they require it. Unilever worked in both countries to change policies, but brought in alternative testing technologies, which have now saved millions of animals. The work has turned one powerful critic, People for the Ethical Treatment of Animals (PETA), into an ally. Consider how difficult it is for PETA to have a productive conversation with the Chinese or Russian government. A company with significant operations in these countries can broach tough subjects that PETA can't. The NGO now allows Unilever to use its cruelty-free label, which attracts customers, on brands such as Dove, Simple, and St. Ives. This is what value from values looks like.

It can be challenging to hold on to your ethics in some situations. Many countries are rife with corruption, and some leaders and governments are doing horrible things to their own citizens. Working with administrations with troubled policies is complicated, but in essence, some things are non-political. When President Narendra Modi in India launched the Swachh Bharat Mission (which means "Clean India"), one key goal was to get a toilet into every household. This was an opportunity for Unilever and UNICEF to expand their sanitation programs. Giving every Indian a toilet is not political. Multinationals see leaders come and go, and a net positive company finds a way to move things in the right direction no matter who is in power.

Did Unilever always succeed? Not exactly. In 2017, when the last US president was about to take the country out of the Paris climate accord, Paul and the chief sustainability officer at the time, Jeff Seabright, pitched the administration on staying in the global agreement. They got in to see the president's daughter and son-in-law. We know how that one ended. Sometimes you succeed, and sometimes you don't.

What Net Positive Companies Do to Work Productively with Governments

- Use their knowledge and skills to help governments develop capacity, improving the business operating environment for all

- Seek areas where the playing field needs to be leveled and governments are willing to actively engage

- Don't walk away from governments they don't agree with, but try to partner and improve the well-being of citizens

- Understand what's short-term and political versus what needs to be focused on for the long term

Partnering with Multistakeholder Groups (Nonsystems)

The most sprawling and complicated 1+1=11 partnerships bring everyone to the table—peers, suppliers and customers, governments, NGOs, academics, and finance. This is when magic can happen, but it's also where too many ingredients can spoil the soup. It's a tough balance. The collaborations we look at here are improving and scaling what works within the current system . . . but are not yet resetting whole systems.

Unilever has found multistakeholder work to be highly effective in the tea industry. It's a big business, but the sector is anchored by more than nine million smallholder farmers around the world.[32] Eastern Africa is a major source, with 500,000 farmers in Kenya and 40,000 in Rwanda (the country's third-largest employer).[33] As a big buyer, Unilever has had a significant presence in the region for a century. Whether these communities thrive reflects directly on the company. Moving to more sustainable practices in farming—managing soil health or reducing pesticides, for example—enhances livelihoods, productivity, and the quality of the tea. But that takes years. Farmers need financial support or guarantees from buyers to shift to better practices.

In Rwanda, Unilever partnered with the national government, the Wood Foundation, IDH (a Dutch NGO), and the UK Department for International Development to develop a new tea plantation. Unilever committed $30 million over four years—what the Wood Foundation referred to as "patient capital"—to develop the farms and a tea processing center in one of Rwanda's poorest areas, the Nyaruguru district.[34]

The collaboration provided tens of thousands of people with livelihoods—farmers, factory workers, and people in support structures, such as schools. It also offered technical assistance and training on the efficient use of resources and how to develop resilience to drought and climate change. Unilever built clean water infrastructure for worker households as well. The program created a virtuous circle of economic, environmental, and social development in one supply chain and region. That's the 1+1=11 outcome. To make it happen, Unilever needed the partnership of NGOs and local governments, but in this case, could do it without peers. This work to create new producers and consumers in Rwanda was the kind of "bottom of the pyramid" market development made famous by C.K. Prahalad, a former Unilever adviser.

Creative multistakeholder partnerships can fill big gaps in a community's development. A lack of safely managed sanitation systems, for example, keeps billions of people from thriving. In many communities, if there's sanitation at all, they treat the sewage and put it back in waterways. They miss out on capturing the nutrients, which can be a feedstock for fertilizer, fuel, and energy (anaerobic digestion turns waste into valuable biogas).

The Toilet Board Coalition (TBC), with founders Firmenich, Kimberly-Clark, LIXIL, Tata Trusts, Unilever, and Veolia—plus fifty stakeholder partners, including UN agencies and the World Bank—is trying to solve this problem by creating a for-profit market for sanitation solutions. The theory of a "sanitation economy" is this: if they unlock previously unvalued assets in the waste system, they'll build more sanitation infrastructure than governments would on their own. As the former TBC executive director, Cheryl Hicks, says, "to reach sanitation for all, we should focus on the value the systems can generate, not just the cost to deliver services."[35]

The TBC is an accelerator of innovative, early-stage companies with waste-to-value technologies, such as smart toilets that capture data on resource flows. The multinationals in the partnership operate as advisers, customers, investors, and partners that can help the new companies ramp up. It may seem wrong to treat a human right as a business proposition, but it's pragmatic: governments and communities lack the resources to fill the gap for billions of people. The fastest way to get sanitation technologies to scale is to turn waste into something valuable, and then leverage the power of business and markets. These approaches do not take value from poorer communities in the way extraction industries often do; they build permanent infrastructure that profoundly improves health and quality of life. It's net positive in all dimensions.

The number of multistakeholder collaborations hoping to solve our largest problems is growing rapidly. Consider a few examples, especially in water, which is impossible to do right without all players in a watershed. These collaborations are worth keeping an eye on and learning from (whether they succeed or fail):

- The World Bank hosts the 2030 Water Resources Group, bringing big beverage companies such as AB InBev, Coca-Cola, Nestlé, PepsiCo, and Unilever together with civil society partners to develop regional and local water resource management strategies.

- Doug Baker, the executive chairman of Ecolab, started the Water Coalition to accelerate the UN-sponsored CEO Water Mandate. Members commit to water stewardship, transparency, and new goals that, Baker says, "mirror the science-based 1.5°C carbon goals." In stressed watersheds, they will target a 50 percent reduction of water use by 2030 and a 100 percent reduction, or "renewal," by 2050. Ecolab's existing work with The Nature Conservancy proves, Baker says, that in watershed protection "you can make a huge difference without huge money."[36]

- The Global Battery Alliance assembles seventy organizations across business, governments, UN agencies, NGOs, and knowledge partners to ensure that the massive carbon reductions the world needs from electric vehicles actually happen.

- The Getting to Zero Coalition connects big maritime shippers (such as Maersk), commodity and product manufacturers, banks, ports, and NGOs to reduce greenhouse gases from shipping by 50 percent by 2050.

What Net Positive Companies Do with Multistakeholder Groups

- Lead multistakeholder collaborations, inviting all the players that are needed, no matter how complicated it gets

- Look holistically at their operations and communities to find gaps and opportunities to improve well-being

- Explore innovative business and financing models to solve societal problems in new ways

Strength and Resilience in Numbers

There are more partnerships to choose from than ever before. It's hard to know where to begin. We can say with confidence that a few key organizations are involved in the majority of efforts that have scale. Look to WBCSD, We Mean Business (or one of its member organizations, such as Ceres or the Climate Group), UN agencies like the UN Global Compact, or other multilateral organizations, such as the World Bank. It's not a big risk to join multiple partnerships. It's important not to spread yourself too thin, but you will know quickly if a group is action-oriented enough for you—or moving too quickly if you're not ready yet.

These groups allow for leadership in a safer environment. Being half a step ahead of the parade, calling the cadence, can create advantage, but you don't want to get *too* far ahead, or you might take all the heat for what doesn't work perfectly. You can push boundaries more by working together. When you gather groups, people are braver, creating what Paul's firm IMAGINE calls "courageous collectives."

That's one of the many benefits of these partnerships. In total, they create resilience for the members. Nothing can protect a company from all possible outcomes—after all, a pandemic was technically foreseeable, but was impossible for sectors like hospitality to fully prepare for. But working together means having allies, the proverbial boats to lash together to ride out the storms. And when seas are calm enough, the group can move fast toward net positive.

7

It Takes Three to Tango

Systems-Level Reset and Net Positive Advocacy

Whenever I run into a problem I can't solve,
I always make it bigger.

—Dwight D. Eisenhower, 34th president of the United States

When India was under British rule, the colonial government was concerned about the number of snakes in Delhi, so it offered a bounty for dead cobras. The program seemed to work, and dead snakes poured in, but the number in the street didn't go down—people were breeding cobras to make money. When the government stopped paying, the breeders released all of their snakes, greatly increasing the numbers in the streets.

It's possible this story of unintended consequences is a myth, but it demonstrates in a simple way that the more complicated the system, the more likely it is that there will be surprises.[1] In transportation planning, for example, when cities build more roads to relieve congestion, the level of gridlock eventually comes back, often worse than before. Additional capacity and speed allows more people to live farther from the city center—more suburbs, more people, more cars.[2] The point here is not some antiregulatory screed. We need rules for the common good and to protect what can't protect itself (the climate, the disempowered, other species). But government setting policies on its own, without considering feedback loops or bringing everyone to the table, will often result in suboptimal outcomes. Likewise, if companies control the agenda alone (through influence or corruption), self-interest might prevail. Unilateral action is entirely unfit for attacking today's toughest problems.

What if communities and businesses took a different approach to the congestion problem? With all stakeholders working together, perhaps they would advocate for more systemic solutions than building more roads. A better policy mix might include incentives for affordable housing downtown, light rail to the suburbs, increased telecommuting, and congestion pricing. As our challenges get bigger and more intertwined, we need broader thinking.

Consider again the Sustainable Development Goals which establish the to-do list of major challenges we need to solve together. The 1+1=11 partnerships within either sector or a value chain are not enough to manage many of these issues. We can't tackle global challenges such as climate change, food security, pandemics, inequality, biodiversity, or cybersecurity by working one company or even one sector at a time. These issues know no boundaries and require unparalleled collective action to solve.

Big picture solutions need all three pillars of society—public sector, private sector, and civil society—working together, dancing a complicated tango. With everyone at the table, we can shift entire systems toward well-being for all. The potential for positive impact is exponentially larger than going it alone. Historically we relied on governments and multilateral institutions to take the initiative. But in an increasingly challenging national and international political environment, we expect that leading companies will step up and help make political action less risky for peers and governments. This is the ultimate work of a net positive company.

The End of Self-Serving Lobbying

Most of what the antibusiness cynics believe about companies has a foundation in traditional lobbying. Beverage companies fight bottle bills that collect fees for recycling infrastructure; agriculture companies demand large subsidies for corn to go into ethanol instead of food; and fossil fuel companies spend endless money convincing lawmakers to give them cheap access to public lands for more exploration.

We've earned the distrust of society.

Companies use basically two tools of influence to create the outcomes they want: corruption and lobbying. The difference between the two is often one of semantics. Corruption is paying lawmakers or civil servants under the table, *after* a law is written, and is deemed illegal; lobbying is paying legislators *before* any rules are enacted (to make sure they're written the way the lobbyists want), which is somehow legal. The United States has legalized corruption in the form of essentially unrestricted corporate giving. Companies collectively spend $3.5 billion a year lobbying the US government.[3] The flow of money might be greater in the United States, but there is self-serving lobbying everywhere—company leaders visit world capitals to advocate for rules that help themselves. Policies set by either corruption or self-serving lobbying protect the interests of those with the biggest wallets; they neither serve the common good nor protect democracy.

Even so, lobbying is not inherently wrong. It's just a tool, and not all current advocacy is done with ill intent. Companies sometimes fight well-meaning regional laws so they can work toward a national standard instead. Or, more important, they actively work with governments to get the right regulation in place. Unilever, for example, advocated actively for elimination of animal testing, and the need to combat product counterfeits globally. In Europe, it pushed for implementation of a circular economy framework. Sometimes business is correct to seek simpler legislation, fewer roadblocks, or harmonized rules that meet a societal goal and help business. Net positive companies understand that getting better legislation that solves our major issues may require them to seek solutions beyond their own narrow self-interest.

The massive political power of business comes from scale (or from buying the power), and it's not going away. Our goal is to add an element of *moral* power, which has ultimate strength, and pivot the whole process toward better outcomes. We propose a new form of influence, *net positive advocacy*—broad coalitions having open conversations about policies that serve everyone's interests. It's time to end the one-dimensional, "just say no" approach to government relations that seeks to avoid all regulations, and shift to one that seeks out shared opportunities to build a thriving world. Companies should absolutely be proactive; it's smart to shape rules before they shape you. But never selfishly try to maintain the status quo at the expense of a thriving future.

Smart stakeholders recognize this tension and want trustworthy businesses to play an active, positive role. Ron Oswald, the general secretary of IUF, the large agricultural and hospitality worker union, says, "We used to complain about companies having too much political influence, but now on critical issues like the environment and human rights, we say, please use it . . . if we trust them."

While there will always be a need for positive unilateral relations between a company and government, we should increasingly initiate larger discussions with governments, peers, NGOs, and labor in the room. If a big company approaches policymakers with an environmental NGO like World Wildlife Fund (WWF) at its side, it sends a signal. It's safer for other companies to take part, and safer for politicians to put themselves out there, even if the action goes against a key constituency.

This is how we "de-risk" the political process.

One way to create this mindset is to apply our net positive core principles to government relationships, and see what changes. For example, companies that take responsibility and own their global impacts will help shape laws that incentivize circular models and embrace extended producer responsibility. Leaders with a long-term view operate on principles and larger policy goals, instead of getting stuck in the time frame of political cycles, in which objectives and politicians change.

Business and government need each other. Countries can sign climate agreements, but without business to implement them, they won't meet their goals. Companies that set aggressive carbon reduction targets also won't get there without policies that move the electric grid toward renewables.

Net positive companies don't view governments as adversaries in a series of one-off antagonistic battles; they see them as partners in an ongoing relationship, working toward shared goals and a better future. And if they are smart, they actively involve civil society to ensure the needed legitimacy. After all, business leaders are not elected.

The Challenges of Public-Private Partnerships

Net positive advocacy, with real partnerships, will feel different than the rhythm of traditional lobbying when a company asks for what it wants and makes clear what it will do for the politician in return. In this new mode, companies will put the needs of a country, region, or community first, and seek policies that solve problems for all. Coalitions between business and governments are not easy. Adding parts of civil society makes it even more complicated, but ultimately more robust. No matter how good the intentions, there are hurdles getting in the way that both sides need to prepare for and navigate.

Power. Business leaders will be trying to influence situations they can't bully their way through. They're not elected and don't have the power most of the time. It's the coalition, working with peers and NGOs for a larger purpose, which gives the effort credibility.

Speed. Business, for all its flaws and bureaucracy, tends to move faster. Government has inefficiencies built in for checks and balances; lawmaking is meant to be deliberate.

Organization. Many in government operate in silos and don't always work in a multistakeholder mode. Government ministers may not talk that often, and may compete for limited budgets. But approach them holistically, and more gets done. Companies and NGOs are often equally siloed.

Ignorance. Lifetime politicians or civil society workers may not understand the private sector. The reverse is also true. Business people don't fully understand the political world and its pressures. Both sides can be naive.

Objectives. A business is generally seeking some concrete outcome and clarity. A politician may only want to be reelected, so making her electorate think she is serving them is the main priority, not effective policy for the greater good. Elected officials can get punished if they step out too far, which is why de-risking provides cover for both business leaders and politicians.

Interdependence. Systems thinking is lacking on both sides. Consider, for example, how often a tariff goes horribly wrong, even when a sector lobbies for it and thinks they want it. Steelmakers may love barriers to foreign steel, but then prices rise and major steel buyers cut back as the economy suffers.

Parties. Until recently, companies almost uniformly avoided siding with a particular party, happy to donate to all sides. In theory, companies should argue for the best policies that need implementing, and work with whomever gets that done. But, in some cases, siding with a policy or principle does mean picking a party. In the current US Congress, for example, nearly zero Republicans have ever voted for climate action or environmental protection. It's unproductive to pretend that conversations about climate, inequality, and democracy are equally fruitful with each side of the aisle.

Money and corruption. Money is everywhere in politics. Even if you walk in with the country's best interests at heart, some officials won't care and will ask what's in it for them. There are no easy answers, but going in with a broad coalition helps. It creates pressure for everyone to work toward the common good.

. . .

With these challenges and differences, it's not surprising that a lack of trust can get in the way. It's a prisoner's dilemma: Who will move first in a spirit of cooperation? Given the justified skepticism about the intentions of the private sector, we in business likely need to extend the olive branch first. Approach governments with multiple stakeholders and a genuine desire to work together, and you will move down the road to net positive.

The Paths to Systems Change

The focus here is on collaborations with all three pillars of society in the room (see table 7-1). These *tangos* of business, NGOs, and governments will aim to reset bigger systems. We identify here four core end goals of collaborations that combine advocacy (the "say") and action (the "do") to bring about real change.

We'll look at partnerships that, for example, work to:

- *Encourage policy makers to think big,* with active advocacy making it clear where business sits on issues like climate change

TABLE 7-1

Two scales of partnership

Chapter 6: 1+1=11 Creating Partnerships with Synergies and Multiplier Effects	Chapter 7: It Takes Three to Tango Systems-Level Reset and Net Positive Advocacy
Scaling with the system	Changing the system
May need competitors to get more done	Need more players (policy, finance)
Solving shared industry risk	Building the greater common good
Localized regions or supply chains	Full systems
Some civil society partners	All participants in the system
Action (More "do")	Action and advocacy (More "say")

- *Guide policy to enable net positive outcomes*, such as working on incentives for more environmentally friendly packaging and recycling, or accelerating specific climate change legislation

- *Help countries thrive*, through public-private partnerships, in ways that support economic growth and build out new sectors or expand ecosystems of business

- *Take on the largest societal problems*, such as the intensely complicated palm oil production system that ties into climate change, inequality, and most other major global challenges

These goals provide guidance on the kinds of partnerships to build and focus all stakeholders on the right outcomes. These are collaborations that are new to most companies (especially in the United States). But the payoff is enormous, for companies and society.

Active Collective Advocacy

The support of business has been integral to making progress on climate change. The Paris climate accord came together in 2015, in large part, because of an unprecedented presence of business and CEOs at the meetings. They spoke with one voice, demanding progress.

The NGO Ceres coordinated a Climate Declaration from 1,600 companies. Specific sectors, such as finance, also put out statements of support.[4] There are good reasons for companies to act proactively. Many regions of the world have some form of carbon tax, but it's not uniform. A quarter of the world's emissions are already under a pricing scheme.[5] Since no business enjoys operating in many different regulatory environments, it makes sense to call for harmonized policies.

Many businesses got vocal when, in June 2017, the president of the United States announced that he was pulling the country out of the Paris Agreement, effectively making the world's biggest economy the lone holdout. In a frantic few days before the announcement, Paul and the then-CEO of Dow, Andrew Liveris, scrambled to get a group of CEOs to speak up. The morning of the decision, the thirty multinationals they gathered ran an open letter as a full-page ad in the *Wall Street Journal*, urging the president to keep the United States in the agreement. They said the Paris accord would create new clean-tech jobs, reduce risk to businesses and communities, and strengthen the country's competitiveness. The ad was signed by the CEOs of big brands such as 3M, Allianz, Bank of America, Citi, Coca-Cola, Disney, Dow, DuPont, GE, J&J, JP Morgan Chase, and Unilever.

A few days later, another coalition created by WWF, Climate Nexus, and Ceres got hundreds of companies to publicly declare, "We are still in" (which has since merged with another pledge movement into "America is all in"). The signatories now number roughly 2,300 businesses, 400 universities, 300 cities and counties, and 1,000 faith groups. CEOs and governors were instrumental in keeping the United States engaged in global climate negotiations after the country pulled out of the Paris Agreement.

For the 2019 climate conference, Paul and Liveris again reached out to CEOs to make their collective voices heard, and a larger group overwhelmingly called for reentering the Paris Agreement. Anne Kelly, the VP of government relations at Ceres, says that having two CEOs pushing so hard was "a real game-changer and integral to its success."[6] In the end, the CEOs of eighty large companies signed a "United for Paris" statement, which added some new, important elements: The statement recognized the climate crisis as a human and inequality crisis, not just an environmental one, and the signatories included the AFL-CIO, a coalition of labor unions representing 12.5 million workers.

It was a powerful message to policy makers to see business and labor together. The statement committed companies to support "a just transition of the workforce that respects labor rights . . . through dialogue with workers and their unions." That phrase was highly unusual. Sharan Burrow, the general secretary of the International Trade Union Confederation, says that American companies generally fight against labor rights policies, and "that's why having signatures of business and the AFL-CIO [together] was so important."[7] During the pandemic, a large coalition of companies, lawmakers, and activists in the EU came out in strong support for a green recovery focused on the clean economy, protection of biodiversity, and a transformation of the agriculture system.[8] The CEOs on the list included Europe's most forward-thinking leaders, such as Danone's then-CEO, Emanuel Faber, Jean-Paul Agon from L'Oréal, and Jesper Brodin from IKEA. Another coalition, Business for Nature, brings seven hundred big companies and major NGOs together to "call for governments to adopt policies now to reverse nature loss this decade."[9]

These public statements are just words, of course. They're not the same as action and measurable changes in outcomes. But they commit companies to support the right policies, which then gives employees and other stakeholders ammunition to hold them accountable. It also makes moving on to more concrete partnerships easier—it all builds momentum from "say" to "do." In the six years since the Paris Agreement, for example, nearly 1,600 companies have signed up to set science-based carbon reduction targets, while hundreds are committed to 100 percent renewable energy.

On climate issues, the business community, in many regions, is ahead of governments. In the United States in particular, companies publicly advanced their carbon reductions and use of renewables while the government was going backward. If any CEOs remain skittish about speaking up, consider that an Edelman survey shows that over 86 percent of people are looking for CEOs to lead on issues like climate change and racial justice.[10]

What Net Positive Companies Do to Speak Out Collectively

- Lead public statements of commitments to large-scale action, and use their leverage with peers to get others on board

> • Use public commitments to draw more stakeholders into the discussion and apply pressure, through net positive advocacy, on governments

Guiding Policy toward Net Positive Outcomes

Unilever launched the USLP with big, hairy, audacious goals. It was clear that many of the targets were impossible to reach without partnering with governments and civil society. Unilever proactively engaged with many stakeholders to build deeper relationships and advocate for change. Miguel Veiga-Pestana, the global head of external affairs and sustainability at the time, led the company's work in Brussels. His goal was to engage with EU leaders on their priorities—such as increasing European competitiveness and participating in the emerging discussion about building a green economy.

Unilever sees policy-making as a funnel. At the top end, as officials get their heads around an issue like climate change, they discuss a wide range of policy options. The funnel narrows to something specific, such as a carbon tax, and then further to minutiae about pricing and mechanisms. While discussions were at the top of the funnel, and nobody had a clue yet about what to do, Veiga-Pestana would bring executives to meet with policy makers. "You can't overstate how important it is to have a CEO like Paul or other senior leaders in the conversation early on," he says.

Unilever offered the EU help in areas where it had specific knowledge: food security and supply chains, deforestation and climate change, hygiene and sanitation, empowerment of women, circular economy, and more. Executives helped EU officials understand how a policy might impact business and markets. Policy makers often expressed surprise at how Unilever approached them. Other business leaders normally came in to complain about legislation or ask for a lower tax rate, but as one government official explained, "Unilever comes in proactively with ideas about how to help Europe." That kind of authentic work builds credibility and earns the right to be a strong voice in the development and implementation of policy. In the climate realm specifically, net positive companies should support an array of existing or potential rules and government actions (see the box "Climate Policies Companies Should Fight For").

Cynics will say that this sounds like the same old self-interested lobbying. Not exactly. The difference is that net positive advocacy does not *solely* benefit the company; it drives changes that make the system more sustainable. There's nothing wrong with advocating for society-improving policies that also help the business meet its goals.

Unilever Russia provides a good example of this balance. To reduce the footprint of its product and please consumers, Unilever wanted to increase the use of postconsumer recycled (PCR) materials in its packaging. Russia's recycling infrastructure, however, was lacking. Irina Bakhtina, then Unilever's VP of corporate affairs and sustainable business in Russia, worked with recyclers and retailers to set up their own infrastructure. Within a year, Unilever launched a portfolio of beauty and personal care products that came in 100 percent PCR bottles.

In parallel, Bakhtina tried to improve policies in Russia that hinder progress. She didn't approach the government to ask for special tax breaks for the recycling infrastructure Unilever built (the company hoped to earn back the investment in sales and brand value). She did, however, want to change the way Russian regulations incentivized choices about material use. The country has an extended producer responsibility (EPR) law that charges manufacturers for each ton of plastic they use. The fee applied to everything equally, both nonrecyclable plastics (such as PVC) and the recyclable plastic Unilever needed for its PCR packaging.

Bakhtina partnered with a professor at St. Petersburg State University to create a detailed formula for collecting fees not based on weight, but on the type of plastic. Easily recycled materials would have much lower fees than plastics that end up in landfills. The incentives would drive businesses to use more of the recyclable materials, providing more feedstock for PCR packaging and lowering the cost of better materials for everyone.

There are miles of space between asking for tax breaks for your business specifically and asking for lower tax rates for *all* recycled content packaging. The former helps shareholders but drains money from the country. The latter increases the incentive to build a circular business around plastics and packaging, creating jobs while lowering both material demand and carbon emissions.

Unfortunately, many companies like to guide policy in the opposite direction, away from net positive outcomes. In the wake of the pandemic, a lobbying group representing the largest chemical and fossil fuel companies—who see their future in producing more plastic—worked to change a US-Kenya trade deal to lift limits on waste. It would greatly increase plastic

CLIMATE POLICIES COMPANIES SHOULD FIGHT FOR

The most productive climate policies will fix market failures, set a high bar for low-carbon products, and help draw out the $1.5 to $2 trillion in capital needed annually to hold warming to 1.5°C. We suggest prioritizing and advocating for the following:

Reducing the economy's carbon and material intensity

- Set a rapidly rising price on carbon, coupled with massive shifts in subsidies from fossil fuels to clean-tech and low-carbon production methods
- Research into and funding for increased material capture (recycling, reuse, repair) to encourage a circular economy

Scaling up

- Unleash public capital that pulls more private investment into clean tech

Reimagining food and land use

- Reverse perverse agricultural policies and provide incentives for farmers to move to regenerative agriculture
- Reduce food waste

Finding nature-based solutions

- Price natural capital and conserve lands (e.g., wetlands) to prevent emissions →

use across Africa. Many of these same companies have signed on to the Alliance to End Plastic Waste.[11] That's a good definition of hypocrisy, which, as usual, transparency helps bring to light.

Like any company, Unilever has had moments, often as part of trade groups, where lobbying has not matched the company's goals to serve the common good. But if differences in philosophies are too big, net positive businesses leave the associations, as Unilever did with the US Chamber of Commerce, Business Europe, and the American Legislative Exchange Council—all were reluctant to fight climate change or actively worked against progress.

Zero carbon mobility

- Phase out internal combustion engines by specific dates (e.g., Norway by 2025) and offer large incentives for electric vehicles of all sizes

Resilient, zero-carbon built environment

- Set high performance standards for building, heating, and cooling systems

- Offer incentives for public transportation and mixed use buildings

- Provide funding for adaptation and city resilience planning

Protecting people

- Ensure reskilling and training for workers displaced by the green transition

- Advocate for climate justice and the rights of vulnerable people

Transparency

- Require climate risk assessments in keeping with the Task Force on Climate-Related Financial Disclosures

- Measure product-level carbon footprints and print data on packaging and labels

The work Unilever does in Russia and China best represents where the company is and wants to be. It has taken this path toward systems reset many times, helping governments, for example, develop better ways to stop product counterfeiting; build more consistent tax policies that attract foreign investment; improve efficiency in government and business; and support laws like the United Kingdom's Modern Slavery Act.

Unilever is often recognized for its policy leadership. For its efforts to reduce animal testing requirements in Russia and China, the animal rights group PETA named Unilever (and a few other leaders, including Avon and Colgate-Palmolive) a "Working for Regulatory Change" company.[12]

What Net Positive Companies Do to Guide Policy toward the Common Good

- Engage with policy makers before laws are written and work together versus coming in afterward to complain or lobby for change

- Proactively propose solutions rather than waiting for regulation that's sure to come

- Advocate for broader solutions to shared problems that, even if they benefit the company, benefit everyone

Helping Countries Develop and Thrive

For businesses to succeed, the countries and communities they operate in need to thrive as well. Without economic development and protection of natural resources, human well-being suffers. Persistent poverty is not good for business.

Your business can create a net positive impact and best help communities and countries develop by focusing on their needs. Never compromise yourself by seeking only self-interest. We offer a few examples of how net positive companies can partner with and help the regions they operate in.

Investing with the government in development. Unilever Ethiopia signed a "memo of understanding" with the State of Ethiopia to build facilities in the country, develop an industrial park, and buy more local goods for its supply chain. The company built a state-of-the-art factory for oral care products, a risky long-term bet in a country where only 3 to 5 percent of people brushed their teeth regularly. Unilever also invested in school programs to encourage oral hygiene and improved nutrition, and provided free products during a cholera outbreak. The mutually beneficial relationship is driving growth and paying off. After five years of investment, the business is profitable, with sales of $100 million annually in the eighth-fastest-growing economy in the world.

Unilever Indonesia made a similar choice in developing a large "fractionation" unit—used to divide palm oil into solid and liquid ingredients—in a remote location in North Sumatra. The company spent $150 million and partnered with the government to build out local infrastructure and port capacity. Unilever Indonesia president director Hemant Bakshi says that the project was also intended to help the thirty thousand smallholder farmers surrounding the plant move to more sustainable practices. It was a multi-pronged approach, including policy changes, to help the region thrive. The work proved they could produce more sustainable, traceable palm oil in the country. Subnational governments see these kinds of commitments and are incentivized to change legislative or regulatory approaches to make it easier for business to invest in the region.

Building ecosystems of industry. A single investment creates ripples and highlights policy and economic needs. In Ivory Coast, Unilever wanted to produce mayonnaise locally, but there was no supply chain. The company worked with the government to increase chicken farming for eggs, creating new jobs. Then, seeing a dearth of supply of bottles, it partnered with the government and other industries to create local, more sustainable supplies of glass.

In Colombia, Unilever attempted to ease tensions between the government and FARC rebels. At the request of then president Juan Manuel Santos, it put forward plans to create more economic activity and jobs, reintegrating former FARC rebels. The plan provided more stability and development, while also avoiding deforestation.

In Russia, Unilever helped found the Foreign Investment Advisory Council, a group of more than fifty multinationals working with the government to create a healthy investing climate. Executives would often come to meetings with the country's leaders and ask for regulatory relief, or talk about what *they* needed. In contrast, Unilever would ask how they could work to help Russia's economy and industries thrive.

Solving shared problems. In the Middle East, Unilever worked with governments on desalination projects to help reduce water shortages. It developed campaigns to change consumer water habits in places with some of the world's highest per capita consumption rates. Has the company benefited from this work? Not in a way that's easily measurable. But giving more people access to affordable water is good for a business selling toothpaste, shampoo, and soap. It helps competitors also, but without a systemic improvement in water availability, every company would suffer (see the box "Water Work").

Being a good friend and partner. Showing up as an ally during emergencies is both humane and it's good business. That's when true relationships are built. One of the critical moments in sustainable business history came out of a natural disaster. After Hurricane Katrina devastated New Orleans in 2005, the CEO of Walmart, Lee Scott, observed that his compa-

---

WATER WORK

Water is life. In many places, there is not enough of it, or its low quality endangers health. Ensuring that this shared resource is available to all is critical for consumer products companies. Sanjiv Mehta, chairman of Hindustan Unilever (HUL) describes how water runs through a typical day—brushing teeth, a cup of tea or coffee, a shower, cleaning clothes, having some soup, cleaning dishes. Unilever makes products relying on water for every step of the way.*

HUL logically picked water as a multibrand, corporate initiative. India, Mehta says, ranks 120 out of 122 countries in water quality. Sixty percent of the country's districts have reached "critical" status on availability. With twenty NGO partners, and national and local governments, HUL reaches more than eleven thousand villages, helping improve water infrastructure and training farmers on crop and water management. In total, HUL has created potential availability of water of 1.3 trillion liters, enough to provide drinking water to all Indian adults for a year.

In Bangladesh, Unilever's water purifier brand, Pureit, works with the UN Development Program to improve water availability. They run a water management program, Innovation Challenge, and train women in rural communities to be "water heroes." Unilever and banking partners offer microfinance for people to buy Pureit purifiers. That brand is not meant to be a moneymaker (but it shouldn't lose money either). It's there to create value for society and build the company brand. When a business protects a natural resource central to so many Unilever products, a low-margin approach is justified as part of a larger net positive portfolio.

*Sanjiv Mehta (Unilever), interview by authors, October 21, 2020.

ny's emergency efforts to bring water and lifesaving supplies into the city were more successful than the government's actions. He started to think differently about the role of his business in society. Walmart began working with NGOs and employees on reducing its environmental and social impacts. The company's scale, and subsequent pressure on suppliers to improve their performance, jump-started corporate sustainability around the world. Unilever has also increased its involvement in disaster relief, in part through a partnership between its Vaseline brand and the NGO Direct Relief, bringing essential medical supplies to health-care professionals during emergencies.

There's nothing more important than executives personally showing support when disaster strikes. Paul and his wife, Kim, were among the first foreigners to visit Fukushima, Japan, after the tsunami-induced nuclear plant meltdown, when most foreigners were leaving the country. A few weeks before he took over as Unilever CEO, Paul also found himself in a terrifying situation while staying in the famous Taj Mahal Palace Hotel in India. During a dinner with company executives and local leaders, terrorists stormed the hotel and held it hostage for days. While everyone at the dinner survived, many others at the hotel were less lucky. Paul insisted on returning to Delhi just six months later to finish the dinner, in the same hotel, but this time, the business leaders served the amazing staff who had saved their lives. It showed a commitment to an important and storied market for the company, and public support for the revival of a famous landmark. It's what you do, not what you say.

Being a friend to the communities you work in is not philanthropic. It's right and good, but also builds the business. It creates trust and goodwill, and it aligns the company with the countries and their development agendas. Being a good partner to host countries means being in for the long haul. The managing director for Unilever Ethiopia, Tim Kleinebenne, regularly meets people from other multinationals who want advice on the market. They will ask him, "How can I get money out of Ethiopia?" If someone thinks like that, they should go somewhere else. It's a long-term journey and commitment to a new market. Unilever, Kleinebenne says, "has been recognized by the Ethiopian government, who knows we're an honest player supporting national development."[13] Helping countries succeed is good for business. Thriving countries expand and reward the friends and partners that helped them get there.

What Net Positive Companies Do to Help Countries Thrive

- Show up as a trusted partner when it's *not* expected or when there's nothing directly in it for them

- Add to the fabric of a country, not look only for opportunities to get money out of the region

Taking on the Largest Problems: The Challenge of Palm Oil

China and the United States are the two biggest economies in the world and, logically, the two largest emitters of greenhouse gases. The next two mega-emitters, however, are *not* the third- and fourth-largest economies, Japan and Germany. No, the honor goes to Brazil and Indonesia because they cut down and burn a lot of trees, which releases vast amounts of CO_2.[14] Deforestation produces roughly one-fifth of the world's greenhouse gas emissions.[15] The drivers of deforestation are complex, but the core reason is clearing land for agriculture—soy and cattle in Brazil and palm oil in Indonesia, which supplies 58 percent of global palm oil (and Malaysia, 26 percent).[16]

Palm oil is an ingredient in a vast range of products—soap, shampoo, cookies, bread and dough, ice cream, lipstick, and on and on. It's basically a list of Unilever products, which is why the company is the world's largest single buyer. But it's not just in consumer products. About half of the palm oil entering Europe flows into the tanks of cars as biodiesel (which means transportation competes for land with food).[17]

Indonesia's palm oil plantations cover sixteen million hectares—an area two-thirds the size of the United Kingdom—up from one million hectares in 1990.[18] Most of that growth came from burning virgin forests. The palm oil problem thus connects to *every* big problem. Inequality and poverty force people to cut down forests for survival, and deforestation contributes to climate change and destroys biodiversity. Stopping deforestation is devilishly hard, and will only happen with the support of a full system of producers, buyers, governments, communities, and finance. After many years of efforts and failure, the industry is finally making headway.

Many NGOs, but Rainforest Action Network and Greenpeace in particular, have focused activism on this issue for decades. Through the 1990s and 2000s, they campaigned against Unilever, Nestlé, their peers, and agribusiness giants such as Cargill and Wilmar. Greenpeace activists scaled Unilever's head office building dressed as orangutans, a species threatened by habitat destruction. The global NGO published two blistering reports in 2007 and 2008 that linked the whole sector, but Unilever specifically, to rampant deforestation.

Unilever was not unaware of the issue. It cofounded the industry Roundtable on Sustainable Palm Oil (RSPO) with WWF in 2004. But in 2007, according to Gavin Neath, Unilever's chief sustainability officer at the time, "We had no *real* consciousness that we were helping to drive deforestation and climate change . . . we believed that climate change was mainly a problem for Shell, Exxon, Ford, or General Motors, but not Unilever."[19] The protests were a "life-changing moment" for Neath; it became untenable for the company, and for him, personally, to maintain the current sourcing practices.[20] In retrospect, it's something the company should have been more proactive about.

At the time, the head of Greenpeace UK, John Sauven, had never met with Unilever management. But soon after Paul arrived as CEO, he and Neath developed a solid working relationship with Sauven and they met regularly. Sauven talks today about how open Neath was when he appeared on TV and admitted that Unilever didn't know precisely where its palm oil came from. "All our suppliers have technically infringed either RSPO standards or Indonesian law," Neath said.[21] This level of transparency built up a trust bank that gave Unilever the benefit of the doubt if something went wrong.

With Sauven's encouragement to "throw down the gauntlet," Unilever took a highly unusual step and canceled a contract with a large supplier that was not meeting the standards. Sauven calls the move "seismic."[22] The Rainforest Action Network released a statement praising Unilever's leadership and pushing other companies to do the same.[23] Unilever, as part of its Partner to Win supply chain program, brought together the big producers for a closed-door meeting in Singapore and got them to sign a moratorium on deforestation. At the 2010 global climate conference, Unilever pushed hard for all Consumer Goods Forum members to commit to eliminating deforestation in palm by 2020. The 2014 New York Declaration on Forests was another big statement and yet, when it published its own five-year review of the program, it concluded that the group had made "limited progress." Or as Sauven concludes more clearly, it's been a failure.[24]

NGOs continue to pressure companies to stop working with bad actors in the value chain. It's easy to demand that companies stop using palm oil, but then what? Palm oil employs millions of people across seventeen countries—4.5 million in Indonesia and Malaysia alone.[25] The net positive view of the world includes improving livelihoods, so cutting off millions of jobs would go in the wrong direction. From a climate perspective, a boycott or shift to other oils could backfire. Dominic Waughray, who runs the Centre for Global Public Goods at the World Economic Forum (WEF), says pulling out would leave "a lot of farmers with no income, and the outcome would probably be a lot worse."[26] People with limited options may cut down even more forest for lumber, fuel, or crops.

Where things stand now is mixed. Unilever and most of its large-company peers are sourcing almost all their palm oil from RSPO-certified plantations. They came pretty far, despite the odds. Yet deforestation continues. The structure of the palm industry is a big problem. Hundreds of thousands of smallholder farmers have to act in their own best interest to survive. On the demand side, big CPG companies do not control the market (Unilever, the biggest, buys 3 percent of global supply). The two largest countries buying palm oil are India and China, and many buyers from those countries don't really seem to care. They want the lowest price and don't worry about certifications.

The only solution is a combination of broader coalitions and better enforcement. Unilever tried using market forces to get to scale, investing in trading GreenPalm certificates, which were similar to renewable energy credits. The company spent millions of dollars, but peers didn't follow, which meant Unilever was just paying more than its competitors. They concluded it wasn't useful anyway. A certificate might make consumers feel better about the product, but it didn't do much for tackling climate change or address livelihood issues like living wages. As former chief sustainability officer Jeff Seabright says, "We can't draw a circle around a few good plantations and say 'we're pure' when, next door, they're slashing and burning and there are human rights abuses."

Unilever needed a different approach to get at the root causes of deforestation. So, it used the $60 million it would have spent on certificates to hire people to explore solutions on the ground and create a global fund with the government of Norway and others to help smallholders convert their operations to better methods. Critics say sustainable palm oil is impossible, but it's not true. The industry and NGOs have gathered best practices. Greenpeace's Sauven says more productive species, for example, double yields and greatly reduce pressure to clear more land.[27] The most successful work today is through another collaboration, the Tropical Forest Alliance (TFA), which Seabright and Marks & Spencer's Mike Barry helped launch in 2012. The goal was to take deforestation out of supply chains by 2020. Nobody has come close to that goal, but TFA is having some success. In fact, deforestation rates in Indonesia have finally dropped.[28] What's working, WEF's Waughray says, is a community-based, "jurisdictional" approach. With smallholder farmers running 40 percent of the acreage, the work needs to happen at the micro local level. But to get to scale, they must also work on entire regions.

TFA assembled a collaboration to support famers with local education programs, national and local government help with land ownership, and purchasing commitments from the buyers. But it needed one more component: financing. Even if farmers are willing to shift to more productive species, what happens during the four years until the trees bear new fruit? They need bridge loans or ways to securitize the future flow of revenue. *The core of the palm oil solution, then, is simple in principle: help farmers transition, and they agree not to burn down virgin forest.*

The Norwegian government and Unilever created the &Green Fund. It's one of the players providing capital and catalyzing investment, especially in jurisdictions where the local government is on board and policies support the efforts. The stability that a full system partnership provides makes it more attractive for companies to invest in the region as well. This multi-stakeholder collaboration seems to be the best path forward on palm oil. As Waughray notes, many NGOs on the ground and farmer associations now choose to work with alliances like the TFA—that, he says, tells us what's really working.

The model can also be effective in other settings. Nutrition company DSM built a factory in Rwanda to produce fortified grains and supplements. As part of the Africa Improved Foods partnership, DSM works with the

World Food Programme, the Rwandan government, and the International Finance Corporation to address stunting, which prevents kids from developing fully, and malnutrition locally (versus flying in food aid, which is inefficient and not consistent with the values of the initiative.)[29] The lessons are clear: systemic solutions require broad coalitions with public, private, and civil society working together; you need a critical mass of buyers and a way to shift the economics on the supply side; it takes patience and time (in this case many years). The good news is that the tools for doing this work are getting better. Satellite data, for example, can closely track deforestation, giving buyers like Unilever real-time data on compliance.

Palm oil is certainly a tough enough issue, but as the world gets more volatile, other more complicated challenges await: race relations, refugees, defending democracy, protecting science from attacks, and many more. The most complicated challenges are increasingly being laid at the feet of business leaders. The ultimate work of a net positive company is to tackle the biggest problems in deep coalitions to heal the world.

What Net Positive Companies Do to Tackle the Largest Societal Challenges

- Lead the work on the biggest, most complex shared problems

- Listen to smart critics to understand systemic challenges and hurdles

- Assemble the full coalition needed, often including finance, to create systemic solutions

- Go beyond just raising standards for suppliers to helping them solve the hurdles standing in the way of more sustainable operations

Business in Service of Others

More than a decade ago, the government of Vietnam commissioned a study on the role of multinationals in the socioeconomic development of the country. It picked Unilever as the case study. The report concluded that unlike many foreign investors, Unilever was working for the long term, developing deep roots in the economy, serving the poor in rural areas, and developing win-win relationships with local small- and medium-sized businesses (instead of crowding them out). "By incorporating selected national priorities into the business agenda and implementing them," the report reads, "Unilever has advanced both national and corporate agendas."[30] That's the result companies should be shooting for. Instead of extracting value from communities and countries, build them up. Being a good citizen attracts talent and creates enormous value for the business. It helps the company move quicker, avoid the many hurdles governments can put up, and gain access to growth markets. Almost none of the It Takes Three to Tango partnerships we've described here have immediate payout. By working with governments and civil society to increase well-being, they build long-term value for the company and the society around it.

Those long-term benefits can show up in surprising ways. During a period of protests in Indonesia in the 1990s, when rioters burned and looted a number of factories, they left Unilever's facilities alone. The company's country general manager at the time asked one of the military leaders why. He said, "It's simple. You take care of your employees and communities. We don't need to protect your buildings with the army. The community protects you." The military leader was General Susilo Bambang Yudhoyono, a big supporter of Unilever who later became the president of Indonesia.

If you approach communities and governments with a genuine desire to help them thrive, and you show up in both good times and bad, they will never forget. Never.

8

Embrace the Elephants

Managing Issues Nobody Wants to Talk About . . . but We Can't Avoid

Not everything that is faced can be changed.
But nothing can be changed until it is faced.

—James Baldwin

In a well-known fable going back at least 2,500 years, blind men who run across an elephant for the first time and try to figure out what it is. As they each explore different parts—the ear, the side, the leg, the tusk, the nose—they come to a different conclusion about what the elephant is. In some versions, they fight over it; in others, they come to a combined understanding.

In this chapter, we address some elephant-size issues that business needs to size up and manage. Leaders pretend to be blind, acting like they don't know what these issues are, but it's not true. They know damn well these are elephants; they know the general shape and size of the problem. But they either don't care or avoid the topic because they don't want to spend money or deal with stakeholders. Getting business to acknowledge and tackle issues like paying taxes, money in politics, or human rights is not easy.

Climate change was once an elephant in the room. Top leaders avoided talking about it. In the early years of climate governance—from the 1992 Rio Earth Summit through the Conference of Parties (COP) meetings that resulted in the Paris climate accord—high ranking government ministers were rarely involved, and business had nearly zero representation (on purpose). If you asked a CEO to speak at a climate event, you *might* get a call back from public affairs. Most companies, except energy giants, didn't think climate applied to them, and they didn't worry about public pressure. The finance world was nowhere near the discussion. Mindy Lubber, president of the sustainability advocacy organization Ceres, says that when it held meetings about financial risk from climate, the banks would say, "We'll send interns."[1] The change in finance has been slow and incremental, she says, until more recently.

But by the 2010s, business got into the game. At the twenty-first COP meeting in 2015 in Paris, business leaders came in force. The UN Global Compact ran a multiday high-ranking business event next door to the government negotiating area (Andrew was a moderator and Paul was a key speaker). Hundreds of CEOs came to support global, coordinated action on climate.

What drove the change? Companies were experiencing the effects and costs of climate change. Stakeholders were asking more questions. Younger employees were pushing companies to do more. But leaders also began to see the business advantage for those who took the lead in the clean economy, a multitrillion-dollar business opportunity. Plus, executives knew that regulations were coming, and they wanted a seat at the table.

As they used to with climate change, too many corporate leaders still act as though the new elephants are not their problem. The question of whether a company pays a fair share of taxes, for example, may not seem like it's on the sustainability agenda, but it is certainly part of being net positive. A company serving society does not employ hundreds of accountants and lawyers just to figure out how to avoid paying anything into the public till. When you find out neighbors are paying no tax, or a purported billionaire pays only $750 for his share of roads, schools, hospitals, or defense, how do you feel? Are you truly purpose driven if you pay no taxes?

We explore here nine issues that we feel can't be ignored anymore: taxes, corruption, executive compensation, paying the wrong shareholders, unprepared boards, human rights, trade association lobbying, money in politics, and broader diversity and inclusion. The elephants share a few key dimensions:

- They are core parts of the current economic system that has created the climate and inequality crises.

- A company can't be net positive without addressing them, since the status quo reduces society's well-being.

- Business either does not want to work on them proactively (at least not transparently) or doesn't know how.

- There's a growing risk to the business and brand for those who do nothing.

- There are few easy answers—these are tough calls with gray areas.

Remember, "You broke it, you own it." These elephants have run through the pottery store of society and contributed to much of what's broken. The system is not working well for all, and companies have a key role to play in tackling these issues. Net positive companies don't shy away from these issues; they proactively address them.

What Makes the Elephants Tough?

None of the items on this list should be surprising. And if they were easy, there would be general agreement on what to do. Let's stipulate up front that there are often no easy answers. Here are some of the good, and not so good, reasons we avoid facing the elephants.

- We bet they'll make you uneasy. Facing the elephants is a process of choosing the harder rights instead of the easier wrongs. It means playing to win, even if uncomfortable, not just playing not to lose.

- It may go against short-term shareholder needs, or threaten the status quo for vested interests. Go too far, and shareholders might rebel, and you'll be fighting some peers or partners. Taking on hard, longer-term challenges doesn't have the short-term dopamine shot to earnings that paying no taxes does.

- It makes you vulnerable. Sticking your neck out to do the right thing, without a coalition behind you, may create short-term disadvantage. The first ones around the bend take all the heat. But they can also reap rewards.

- There are not always great metrics. It can be hard to know what goal you're chasing. Saying "zero human rights issues" sounds good, but the world is rarely that clear. Is it a human rights violation, or child labor, if a teen works on a family farm, but still goes to school?

- Other partners, such as governments, may stand in the way or create disincentives. Companies find themselves competing in a race to the bottom. Few business leaders are comfortable taking political positions to improve the rules. It's a systemic failure.

There's no clear path to addressing the elephants, but there are actionable steps to take now, even if they only solve part of the problem. For each topic, we lay out the issue with some data, where available, on the scale of the problem. We ask why this matters to society and how it keeps the world from thriving. Then, we offer some topline ideas for how companies can do better, even without definitive answers.

Each one of these issues could fill a book. Our goal here is to put them firmly on the business radar, not as nice-to-haves, but as requirements. The nine elephants we highlight are contributing mightily to many of our largest challenges, most pointedly inequality and justice. These are failures of our economy and society that move wealth and capital upward to the richest, keep the poorest stuck in poverty, or maintain control in the hands of a small number of mostly white people. This is hoarding money and power.

Before diving in, remember, you can't do these things alone. Many of these topics should increasingly be part of the partnerships and net positive advocacy strategies from last chapter. Don't worry about being a paragon of perfection. Acting in good faith on taxes does not mean paying 100 percent tax. But it does mean taking an active role in a system that ensures taxes are paid. Let's start there.

1. Paying Taxes

The Problem

Over eight years, Amazon paid $3.4 billion in taxes on $960 billion in revenues and $26 billion in profits. Some years, it paid zero. An NGO campaigning for transparency, Fair Tax Mark, labeled Amazon the "most aggressive" company in avoiding taxes, but also said many tech giants were nearly as bad. Facebook, Google, Netflix, and Apple, the *Guardian* reported, are "avoiding tax by shifting revenue and profits through tax havens or low-tax countries, and delaying the payment of taxes they do incur."[2]

Tax avoidance is hardly just a tech company thing. Starbucks has been singled out often, and fought a court battle with the European Commission and Dutch authorities. The company threw a relatively tiny $28 million settlement at the problem to make it go away.[3] The UK tax authority sued GE for fraud in 2020, demanding $1 billion in back taxes.[4] With budget holes to fill after massive pandemic stimulus spending, governments will likely get more vigilant about lost revenue. But until they come down on companies systematically, rampant tax avoidance will remain common—and it is very common. In a 2018 analysis, of the 379 profitable companies in the *Fortune* 500, almost one-quarter paid an effective tax rate of zero percent or less. They paid no taxes or got money back.[5] These ninety-one companies include many well-known names—AEP, Chevron, Deere, DowDuPont, Duke Energy, Eli Lilly, FedEx, IBM, JetBlue, Levi Strauss, and McKesson.

Judy Samuelson, the founder of Aspen Institute's Business and Society program, talks about "blind spots" in business, including, prominently, taxes. As she told *Fortune*, "a reckoning on taxes" is coming. Advocates like Samuelson have sometimes supported policies that *reduce* corporate tax rates, but only "to make sure we brought everybody up to that rate." Unfortunately, she says, international tax shelters and other games have continued to undercut that goal of fairness.[6]

What these companies are doing is generally legal. But is it right or responsible? How can you be a purpose-driven company when you don't pay much to the society that makes it possible for you to do business? Whatever your opinion is about government efficiency, it's undeniable that it provides immense public services—education, hospitals and health care, police and fire departments, defense and the peace, social safety nets, and a sprawling, modern infrastructure to move energy, water, waste, and people around. We need to transform the image of taxes as costs to minimize to thinking of them as investments in our health, well-being, and society.

Amazon literally depends on roads to deliver products. Those who don't pay leave the bill for the rest of us who do, and that bill is not small. Countries make choices about the scale of services and protections the state will provide. In the Organisation for Economic Co-operation and Development (OECD) countries, the ratio of tax collection to total GDP averages 34 percent. The United States sits near the bottom at 24 percent.[7] Sweden, a country with a larger safety net and better public services, collects 44 percent.[8] Lower-income countries, the OECD says, need at least 15 percent to provide bare-bones services. But in thirty of the seventy-five poorest countries, tax revenues fall below that low bar.[9] Meanwhile, an estimated 10 percent of world GDP is held in offshore accounts, and countries lose $500 to $600 billion of corporate tax revenue annually from profit-shifting.[10] The OECD created a framework called BEPS, which stands for base erosion and profit shifting. The "base" here is the money that supports society.

There has been some progress. Janine Juggins, Unilever's head of tax and treasurer, says countries are adopting the OECD's recommendations, so many tax planning tools that relied on tax law mismatches—to create double deductions or nontaxable income—no longer work. What's remaining are, in our words, games to play around where the business resides or generates profits. Ignore the calls for fiduciary responsibility that supposedly force a company to drastically minimize taxes. Dr. Robert Eccles, a leading expert on sustainability and finance, says that "fiduciary duty actually suggests the board should ensure the company is paying an appropriate level of taxes to avoid unnecessary reputational risk," as well as operational risk in underfunded countries.[11]

Instead, take pride in paying a reasonable amount of taxes and appreciate the infrastructure you helped fund. You're contributing to society. Juggins says that environmental, social, and governance (ESG) rating methodologies treat tax as a governance issue. But, she says, "I think it should be part of the 'S,' the social contract."[12]

Let's be clear. A company can't be net positive if it avoids paying taxes. It's literally taking more than you give.

The Solutions

First, start with transparency. Unilever posts detailed tax principles, its effective tax rate (27.9 percent in 2019), and details on the facilities, sales, and taxes paid in dozens of countries.[13] You can endorse a set of Responsible Tax Principles, such as those the B Team developed. A report from the sustainability nonprofit and consultancy BSR, *The Business Role in Creating a 21st-Century Social Contract*, recommends adjusting tax strategy so you pay taxes "commensurate with the amount of revenue in a tax jurisdiction."[14] That means no games, such as moving all profits to one low-tax region. Investors can help, Juggins says, by "taking notice of companies with unusually low tax rates" to assess audit risk or risk of reputational damage from irresponsible tax behavior.[15]

Second, to make profit-shifting less useful, support a mandatory minimum rate globally. The OECD is working on the idea, and supporters are pushing for a 21 percent floor on taxes. It looks more likely, however, that countries will support 15 percent, which the US Treasury and President Biden have called for. It's not high enough, but it's better than nothing. So, publicly advocate for this effort to level the playing field. Third, BSR also recommends using the standards and reporting guidelines from the Global Reporting Initiative and the BEPS program.

Being a good actor builds trust with tax authorities and governments. Companies with the skills and capacity can help countries develop their tax systems and broaden the tax base. As we've described, Unilever has trained tax inspectors in multiple countries. Part of that work leads right into the biggest source of tax loss, corruption.

2. Corruption

The Problem

One of the toughest challenges a multinational faces is how to do business consistently and ethically everywhere. Standards vary greatly by country and culture. Transparency International's ratings of corruption levels (low corruption = 100) range from Denmark and New Zealand at 87 to Somalia at 9. In some places, paying someone in the government to allow your products into port is expected. Giving someone money to accelerate a visa application is dubbed a "facilitation payment" and treated like a normal aspect of doing business (the UK Bribery Act made facilitation payments illegal, but they're allowed in the United States).

Corruption, bribery, theft, and tax evasion siphon $1.26 trillion away from developing countries every year, enough to lift the 1.4 billion poorest people in the world above the poverty line.[16] Corruption adds 10 percent to the cost of doing business globally, and 25 percent to the cost of procurement in developing countries. The "envelope of money under the table" is still a problem, but a B Team report, *Ending Anonymous Companies*, highlights a larger issue.[17] About three-quarters of bribery and corruption cases involve companies whose ownership is hard to identify. Shell companies, the report says, are "getaway vehicles" for corruption and money laundering. The B Team and the World Economic Forum's Partnership Against Corruption Initiative (PACI) are working to eliminate this problem.[18]

Corruption is not just a developing country issue. Half of foreign bribery cases since 1999 involved public officials from highly developed countries.[19] The free flow of money to politicians in the United States is legalized corruption. Using unique access to the power of government is morally hazy. For example, when the United States threatened to ban the social media app TikTok during a trade battle with China, software giant Oracle ended up with a minority stake in TikTok. What didn't go unnoticed was Oracle CEO Larry Ellison's cozy relationship with President Trump or, as Ellison was moving to close the deal, his donation of $250,000 to support the reelection of Trump ally Senator Lindsey Graham.[20] For every corruptee, there's a corruptor. Call it what you may, but as the old phrase goes, if it looks and quacks like a duck, it's a duck.

The Solutions

There are structural and policy-based ways to fight corruption (the hardware) and ways to educate and influence people through culture change (the software). In both cases, transparency is the best antidote. One step is to join groups such as PACI and endorse efforts to enforce ownership transparency.

On the structural side, start with a strong code of conduct and business principles to hold employees accountable. It's necessary but not sufficient. Unilever investigated hundreds of code violations annually, dismissing more than one hundred employees one year. The code gave everyone a defense against corruption. When Unilever execs were asked to do something for a community or company that felt wrong, they could say, "That won't fit our global standards, and we would have to ask our shareholders, which would be in the public domain. Would you feel comfortable with that?" If the answer was no, the request was likely a bribe.

Preparing a response like that for employees to have ready is part of a well-thought-out resistance plan, according to David Montero, author of *Kickback: Exposing the Global Corporate Bribery Network*.[21] To help someone who is asking for a bribe save face and feel respected, he says, find another way to do something for them that is legal. Create more jobs in their community, or provide training and technical advice. In Kenya, Unilever trained police on how to enforce a law on counterfeit products, a problem that was costing the company and the country money. Montero also suggests building the costs of avoiding bribery, such as delays at the border and additional bureaucracy, into the business plan. Identify places that he calls "moon markets"—so corrupt that you treat them as if they're as inaccessible as the moon. In fact, despite many requests, Unilever never entered the Democratic Republic of the Congo (DRC) because of the level of corruption. DRC was Unilever's moon market.

People are the software of fighting corruption. Find allies in countries willing to challenge the status quo. Support their efforts, which are personally dangerous. When Ngozi Okonjo-Iweala (now head of the World Trade Organization) was Nigeria's finance minister, she refused to make payments to fuel importers. Her mother was kidnapped in an attempt to pressure her to quit—she didn't, and her mother was released five days later in good health.[22]

To protect your own people, create a "speak up" culture where everyone feels open to voice their concerns if something doesn't feel right. Build in tools such as a complaint line and regular employee check-ins, like Unilever's "dipstick" surveys (a quick measurement), every three or six months. Build a continuous feedback loop. Beware of creating a culture of financial performance above all, which can drive people to do the wrong things. At the bank Wells Fargo, the pressure of ever higher sales targets was so intense, salespeople created millions of fake accounts. At times, Unilever has experienced cultural disconnects like these, but at a much smaller scale.

It seems counterintuitive, but when Unilever's enforcement rose and the number of code violations increased, it was a good sign—people felt they could speak up. Make it clear that every employee is expected to comply with the Code. Failure puts the company and the employee at risk.

Make sure everyone knows that success without integrity is failure.

3. Overpaying Executives

The Problem

CEOs make too much money. In the 350 largest companies in the United States, CEOs made 320 times more than their average worker in 2019 (up from 61 times in 1989 and just 21 times more in 1965). CEO compensation rose more than 1,100 percent over forty years, while typical worker wages stagnated at 14 percent growth (not annually, but total).[23] In the United States, inflation-adjusted worker wages peaked in 1973 and flatlined since.[24] The trend isn't stopping yet, and it got worse during the pandemic—in 2020, median pay for CEOs of three hundred of the largest US public companies rose $0.9 million to $13.7 million.[25]

The United States may be the biggest offender, but other countries have seen large pay increases as well—Indian CEOs receive 229 times as much as the average worker, and UK CEOs get 201 times more.[26] Lynn Forester de Rothschild, founder of the Coalition for Inclusive Capitalism, says the creation of personal wealth for CEOs "became the objective, as opposed to [asking], What wealth have you left behind in society? How have you made the world better?"[27] If the top earners in the business world take all the salary growth, it makes inequality a lot worse. Without some change, executive pay will remain a flash point for issues relating to inequality, mistrust of elites and business, and economic insecurity.

Most economists agree that the core problem has been the rise of stock options as compensation. It was meant to align executive incentives with shareholders, which certainly worked—it made companies even more short-term focused and prone to abusing the system. GE has often awarded enormous pay packages for executives to hit short-term goals that haven't necessarily helped investors over the long haul.[28] The pandemic brought out the worst in some companies' cultures. A number of CEOs kept salaries and bonuses while shuttering parts of the business. After laying off thousands, GE's CEO, Larry Culp, received a $46.5 million bonus (with potential for $230 million), largely because the board had dramatically lowered the stock strike price that triggered the bonus. It was adjusted, in theory, to reflect a bad pandemic economy . . . which then wasn't as bad. Culp defended himself to the *Financial Times*, talking about the sacrifices he made (such as giving up his $2.5 million salary during the year).[29] It's hard not to see a system with boards filled with fellow CEOs, adjusting the targets, as rigged.

The Solutions

Be prepared to lead, or prepare to be restrained—in recent months, shareholders have rejected management compensation proposals at AT&T, GE, Intel, and many more—and accept that this issue affects license to operate.[30]

Only a few places in the world put a cap on salary, but eventually most governments will do something like taxing compensation above a limit. Be proactive and control top salaries. Pay the top exec less, and peg the ratio at a reasonable level (and maybe develop a sense of shame). Unilever did not actually have a set ratio, but Paul's approach was unusual and, against the board's wishes, he held his own salary flat.

Don't just use a formula. Innovate. The traditional pay structure is too short term-focused and too complex. We need simpler structures that make executives long-term shareholders. The board should look at pay in context and apply discretion to ensure the outcome is fair. Focus on succession as well. Boards can get in trouble if they have to overpay for an external hire.

Most important, focus not just on top salaries, but on improving the living standards of employees, raising wages to fair, living levels throughout the business. It would be naive and counterproductive to advocate for absolute income equality, but at a bare minimum, the people regularly left behind should gain ground, not lose it. Be transparent. In its 10-K, Unilever was clear about linking performance criteria to pay. Slowing the growth of executive salaries and shifting funds downward to balance the overall ratio sets the right tone, and it goes further than you might think. When CareCentrix, a health-care services company, froze pay for twenty top execs, the savings from just holding those twenty high salaries flat was enough to increase the wages of *five hundred* entry-level employees from the US minimum of $7.25 to $16.50 per hour. It also offered profit sharing to all employees.[31]

A Seattle-based credit card processing company, Gravity Payments, took the idea of raising wages to a new level. In 2015, its CEO, Dan Price, took a $1 million pay cut and raised the minimum wage for a highly educated employee base to $70,000 a year. When Gravity bought a small firm in Boise, Idaho, where the cost of living is much lower, Price kept the minimum for everyone. He told *Fast Company*, "I struggled to understand how we could keep our integrity if we couldn't find a way to do it."[32]

Large companies should also stop playing games with options or hiring remuneration consultants to design golden pay packages. At Unilever, Paul moved senior executives to just salary—no cars, no pension, no options. It was a take-it-or-leave-it approach. There was senior-level turnover as the company embraced its new mission, but rarely was pay the issue. As we said before, Unilever made sure that executives at the same level got the same salary after tax, globally, which made choices about international jobs easier. The company also matched any bonus the executive chose to put into Unilever shares. Execs were required to build their stock portfolio to three times their salary and hold shares for five years (which fostered long-term thinking).

Executives in successful companies can still enjoy high wealth generation without making inequality worse.

4. Paying the Wrong Shareholders

The Problem

Companies often use quasi-legal means to "manage" earnings to give Wall Street a good story of steady growth. For years, GE didn't miss a quarter because it could turn the dials on profits from its financial division. In many boardrooms, it's a sport.

Another tool for keeping the share price up, stock buybacks, has become the norm, and it's sucking up an incredible amount of capital. From 2009 to 2018, the 466 companies that remained in the S&P 500 the whole time spent $4.0 trillion buying back stock and $3.1 trillion on dividends—a total of 92 percent of profits. In the early 1980s, buybacks were just 5 percent of profits.[33] What changed? Stock options and a focus on maximizing shareholder return at the expense of long-term growth.

Shareholders should do well—no argument there. But short-termism creates an ugly culture that sacrifices investment in the future. In a survey a number of years ago, 80 percent of CFOs admitted they would decrease spending on R&D, advertising, maintenance, or hiring to ensure hitting a quarterly target.[34] The buybacks would be fine if companies were first funding investment in the business or in their people, but they're not. Trillions of dollars that could have enhanced the business—raising its value and the stock price more over time, and thus serving long-term investors, such as pension funds—paid off short-term investors instead.

In their article "Why Stock Buybacks Are Dangerous for the Economy," three economists found that, in some years, 30 percent of buybacks were funded by corporate bonds. Companies are taking on debt to finance buybacks, they observed, not to create "revenue-generating investments that pay off the debt." They called this out as bad management. Meanwhile, corporate R&D spending has gone nowhere, with 43 percent of the S&P 500 companies spending zero on the future.[35]

This strategy can take companies down a dangerous path. From 2013 to 2018, Boeing spent $43 billion to retire stock, and just in that same period, spent $20 billion on R&D.[36] In an industry where a new plane model also requires many billions of investment, it seems like a strange allocation. Is it surprising that Boeing ended up taking major shortcuts on design and safety, resulting in grounding the 737 Max after two crashes? In a highly unusual move, David Calhoun, the Boeing CEO who took over after the debacle, publicly criticized his predecessor for chasing stock price above the company's future.[37]

Most analyses on buybacks show that they're not good for business. Paul was a founding member of the organization Focusing Capital on the Long Term (FCLT), which calculated that companies that "reinvest greater portions of their earnings back into the company outperform their peers in ROIC by an average of 9% per year."[38] The companies in the S&P Buyback Index (the hundred companies buying back the most stock) have significantly underperformed the market in one-, three-, and five-year periods.[39]

In the end, who does it serve to send all the profits back to shareholders? Certainly not long-term investors. It just pays the speculators, gamblers, and instant traders that make the market irrational.

The Solutions

The simplest answer is for companies to reduce buybacks and special dividends, and instead invest more in making their businesses fit for the future. There are many better uses of capital: increase R&D to pivot your portfolio to more sustainable products and services, accelerate the move to 100 percent renewable energy and zero-carbon operations, invest in employee development and training, or fix human rights challenges and pay workers living wages in the supply chain.

Slowing buybacks is important, but we should also address the underlying problem, the continuing obsession with short-term performance. A two-year hurdle rate on investments is arbitrary. Some things may pay back more quickly, but many important investments pay out after a few years or more. So, as we've discussed, help the organization extend time horizons and create the needed space for people to make longer-term decisions by, among other things, pushing back on quarterly guidance and shifting compensation to incentivize long-term thinking. Extend reporting and strategy timelines to three to seven years or more, rather than single quarters. It would encourage companies to define corporate purpose and objectives, and set long-term strategy to build resilience and create enduring value.

A core problem is that many investors have a short time horizon (weeks or months, not years). The average holding period of stocks has plummeted from up to eight years in the middle of the twentieth century to about five months in 2020.[40] To combat this unhelpful trend, companies can cultivate longer-term investors, which Unilever did for years. Financial institutions can also adopt stewardship codes, an emerging governance tool that the asset management firm Robeco defines as "requiring institutional investors to be transparent about their investment processes, engage with [their investors], and vote at shareholder meetings."[41] By focusing on longer-term measures of success, stewardship codes can help companies and investors think differently about value. The codes can guide asset owners to seek long-term value creation for their investors, communicate more, and develop rigorous monitoring practices.

Investors can create their own stewardship principles to emphasize the issues that are important to their organization and ensure that stewardship codes around the world are harmonized. If short-term pressure from markets is the monkey on company's backs, and the thing forcing poor decisions about where to direct capital, let's get rid of the monkey.

5. Unprepared Boards

The Problem

In 2020, mining giant Rio Tinto made a huge mistake in Australia. It excavated a mine and destroyed two ancient caves—significant archaeological sites—over the opposition of the Aboriginal people who had owned the land. A few months later, the CEO and some other senior executives were forced out.[42] The board chair also stepped down, saying he was "ultimately accountable" for the scandal.[43] This kind of executive ousting, and especially repercussions for the board, hasn't happened over ESG issues often, if ever. They are almost never held accountable for how the company serves (or mistreats) the world. It's a new day.

Today's boards are unprepared for the rising expectations of the outside world. They have shockingly limited knowledge of ESG issues. A study from the NYU Stern Center for Sustainable Business reviewed the bios of 1,180 *Fortune* 100 directors. While 29 percent had some relevant ESG experience, it was almost entirely in the "S" category. Only *five* directors across all one hundred companies had climate knowledge, and a paltry two in water.[44] (Dow Inc. alone had three of the people with serious qualifications in environmental issues, such as a former administrator of the US Environmental Protection Agency.) Study author Tensie Whelan said that boards without relevant knowledge "won't know the questions to ask, or understand what potential risks might exist."[45]

Many boards have corporate social responsibility committees, but the people on them generally aren't qualified. Imagine putting people who haven't looked at a balance sheet on the finance committee. Most directors don't really care about ESG. In a report by the NGO Ceres, 6 percent of US directors chose climate change as a focus area for the coming twelve months, and 56 percent thought "investor attention on sustainability issues is overblown."[46] They may even feel that talking about ESG issues is a risk, but it's the opposite.

Given their role as safeguards of the business, board members are remarkably short term in their focus. Boards are applying significant pressure on senior executives to hit short-term profit goals. And more than half of boards globally, and 70 to 80 percent in some EU countries, do not have succession plans in place for the CEO, even as tenures have dropped from eight years in 2000 to just five years today.[47]

Boards are also low in diversity and lack perspective. In the *Fortune* 500, just 23 percent of board members are women, and 16 percent people of color.[48] In sum, few boards represent the world around them, most don't know what ESG means, and very few can tie it to strategy or long-term value creation. They're grossly out of touch with what's happening out there.

The Solutions

Boards need more people of color, more women, and younger members. That diversity will help the company navigate the world. But there's also diversity in perspective and knowledge. Having one person who may look different, but who understands the world the same way as the rest of the board, doesn't help enough. You need a critical mass of members with diverse knowledge and interest in the world's social and environmental challenges.

A new batch of people will bring a different and broader understanding of governance and fiduciary duties.

For current board members, we recommend mandatory training in ESG and on climate change specifically. Both of us have worked with Competent Boards in Canada, which trains executives and board members. Other organizations, such as Ceres, produce educational resources, like its paper *Getting Climate Smart*. Boards must also become familiar with rising standards and guidelines, such as the Task Force on Climate-Related Financial Disclosure (TCFD) and the Global Reporting Initiative (GRI).[49] It's also important to get board members thinking more about purpose. Programs like the Enacting Purpose Initiative out of the Saïd Business School at Oxford can provide perspective and training.

In short, boards should meet certain qualifications—just as lawyers and doctors do. Portfolio traders have to go through training. People working at hair salons need a license. Board members should no longer be driving companies without their own net positive license.

6. Human Rights and Labor Standards

The Problem

Imagine you're a migrant worker who pays an employment agency a "finder's fee" of $5,000 to get a job in a factory or farm. You then make $250 per month, too little to ever pay back the debt. You have zero rights in the country you're working in, and the agency took your passport. That's what forced labor looks like *today*, in the 2020s.

It's been twenty-five years since *Life* magazine ran a story with a picture of a boy sewing a Nike soccer ball (for which he was paid 60 cents a day), and eight years since the devastating Rana Plaza collapse killed 1,132 apparel workers in Bangladesh. Yet the number of people in horrific working conditions remains outrageously high. The International Labour Organization (ILO) estimates that 150 million kids, 1 in 10 worldwide, are working in conditions that are dangerous or deprive them of schooling.[50] Over a five-year period, eighty-nine million adults experienced modern slavery—forced work or forced marriage—at some point.[51] And taking a broader view of human rights issues, 1.6 billion workers are vulnerable; they're part of the "informal economy," with few protections or rights.[52]

Rosey Hurst, founder of ethical trade and human rights consultancy Impactt, describes the harsh reality: "the global supply chain is based on the use of forced labor."[53] Unilever's global VP of integrated social sustainability, Marcela Manubens, adds that billions of profits have come on the backs of people making poverty wages, which contributes mightily to inequality.

Companies have done shockingly little to address this tragedy. The Corporate Human Rights Benchmark (CHRB) assesses and ranks the two hundred largest companies in high-risk sectors—agricultural products, apparel, extraction, and ICT. Overall performance is abysmal. The average score out of 100 is 24.

Steve Waygood, the chair of CHRB and chief responsible investment officer at Aviva, concluded that the report paints a "distressing picture," given how few companies are even trying—most "have not taken part in the race."[54] A large part of the assessment scores companies on how much due diligence they conduct in supply chains—that is, are they even looking for human rights problems? Almost half the companies got a zero. In contrast, the top three ranked companies, Adidas, Rio Tinto, and Unilever, scored full points on due diligence. Close to half of the companies had at least one allegation of a serious human rights violation, and almost none had remedied the situation—less than a third met with stakeholders and only 4 percent of cases resulted in a satisfactory outcome for victims.[55]

In one rare piece of recent good news on human rights, some big investors are applying pressure on companies to do better. In 2021, BlackRock and CalSTRS (the California pension fund) voted against the directors of the large manufacturer Top Glove after a quarter of its workforce got Covid-19.[56] But companies should not wait for stakeholders to force them to fix this.

The Solutions

It's hard to face, but you know that slave and child labor are wrong. Don't behave like an ostrich. Sharan Burrow, the general secretary of the International Trade Union Confederation, says, "If you don't know because you don't ask, does that absolve you? No. It makes you even more guilty."[57]

Learn what laws are in place and advocate for more. The UK's Modern Slavery Act cracks down on slavery and trafficking. After some political wrangling, it included requirements on transparency (reporting) and supply chains.

Find organizations, such as the Fair Wage Network, to help educate you, and share what you know publicly. When Unilever issued the first stand-alone human rights report, it was scary, but it didn't hurt the company. It helped Unilever identify the human rights issues it needed to focus on, including forced labor, discrimination, harassment, and working hours. Once you have a handle on the scale of the problems, become an active part of eliminating modern slavery from your value chain.

Another solution, in theory, is audits. There are many international standards and firms that audit factories for violations. Human rights advocates are skeptical, because audits have a mixed reputation for efficacy. Hurst from Impactt says that off-the-shelf audits don't work: "You have to do something far more engaged, with the worker voice at the center." Workers need a way to speak honestly, without fear of retribution. Better technology—mobile, anonymous surveys, video feeds—can help get closer to the reality on the ground and improve traceability and transparency.

Rather than rely on audits, you should build deeper relationships. The Gap, after releasing detailed supply chain data, reduced the number of major supplier relationships from two thousand to nine hundred, allowing the company to focus, build trust, and fix problems together.[58] The culture of procurement needs to change to make these better relationships the norm.

Companies can work in partnership, precompetitively, to get better information from shared suppliers, or raise wages and improve job security by reducing contract labor. Burrow believes that living wages help solve child labor issues, saying, "If people were paid enough for their family to live on, they wouldn't need the income from their kids." Putting a survival floor of living wages under 250 million people in the world, Burrow says, would cost about $37 billion (less than 1 percent of the $4 trillion *increase* in the wealth of the world's billionaires during the pandemic).[59]

7. Trade Association Lobbying

The Problem

All the good work a company does on climate—setting science-based goals, issuing public statements in support of the Paris Agreement, buying renewable energy—is undermined if its trade associations lobby against climate action. If the policies they push are not consistent with a company's own statements, how can governments, NGOs, or employees take the company seriously?

The gap between company statements and industry lobbying has been large, especially in the fossil fuel business. Most oil and gas companies say they support a carbon price, but when there's an actual policy in the works, the groups representing them mobilize to oppose it. A proposed carbon tax was on the ballot in Washington State in 2018, and it was leading in the polls. The Western States Petroleum Association poured $30 million—$13 million from BP alone—into convincing people it would be bad for them.[60] The ballot initiative failed.

For many years, the US Chamber of Commerce, the top-spending lobbyist in the United States, fought hard against environmental and climate policy.[61] Through some hard work by a few dedicated companies, in particular DSM North America and its president, Hugh Welsh, the chamber admitted that climate change is a real problem caused by humans. Still, late in 2020, the World Resources Institute (WRI) wrote that the chamber was at odds with the Business Roundtable (BRT) over climate. The BRT laid out climate policy principles that the WRI said, "go further in addressing climate change than any other major trade association to date."[62]

Companies still hide sheepishly behind organizations, with execs saying something like, "I don't agree with them on climate, but I need them for lobbying on trade." This is cowardly and it undermines trust. Stakeholders will ask: Who are you funding? What do associations or PR firms do in your name? How much are they fighting policies that slow climate change or reduce inequality (such as minimum wages)? Be prepared to explain any disconnects.

The think tank InfluenceMap has gathered extensive data on corporate and trade association lobbying on climate and environment. It consistently highlights how trade groups, especially in fossil fuels, try to weaken environmental regulations. Some climate change deniers, who may have moved away from directly funding candidates or campaigns, have weaseled their way into trade associations to assert their influence. Nobody is fooled.

The Solutions

Sometimes engaging with trade groups to hash out disputes over policy is worthwhile. DSM's work to nudge the Chamber of Commerce was important. So, first try to shift their thinking. Make the argument that you want to work together on multiple issues, but since climate change is the biggest crisis, industry has to speak with one voice in support of action. After trying to change their views it may be best to break ties from groups that hold on to antiquated ideas. More than a decade ago, Apple, Nike, Unilever, and others left the US chamber over its climate stance.[63] As we said earlier, Unilever also left BusinessEurope and the notorious American Legislative Exchange Council, which lobbies at the local level for lower environmental standards and regressive social policies. Similarly, health-care colossus CVS Health exited the US chamber over its efforts to ease regulations on tobacco, a position in direct conflict with the company's commitment to take cigarettes out of its stores.[64]

It's never too late to have a "Road to Damascus" moment and realize you're on the wrong side. Sixteen months after funding the campaign against a carbon price in Washington State, BP left the Western States Petroleum Association. BP said their policies were no longer aligned. The company then started advocating for a price on carbon.[65] French oil giant Total left the powerful American Petroleum Institute over its opposition to carbon pricing or subsidies for electric vehicles, and for its donations to American politicians who supported the United States' exiting the Paris Agreement.[66]

Besides the nuclear option of leaving these groups, companies can pressure associations to change their ways. Call on them to be open about their stances. Unilever forced transparency by commissioning a study on trade association positions on climate and releasing it at the 2018 climate summit in Poland. The company asked its trade associations to assess if their views were consistent with climate science.

Going public is a good way to force their hands and find out what the associations really believe. As early-twentieth-century jurist Louis Brandeis famously said, "Sunlight is the best disinfectant."[67]

8. Money and Influence in Politics

The Problem

In 2010, the US Supreme Court case *Citizens United v. FEC* declared political donations as a protected form of free speech. The decision unleashed billions of dollars and gave companies enormous influence over policies and politicians. Legislators desperately need the money to fund campaigns that go on for much longer than in other countries. Representatives in the US Congress spend hours every day, begging for money to fund their never-ending campaigns.

Companies can influence the political process in other countries as well. An OECD report, *Financing Democracy*, warns of the risk of "policy capture" by well-funded vested interests. Among the OECD countries, only 35 percent ban corporate donations to political parties and candidates.[68] Still, the problem is noticeably worse in the United States. For companies, the return on spending on influence is high—every dollar they use to get that big tax break can yield hundreds of dollars of savings.[69] The legalized corruption doesn't stop there. More than half of the politicians who take a job after leaving Congress immediately become lobbyists and see their salaries go up dramatically.[70]

Companies are not using their influence for good. In InfluenceMap's report on the 50 most influential companies, 35 were named as negative influences, while 15 multinationals played a positive role, including Iberdrola, Phillips, Royal DSM—and Unilever in the top spot.[71] It's time to reset the private sector's relationship with US politics to ensure the government runs on the will of the people, not the power of the dollar.

The Solutions

A century ago, IBM decided it would play no role in politics. In 1968, CEO Thomas Watson Jr., the son of the founder, said a company "should not try to function as a political organization in any way."[72] Even without political donations, as a corporate leader, IBM still holds a seat at the policy table. Companies should follow this example and commit to making no political donations and being much more transparent. Publish any and all donations to any cause, political or not. Companies should also dissolve corporate political action committees—which Unilever stopped donating to many years ago—to separate policy from politics. Don't wait for events to force your hand. The attempted coup in the United States was a moment of clarity. Dozens of companies paused all donations to politicians.

The Brennan Center for Justice, League of Women Voters, and People for the American Way have all created similar lists of ways to get money out of politics. Disclosure and transparency are their top choices as well, but they also suggest moving to public financing of elections. We need to think even bigger and advocate for a constitutional amendment to overturn the absurd *Citizens United* verdict. Unilever's Ben & Jerry's is trying to foment a grassroots movement to support such an amendment. The maker of cookie dough ice cream has been a vocal advocate of "Getting the dough out of politics."

9. Broader Diversity and Inclusion

The Problem

Everyone has experienced the frustration of speaking on a video conference and realizing they were on mute. Imagine being on mute permanently, and you get a sense of what it's like for groups that are systematically excluded from the economy.

In this global age, diversity is our greatest asset. Look around the world and see a rich, vibrant, and diverse world with many languages and cultures. This brilliance is good for business. The business case for diversity and inclusion is overwhelming. It's a multitrillion-dollar opportunity. A McKinsey study found that top quartile companies in ethnic and cultural diversity outperformed the bottom quartile by 36 percent in profitability.[73] A BCG study concluded that companies with more diverse management teams have 19 percent higher revenues from innovation.[74]

But business is underperforming on inclusivity, especially in its own senior ranks. Women fill 47 percent of entry level jobs in corporate America, but they occupy only 21 percent of the C-suite roles.[75] Underrepresented groups fare worse. Women of color make up 18 percent of entry-level positions and just 3 percent of the C-suite. White men hog two-thirds of the top positions. This reality has created a small challenge for us in writing this book. We focus on large companies and quote many CEOs. We want diverse voices, but the *Fortune* 500 CEO pool is anything but. A few years ago, there were more CEOs named John than there were women.[76] Today, there are only four Black CEOs (and only nineteen in the history of the *Fortune* list since 1955).[77] The third Black female CEO ever, Roz Brewer of Walgreens, started in 2021.

Companies are embracing diversity and inclusion (D&I) rapidly, increasingly tracking performance, and setting quantitative targets, such as HP's goal to double the number of Black executives by 2025.[78] But companies are generally not looking at the full world of inclusion: differences in culture, race, socio-economic background, gender, sexuality, disability, neurodiversity, and more. It's a holistic view, not a siloed project of addressing, say, gender balance this year, LGBTQ another, and race when the Black Lives Matter movement applies pressure. We need consistent efforts across all groups to bring more perspectives into business.

Without a total inclusion mindset, companies overlook people. Only 4 percent of companies have focused on inclusion efforts for the disabled.[79] In countries with legal obligations to hire the disabled, a report from the World Health Organization found, many companies would "rather pay a fine than attempt to fill their quotas."[80] The results of that attitude are clear: only 29 percent of working-age Americans (between ages sixteen and sixty-four) with disabilities were employed versus 75 percent of those with no disability.[81] It's a big mistake. Disabled employees have equivalent or higher productivity, lower absenteeism, and lower turnover—the opposite of the stereotypes.[82] The one billion people making up the disabled community, along with their families, control more than $13 trillion a year in disposable income—about the size of household spending for the entire EU.[83]

A workforce that looks like the world will better serve the world. Apple's CEO Tim Cook has said, "An inclusive workforce will make the next generation of innovation possible . . . the best products in the world will be the best products for the world."[84]

The Solutions

Start by speaking to everyone. Recognize underrepresented groups in corporate marketing and communications, and acknowledge everyone's humanity and dignity. This is an important foundation, but language only goes so far.

Use the business to support diversity in your business ecosystem. Spend money with minority-owned suppliers. Buy businesses started by disabled people, people of color, or from the LGBTQ community. Invest in geographies with diverse communities. Set standards for who you'll do business with—Goldman Sachs, the top underwriter of initial public offerings

(IPOs) in the United States, will not take a company public unless it has one diverse board member today, and two starting in 2022.[85]

Change policies internally. Look carefully at who is being promoted. Is it weighted toward majority demographics? Are you implementing hiring quotas to get more people from underrepresented groups? Hire people not like you. Keep an eye out for groups that are falling behind. The global pandemic was a disaster for women in the workplace. The McKinsey report concluded that the Covid-19 crisis "could set women back half a decade."[86]

Unilever's pursuit of gender parity has been a case study in driving diversity. The company created a committee under the CEO, and Paul purposely included some executives with bad records on diversity hiring. In 2010, women made up 38 percent of company management (and none of the board). With new targets to make women 55 to 60 percent of all new management hires, the ratio increased, and in March 2020, Unilever reached 50 percent women at management level globally.[87] In a survey of UK companies, Unilever was the only one that paid the same or more to women. It made even larger progress in regions with extremely low representation. In North Africa and the Middle East, the ratio of women in promotions to manager level jumped from 9 percent to 48 percent. Unilever also made half of the board women, and added three Black members.

You can help change the system by advocating for smart government policies, such as California's requirement that companies headquartered in the state have underrepresented groups on their boards.[88] We also need policies that build the social infrastructure to support inclusion. Universal child care and parental leave laws can reduce the number of women driven out of the workforce. Consider also what laws might make it easier for the disabled to work in your business.

Join a movement. Ursula Burns, the former CEO of Xerox and first Black woman to run a *Fortune* 500 company, cofounded the Board Diversity Action Alliance. Companies that have signed on to diversify boards include Dow, Mastercard, Mondelez, PepsiCo, PNC, Starbucks, Under Armour, and UPS. Another group, OneTen, has gathered large companies "to upskill, hire and advance one million Black Americans over the next ten years."[89]

For disability inclusion, look to The Valuable 500, the largest collective of CEOs and brands creating lasting change for people living with disabilities. Founded by Caroline Casey and chaired by Paul, the group (with a combined 20 million employees) will innovate together to incorporate disability inclusion into recruitment strategies and product designs; improve accessibility; and transform business systems to ensure nobody is left behind.

When Paul retired, he requested that they avoid the normal corporate celebratory jazz. As a more meaningful good-bye present, the company surprised Paul with a commitment to hire eight thousand people with disabilities. They knew the way to a net positive CEO's heart.

Working New Muscles

The companies that take a hard look at these nine issues will start to see how they connect and build on one another, for good or bad. Transparency is a theme that runs through them all. These are not easy issues, so be open and work with others. But take responsibility. You can't be net positive and avoid taxes, tacitly support corruption, be willfully ignorant of slave labor in the supply chain, overpay everyone but workers, and dump all bad effects from the company on the commons.

Many of these problems can be turned into opportunities. Doing the harder right thing builds trust with external stakeholders and makes employees proud. The more of the hard things you address, the easier it becomes. You're building organizational and moral muscle and experience. It's this strength that supports and maintains a new, more courageous culture.

This new strength will come in handy as more issues come at us faster than ever. The list of topics to address as a purposeful, multistakeholder company is not static. Getting engaged on the elephants will help you see around the corner a little better and get ready for action.

What Net Positive Companies Do to Tackle Critical, Ignored Issues

- Proactively face those "elephants in the room" that most have avoided and work in an authentic way to address them

- Identify how their businesses contribute to our largest challenges, and, in particular, focus on inequality driven by the hoarding of money and power

- Look honestly at how they spend their money—through taxes, corruption, overpaying executives, money in politics, short-term share buybacks, and so on—and consider how they undercut the company's long-term prospects and damage society

- Lead on human rights and valuing the people in their supply chains

- Develop an inclusive workforce and value chain, identifying those most often left behind and bringing them into the system to share their skills

9

Culture Is the Glue

Putting Values into Action, Deep in the Organization and Brands

If we are to preserve culture we must continue to create it.

—Johan Huizinga, Dutch historian

When you walk into an office or factory, you can sense the culture—it's the smell of the place. Look around the lobby for cues about how the organization feels about itself. Are the company's products proudly on display?

Look at the purpose or mission statement. If you see something that basically says, "We pursue excellence to be the best at what we do," you're looking at a rigid organization with narrow boundaries. Patagonia's says, "We're in business to save our home planet." That organization will have no problems blowing up boundaries and thinking big.

Listen to people. Talk to the receptionist. Do employees seem happy to be there? Are they speaking the same language from the heart, not just parroting what the CEO says? As Andrew interviewed dozens of current and former Unilever employees around the world, he was struck by how alike they sounded—not as automatons, but with a clear sense of what the company was all about. The people leading the businesses in Ethiopia, India, Indonesia, and Russia all sing from the same hymnal.

When Paul left Unilever, the sustainability community and many of the company's investors were concerned that the sustainable living focus would wane. It's now clear that it won't happen—employees won't allow it. Paul's successor, Alan Jope, fully believes in the net positive business model, but also says, "If I tried to change direction now, the company would not accept it . . . about 70 percent of our people joined because of the mission. If we backed off being driven by purpose, I would get kicked out by a people's revolution."[1] It's the best proof point that Paul's bet on Unilever and the Unilever Sustainable Living Plan (USLP) transformed the company. If somehow the commitment to the USLP did fade, the performance of the company would go down as well—the USLP, a commitment to a powerful purpose, and a net positive culture have all driven the success of the business.

A common model of corporate culture is an iceberg. Above the water are things you say. At the waterline are the things you do. The majority of the iceberg, deep below, is what everyone believes. Leaders can say whatever they want, but how the organization acts and what people really believe will control the iceberg. That's what people mean when they quote Peter Drucker's famous line, "Culture eats strategy for breakfast." It's basically true, but lacks nuance—culture and strategy are *both* stronger if they're in sync. Over time, strategy and values, regularly applied through action, build the culture. If you eat a better breakfast for years, you'll be healthier.

Let's be clear about the terms we're using. As we see it . . .

- *Values* are fundamental beliefs underpinning an organization. They should change rarely, if ever.

- *Purpose* is the meaningful and lasting reason for an organization to exist, providing clarity on how you fill a need in the world. It motivates people and directs the strategy and priorities of the company. Employees working on the Lifebuoy soap brand aren't just pitching the functionality of soap, they're pursuing a net positive purpose, saving millions of lives through better hygiene.

- *Culture* is values in motion. If values are core beliefs, and purpose is your "why," then culture is how you show it all through behaviors. It's an aggregation of company beliefs consistently put into action.

Of these three, culture is the one that can, and should, change. The behaviors that make values come alive can vary based on what you sell, the regions where you operate, the types of businesses you're in, and the mix of people. One company can house multiple cultures. Culture changes with acquisitions, when you hope to combine the best of each organization. When Unilever bought prestige beauty brands and many mission-driven, entrepreneurial businesses, they contributed new elements to the culture. The culture also evolves with changing societal norms. With awakenings like the #MeToo and Black Lives Matter movements, the company's behaviors *must* change. In this time of extraordinary volatility, you have to refresh the culture regularly.

A net positive culture consistently acts on values such as responsibility, care and empathy, service, trust, openness, and high performance. Building this culture takes time and commitment to the strategies we've laid out— blowing up boundaries, building trust through transparency, forming deep partnerships, and embracing the elephants. Net positive culture is the culmination, not the beginning, which is why we waited until this point to dig into it.

When the values, purpose, and culture all align, the business becomes a place where people want to work. It's a place where every person can develop to their full potential, finding that sweet spot of overlap between values, what the world needs, and what they're good at. When you create a culture that fits the mission and responds to the world and the moment we're in, it provides a common language for everyone in the company. It's the glue that binds people together to serve the world.

When Values and Behaviors Collide

Communication. Respect. Integrity. Excellence.

That was the stated list of values at Enron, the energy and commodity trading giant that unleashed one of the greatest frauds in corporate history. Statements are lovely, but if values and behaviors don't match, and those behaviors are toxic, a company can implode. Enron's true value was greed, its purpose was to maximize shareholder return no matter what, and the culture was winning at any cost. It was malignant.

In recent years, something went wrong with Boeing's culture as well. When the government investigated the safety problems of the 737 Max plane, internal messages showed employees ignoring federal rules and deceiving regulators. Some mocked their peers, saying, "This airplane is designed by clowns, who are in turn supervised by monkeys."[2] A crisis tests the culture.

A pandemic, a hostile takeover, a huge failure, a new successful competitor—when things get rough, do you blame each other in a circular firing squad, or rally together?

Values on the wall are worth nothing unless they're endorsed by leadership and then shared, understood by all, and reinforced. When Paul arrived at Unilever, the company had good values, but they were implicit, not spelled out, and not aligned. As a result, a lot of the behavior did not match what the company stood for. He asked each person in the leadership team to write down the company's values. They produced a soup of ideas. It's hard to make purpose come alive if the values aren't clear and agreed on.

Culture Is Consistency

There is no effective culture without the vast majority of employees on the same page and connecting to the purpose. That builds trust in management and engagement, which is the glue holding the organization together and the hallmark of a net positive company. Unfortunately, a Gallup study found that only 15 percent of employees globally say they're engaged (what an opportunity to engage the other 85 percent).[3] That's a failure of both culture and values. When people see the company doing things that are not aligned with what it says it stands for, employees either put on a mask and fake it, which makes them deeply unhappy, or they leave.

To inspire people and get them moving in the same direction, the organization has to be consistent in its culture, and have a bias toward doing over just saying. Employees will not believe or embrace the culture if they don't see their leaders live the values, and see consistency across thousands of everyday decisions. Jeff Hollender, cofounder of Seventh Generation, says that "every single thing a company does is an expression of its culture."[4] Being consistent creates a strong, clear culture, which can be polarizing; not everyone will fit. If someone's not proud of the company's work and culture, they will weaken that culture. It was known in Unilever that not fitting the culture was often a better reason to leave the company than poor performance. And for top performers, don't make the mistake of sweeping bad behavior under the carpet—that's a poor tradeoff. The best legacy CEOs can leave an organization is embedded values, which results in a stronger culture, and better people than when they arrived.

Let's look now at building consistency and demonstrating a deep culture in four areas: engaging people, building the organizational infrastructure to support culture, developing purpose-driven brands, and connecting to and influencing the cultures in the communities around the business.

Engaging People

We have little time to solve our biggest issues, especially climate change. We wish we could say that building a net positive culture is a quick job. It will get easier as younger generations that seek purpose and impact fill the workforce. But it takes time to get to critical mass, where the large majority of employees and execs are on the same page.

Current Unilever CEO Alan Jope has a good perspective on the company's evolution. He was one of those senior executives when Paul brought in a strong growth and responsibility message. Jope comments that after the first four years—which was already two years into the USLP—many people still thought, "This too shall pass." But, he says, there's a distribution curve of buy-in. The early adopters got it immediately. The middle of the curve kept moving, and by the end of eight years, the large majority were on board (or presumably had left) and wanted to do more. "It's now part of the fabric of the company," Jope says.[5]

Unilever needed years to get there, but that's not particularly surprising. Cultural norms take a *long* time to move, but when they finally do, they can flip shockingly fast. Throughout history, big shifts in values—such as the abolition of slavery, civil rights, equality for women, marriage equality for the LGBTQ community, and now climate action and justice—happened suddenly it seemed . . . after forty years of intense work leading up to it.

Society is changing around us, with multiple shifts in attitudes happenings at once—on race, sexuality, our relationship with the natural world, and more. To match the revolutions in the outside world, corporate culture has to adapt (quickly), just as the USLP had to evolve. The philosophy of net positive is far more evolved than the typical CSR approach, which is mainly a "check the boxes" exercise.

The real change won't happen top down, where an older executive crowd may not fully identify with the new values in the world. With new people coming into an organization constantly, the culture is not imposed upon people; it's built from the bottom up. So, it matters who those people are, who they want to become, and what you incentivize them to do.

Who They Are—Diversity, Inclusion, and Parity

As discussed in the last chapter, inclusion is one of those elephants you need to face, and it's core to business success—a company and culture that serves the world needs to look like the world. We want to focus briefly here on how the right culture feeds diversity . . . and how diversity drives culture.

Without broad representation in the business, a company is more likely to show insensitivity or lack of awareness. Unilever has made some mistakes. A Dove ad for body wash showed a Black woman who removed a brown shirt and turned into a white woman in a light-colored shirt. It wasn't the intention of either Unilever or the ad agency to indicate that after using the body wash, the preferred state equated with being white. But mistakes like this are more likely to be caught with the right mix of people in the room.

A diverse and welcoming company changes the culture and the people in it. Total inclusion lets people flourish with no barriers and no biases in hiring and promotion. They are respected and treated with dignity. Many people tell us how much they've learned seeing the openness and tolerance at Unilever on gay rights and marriage (which is illegal in many markets). The extensive efforts Unilever made on gender parity also changed internal attitudes toward women—you know, the people that make up 70 to 80 percent of Unilever's consumers. Paying women the same makes it clear to your employees what you value. And hiring from the large, qualified pool of disabled people sends a message internally about valuing everyone.

Diversity efforts shouldn't be as hard as companies make them out to be. Good leaders make parity happen. When Canadian prime minister Justin Trudeau built his first cabinet in 2015, he fielded a question from a reporter asking why it was 50 percent women. Quite literally, his entire answer was "Because it's 2015."

When Unilever built a new toothpaste plant in Ethiopia, they hired an all-female workforce. The factory was meant to help local communities, but it was also a culture-building effort to challenge people. As the managing director for Unilever Ethiopia, Tim Kleinebenne, says, "We were trying to break down limiting beliefs" about women in society and as employees.

Unilever's personal care factory in Haridwar, India, is also all-female—even as CEO, Paul had to get permission to enter the building.

Inclusion initiatives for gender, race, sexuality, and abilities can take companies too long if they're forced or don't fit the values. Unconscious bias is a cultural problem. Real skeptics are dying out, but many still ask about the value of diversity. This should be treated, vocally, as an absurd question—that reaction will also send a message about values and culture. Ask them: Why do we have to prove that having more women is a good thing? What's the business case for all men? It's silly because the proof is there. A Goldman Sachs study found that the stock prices of companies with more women in management and on boards rose 2.5 percent per year faster than at male-dominated companies.[6] There's always a challenge of causation versus correlation, but Bloomberg believes in the data. In 2021, the company launched a Gender-Equity Index (with 380 companies in forty-four countries) to "track the financial performance of public companies most committed to gender equality."[7] These financial giants are helping shift thinking to see equality as an opportunity, not a burden.

Diversity also creates more open attitudes and wider perspectives, which is essential in a global company. People who don't enjoy understanding different national cultures and markets, or don't embrace diversity, don't belong in a place like Unilever. *There are not many xenophobes in a successful multinational.*

Who They Can Be—Purpose and Empathy

Employees with a dated view of a business stand in the way of a culture shift toward net positive. But they can evolve. Doing the work to discover personal purpose, and its connection to the organization's mission and soul, is an important step. The extensive purpose work that the Unilever leadership team went through (chapter 3) was a turning point. The organization increased its commitment to serving the world. Now that sixty thousand employees have gone through a similar process, having a personal purpose is an important part of the culture. The multiple layers of purpose—individual, brand, and company—reinforce one another.

They don't all have to be the same, however. Jonathan Atwood, the former VP of sustainable living and corporate communications for Unilever

North America, says the personal purpose is the glue that holds the whole thing together and is the real unlock for the organization. The company becomes an amalgamation of individuals with their own purpose. They can put their own twist on it, but they still need to align with the company's overall purpose and have a commitment to serving the world. That may require helping employees develop empathy and understanding. Hindustan Unilever has a powerful way to do that.

In India, most new management hires come from top schools and from cities. They are urbanites. But 40 percent of Hindustan Unilever's sales come from the rural areas that make up two-thirds of the country. So, the company sends new hires to live with a rural family for four to six weeks. They bring no money and live as their hosts do. Sanjiv Mehta, the chairman and managing director of Hindustan Unilever, says the program helps people develop a deep understanding of the life of a rural Indian and how the local economy works. It also, he says, "makes you empathize much more with your consumers . . . and that makes you grounded." Giving managers an outside-in view broadens their thinking and makes the business more human. The program has deeply affected people.

Thirteen years before he was running the Lifebuoy brand, Samir Singh was new to the company and was sent to live with a family in a remote village in India. There was no power, no toilets, and it was very cold. He shared a room with a buffalo for six weeks. Today, whenever he faces a decision about a brand that serves rural consumers, he says, "I go back to those days and the everyday reality of people's lives—so different from our romantic notions of idyllic village life. This is what keeps me real and grounded."

Imagine being a new hire and having that experience (with or without the buffalo). If it changes you, you will help build a culture that serves consumers and values deep understanding and empathy. If it's not your thing, you don't last long. Either way, the program creates a consistent culture. It's one reason Unilever brought back consumer immersion and customer development training for all. It's an important way to bring an outside-in perspective and remind everyone to take a broader view.

A net positive culture also has to value long-term thinking over short-term profit maximization. Making that shift is not easy in any sector, and the existing culture can push back powerfully. Hiro Mizuno led the world's largest pension fund, GPIF, for the Japanese government. Mizuno shook up the $1.5 trillion fund when he brought a focus on environmental, social, and governance (ESG) performance into the core of its investing strategy. With that much money under management, his fund couldn't do well unless society did well—his first priority for returns was to ensure that the world thrived. Mizuno knew that managing ESG well was core to that goal. He took heat from the media for the new focus, so you might think that managing outside pressure was his biggest struggle. Instead, he says, "the people who pushed back the hardest were in my own investment team [and its governance body]."

Mizuno almost gave up and then realized he could bring other stakeholders to bear—especially those who want pension managers to avoid risk. He reached out to the biggest pension contributors, the unions, and asked them to embrace ESG as a way to both create long-term value and build the inclusive society they advocated for. As GPIF customers, unions then put pressure on Mizuno's own asset managers. He also worked with the business and political media, holding events to change views and make ESG a buzzword. The more normalized it became, the less asset managers could drag their feet.

A combination of personal purpose work, redefining roles, and external pressure can unleash a better, more empathetic and productive culture and workforce.

What They're Rewarded For
(Encouraging Net Positive Behavior)

For a number of years, Unilever had no link between the USLP's goals and bonus compensation. The thinking was that you shouldn't have to pay people to do the right things. Why give a bonus to a factory manager for a good safety record or to a brand executive for improving racial diversity? These things should come from cultural values of dignity and respect. That's how you embed the right culture, even if it takes longer. (It may be more of an American concept to just throw money at something to fix it.)

Financial motivation is a blunt force instrument that outsources a leader's responsibility to inspire people in a deeper way. Money is a poor tool for that. If a doctor hands you a bill for treating your cancer, you don't say, I'll pay you 50 percent more to make sure I stay alive. For most doctors, as long as they make a fair amount for the service, money isn't a motivation. For those with a net positive view, purpose and mission are the core goals, not profit.

It's the same in business. Bonuses at lower levels may be an important motivation. But for most, and especially senior managers and executives, the drive will not be monetary, so long as they are fairly paid compared to other companies and versus colleagues (which is why a gender pay gap is totally unacceptable). Unilever harmonized the performance management system and made salaries more uniform globally so everyone was on the same footing.

If basic financial commitments and fairness are met, then money does not keep people around. People ultimately stay because they buy into the purpose, they feel they can make a difference, their work matters, they're being heard, and they can develop themselves to their fullest potential. They also need a good relationship with their managers—people don't quit companies, they quit bosses.

You can reward people for success and net positive work, but it doesn't have to be a targeted, separate bonus. Assess people on their values and behavior, giving multiple dimensions of performance weight. The better performers should rise through the ranks. If a factory head gets to zero waste and is performing better, or a buyer hits a sustainable sourcing target quickly and in an innovative way, give them a promotion, more responsibility, and more salary (a permanent shift in competition). Those who don't share the values and commitment to sustainable performance will get the message—they don't belong there anyway.

If you pay just for specific metrics, it might narrow the focus in an unhelpful way. Pay people for gender diversity and climate, for example, and you may lose focus on other elements of a multistakeholder, long-term-value approach to business (such as human rights or biodiversity). At nutrition company DSM, 50 percent of the executive bonus was once based on being number one in the Dow Jones Sustainability Index for its sector. That's too narrow for running a business. When DSM fell to number two, it decided to stop chasing rankings. The goal should be holistic, systems-based leadership, not managing to narrow measures or some outside ranking.

Even though Unilever did not pay directly for specific sustainability metrics, the company did measure success against key performance indicators and hold people accountable. Tracking progress was more a conversation than a scorecard. Management sat down quarterly to look at progress on issues like diversity and flag the departments or functions that were lagging. The leadership met with procurement, for example, every few months to discuss progress and look at metrics such as water use, waste, energy, and sustainable sourcing.

Unilever developed benchmarking and real-time data for transparency, identifying high performers and letting people see their progress. These methods were better for engraining the USLP principles into the culture. At the end of Paul's tenure, the company did add sustainability performance to incentive compensation for the top 100 executives. The board requested it to maintain focus on driving business results through the USLP.

With broader reporting and increased understanding of materiality issues in the investment community, we will see more companies making ESG performance a direct part of compensation. That's fine, but in the end, if people are not bought in and aligned, the incentive pay won't matter much.

The Infrastructure of Culture

People talk about building something like innovation or responsibility "into the DNA of the organization." But many things, like purpose, that seem core to a business get lost over time. As Jeff Seabright, former Unilever chief sustainability officer (CSO), asks, "Is the culture of purpose a recessive gene or a dominant one?" If you don't build the structures to reinforce the culture, it may fade into the background.

A dominant gene is impossible to uproot. That means getting the culture of net positive into every aspect of the business. It's helpful to rotate people out of sustainability and into other functions and geographies. Seabright says the ultimate goal of the CSO should be to work oneself out of a job. It's partly hyperbole, since there will always be some need for centralized knowledge and planning for long-term trends. But execution on sustainability should be deeply embedded. It slows down progress if the attitude in the business is "the sustainability folks will take care of that." Everyone needs ownership.

To unlock organizational potential, you need a high degree of trust, which allows you to drive decision-making down to the level where knowledge is instead of micromanaging. It allows for complexity to be pushed up, not down (which is what most organizations do). You want to give people freedom to make long-term, net positive choices without getting bogged down in things that make their lives difficult.

Pushing decisions down only works in a principles-based organization, not a rules-based one. Unilever introduced the Compass tool (chapter 3) as a guide to its values and standards of leadership. The name Compass was deliberate—finding your way is not a straight line and you will need to navigate around some trees. Everyone at Unilever is expected to live up to the ideals of the Compass: integrity, respect, responsibility, pioneering, a growth mindset, a bias for action, and a consumer focus. These values supported the performance culture that the company needed to revitalize the business.

The USLP brought a focus on the outside world, and a culture of serving the world, into the organization with specific measurable objectives. The right organizational structure and tools also create positive feedback loops in the culture. Break down silos between brands or geographic regions. Consider whether decentralization is hindering the quest to find and deliver on a common purpose.

Building the culture should be on the desk of the CEO, not just HR. All major functions are key to embedding a net positive culture into the business, but some—core areas such as finance, R&D, and M&A—are not engaged on environmental and social issues enough today. They should be.

Net Positive Finance and Budgeting

Purpose-driven brand projects, such as Lifebuoy's global hand-washing programs, will pay back in brand value and increased sales, but there is a cost. Investments in facilities to help countries develop take a lot of capital. So, net positive budgeting is a structural culture issue. Unilever brands find the money for these investments, in part, by not treating a purpose-led initiative like something that requires a separate budget. If it's seen as part of doing business, it may be included in the marketing budget or in capital expenditures.

Net positive companies break up mental and organizational silos and look at things holistically. A zero-waste factory may cost more up front, but it yields higher quality, less waste, better corporate reputation, and much more. Investing in living wages, or reducing contingent labor in the supply chain and adding people to the payroll, raises costs in the short run. But lower turnover and higher productivity pay back.

In the trenches, you have to give managers ownership of more of the business and its P&L, so they can allocate funds as they need to. When Unilever first considered putting solar panels on factories, the head of manufacturing faced a hit to the capital budget. But he also had responsibility for the electricity bill and costs (including a price on carbon). He had to develop five- and ten-year risk plans that included the environmental impacts of the factory on communities. With that broader perspective, he could take a holistic view and make better, well-rounded choices (they put up the solar panels).

Sanjiv Mehta from Hindustan Unilever, talking about budgets and water availability, says, "If you come from a perspective that without water, there's no business, why wouldn't you spend money on projects to protect that resource and the future of the business?" Making these investments the normal way of doing business stems from and reinforces a culture of purpose. Mehta also says that if you want to be part of the solution, "you will find the money."

It's a leadership and organizational decision to give people the freedom to work for the long term (not reporting quarterly gives them that space). It helps your people step back and see the forest from the trees.

Net Positive R&D

The USLP brought an outside-in perspective to innovation. An understanding of planetary boundaries, and how they affect people in the real world, helps researchers identify needs to fill and opportunities to rethink products. To make sure that brands and R&D were in sync and serving the USLP, Unilever embedded a director of R&D with brand teams. It was another way to break down silos, make innovation more relevant, and get to market faster.

For example, brand managers who worked on the Lifebuoy hand-washing initiative identified a challenge that a product innovation might fix. The program teaches kids to wash their hands for thirty seconds. But in some locations, there may not be enough water for every kid to wash for that long. And they're kids, so they may not stay put for thirty seconds anyway. Fixing these issues, the brand managers believed, would help Unilever achieve the USLP goals on human well-being.

Geneviève Berger, the head of Unilever R&D at the time, tasked the Lifebuoy team with finding a way to kill germs faster. They identified a combination of molecules from natural ingredients (thyme and pine trees) which could kill *E. coli* and other germs on hands in just ten seconds of washing. That assignment to "fix" Lifebuoy was not a one-off. To build net positive thinking into the organization, Unilever was using a "green funnel" in R&D, a step in the process to formally include environmental and social needs. New innovations had to add to margins *and* pass the funnel.

Another one of Unilever's chief R&D officers, David Blanchard, established an annual Green Funnel Review that helped researchers from different product categories share knowledge about new products, technology platforms, and challenges that consumers faced around the world. For example, in many communities where people wash clothes in a bucket—and may walk miles to get water—it took one bucket to wash the clothes and six more to rinse them. So, at a Green Funnel Review meeting, the laundry team set up six buckets of water and asked both the marketing and R&D teams to carry them to another room, telling them, "This is what we're trying to solve for." It gave the teams a sense of urgency and empathy. They developed a new "one-rinse" technology, which reduced soap foam quickly so people in water-stressed areas could rinse their clothes with much less water. Seeing this innovation, brand managers from personal care asked whether the new technology could cut rinsing time in soaps and shampoos in showers as well. The technology made its way into other brands.

Of course the Green Funnel process did not always produce winners. The teams were sure that a new compressed deodorant, which reduced packaging volume and shipping emissions, would be, as Blanchard says, "a slam dunk." But consumers thought they were getting less product and didn't buy it. Lesson learned. With embedded R&D, brand teams learn from failure more quickly as well.

M&A: Culture Is an Inside Job

As the USLP gained steam and the business grew, Unilever accelerated its mergers and acquisitions (M&A) activity. During Paul's tenure, they sold fifty-two brands and bought sixty-five—far more M&A activity than in the previous twenty years—and dramatically shifted the portfolio to position Unilever better for the future. The acquisitions included many founder-led, purpose-driven businesses, extending some categories and venturing into new ones.

Sundial Brands was a successful hair and skin care company that served a younger, multicultural consumer base. The founder, Rich Dennis, emigrated from Liberia and started the business with nothing, selling shea butter from a folding card table on the streets of Harlem in New York City.[8] Dennis stayed on after the acquisition. He and his company bring additional diversity and knowledge of new, growing markets to Unilever.

Many of these entrepreneurial CEOs expressed clearly that they were only interested in joining Unilever. Mark Ramadan and Scott Norton, the founders of natural condiments company Sir Kensington, said that "our company was not for sale." But when Unilever approached them, they realized that joining the company would "allow us to more rapidly expand distribution while holding true to our values."[9]

Jeffrey Hollender, as cofounder of the purpose-led company Seventh Generation, had always been suspicious of big companies. For many years, he refused to sell his products at Walmart. Hollender says, even more bluntly than Ramadan and Norton, "There weren't multiple companies to buy Seventh Generation that wouldn't give me a lump in my throat . . . there was *one* option."[10] John Replogle, the CEO of Seventh Generation at the time, says they were not for sale. When approached, they embarked on six months of conversations with Unilever leadership about being a B Corp and their values. Only then did they talk about purchase price.[11] In the five years since Seventh Generation was acquired, sales more than doubled and its products are now sold in forty countries, many more than they had been in before.

Unilever has generally allowed acquisitions to operate independently of the mother ship, but draw on the knowledge and resources they need to scale up. Kees Kruythoff, former president of Unilever North America, says the company wanted to serve these newly acquired businesses and help them grow. He told Seventh Generation leadership, "Congrats, you just bought Unilever—our resources are at your disposal." Kruythoff also told Jostein Solheim, CEO of the activist Ben & Jerry's brand, "Your job is to be the insurgent in Unilever."[12]

Founders generally leave the big companies that buy them, but most of these CEOs stayed with Unilever because of the culture. These entrepreneurs feel more affinity with each other than with a typical Unilever brand team. As more stay, they attract others; it's a multiplier effect of competitive advantage.

A net positive company looks at M&A differently, with a higher success rate for adding new companies into the culture and learning from them as well. Bringing in successful, purpose-led businesses and founders—with their pioneering, risk-taking mindset—adds something new to Unilever's DNA. Executives see the passion and excitement, and it rubs off. They hear a different language that big companies don't speak anymore.

The more purpose-led organizations Unilever envelops—ones that have clear missions to serve stakeholders—the faster the organization's purpose flywheel spins, and the closer it gets to net positive.

Purpose-Driven Brands

Purpose work starts at the corporate level. Taking a stand on issues such as human rights, diversity, and climate has to be company-wide. Brand-level work alone will look empty and half-baked. You can't be credible with one product using sustainable palm oil but not another. The company is only as good as its worst brand.

But once you have a consistent corporate agenda, you can effectively drive purpose at the brand level and develop the depth of commitment that supports a net positive business. The brand level is where most people interact with the company and its mission and where it all comes alive. Bringing meaning into the products is the ultimate demonstration that the culture of purpose has taken hold. You know it's embedded when the purpose work goes beyond training programs or grand statements from the CEO and moves into the brands. Purpose at Unilever truly took off when the marketers came on board.

Unilever has gained momentum by identifying societal issues for products to take a stand on and work to solve. But a brand with purpose is *not* CSR or philanthropy. It works authentically to serve people in a way that ties to what the product is all about. Doing it right drives sales also. For a number of years, the purpose-driven brands have grown 50 to 100 percent faster than the rest of the business, delivering 75 percent of the company's growth (and with higher margins).[13] This is profits through purpose.

The two longest-standing brand purpose programs, run by Dove and Lifebuoy, existed before the USLP, but they were small and not consistently applied. Lifebuoy went from a respectable reach of maybe thirty million people, mainly in India, to a global program that reached a billion people. Net positive companies embed programs like this throughout the business.

Unilever now has twenty-eight brands designated as purpose-driven. To get the internal label, they've shown they can hit certain high markers and take big steps with partners. But there is purpose work across the whole organization; it's a part of all three hundred brands. All have USLP-related targets, and the big goals, such as improving the life of a billion people, are measured across the company.

The Development of Purpose-Driven Brands

Marc Mathieu, the global head of marketing in the early days of the USLP, played a critical role in driving purpose down to the brand level. He's a respected thinker on what brands mean, and he knew Unilever needed to change how it thought about itself before it could convince consumers of anything. To help the organization evolve, build a different culture, and develop brands that deliver on the USLP, he created a narrative he called Crafting Brands for Life. It was an internal marketing campaign with videos asking everyone, "Are you willing to change the world again?" (referring to Lord Lever's commitment to hygiene at Unilever's founding).

A brand is a product to buy, of course, but also an idea to buy *into*, Mathieu says. The idea needs to be bigger than the product to add value. To expand thinking, Mathieu redesigned Unilever's "brand key," one of the core tools the company's marketers use to shape brand positioning. The original chart had fourteen boxes and was overly complicated. Mathieu reduced it to a triangle with a focus on product, brand, and human truths. To drive toward purpose, he added a heart with a larger ambition, and some additional elements to bring it to life.

Unilever calls this the brand *love* key (see figure 9-1). We show here a version for Rexona, an Australian antiperspirant brand (known as Sure, Degree, or Shield in other countries). The brand's purpose is to help people live a better life, "do more," and push their limits, with confidence and no odor. Rexona's USLP ambition is to "enable doers to live a more physically active, socially connected, and emotionally engaged life." Rexona supports personal hygiene education programs as part of its work.

You'd be forgiven for saying, "Oh, come on, it's deodorant." Fair enough. This is not one of the most world-changing brand missions, but that makes it a good example of the challenge. A purpose-driven brand connects to and

FIGURE 9-1

Brand love key

Sample Unilever Brand Love Key, Rexona

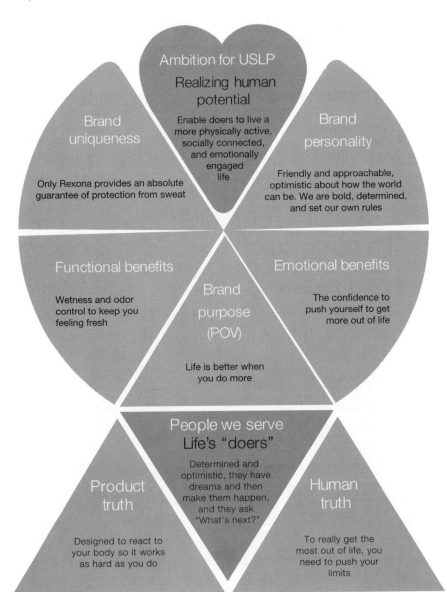

helps solve a larger problem in the world or in people's lives. Deodorant ties to self-image and comfort in social engagements, which matters to people. Sure, some brands connect to bigger goals. Lifebuoy can literally save lives through hand washing. Vaseline provides medical supplies to sites of natural disasters and refugee camps. Domestos cleaning products can credibly have a purpose to "win the war on poor sanitation."

But Rexona deodorant? Or, more to the point, Axe body spray?! How can a brand that lived off misogynistic advertising images for years find a good purpose? Yet somehow it did, flipping the messaging to question toxic masculinity and support multiple meanings of manhood. Norms often change, or in some cases, they need to. Axe had to show humility and acknowledge how it had portrayed women. Finding a larger mission for some brands, like Axe, has not been easy or obvious. It takes time. The ones that have figured it out have a mission that is clear to everyone internally and to their consumers. They've found a purpose that fits the history and functional benefits of the product.

Many of Unilever's brands have used the Sustainable Development Goals (SDGs) as a tool to find their larger mission. Knorr food, with supply chains in agriculture, is working on SDG 3 (good health & well-being) and SDG 15 (life on land). Domestos is fighting a war on poor hygiene, which ties to SDG 6 (clean water and sanitation).

The process of finding a purpose that works for a brand is an evolution. Karen Hamilton, Unilever's global VP of sustainability, groups the brands on a purpose journey into three buckets: *crafting* the purpose and building the brand key; *learning* (with humility) more about an issue and working with partners to build programs; and, for the most advanced brands, such as Dove, Lifebuoy, Domestos, and Seventh Generation, *scaling* their initiatives. The further along the path a brand is, the more it closes the "say/do" gap, clearly stating what it stands for and creating programs that deliver real impact.

The "do" part, the action on the ground and programs that improve lives, is what gives them credibility to keep raising the bar and address bigger and deeper issues. Dove can legitimately talk about self-esteem because it has held classes for sixty-nine million young people. Lifebuoy can engage on improving child mortality rates because it has taught hundreds of millions of people about hand washing with soap. Domestos can work on the larger issue of open defecation because it helped build millions of toilets in India and developed many school cleaning programs. Brooke Bond Red Label tea can work on racial and gender bias after using its ads and marketing to take the issue head on.

Brands with purpose create a virtuous circle that leads to more purpose work and more net positive outcomes.

Revitalizing Brands

Moving perceptions and financial results for a big, mature brand is hard. None of Unilever's products is more mature than Lifebuoy soap. Its journey from the 1800s is a microcosm of the Unilever story. It combines history and real progress for society with business growth. Finding a brand purpose can revitalize stagnant brands and reanimate the culture, as long as there's a good, authentic story and real action.

The challenge Lifebuoy has long focused on is the heartbreaking death of millions of children before age five from preventable diseases.[14] Regular hand washing can reduce the incidence of two big killers, pneumonia and diarrhea, by 23 and 45 percent, respectively. Teaching new mothers and midwives better hand-washing behavior can prevent 40 percent of the 2.5 million deaths that happen within the first month of life.

Lifebuoy's program has centered on a few actions: events to train kids and mothers on hygiene; extensive outreach through media; a comic book, *School of Five*, that promotes hand washing at five key times (after toilet, before each meal, and during bathing); and product innovations, such as a Mickey Mouse dispenser, to help make hand washing commonplace and fun.

Since 2010, the program has reached about half a billion people—a large part of the 1.3 billion people Unilever reached through all its hygiene and health programs—in twenty-nine countries across Asia, Africa, and Latin America. Unilever built partnerships around the programs, including a collaboration with the Global Vaccine Alliance in India to promote both washing with soap and immunization, two of the most cost-effective solutions for avoiding disease. A newer £100 million partnership with the UK government worked specifically on reaching one billion people to raise awareness and change behavior to fight Covid-19.[15]

The results of the full program, as part of the world's efforts to reduce unnecessary deaths, have been outstanding. Globally, 36 percent fewer children die from diarrhea. A study of two thousand families in India showed that those who went through a Lifebuoy training program reduced cases of diarrhea by 25 percent, acute respiratory infections by 15 percent, and eye infections (from touching eyes with dirty hands) by 46 percent. New mothers who are educated are dramatically more likely to wash their hands after changing diapers and before breastfeeding.

The financial resuscitation of the Lifebuoy brand has been remarkable. Revenues were flat or slightly declining for decades. As it leaned into purpose, Lifebuoy sales started growing a double-digit percentage per year. It became the twelfth product to join the pantheon of Unilever's €1 billion brands. When he left Unilever, Lifebuoy gave Paul a custom-made package of soap picturing Paul and his wife, Kim, on the cover (not a gold watch, but nice). The packaging brags that Lifebuoy had achieved the core USLP goal of reducing footprint while doubling sales.

Many of Unilever's purpose-driven brands have started growing again after years of going nowhere. The Knorr brand of soup and meal mixes adopted a purpose of making "wholesome, nutritious food accessible and affordable to all," and worked on issues of food quality, access, and health. After decades of flat sales, it is doing well in tough markets, even as competitor sales drop. Hellmann's mayonnaise, a 125-year-old brand, found new energy after Unilever figured out that the brand could play a big role in the fight against food waste. The leadership team visited farms and began connecting the brand to its roots, with ads featuring farmers who supply the eggs. Hellmann's worked to "defend real food" through its sourcing and messaging. With these efforts, and walking the talk with 100 percent cage-free eggs and 100 percent recycled plastic packaging, Hellmann's started growing again.

These successes do amazing things for the culture at Unilever. More than forty thousand employees have participated in hand-washing events as Lifesaver volunteers. Everyone can feel pride that the company has helped save millions of lives. They know their employer stands for something and that they can take part. They also see the business succeed financially, which increases buy-in and convinces even the skeptics that net positive work is good business . . . and that they should do more of it.

Home-Grown Purpose

Net positive thinking drives innovation and inspires companies to do more than just revitalize existing brands. Kees Kruythoff says that the portfolio of purpose-driven products comes together from three areas of work: strengthening core products such as Dove and Ben & Jerry's, acquiring brands like Seventh Generation and Shea Moisture, and crafting new products from the ground up. This last one may be the most fun.

The company started with a blank sheet of paper when it developed Love Beauty and Planet hair and skin care. The packaging is 100 percent recycled content. Ingredients are vegan and cruelty-free, with no parabens or dyes. Everything is sourced to reduce impact and promote livelihoods. Vetiver plants, which provide oil with a woody scent, come from Haitian farms. Unilever pays a premium for the oil and supports community development projects, such as roads, better access to health care, sanitation, and electricity.

As Kruythoff says, "The freedom to start from scratch, without any legacy, and design from societal needs back into formulation, packaging, and communication—that's the ultimate in crafting brands for life!" The clean slate also gave them flexibility on where the brand could go, leading to extensions such as Love Home and Planet cleaning products. The Love Beauty and Planet line made $50 million in its first year. Global shampoo and conditioner sales were down, but the new product grew fast, climbing into the top 20 shampoo brands in its launch year.[16] After just two years, it was on the shelves in forty countries.

The whole new line of products was created by a half dozen people in a room asking what a from-the-ground-up, purpose-driven brand could look like. They were given the space to think big. Similarly, a single, passionate employee, Laura Fruitman, created The Right to Shower, which makes soaps and body washes with names such as "Hope" and "Dignity." Thirty percent of profits go to initiatives that help homeless people get access to services, including showers. Fruitman was a global brand manager at Dove when she made the pitch based on her personal purpose to help the homeless. She found a perfect way to live that mission within Unilever. Now she's the product general manager and an "entrepreneur in residence" at the company.

It's a good example of what can come from a culture of compassion, service, growth, and creativity.

Internal/External

Company cultures do not exist in a vacuum. They're part of the larger culture of their communities. Connecting internal and external cultures has risks and rewards, including disconnects that are hard to reconcile. A net positive business won't back down on its principles. It will fight injustice to protect rights, challenging norms and finding the courage to do what's right.

Challenging the Norms around You

Executives often fear that if they put their values out there, they will step in hot water. Things get tricky if the culture of the business—diversity and tolerance, for example—clashes with the cultural norms in the society around the business.

Brooke Bond is one of the largest tea brands in the world, with a huge presence in India. The company has made a mission of "standing for inclusion in a world of prejudice." It uses its marketing machine to run campaigns about tolerance, showing how sitting down to tea can help people come together. In India, religious violence against Muslims has been tragically common. This is, to put it mildly, a contentious situation. Yet, Brooke Bond dove into the issue. One ad shows an Indian family, presumably Hindu, locked out of their apartment. A Muslim woman next door invites them in for tea. They are hesitant, but go in and share a cup. The tagline is the "taste of togetherness."

Another Brooke Bond campaign takes on discrimination against transgender people. A grandmother and child are stuck in a cab in bad traffic in the rain. A transgender tea vendor knocks on the window and the old woman waves her away and mutters in a disgusted voice, "those transgenders." But the vendor is offering free tea for people stuck in the traffic. The woman takes it, loves it, and calls the vendor back over. She gently touches the tea vendor's face and says "bless you" while the little girl watches and learns tolerance. Hindustan Unilever's inclusion work is broad; it helped support the creation of India's first transgender band. A film about the group won a Grand Prix prize at the Cannes film festival.

These ads can sound like gimmicks, but they feel genuine and are effective. Brooke Bond recently became the largest tea brand in India. Hindustan Unilever chairman Sanjiv Mehta says that he can't say it's because of the transgender or religious tolerance work, but the success is about having *"brands with purpose at heart, which is not just brand say but brand do."*[17]

Taking a stand has risks. A Unilever ice cream brand ran a campaign in Australia in support of gay rights. The product was made in Indonesia, and some was sold in that market. When the Australian ads were posted online, anyone could see them . . . including people in Indonesia, where being gay is illegal. Unilever eventually removed the ads, but it did not back down from inclusion in its business. The company, in its hiring and benefits, recognizes gay marriage globally. In Indonesia, it's clear to the gay community which companies are welcoming, and those organizations get access to more talent.

Still, it's a tightrope to walk, and a company must maintain its principles, while being careful about messaging that may offend different cultures. A net positive business will be an advocate for change and is willing to face tougher challenges, especially if it can lead a group to take on cultural norms together. In Uganda, being gay used to carry the death penalty. The B Team, a group of global leaders advocating for more human-centered business practices, wrote a letter to the Ugandan government threatening a boycott. It was not the only factor, but it helped, and the law changed.

A cultural commitment to equity runs across Unilever. Domestos, in its sanitation and hygiene work, took on India's caste system in a clever way. As the brand helped get millions of public toilets built, there was an issue with maintenance. In India, it was taboo for anyone but untouchables to clean a toilet. To encourage everyone to take part in community hygiene and well-being, Domestos created a new campaign, Pick up the Brush. The ads show A-list Indian stars cleaning their toilets.

Caste is a difficult stereotype to break, but gender stereotypes may be even harder. Unilever's former chief marketing and communications officer, Keith Weed, says that the majority of advertising has been stuck in a dated, 1950s worldview, where Dad can't operate a washing machine and Mom is always in the kitchen. In a global survey, 40 percent of women said they did not see themselves in most advertising—only 4 percent of ads showed women in leadership positions.[18]

To battle this twisted view of reality, Unilever cofounded the Unstereotype Alliance with UN Women, major ad agencies like IPG and WPP, and big ad buyers, such as Google, Mars, Microsoft, and J&J. With the UN as a convener, they got rival P&G on board (for context, Unilever and P&G are the two biggest advertisers in the world). The alliance hopes to "banish stereotypical portrayals of gender in advertising."[19] It's a powerful idea: ensure that hundreds of billions of ad dollars support equality.

The initiative has tested and measured the effectiveness of more inclusive communications. Ads that represent people well generate 25 percent more engagement and purchase intent.[20] The Unstereotype Alliance is challenging norms and a cultural system that keeps people in little boxes. Unilever has also worked on messaging about inclusiveness for the disabled in countries as diverse as Mexico and Egypt. In 2021, Unilever also committed to a global ban on the word "normal" in advertising or on packaging, as part of its Positive Beauty work.[21] As these initiatives and commitments grow, they help shift the culture in society and inside companies to be more inclusive, respectful, and equitable.

That's an inspiring net positive outcome.

Moments of Net Positive Courage

The website BabyNames does exactly what it sounds like; it offers expectant parents data on the frequency of names and their meanings. It's not a controversial company. But after the murder of African American George Floyd by police, BabyNames created one of the most powerful messages of support for Black Lives Matter. The site put a simple black box on its home page, listing dozens of Black Americans killed by racism and hatred, going back to the 1960s. The top of the box said simply, "Each one of these names was somebody's baby."

Companies generally avoid calling attention to themselves on contentious issues. But that's a mistake. Standing for something matters to stakeholders, especially employees. Like Dick's Sporting Goods (chapter 2), Levi's decided to use its brand reach to speak out on gun violence in America. The company partnered with a gun safety NGO to form a coalition of business leaders committed to action. They encouraged employees to use their five hours a month of paid volunteer time to get politically active. CEO Chip Bergh, a sustainability leader, said "We simply cannot stand by silently when it comes to issues that threaten the very fabric of the communities where we live and work . . . taking a stand can be unpopular with some, but doing nothing is no longer an option."[22]

Businesses in the services sector—consultants, banks, PR and ad firms, and so on—face tests of courage every time they choose to work with troubling clients. Pursuing customers to generate revenue at any cost is not a good choice. These situations make for tough decisions, and some companies seem to be consistently making the wrong ones.

Consulting giant McKinsey keeps finding itself on the losing end of moral choices (a *New York Times* headline, "How McKinsey Has Helped Raise the Stature of Authoritarian Governments," is a good example).[23] The company was fined $559 million because of "advice" it gave Purdue Pharma on how to increase sales of OxyContin, the prescription opioid.[24] McKinsey calculated that the company could afford to pay "rebates" to pharmacies for every patient who overdosed. The strategy guru and former McKinsey consultant, Tom Peters, wrote an open letter in the *Financial Times* effectively renouncing his association with the firm, asking, "Should I remove McKinsey from my CV?"[25] When you lose one of your most famous alums, it's not good.

The math on the number of pills sold per person was clear to many companies in the opioid value chain (including J&J, which also got fined). A consulting firm acting as a real partner to these companies, serving their best interests and the interests of society, would have helped them rethink their stance on opioids . . . or walked away. McKinsey helped Purdue go down an immoral path that was potentially devastating for the brand and its long-term financial performance.

Unilever has faced many situations that force a choice between doing the right thing versus immediate business results. When a courier service in London did not pay its delivery people minimum wages, Unilever stopped using the company to deliver ice cream. In another case, facing demands for bribes in Kenya, it stopped shipments from leaving the country. Choices like these set a moral standard that works better for the business in the long run because it gets reflected in the whole organization. Your people watch closely the way you do business.

Evolving Culture

Culture is not a fixed mark. It should change over time as people and the business models shift. But your values remain, and they come out in every decision you make, every organizational choice, and what kinds of businesses you build or buy. But the culture does evolve in different countries and business units around those values and the commitment to being net positive.

Being net positive means consistency, even in tough areas. It's important to constantly monitor the culture for disconnects. Survey employees and hear what they say—are you too slow in decisions, too consensus-driven, or maybe not values-driven enough? It's a perpetual process.

A strong enough culture will affect the communities around it. As more companies take a stand on race or inequality or climate change, they shift the discussion. The people in net positive companies go out into the world and change it. Many operational executives who leave Unilever focus on sustainability and net positive work. The former head of R&D is now chairing a regenerative agriculture company. Kees Kruythoff, is running a fast-growing plant-based food business, LIVEKINDLY. Others who took on CEO or C-suite roles elsewhere, such as former chief supply chain officer Pier Luigi Sigismondi who now leads Dole Packaged Foods, have developed sustainability plans inspired by the USLP. When Paul left Unilever, he cofounded the foundation and for-benefit company IMAGINE to bring together CEOs from entire sectors, such as agriculture or apparel, to tackle systems change.

For decades, GE and other blue chip companies that focused on leadership development spun out executives trained in their way of thinking to run other businesses. Today, Unilever's way of business is spreading. A culture that propels people to change other pockets of the world is a powerful tool. Building that kind of culture takes courage, consistency, and humanity.

What Net Positive Companies Do to Build a Powerful, Purposeful Culture

- Demonstrate values and culture through leadership, role modeling, and consistent behavior

- Embed a culture of purpose and service to the world by using business processes and tools that drive it into the core of the business

- Incorporate a net positive mindset into all activities—R&D, marketing, finance, and so on; this is a team sport

- Revitalize old businesses through purpose and culture, acquire purpose-led brands that bring entrepreneurial spirit into the culture, and build new products from the ground up, aiming for net positive in every dimension

- Connect the company's culture (values in motion) to the world in ways that inspire and motivate employees and stakeholders, and help reinforce and deepen that culture

- Influence the culture in the communities or countries around the company, and challenge norms that are discriminatory or go against their values—they stand up for what's right

10

Net Positive World

Looking Around the Corner to Greater Challenges and Opportunities

We stand now where two roads diverge. But . . . they are not equally fair. The road we have long been traveling is deceptively easy, a smooth superhighway on which we progress with great speed, but at its end lies disaster. The other fork of the road—the one less traveled by— offers our last, our only chance to reach a destination that assures the preservation of the earth.

Those who contemplate the beauty of the earth find reserves of strength that will endure as long as life lasts.

—Rachel Carson, author of *Silent Spring*

When you set a big goal—running a marathon, writing a book, or mastering a new language—it's exciting, but daunting. There are painful points along the way, like the famous "wall" in marathons, or moments of self-doubt. But when you get there, the feeling is amazing. All the training and late nights were worth it. It inspires you to shoot higher—maybe a triathlon this time? It's exciting to feel like you have more in you.

The journey toward net positive is similar. If you've come this far, it's impressive, and you should enjoy it. All of that work—to take responsibility and serve others, focus on the long term, blow up boundaries and set big goals, build deep trust, partner in dramatically new ways with all stakeholders, tackle the "elephants" that nobody wants to face, and develop a strong culture—will take you far. You've increased the good your business does for all stakeholders, and you're seeing new growth and excitement among employees. You have credibility and the trust of stakeholders. Your business is stronger and the world is a better place because you and your company are in it.

You're ready for more, and you'd better be. With expectations running high and the world moving fast, this level of performance will increasingly become the norm. It will get you invited to the party, but it's not quite enough. The tough reality is that even if every company became a B corporation immediately and matched today's most sustainable companies, we would still be on a dangerous trajectory. Here's the main question: If companies move toward net positive, will we have changed the systems *enough* to create a thriving, equitable, just, healthy, and carbon-free world that works for all, now and for generations to come? Maybe not, but we have ideas on how to get there and what issues to address.

The elephants in the room, such as taxes, corruption, corporate power, and human rights, create risk for any company that doesn't take part in the conversation. You can't build a net positive business and society without tackling them. These issues are also, increasingly, draining financial and moral capital from business—the cost of doing nothing is continuing to rise. The issues we take up here, including reforming capitalism and defending democracy and science, go even further beyond business and the economy—the cost of inaction is reduced freedom and a dysfunctional society. They're about long-term thriving for *everyone*. That scale of work needs credible net positive companies taking the lead.

The closer you are to net positive, the better able you are to drive the changes that need to come. You're more resilient and can contribute even more to the larger good. You'll also get a better look around the corner at what's coming in the future, and receive an invitation to help design it.

We cannot shy away from the biggest of challenges, the ones that society increasingly expects business to help solve. There are big forces at play, and we have to push on. We must work to build not just net positive companies, but a net positive world.

Everything Is Accelerating

If things were static, or we had started earlier, we could move toward net positive at a good pace and be fine. But everything is still speeding up and our existential challenges are growing. Inequality somehow got much worse during the pandemic, as trillions of dollars rushed to the richest hands, while the bottom quartile went into a depression and more people fell into poverty. The world's biophysical health keeps declining. We're cutting down more forest annually than we did ten years ago.[1] Climate change and extreme weather are speeding up—five of the six largest fires in California history happened in 2020.[2]

The seas will continue to rise and we are close to dangerous feedback loops in our natural systems. We've boxed ourselves in and things will get worse before they get better. How much worse is up to all of us and how fast we race to net positive.

At a time when we need to come together as a species, we are moving apart through declining democracy, accelerating nationalism, and separation of people by ideologies (made worse by bubbles of misinformation). This dysfunction is dangerous. The surprise of the pandemic was not how it spread or the disease itself, but the utter inability of the world's governments to work together.

But some upward trends are speeding up as well. Every day, we have more tools at our disposal, as technology gets smarter and more efficient, and the costs of building a clean economy continue to plummet. As Al Gore has said, "We're at the early stages of a technology-led sustainability revolution, which has the scale of the industrial revolution, and the pace of the digital revolution."[3]

The pressure on business to take more responsibility is growing, especially coming from employees. About one-half of millennials in the United States say they have spoken up to support or criticize their employer's actions over a social issue.[4] What happens when the more activist Gen Zers fully join the workforce?

In total, the case for action versus inaction strengthens daily, and we are gaining momentum. Most large countries have made carbon neutrality commitments (China will aim for 2060). Policy is likely to accelerate and we'll see more rules that increase efficiency in transportation and buildings, promote nature-based solutions for farming and forests, regulate product end-of-life and circularity, mandate the mix of renewable energy on the grid, and more. At the company level, commitments on everything from carbon emissions to diversity levels are proliferating rapidly.

Finally, investors are, at long last, diving in. PwC estimates that sustainable investing will make up more than half of global assets by 2025.[5] Moody's predicts that the sustainable bond business will top $650 billion–plus in 2021; that's 8 to 10 percent of the total bond market.[6] Experience shows that at about 20 percent, we'll see a tipping point and acceleration.

Net positive companies will be best positioned to match the moment. The leaders will create a continuously growing positive impacts and see consistent improvements in their performance, their connections to stakeholders, and their opportunities for growth. As the work to build a net positive world gains speed, like a train moving out of the station, it will leave behind those that don't jump on. The positive flywheel spins faster and faster.

Here's the wild part: the pace of change may never again be as slow as it is now.

Net Positive 2.0: Working on the Biggest Systems Changes

We started this journey with five key principles of a net positive company: take responsibility for your full impacts; work for the long-term benefit of society; create positive outcomes for all stakeholders; improve shareholder return as a result, not an objective; and embrace transformative partnerships. In an accelerated world, the principles will remain the same, just more so.

We address here six society-level challenges that a net positive 2.0 company will take on:

- Be even more responsible for broader impacts (do more good)
- Challenge consumption and growth
- Rethink the measures and structures of success (such as GDP)
- Improve the social contract: focus on livelihoods
- Bend the curve on capitalism and overhaul finance
- Defend democracy and science, two critical pillars of society

Companies that go faster toward net positive will have more capacity and skills to work on these society-wide issues. They will redefine what a corporation stands for, and their collaborations will expand and aim for full systems change and regenerative models. Achieving the SDGs will become a given. Business will truly be part of the solution and not just less of a problem, helping the planet thrive and society function for all.

These are the biggest of all systems, so they can be intimidating. Break them down into pieces to address your contribution to the larger goal. Keep the larger missions in mind, but act at your scale. For example, you might start using different measures of success to fit into and encourage stakeholder capitalism. Or you could engage with customers and citizens about what they really need, and whether some consumption is necessary.

A CEO who talks about these issues might take some heat. Paul was sometimes criticized for "taking his eye off the ball" and focusing too much on meetings with the United Nations, leading task forces for the G7 or G20, or championing broader societal causes. But whose interests were the detractors defending? Not the common good.

It's also an odd criticism when trust in business is so low (and trust is the ultimate currency). How will business regain society's support? Through more focus on profits? By staying in its own bubble? No, it's through working authentically to improve the world.

If we contemplate the big picture, the opportunities are vast. Donella Meadows, the environmental scientist who helped create the field of systems thinking, identified the top three leverage points for changing a system: its goals, its paradigms, and "the power to transcend those paradigms." The last one is powerful. What if we looked closely at today's economic paradigm—that our economy should maximize GDP and companies should be short-term profit maximizing machines—and understood that it's just a story a small cadre of economists (all white men) essentially made up? We can transcend it and tell a different story. As Meadows said, "Everyone who has managed to entertain that idea . . . has found it to be the basis for radical empowerment. If no paradigm is right, you can choose whatever one will help to achieve your purpose."[7]

So, let's make our purpose thriving for all.

It's freeing to look at the largest issues, with humility, and say, "Why can't this be completely different?" In the end, we are talking about a new partnership with society where we put the interest of others ahead of our own (which will ultimately benefit us as well) and treat all players as equal, regardless of size or economic power. It might mean short-term sacrifices. But if you want to jump high, you have to bend the knees, do the work, and commit.

Are you willing to tackle the toughest issues and, more important, be a part of the solutions? Then, read on.

1. Be Even More Responsible for Broader Impacts (Do More Good)

The first commitment of a net positive company is responsibility for the impact is has across its value chain. But a company contributes to (or deducts from) the world in larger ways. Let's use the Greenhouse Gas Protocol, which provides standards for how companies should measure carbon emissions, as a way to talk about broader responsibility.

The protocol puts corporate emissions in three categories, called "scopes": direct burning of fossil fuels in your facilities and vehicles (Scope 1), emissions from purchased energy that you bought from the grid (Scope 2), and emissions from your suppliers and from your customers when they use your products (Scope 3). For most companies outside of heavy industry, transportation, and utilities, Scope 3 is the largest slice of the life cycle emissions pie. It's weighted upstream for sectors like agriculture and apparel with heavy emissions in the supply chain, and downstream for those who sell energy-using products such as tech companies.

Companies can influence value chain emissions by working with suppliers on systemic change or by designing products that help customers reduce *their* impacts. Tech companies, for example, by enabling virtual meetings, help companies cut emissions from travel. And AI tools for precision agriculture reduce energy use on farms. Some refer to these as "avoided emissions" or, unofficially, as Scope 4. When Unilever helps Rwandan or Indonesian smallholder farmers get more productive, it reduces Unilever's Scope 3 emissions. But it also helps communities avoid the emissions that come from cutting down forests—that's Scope 4.

Two founders of the climate change NGO Extinction Rebellion, Roc Sandford and Rupert Read, have proposed that companies address two more levels of carbon emissions.[8] Scope 5, they suggest, includes political influence. When a company lobbies against action on climate, it can lead to far more economy-wide emissions than the company's own footprint. The net positive advocacy we proposed in chapter 7 is a Scope 5 activity, but a good one. Scope 6, Sandford and Read continue, is the influence companies have through advertising and messaging—do they support a consumption-based culture and energy-intensive lifestyles? Solitaire Townsend, founder of sustainable branding firm Futerra, has called for addressing what she dubs Scope X emissions, which would involve "work that restores and regenerates . . . healthy ecosystems and . . . takes responsibility for system level emissions."[9]

This idea of scopes is powerful. Since that terminology is used mainly for carbon emissions, and we'd like to broaden the discussion, let's call them Impact Levels. Consider six spheres of influence starting with a core of direct operations and moving out to include indirect operations, value chain, sector and community, systems and policy, and the world and society (see figure 10-1). As you move outward, your control greatly diminishes, and your focus will turn to influence, advocacy, and partnership.

In figure 10-1, we show the emissions example in line with the scopes framework. But we also give an example along a dimension of well-being, starting with employee safety at the core and extending out to human and natural world thriving at the largest level. Let's consider a few examples of what these scopes mean in practice.

Some of our thought partners on this model, Daniel Aronson of Valutus and P. J. Simmons from Corporate Eco-Forum, explored with us how one company, Facebook, affects the world. At the core, employees have livelihoods, which is good. But, as Aronson points out, "the content moderators who have to read racist, sexist stuff all day suffer wellness consequences," and that's also Impact Level 1. Further out in Levels 3 and 4, we see the well-being of Facebook members and their communities, both the good (staying in touch with loved ones) and the bad (algorithms that show them things that make them angry so they'll click more). Furthest out, Facebook has an impact on democracy itself. So far, Facebook has not taken responsibility for the outer levels.

Net positive companies address the outer impact levels, and you can tell when a company is taking ownership. When Microsoft pledges $500 million for affordable housing near Seattle, it's acknowledging some responsibility for increasing living costs and pricing people out of the local housing

FIGURE 10-1

Impact levels 1 to 6

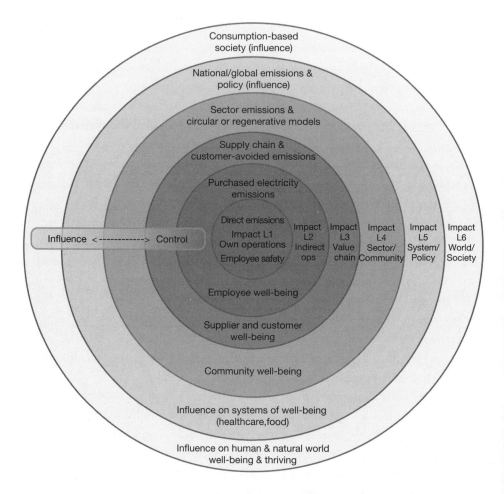

Consumption-based
society (influence)

National/global emissions &
policy (influence)

Sector emissions &
circular or regenerative models

Supply chain &
customer-avoided emissions

Purchased electricity
emissions

Direct emissions
Impact L1
Own operations
Employee safety

Influence <-----------> Control

| | Impact L2 Indirect ops | Impact L3 Value chain | Impact L4 Sector/ Community | Impact L5 System/ Policy | Impact L6 World/ Society |

Employee well-being

Supplier and customer
well-being

Community well-being

Influence on systems of well-being
(healthcare, food)

Influence on human & natural world
well-being & thriving

market.[10] When executives announce efforts to reduce systemic racism and increase diversity, they are talking about the outer levels of impact. Unilever was the first to issue Green Bonds in the consumer goods sector, and it required partner banks to commit to eliminate deforestation from their lending. When it selected an advertising or PR agency, it insisted they drop clients that were active climate deniers. Those are examples of using one's influence to affect Impact Levels 5 and 6.

Thinking this broadly about responsibility will lead to some tough conversations. When Disney launched the movie *Mulan* in 2020, the media reported that the company had filmed in China's Xinjiang region,[11] where the Chinese government is holding in detention camps at least a million Muslims from the Uyghur minority. Was Disney wrong to film there? Is it the company's responsibility to avoid working with governments with human rights abuses? We're not sure, but by that standard, it would rule out a lot of countries, including, at times, the United States.

There really is no choice on all of this. Stakeholders will expect companies to address the broadest impacts. They are watching, and the questions will keep coming. So, get out ahead of it and think through the impact levels now.

What Net Positive Companies Do to Take More Responsibility

- Expand their visions and look hard at how the existence of the business affects society; they cast a wide net and look at the effects of effects of effects

- Consider their influence on policy and systems through action *and* inaction, asking, What are we enabling through silence?

- Ask how to improve their societal footprint, the broadest level of impact, and what they would need to do to create positive Scope 6 value

2. Challenge Consumption and Growth

We humans like stuff. The way we buy and use things has been getting more resource intensive—mindless consumption; fast fashion, where every day becomes a season; and same-day delivery of things we probably didn't need anyway.

The planet's limits are getting clearer. The amount of copper in every ton of ore has declined more than 25 percent in a decade, for example.[12] Yet we continue to dig up more while the world is supposedly getting less physical and more digital. *The "cloud," it turns out, is not very light.* We're not living on the interest the world gives us, but drawing down capital and diminishing the capacity of the planet to support us. At current consumption rates, we would need multiple planets to support what will be nine or ten billion people living a decent quality of life.[13] Earth is finite, and it won't support our needs unless we rethink how we consume and start regenerating resources.

To thread this needle and allow our one planet to support us, the classic book *Natural Capitalism* provides a plan. Coauthor Hunter Lovins says it's three steps: "buy time with efficiency, redesign how we make and deliver all goods and services, then manage all institutions to be regenerative of natural, human, and all forms of capital."[14] Agreed. There's so much potential to improve efficiency: less than nine percent of everything produced gets reused, less than a fifth of electronic waste gets recycled, and upward of 40 percent of food is lost between farm and table.[15]

To address the drawdown of resources, we can pursue three paths of increasing difficulty: decoupling production from resource use (like the overarching goal of the Unilever Sustainable Living Plan [USLP] to double sales while holding footprint flat), building circular economies, and finding regenerative solutions.

A decoupled product is primarily made with renewable energy from recycled and renewable materials. It should also provide a living wage to everyone along the value chain. A circular model reuses or recycles all materials in an endless loop. Regenerative practices, most often mentioned with agriculture, could improve the world with every item consumed. Eating food from a farm or ranch that sequesters carbon in soil can be net positive on climate. The cutting-edge companies are already building these products. Shoe company Timberland is selling a Heritage Boot made with recycled content, insulation from PrimaLoft produced using air instead of heat (so it generates drastically lower carbon emissions in manufacturing), and leather from farms using regenerative agriculture practices.

We need to question growth, but ask a more nuanced question about what *kind* of growth we're pursuing. If your company can produce a circular or regenerative product, then please grow. We want companies like Timberland and Patagonia, which have worked tirelessly to move toward a net positive model, to take a bigger market share. Ditto for one-for-one businesses like eyeglass chain Warby Parker (every pair of glasses you buy triggers a donation of a pair to someone in need). Growth can sound like the wrong goal. But we want good companies to be around for a long time, and that's difficult to do by shrinking.

Clearly we have to look at growth differently. Some measures of company success should grow almost without limit—engagement and purpose of employees, customer satisfaction and joy, and community well-being. This is net positive growth. But in terms of physical material, the world is not regenerative, circular, or decoupled today's growth. The harder question on consumption, the truly heretical one, is how much stuff we need. A thriving world is one where every person has their basic needs met. Even that low bar would vastly increase material demand, as billions rise out of poverty.

Therefore, our two grand challenges are on a collision course. Since sincere climate action has started too late, we can't hit the targets we need *and* reduce inequality to increase quality of life for billions without something giving. That something may need to be the consumption of the richest billion among us.

In the future, when regenerative agriculture is dominant, or when the grid and cars are completely clean, then current levels of consumption may be possible within our shared carbon budget. Since we can't wait for those better technologies to get to scale. Instead, can we ask the well-off to check their wants versus their needs? Do the wealthiest *need* a lot of industrial grown meat in their diet? Do they *need* the third car or another thousand square feet in a house that's already too big?

A tiny number of companies have been willing to pose these heretical questions . . . Patagonia famously said, "Don't buy this jacket" in a Christmas ad. Eileen Fisher, founder of the apparel company that bears her name, said, "We think maybe we don't have to sell so many clothes."[16] Dutch airline KLM ran a campaign (before Covid-19) asking people to fly less, suggesting they use digital technology or take the train for shorter distances.[17] IKEA is launching a buy-back scheme for some used furniture (with a goal of full circularity by 2030).[18] These leaders are suggesting that we make fewer, better, longer-lasting things and think hard before using a nonrenewable resource like jet fuel. But stories like this are scarce, and almost always come from privately held businesses. It's hard to imagine big, public business taking the lead. But consumers may force the issue.

Eighty percent of respondents in a survey of US and UK citizens said they would make lifestyle changes, as they did during the pandemic, to stop climate change. They would avoid plastic, eat less industrial meat, and switch to green energy.[19] Younger people who are more concerned with environmental degradation may challenge a consumption-based society, seeking a different path to happiness. Economist Juliet Schor, who studies attitudes on consumption and wealth, has shown that people who already have the basics can improve their well-being by taking a different path: "Earn less, spend less, emit and degrade less. That's the formula. The more time a person has, the better [the] quality of life, the easier it is to live sustainably."[20] There's a reason the "simplicity" movement is popular.

Companies are increasingly giving consumers more information to make better choices. Amazon launched a "climate-friendly" label, based on reliable certifications such as Cradle to Cradle, Fair Trade, Rainforest Alliance, FSC, and Green Seal. Unilever's effort to put carbon footprint data on seventy thousand products will raise awareness. These things will help, but to date, inviting people to consume less has not worked well. It's one of the noticeable failures of the USLP—it couldn't budge people's showering or washing habits, and selling less wasn't much of an option either (people do want to get clean).

When $600 billion is spent annually on advertising to make us desire more things, a small campaign about reducing consumption doesn't stand a chance. What if that marketing machine were turned toward creating demand for net positive products and services, or toward finding less meaning in stuff, and more in people and living in service of others?

This is tough and uncomfortable. The wealthiest of the world can and should ask themselves hard questions about what they can do without. As Mahatma Gandhi said, "The rich must live simply so that the poor can simply live."[21]

What Net Positive Companies Do to Challenge Consumption and Growth

- Make regenerative approaches the default option in all they do; they seek to become net contributors, not takers

- Proactively use renewable or alternative materials

- Talk to customers and consumers to understand what they really want out of a product or service, a need that may be satisfied with less material use

- Set clear goals around *absolute* resource reduction and also ensure full recyclability and reuse (the fashion sector, for example, is moving toward recycling, rental, and resale of materials as their business models)

- Integrate nature positive and climate positive solutions into design

3. Rethink the Measures and Structures of Success (such as GDP)

The way we view progress is deeply flawed. We measure how successful people are by the number of dollars or followers they have. For companies, we focused on stock price and shareholder value. At the macroeconomic level, countries obsess over gross domestic product (GDP), which is a horrible measure of well-being of a society. It's time to rethink these metrics. *We need to measure what we treasure.*

Reframe GDP and Well-Being

Having a sense of total economic activity is fine, but GDP is a dated measure from an era of manufacturing, before the rise of intangible value. It counts *everything* that raises spending as a good thing. More cancer and medical costs, reconstruction after giant storms, wars and conflicts, and liquidating other forms of capital like cutting down old-growth forest—these all *increase* GDP. It does not measure peace, justice, quality of education, mental health, air quality, or the protection of natural capital needed for our survival. It measures, in the words of Robert F. Kennedy, "everything except that which makes life worthwhile."[22]

In using GDP, we're also fooling ourselves. As Hunter Lovins, president of the Natural Capitalism Solutions, writes in her book *A Finer Future: Creating an Economy in Service to Life*, "Our mental model of how the world works tells us we're winning when we're really losing. GDP measures nothing more than the speed with which money and stuff pass through the economy. So the real question is, do we have the courage to create an economy in service of life, not consumption?"[23] Can we manage societal systems to maximize happiness, health, and well-being?

Many people, including Nobel Prize–winning economist Joseph Stiglitz, have spent years advocating for a move away from GDP. Even the creator of the metric, Simon Kuznets, said it had nothing to do with well-being. But what do we replace it with?

There are a number of robust alternative measures for an economy:

- Genuine Progress Indicator, which looks at a country's performance on broader economic, environmental, and social variables

- UN's Human Development Index, which includes life expectancy, education, and income levels

- Happy Planet Index, which makes a formula of well-being, life expectancy, and reduced inequality, divided by ecological footprint/damage

- Gross National Happiness, which the small nation of Bhutan started measuring in 1972

The world is not debating the need for broader sustainability measures anymore, especially as the materiality of many of them continues to rise. We're tracking over six hundred of these new metric efforts, as everybody joins the race to the obvious. The Wellbeing Economy Alliance is a group trying to coordinate multiple efforts to redefine measures of societal health. Most new initiatives are focusing on a wider list of measures of success in categories such as prosperity (including health and well-being), planet, people, and principles of governance.

What do these broader measures tell us? Mostly that people want the same things, and it's not actually about money. The OECD developed a Happiness Index and measured well-being in all member countries. It found that people had similar priorities across cultures, and that health, security, freedom, and connection drove life satisfaction more than economics.[24] People need dignity more than money. At low incomes, especially below subsistence, of course income and happiness are correlated. But once people have "enough"—which varies by country and one analysis pegs at around $75,000 per year in the United States—the correlation between happiness and income is nearly zero.[25]

A few midsize countries are working toward a fuller set of metrics. Most notably, New Zealand's prime minister Jacinda Ardern announced in 2019 a first-ever "well-being budget." The government, she said, should ensure health and life satisfaction, not just wealth and economic growth.[26] Some cultures have informal ways of talking about more humane priorities—in Costa Rica, the phrase *pura vida* ("simple life") is used as a greeting and philosophy.

In a finite world, we can't increase the traditional economic metrics forever. But we can seek limitless growth of the intangible elements of a good life, such as well-being, joy, connection, meaning, and love.

Redefine the Corporation

The corporate world is also zeroing in on better metrics, with a soup of new initiatives and acronyms popping up. The EU's Non-Financial Reporting Directive, the Task Force on Climate-Related Financial Disclosures, the EU Taxonomy (2020), the IFRS Foundation's work to create a Sustainability Standards Board—all are driving a shift to better measurement. Europe leads, but there is new interest in the United States Securities and Exchange Commission as well. These groups will force transparency and help business get better at measuring and understanding its true costs and benefits to society—and those societal impacts are not small.

According to a study by TruCost, if companies had to pay for the natural capital and resources that they use for free, none of the biggest industries would be profitable.[27] (It's time, perhaps, to question the idea of "profit" as currently pursued. See the box "What Is the Right Level of Profit?".) The cost of food, for example, would be double if externalities were factored in. This is a feature of our system, not a bug. All the major corporate forms—such as LTDs, LLCs, or C corporations that aim to maximize shareholder returns—are externality-generating machines. They're not fit for a thriving future. It's a stretch, but if we priced externalities and *all* the players in the system, including finance, were long-term focused, those current forms might work. But they probably wouldn't get us to net positive quickly enough anyway.

So, what would a company look like if citizens, not shareholders, were the focus? A few other business structures have cropped up to try to answer that

WHAT IS THE RIGHT LEVEL OF PROFIT?

John Mars, one of the family owners of pet food and candy giant Mars, once posed the question "What should the right level of profit be?" In the modern mindset of unfettered capitalism, that question does not compute; the answer is: "As much as possible." But Mars was asking an important, nuanced question. Mars exec Jay Jakub, coauthor of the book *Completing Capitalism: Healing Business to Heal the World*, says that John Mars's point was that "we're only as strong as the weakest link in our value chain, and if we're taking too much . . . [it] can create a squeezing effect among partners that actually disadvantage[s] the company."* So, wringing every cent from suppliers might maximize short-term returns, but it weakens the system. This question is core to a philosophy that Mars developed, "the economics of mutuality," which is, like net positive, about purpose and a better, fairer form of business and capitalism.

*David Gardner and Jay Jakub, "How Social, Human, and Natural Capital Create Value," Rule Breaker Investing—A Motley Fool Podcast, accessed March 7, 2021, https://www.fool.com /investing/2020/08/10/how-social-human-and-natural-capital-create-value.aspx.

question by allowing companies to serve all stakeholders. The most prominent alternative is the legal designation of "benefit corporation" and the closely allied B corporation certification. Benefit corporations commit publicly to serve multiple stakeholders. In addition, France created a new form of governance that's similar in spirit to B Corps—the Entreprise à Mission explicitly embeds purpose and a multistakeholder model into governance.

As we mentioned, two high-profile parts of Unilever—Ben & Jerry's and Seventh Generation—are B Corps, and Danone became the largest B Corp in the world when it certified its $6 billion North American operations. Every company should consider getting certified as a B Corp, at least in spirit and approach. Even without the label, you can still take voluntary actions to support deeper change. Patagonia donates 1 percent of sales to environmental activists, Generate Capital dedicates 6 percent of profits to promote sustainable capitalism, and Unilever's Ben & Jerry's has a social mission fund that supports organizations fighting for a more just society.

A stakeholder-driven, net positive company might need a different ownership structure entirely. Family-owned businesses are more naturally aligned with long-term thinking, but the rest need new options. Dozens of multibillion-dollar organizations are owned by customers in co-ops. The world's largest, Crédit Agricole Group, is a network of 39 regional banks and 7.4 million customer owners.[28] A handful of companies have embraced employee stock ownership plans (ESOPs) where the workers get some part of profits and possible control. We also may see more pressure to put employees on boards; there are examples, such as transport operator First-Group, but it's still rare.[29]

A more radical shift would be changing the ownership structure for large, public companies to free them to operate for the long term. John Fullerton, a former managing director at JPMorgan and founder of the Capital Institute, questions traditional ownership and financial models. He promotes an alternative called Evergreen Direct Investment (EDI).[30] In this novel structure, a small number of long-term investors, such as pensions or national sovereign funds, would own "a share of the stream of the [company's] cash flows." There would be no public markets demanding unrealistic growth targets—just a handful of long-term investors wanting a reliable return. It's a perfect match between older, cash cow brands and investors with long time horizons.

A company is just a construct, dating back to the Dutch East India Company of the 1600s. It has evolved many times and can again. The current form encourages incremental approaches to be less bad. That's not good enough.

What Net Positive Companies Do to Rethink the Measures of Success

- Actively engage in the development of a fuller set of metrics to measure company success, stakeholder well-being, and a thriving economy and society

- Consider what alternative ownership and incorporation models like Benefit and B corporations, co-ops, ESOPs, and Evergreen Direct Investment would mean for the business

- Go well beyond minimal requirements to publish broader environmental, social, and governance measures, and clearly link them to value creation

4. Improve the Social Contract: Focus on Livelihoods

One of the world's most pressing issues going forward will be social co-hesion. Covid is pushing upwards of 150 million people back into extreme poverty.[31] Unemployment has increased as the world lost work hours equal to hundreds of millions of jobs. The most vulnerable, especially women and youth, suffer disproportionately. Many of these jobs will not come back.

All organized societies have written and unwritten agreements between citizens and governments. Individuals give up the "freedom" to let our id run wild and do whatever we want; in exchange, the government provides the security of structure and rules. We function best when treating everyone with dignity and respect, using some form of the Golden Rule. We also have an unspoken contract with Mother Nature: we won't use too much or abuse the privilege, and all we ask is that you please keep us alive.

The deal between business and workers once offered stability. Andrew's father worked for IBM for thirty-five years, retiring with a pension (remember those?). He spent most of his career in a company that promised lifetime employment. But in 1990, IBM laid people off for the first time. In the decades since, union membership dropped and layoffs somehow became a sign to investors of good management. We need to rethink that.

The nature of work is undergoing deep change. New technologies, par-ticularly AI and automation, are upending entire sectors. McKinsey es-timates that as many as 375 million people will need to switch jobs and acquire new skills by 2030.[32] The great paradigm shift in work will leave younger people particularly at risk. The International Labor Organization estimates youth unemployment at 13.6 percent, with another 12.8 percent in households below the poverty line.[33] It's rarely good for society to have a large number of idle people. Forty percent of youth who join rebel groups are motivated by unemployment and idleness—too few jobs leads to lower lifetime earnings, less success, unrest, radicalism, and migration.[34]

Focus on Livelihoods

To build a stronger social contract, we need to create jobs and consider how choices in business affect people. Agribusiness Olam once needed seven workers to produce one bag of cashews in Africa, but now only needs one. Olam's CEO Sunny Verghese asks and answers a core question: "Do I have no accountability for the people displaced? No. The company's responsibility extends to finding a viable option for people laid off because of new technologies."[35]

Like Olam, Unilever has increased automation, and it has looked for ways to protect and create jobs throughout the value chain. The needs of business force tough calls like closing a plant to stay competitive, which critics may decry as hypocrisy for a purposeful company. With a larger view on job creation, the USLP had a goal to create five million livelihoods. Paul kept the tea business in the Unilever portfolio, not only because it serves a growing health drink market, but because it supports many thousands of tea farmers. A well-managed tea plantation can also be good for the planet. That doesn't help the factory workers laid off from automation, though. Leaders must make hard choices, but need to explain them clearly and transparently, and do things with strong values and principles—like helping those displaced transition to new work.

The most innovative and counter-intuitive approach to creating jobs may be open hiring. Greyston Bakery in New York, which supplies brownie bites to Ben & Jerry's for its ice cream, offers jobs "first come, first serve." Anyone can sign up for an entry-level job. The company has hired people who served time in jail, lived in homeless shelters, or who have never held a legal job. Mike Brady, the former CEO of the bakery, points out that companies spend $3 billion annually keeping people like this *out of work* through roadblocks like background checks.[36] Invest the money in people instead, Brady says. The company has thrived, and the stories of lives turned around are inspiring.

Net positive advocacy supports livelihoods as well. Unilever helped drive the passage of the Modern Slavery Act in the United Kingdom, and encouraged Consumer Goods Forum members to commit to the Ruggie human rights framework.

One of the biggest tests of our humanity and our social contract will be refugees. Roughly eighty million people—about as many as live in Turkey, Iran, or Germany—have been forcibly displaced today.[37] The number of climate refugees in the coming decades could rise to a billion people or more.[38] Some leaders hope to alleviate the refugee crisis through work. Hamdi Ulukaya, the billionaire founder of Chobani yogurt, created the

NGO Tent Partnership for Refugees, which Unilever joined. As Ulukaya told *Bloomberg*, "a job, for a refugee, is day and night . . . that's the point at which they find their life can continue."[39] Unilever's Ben & Jerry's created a four-month training and mentoring program, the Ice Academy, for "aspiring entrepreneurs who arrived in the UK as refugees."

The idea of a social contract revolves around one core question: What do we owe each other? The answer is complicated, but given how connected everything is—we basically have one planetary and human immune system—we should make sure everyone has enough to survive and an opportunity to thrive. It's one reason why Unilever recently told all suppliers that they must pay living wages by 2030.[40] Earning money on the backs of others is not acceptable.

The International Trade Union Confederation (ITUC) has issued five demands for a new social contract: climate-friendly jobs as part of a just transition; rights and protections for all workers; universal social protection (that is, a floor on basic human needs and dignity); equality of incomes, gender, and race; and inclusion. These make a great framework for building a world where we leave nobody behind.

What Net Positive Companies Do to Improve the Social Contract

- Think of labor not as a cost, but as an asset to nurture

- Ensure basic principles of human rights and livable wages across the value chain

- Actively develop strategies to combat inequality and ensure just transitions where jobs are changing

- Collaborate with suppliers, governments, and civil society to eradicate modern slavery (by 2030)

- Embrace the challenge of solving broader social challenges like refugees, youth unemployment, and skill development

5. Bend the Curve on Capitalism and Overhaul Finance

During the pandemic, we all became amateur statisticians, talking about flattening the curve of Covid-19 case growth. It means doing what's necessary to slow the exponential growth of something dangerous.

We have other curves to bend.

Carbon emissions grew for decades in a roughly exponential way, tracking with the growth of population and economic output. The percentage of income and wealth flowing to the top 1 percent has grown more than linearly for decades. While some developed countries have flattened the carbon curve, holding emissions per dollar of GDP steady, the world is still driving toward a climate and inequality cliff.

Capitalism has been the superior economic system for generating well-being, at least compared to the others humanity has tried. But the recognition that something is wrong at the core of the system is growing. Not just NGOs and academics point this out, but CEOs and governments. Many of the largest companies are talking, even if superficially, about stakeholder capitalism. It's no sexier a term than "sustainability," but it makes the point that shareholders should not be the focus of strategy. Walmart's CEO Doug McMillon has supported the logic of stakeholder capitalism, saying, "We simply won't be here if we don't take care of the very things that allow us to exist, our associates, customers, suppliers and the planet."[41]

Salesforce CEO Marc Benioff says that "capitalism as we have known it is dead" and laments the "obsession we have with maximizing profits for shareholders alone . . . stakeholder capitalism is finally hitting a tipping point."[42] His enthusiasm is welcomed, but he may be ahead of himself. A multistakeholder approach is less alien to company leaders, but we're far from the death of short-term, profit-maximizing capitalism.

Business leaders should take note of how deep the skepticism *outside* the business world runs. In the *2020 Edelman Trust* report, 56 percent of respondents from around the world agreed that "Capitalism as it exists today does more harm than good." Only 18 percent think the system is working for them.[43] A quarter of Americans support the "gradual elimination of a capitalist system in favor of a more socialist system" and 70 percent of millennials say they're likely to vote for a socialist.[44] Most of them do not likely support the literal definition of socialism, government owning the means of production, but are attracted to Scandinavian-style democratic socialism. However they define it, these numbers are a warning.

We can only scratch the surface of a discussion on how to "fix" our system. There are a number of important thought leaders on reimagining capitalism for a finite planet under siege. It's worth exploring their writings and thinking (see note for a partial list).[45] In our admittedly abridged version of what is easily a book-length discussion, we'll focus on two failures of capitalism that business can work on: failing to price valuable resources, and a financial market stuck on the short term.

The Original Sin of Capitalism: Externalities

For those who pray at the altar of the dominant, neoliberal-inspired economic model, two tenets are unquestioned: shareholder value is all that matters, and free markets (or freedom in general) will solve everything.

In that worldview, if a company does wrong by society, people will buy from someone else. If the environment is damaged, property rights and legal action will stop polluters. But no matter what, liberty remains more important than the environment (this is a narrow liberty that only applies to companies only, since people deserve freedom from pollution as well). The theory says that unfettered markets will magically take care of these issues.

To buy this story, you have to believe in multiple fairy tales, including the demonstrably false idea that markets function seamlessly, with perfect information flows and perfect competition. In the real world, market power is heavily concentrated in a few hands, we don't have all the information we need, and markets were never free. They are plagued with the fatal flaw of externalities. Many societal costs and benefits from a company's operations are not reflected in the price of goods or services. The atmosphere has been a free landfill for our carbon emissions, and something that costs zero gets used a lot. The societal bill for climate change will be many trillions of dollars, and the cost is effectively infinite in uninhabitable places. But polluters don't pay for any of that.

Climate change is the greatest market failure in history. Inequality is a close second, and the market for wages does not reflect real value. Essential workers who risked their lives during the pandemic often held minimum-wage jobs. They kept the rest of us who can work by Zoom alive.

To change how we use the world's bounty, we need to value scarce resources, either through voluntary pricing or by regulations or pressure from customers. Hundreds of companies have voluntarily added internal carbon fees, but generally as a "shadow price," which calculates what a project would cost if there were a tax. A smaller group of companies collect real cash from business units to invest in climate action, including the following:

- Unilever: €40 per ton fee, with the money funding eco-efficiency projects

- LVMH: €30 per ton price that its luxury brand "houses" have to invest in carbon reduction[46]

- Siemens: £31 per ton fee in the UK alone[47]

- Microsoft: $15 per metric ton, charged to divisions, with the funds going to investments in energy efficiency or clean tech. In 2021, it added a $5 per ton tax on value chain (or Scope 3) emissions as well.[48]

These are important efforts, but economists estimate that the price of carbon needs to be upwards of $100 per ton to reduce emissions fast enough.[49] Carbon is theoretically easy to put a price on. The emissions from different forms of energy are a matter of physics, and a tax can be administered at the refinery, gas pump, or other logical, trackable point in the chain.

Natural capital is much more complicated. How much are healthy forests that cleanse groundwater, or provide flood protection, worth? A World Economic Forum report estimated the value of natural capital that underpins all economic activity at $125 trillion, much bigger than the global economy.[50] Finding better estimates of the value of natural capital has been in the works for years. The Capitals Coalition developed a protocol for companies to measure how they affect and depend on the natural world.

A decade ago, Kering's Puma brand created an environmental P&L to estimate the value of natural resources it relied on in its value chain. The unpaid services from nature were roughly $100 million, a sizable chunk of profits. This knowledge was interesting, but didn't change the company or sector's practices much—without pricing externalities, why would behavior fundamentally change?

Over time, though, companies will be held accountable for their impacts. Even if there's no dollar value or market, the "price" of misusing resources could be loss of sales, reputation, employees, or license to operate. As Peter Bakker, president of the World Business Council for Sustainable Development, says, "The days where we can only optimize returns on financial capital are over."[51]

We can't perfectly assess the price of the resources we draw on, but it's clearly not zero. Companies should use net positive advocacy to push for real prices, even if imperfect. We can wrangle about the size of the fee, but with some cost on externalities, the financial world can create markets at scale—and if there's real money involved, you can bet they will.

Finally, some things cannot be priced, but need to be protected or re-generated. Preservation of rare species would qualify. Not everything has a measurable value or can be regulated away. Net positive companies understand this.

Overhaul the Financial System

John Fullerton of the Capital Institute developed a framework for "regenerative finance."[52] He hopes to bring the financial system in line with, and in service to, people and planet. Fullerton challenges the "assumed truths about finance," such as the idea that financializing everything, and continually increasing the size and influence of finance on the economy, automatically leads to efficiency, growth, and prosperity. It hasn't done that at all, unless you count the prosperity of bankers themselves.

Fullerton advocates for principles like more transparency; generation of real, long-term wealth; collaboration; resilience; making finance a *means* to a healthy economy, not the end itself; and keeping finance at the right scale within the economy (at the time of the 2008 financial crash, banks reaped an absurd 30 percent of total corporate operating profits).[53]

In line with Fullerton, we believe that the idea of "fiduciary duty," interpreted as maximizing short-term profits, needs a rethink. As one of the world's top experts on integrated reporting, Bob Eccles, has written, the idea that fiduciary duty equals shareholder primacy "is an ideology, not the law."[54] It's yet another story that we can rewrite.

A group led by Generation Foundation (part of Generation Investment Management), the UNEP Finance Initiative, and Principles for Responsible

Investment (PRI) is working to challenge the traditional view. The CEO of PRI, Fiona Reynolds, says the project means to "end the debate about the inclusion of ESG factors in fiduciary duty."[55]

Andrew Liveris, former CEO of Dow, helped found Focusing Capital on the Long Term (FCLTGlobal), and works to fix the financial system. As Liveris sees it, we need two points of attack on investors: new government policies and higher transparency—"We need to shame them," he says. He suggests regulations on short-term trading and hedge funds because "stock markets are like Las Vegas and bear no resemblance to reality." He wants more disclosure on risks like climate change, better metrics on company progress against the SDGs that pension funds can incorporate in investment decisions, and new incentives for asset owners to stop rewarding them for short-term performance. We need two points of attack on investors, Liveris says, government changes in policy and, "we need to shame them."[56]

Some long-term investors are trying to change the system from within. When Hiro Mizuno ran Japan's $1.5 trillion government pension fund (GPIF), he shifted it toward ESG, but he didn't come at it with a sustainability lens. His interest was in managing long-term risk since GPIF's size made it what he called a "universal owner"—that is, at their scale, they basically were the market. If you own that much for a long time, only systemic risk matters. But, Mizuno says, the conventional portfolio management strategy focused only on how to beat the market, not how to make it better. ESG was the best way he found to communicate his point about long-term value management, since every dimension of ESG "becomes relevant in the long-term scale."[57] But if ESG is a relevant risk, he asks, "how do you hedge it?" A brilliant observation we could apply to climate, pandemics, and supply chain disruptions. How do you hedge those risks? (Becoming a net positive company is a good start.)

The current short-term approach, Mizuno says, is a systemic failure and a "tragedy of the horizon." Managing assets for the quarter is "technically right, but holistically wrong." That sounds like our entire economic system.

What Net Positive Companies Do to Bend the Curve on Capitalism

- Price externalities, put a price on carbon in their operations, collect real money, and invest it in reducing carbon emissions more

- Use corporate political power to aggressively advocate for a regulatory price on carbon

- Work in collaboration with NGOs and others to put directionally correct prices on hard-to-measure natural resources like water and land use

- Encourage the financial system to value ESG and the long-term by shifting their own investments to sustainable investing and by proactively talking to investors about how the company's ESG work creates value (don't wait for analysts to ask)

6. Defend the Pillars of Society

The list of principles that underpin a just society would be long, but would certainly include democracy, protected freedoms, equality, a free press, and a commitment to science and fact. All of these societal pillars are under attack in increasingly blatant ways. Calling the press the "enemy of the people" is not subtle.

The global rise of autocratic leaders creates tough choices for companies. It's bad for business and society. In the B Team's report, *The Business Case for Protecting Civic Rights*, they conclude that "countries with higher degrees of respect for civic rights experience higher economic growth [and] higher levels of human development."[58] During the pandemic, rights deteriorated everywhere, and 87 percent of the world's population is living in countries now rated "repressed," "obstructed," or "closed."[59] More than half the world lives under regimes with significant human rights violations: concentration camps of Uyghurs in China, violence against Muslims in India, and children separated from their parents at the US-Mexico border. Russia, Turkey, Hungary, Brazil, and others have shifted toward autocracy and reduced freedoms (as did the United States for four years). Should companies stop working with these governments? Perhaps, but if you do, you abandon half the world.

Business leaders can't sit it out, but they need to be statesmen, not politicians. So, stay true to your values. Think hard about what you won't accept from government partners. It's a fine line. Say too much, and you may alienate leaders and reduce any influence you have; say too little, and you tacitly support autocracy and repression. When McKinsey told its Moscow employees not to join protests in support of Putin's opposition, the *Financial Times* likened it to propaganda, and a US senator sent the company a letter saying the incident "raises serious questions about McKinsey's core values."[60]

Companies can challenge attacks on freedoms and fight for justice. Unilever has used its advertising to promote inclusion. It has spoken out against intolerance, including in India as violence against Muslims rose. Companies are coming out of their shell when the attacks on the pillars of society are obvious. Unilever's Ben & Jerry's fought voter suppression in the United States, working to help citizens who once were barred from voting (because of a criminal record) cast their ballot once again. The B team often speaks up on corruption, human rights violations, or money in politics. These are all cancers on society that undermine democracy.

In the run-up to the 2020 election in the United States, some organizations used their voices for the first time. The magazine *Scientific American* and the *New England Journal of Medicine*—both of which had never made a political statement in their history, going back to the 1800s—endorsed Joe Biden, because they feared that science was being undermined. Business leaders signed statements in support of free and fair elections (the Leadership Now Project) and civic participation (the Civic Alliance). The US Chamber of Commerce and the union AFL-CIO, in a rare combined statement, called for all votes to be counted when the sitting president questioned, without basis, the legality of mail-in ballots.

After losing, Trump and his enablers perpetrated the big lie that he had actually won the election, instigating an armed insurrection and takeover of the US Capitol building on January 6, 2021. An appalling 147 members of Congress (all Republicans) voted, *after* the deadly attack, to overturn the election results. As we've mentioned, many businesses paused political donations. But an impressive list of big companies stopped donating only to those 147 members. (Shamefully, some companies have already started donating to the insurrection supporters again.) In the following months, some US companies also opposed numerous laws passed by state Republican parties to restrict voting rights.

Business can also take action in its operations to counteract bad policy. As deforestation in the Amazon increased under Brazilian president Jair

Bolsonaro, soy and meat buyers increased pressure on their suppliers to stop deforestation and respect human rights. Those are legitimate business choices that don't address politics. Unilever often continues doing projects that improve lives, such as nutrition or health and hygiene initiatives, no matter what's going on with the government. In places with human rights concerns, these projects are needed even more. Change happens from within, and leaving those regions to suffer won't help.

Attacks on democracy and the press are grave, but we're most concerned about efforts to undermine fact and science. The rise of "fake news"—meaning doctored and fabricated information, not just stories you don't like—has led to vast misinformation. In the United States, those peddling the insane QAnon conspiracy convinced millions of people that Democrats were running a child-trafficking ring out of a pizza restaurant. In Myanmar, after mobile phone penetration skyrocketed from 1 to 90 percent in just seven years, Facebook became the primary source of information.[61] The UN determined that fake, incendiary news on Facebook led to genocidal violence against the Rohingya people.[62] Unilever was one of the first to stop advertising on platforms that incite hate and spread misinformation.

Populist politicians have long tried to confuse citizens about what is true, making the case that nothing is known for sure. And companies have cast doubt on facts that they find inconvenient, such as ExxonMobil waging a despicable war on the science of climate change for decades. Public trust in information is at a low.

None of this is good. Every company with a stake in science and truth—which is everyone, but some sectors more than others—must defend reality. Go public and say out loud, "We believe in facts and science." If that's a political statement, then so be it. Speaking out is, paradoxically, how we can best depoliticize it. After Trump made statements about rushing a Covid-19 vaccine to market, a group of the world's largest pharma companies issued a statement that they would follow the science, not politics. It's disturbing that they even had to say it.

How can we possibly tackle global, shared challenges and seek a just, equitable world if we can't operate from a single basic set of facts on everything from climate change to pandemics to racism?

What Net Positive Companies Do to Defend the Pillars of Society

- Get off the sidelines and speak out publicly, alone or collectively, to protect democracy, freedom, science, and truth. This isn't only an issue for science-based companies; all are at risk when politicians declare their own reality.

- Work to correct misperceptions that their own employees may have

- Find ways to use the power of the business, like supply chain purchasing, to fight dangerous policies

- Take the long-term view and continue to work directly with communities, even in countries with serious human rights or democracy issues—it's better to be part of the change than run away from it

"A Higher Moral Ground"

Throughout history, every generation feels that it's living in the most important time ever. But perhaps now it is true. Technology has never advanced so fast. The world has never moved so quickly. We have never known so much about our world as scientific insights change our understanding of reality. There have never been so many people—almost eight billion people—competing for space and resources, an unimaginable number to the ancient Greeks.

Even citizens at the dawn of the twentieth century—when the world discovered much of what we consider modern, such as electricity, cars, and planes—would be shocked. At that time, about 1.6 billion people roamed the planet, but spread out, with days of travel between them. Now, about one long lifetime later, the majority of humanity is essentially connected in one global organism (two-thirds of all people now have mobile phones).[63]

The two of us have worked for decades to help the business community evolve, thrive, and bring about a new world—to make business a force for good. We do not believe humanity will make it through the gauntlet of the mid-twenty-first century without business taking a prominent role in solving our shared challenges instead of contributing to them.

We're facing existential issues. Will things get worse or better? It's in our hands. The solutions to our decades-long global crises—climate change, biodiversity loss, inequality, the racial divide, and poverty, among others—lie in empathy and compassion, in systems thinking, and in collective action. We can choose the direction we go and what kind of world we create. We can have a net positive impact on all around us and build a place where people and organizations give a lot, but also receive a lot in return. We have the tools to make enormous progress on everything that ails us. We can eliminate dire poverty, we can decarbonize, we can protect land and species.

We will choose our destiny, together. We're asking for more trust, more courage, and more humanity. Do you care? Do you have the willpower? Can you find the moral leadership to do what we must? If you join us in this most critical journey to net positive, you may open yourself up to criticism. You'll make mistakes. But the rewards are enormous, for you, for your business—which will thrive in a whole new way—and for all of us living together on this spinning, imperfect ball.

In 2004, the Nobel Prize Committee awarded Kenya's Wangari Maathai the Peace Prize for her life's work, the Green Belt Movement, which planted more than thirty million trees and improved the lives of a million African women. In her Nobel address, Maathai noted that the committee, by giving her this award, was challenging the world to broaden the understanding of peace.

"There can be no peace without equitable development," Maathai said, "and no development without sustainable management of the environment in a democratic and peaceful space. . . . In the course of history, there comes a time when humanity is called to shift to a new level of consciousness, to reach a higher moral ground. A time when we have to shed our fear and give hope to each other. That time is now."[64]

Yes, it is.

ACKNOWLEDGMENTS

A surprising number of people help make a book happen. We've relied on many others to provide us with inspiration, ideas, and stories, as well as act as sounding boards, editors, thought partners, and friends (the ones who tell you the hard truths). This book would not have become a reality without all of them.

We have enormous gratitude for Jeff Seabright, who should really be the third author. Jeff was on every call, read every draft, offered new ideas, and provided guidance on every theory and idea we had. Jeff's combination of experience is unique, including time as chief sustainability officer at Unilever, previous roles in multinationals in consumer products and energy, and work inside the US government. Jeff kept the rudder straight on this project, helping it, as he says, "lurch toward greatness." If we got anywhere near that mark, it's because of him.

We spoke to a large number of people who generously gave their time and very honest perspectives on sustainability in general, and on Unilever's place in the story specifically. As any writer knows, it's painful to have a long, fascinating conversation with someone and boil it down to a single quote—or have to leave a great story on the cutting-room floor. We wish we could have shared much more of all of these contributors' views. Thank you to James Allison, Jonathan Atwood, Doug Baille, Doug Baker, Peter Bakker, Irina Bakhtina, Hemant Bakshi, Charlie Beevor, David Blanchard, David Blood, Romina Boarini, Sharan Burrow, Jason Clay, Doina Cocoveanu, Jonathan Donner, Tony Dunnage, Marc Engel, Karen Hamilton, Rebecca Henderson, Cheryl Hicks, Jeff Hollender, Rosie Hurst, Alan Jope, Janine Juggins, Anne Kelly, Tim Kleinebenne, Kees Kruythoff, Angélique Laskewitz, Andy Liveris, Mindy Lubber, Rebecca Marmot, Marcela Marubens, Marc Mathieu, Sanjiv Mehta, Steve Miles, Hiro Mizuno, Kumi Naidoo, Leena Nair, Gavin Neath, Frank O'Brien-Bernini, Sandy Ogg,

Ron Oswald, Miguel Veiga-Pestana, John Replogle, John Sauven, Pier Luigi Sigismondi, Samir Singh, Jostein Solheim, Emilo Tenuta, Harold Thompson, Sally Uren, Sunny Verghese, Jan Kees Vis, Dominic Waughray, and Keith Weed. We also extend a thanks to the many other leaders from business, NGOs, academia, and government who inspired us with their work to write this book.

With nearly five hundred endnotes, this book required a great deal of detailed research to get all the statistics we needed and ensure the stories we told were accurate. We relied heavily on our research director, Jennifer Johnson, and research assistant, Laura Zaccagnino, both of whom could find any obscure statistic we wanted and provided feedback as really the first readers. Thanks to designer Fiona Fung, who made our graphics and ideas for frameworks look good. And thank you also to a few people who helped us track down or confirm information at Unilever, including David Courtnage, Cliff Grantham, James Hu, and Ishtpreet Singh.

Once we had a full rough draft—which needed a lot of work—we asked some brave souls to read it and give us their unvarnished perspective. We can't thank enough the following people who spent a lot of time providing detailed feedback: Matt Blumberg, Mats Granryd, Jeff Gowdy, Andy Hoffman, Hunter Lovins (who went above and beyond providing much needed tough love), Henrik Madsen, Colin Mayer, Jeremy Oppenheim, Jonathan Porritt, and P. J. Simmons.

We also want to thank our teams that kept our businesses going while we wrote. Andrew could not do his work without his core team of Aleise Matheson, Sharon Parker, and Dina Satriale. Paul's support at IMAGINE includes Kelsey Finkelstein, Jenna Salter, and cofounder Valerie Keller. Zena Creed helped kick off the book process, had a son and took parental leave, and came back . . . and we were still writing. She has been an important thought partner on getting our book out there and developing our story and communications.

The team at Harvard Business Review Press is world class. Our strategic adviser throughout the process was our editor Jeff Kehoe, who showed great patience. A large team produced this book and made it better. Thank you to Stephani Finks for another great book cover design, and to press editorial director Melinda Merino and production manager Jen Waring, as well as Christine Marra from *Marra*thon Editorial Production Services. We also want to thank the business operations and marketing teams that shepherd the book and sell it around the world, including Press Commercial Director Erika Heilman, Sally Ashworth, Julie Devoll, Lindsey Dietrich, Brian Galvin, Alexandra Kephart, Julia Magnuson, Ella Morrish, Jon Shipley, Felicia Sinusas, and Alicyn Zall. Our gratitude as well to the leadership team at HBR, Adi Ignatius (who was key in convincing Paul to do the project), and Group Publisher Sarah McConville.

Finally, we thank our families, who are the inspiration for all we do and support us during the long and strange work hours of writers who are six hours apart. Andrew's parents, Jan and Gail Winston, deserve endless thanks for decades of unconditional support, and for instilling a sense of morality that guides Andrew's work and life. Christine Winston, an experienced businessperson, has long been Andrew's best editor and sounding board. While working full-time, she has taken on more than a fair share of the effort keeping the home going while Andrew has been distracted, typing away. Their boys, Joshua and Jacob, have grown from toddler and newborn when Andrew published his first book, to teenagers who can ask tough questions about the content and purpose. We all will rely on Gen Z to pick up the fight for a thriving world, and Andrew looks to his own two members of the action generation to go out and do good in the world.

Paul could not be prouder and more grateful to his family who not only contributed greatly by instilling values, but also by being great examples themselves. His parents, Bertus and Ria Polman, had a simple mission—to give their kids a better and meaningful life and tirelessly put themselves to the service of the greater good. Kim Polman has her own incredibly busy life as founder and chair of Reboot the Future, a social enterprise with a mission to create a more compassionate and sustainable world, via a radical shift in mindset founded on a rule as ancient as humanity itself: the Golden Rule. She is also chairing the main family foundation, Kilimanjaro Blind Trust, focused on unlocking literacy in Africa for the visually impaired. She herself knows what it takes to author a book and has published *Imaginal Cells: Visions of Transformation*, which gave us lots of inspiration. Whilst showing more than patience during our late hour book discussions and missed dinners, she also stimulated the creative flow with her live cello music.

Paul and Kim's sons, Christian, Philippe, and Sebastian, despite having busy family lives, have been good sports in encouraging the work and forcing us to go the extra mile. They are each, in their own way, trying to live the net positive life. Millennials might have started a bigger trend than we realize. For that, a big thanks.

And thank you to all the readers who will do the work of building a net positive, thriving world.

NOTES

Introduction: Why Mayo Beat Ketchup

1. Arash Massoudi, James Fontanella-Khan, and Bryce Elder, "Unilever Rejects $143bn Kraft Heinz Takeover Bid," *Financial Times*, February 17, 2017, https://on.ft.com/3eHeNM4.

2. Daniel Roberts, "Here's What Happens When 3G Capital Buys Your Company," *Fortune*, accessed March 3, 2021, https://fortune.com/2015/03/25/3g-capital-heinz-kraft-buffett/.

3. Arash Massoudi and James Fontanella-Khan, "The $143bn Flop: How Warren Buffett and 3G Lost Unilever," *Financial Times*, February 21, 2017, https://www.ft.com/content/d846766e-f81b-11e6-bd4e-68d53499ed71.

4. Ron Oswald (IUF), interview by author, September 28, 2020.

5. Harold Thompson (Ash Park), interview by author, April 24, 2020.

6. Vincent Lee (Bernstein), email communication with author, March 3, 2021.

7. "Unilever Announces Covid-19 Actions for All Employees," Unilever global company website, accessed March 3, 2021, https://www.unilever.com/news/news-and-features/Feature-article/2020/unilever-announces-covid-19-actions-for-all-employees.html.

8. "From Our CEO: We Will Fight This Pandemic Together," Unilever global company website, accessed March 4, 2021, https://www.unilever.com/news/news-and-features/Feature-article/2020/from-our-ceo-we-will-fight-this-pandemic-together.html.

9. Uday Sampath Kumar and Bhattacharjee Nivedita, "Kraft Heinz Discloses SEC Probe, $15 Billion Write-Down; Shares Dive 20 Percent," Reuters, February 22, 2019, https://www.reuters.com/article/us-kraft-heinz-results-idUSKCN1QA2W1; Gillian Tan and Paula Seligson, "Kraft Heinz Taps as Much as $4 Billion of Credit Line," Bloomberg, March 16, 2020, https://www.bloomberg.com/news/articles/2020-03-16/kraft-heinz-is-said-to-tap-as-much-as-4-billion-of-credit-line.

10. Mark Engel (Unilever), interview by author, May 14, 2020.

11. William McDonough and Michael Braungart, *The Upcycle* (New York: North-point Press, 2013), 35–36.

12. Kim Polman, *Imaginal Cells* (self-published, 2017), 8.

13. "Unilever, Patagonia, Ikea, Interface, and Natura &Co Most Recognized by Experts as Sustainability Leaders According to 2020 Leaders Survey," *GlobeScan* (blog), August 12, 2020, https://globescan.com/unilever-patagonia-ikea-interface-top-sustainability-leaders-2020/.

14. Dominic Waughray (WEF), interview by author, September 25, 2020.

15. *The Private Sector: The Missing Piece of the SDG Puzzle*, OECD, 2018.

16. "Citing $2.5 Trillion Annual Financing Gap during SDG Business Forum Event, Deputy Secretary-General Says Poverty Falling Too Slowly," UN, Meetings Coverage and Press Releases, accessed March 4, 2021, https://www.un.org/press/en

/2019/dsgsm1340.doc.htm; "International Aid Reached Record Levels in 2019," *New Humanitarian*, April 17, 2020, https://www.thenewhumanitarian.org/news/2020/04/17/international-aid-record-level-2019.

17. Emily Flitter, "Decade after Crisis, a $600 Trillion Market Remains Murky to Regulators," *New York Times*, July 22, 2018, https://www.nytimes.com/2018/07/22/business/derivatives-banks-regulation-dodd-frank.html.

18. *2020 Edelman Trust Barometer*, Edelman, January 2020, https://www.edelman.com/trust/2020-trust-barometer.

19. "A Message from Our Chief Executive Officer," 2020 ESG, accessed March 4, 2021, https://corporate.walmart.com/esgreport/a-message-from-our-chief-executive-officer.

20. Eben Shapiro, "'It's the Right Thing to Do.' Walmart CEO Doug McMillon Says It's Time to Reinvent Capitalism Post-Coronavirus," *Time*, October 21, 2020, https://time.com/collection-post/5900765/walmart-ceo-reinventing-capitalism/.

21. "Earth Overshoot Day—We Do Not Need a Pandemic to #MoveTheDate!" Earth Overshoot Day, accessed March 14, 2021, https://www.overshootday.org/.

22. Kenneth Boulding, "The Economics of the Coming Spaceship Earth," in *Radical Political Economy*, ed. Victor D. Lippit (Armonk, NY: M. E. Sharpe, 1966), 362.

23. Niall McCarthy, *Report: Global Wildlife Populations Have Declined 68% in 50 Years Due to Human Activity* [Infographic], *Forbes*, accessed March 7, 2021, https://www.forbes.com/sites/niallmccarthy/2020/09/10/report-global-wildlife-populations-have-declined-68-in-50-years-due-to-human-activity-infographic/.

24. "Rate of Deforestation," TheWorldCounts, accessed March 7, 2021, https://www.theworldcounts.com/challenges/planet-earth/forests-and-deserts/rate-of-deforestation/story; Alexander C. Kaufman, "Fossil Fuel Air Pollution Linked to 1 in 5 Deaths Worldwide, New Harvard Study Finds," HuffPost, accessed March 5, 2021, https://www.huffpost.com/entry/fossil-fuel-air-pollution_n_6022a51dc5b6c56a89a49185.

25. These systemic connections between natural systems and human health are the focus of the emerging field of planetary health. To learn more, see www.planetaryhealthalliance.org.

26. Luke Baker, "More Than 1 Billion People Face Displacement by 2050—Report," Reuters, September 9, 2020, https://www.reuters.com/article/ecology-global-risks-idUSKBN2600K4; see also Chi Xu et al., "Future of the Human Climate Niche," *Proceedings of the National Academy of Sciences* 117, no. 21 (May 26, 2020): 11350–55, https://doi.org/10.1073/pnas.1910114117.

27. Tim Cook (Apple), in keynote speech at Ceres 30th Anniversary Gala, October 21, 2019.

28. "Cases, Data, and Surveillance," Centers for Disease Control and Prevention, February 11, 2020, https://www.cdc.gov/coronavirus/2019-ncov/covid-data/investigations-discovery/hospitalization-death-by-race-ethnicity.html.

29. "Indigenous Tribes in Brazil Are Dying Twice as Much as the National Average Due to COVID-19," World Is One News, May 25, 2020, https://www.wionews.com/world/indigenous-tribals-in-brazil-are-dying-twice-as-much-as-the-national-average-due-to-covid-19-300952.

30. *SDG AMBITION: Introducing Business Benchmarks for the Decade of Action*, UN Global Compact, 2020.

31. "Nearly Half the World Lives on Less than $5.50 a Day," World Bank, accessed March 14, 2021, https://www.worldbank.org/en/news/press-release/2018/10/17/nearly-half-the-world-lives-on-less-than-550-a-day; "Learning Poverty," World Bank, accessed March 6, 2021, https://www.worldbank.org/en/topic/education/brief/learning

-poverty; *World Hunger Is Still Not Going Down after Three Years and Obesity Is Still Growing—UN Report*, accessed March 6, 2021, https://www.who.int/news/item/15 -07-2019-world-hunger-is-still-not-going-down-after-three-years-and-obesity-is-still -growing-un-report; "Children: Improving Survival and Well-Being," source: World Health Organization, accessed March 6, 2021, https://www.who.int/news-room/fact -sheets/detail/children-reducing-mortality.

32. "Secretary-General's Nelson Mandela Lecture: 'Tackling the Inequality Pandemic: A New Social Contract for a New Era' [as Delivered]," United Nations Secretary-General, July 18, 2020, https://www.un.org/sg/en/content/sg/statement /2020-07-18/secretary-generals-nelson-mandela-lecture-%E2%80%9Ctackling-the -inequality-pandemic-new-social-contract-for-new-era%E2%80%9D-delivered.

33. Mellody Hobson, "The Future of Sustainable Business Leadership," Ceres 2021, Virtual event, https://events.ceres.org/2021/agenda/session/430203.

34. Nick Hanauer and David M. Rolf, "America's 1% Has Taken $50 Trillion from the Bottom 90%," *Time*, accessed March 7, 2021, https://time.com/5888024/50-trillion -income-inequality-america/.

35. Rick Watzman, "Income Inequality: RAND Study Reveals Shocking New Numbers," accessed March 7, 2021, https://www.fastcompany.com/90550015/we-were -shocked-rand-study-uncovers-massive-income-shift-to-the-top-1.

36. "A Fifth of Countries Worldwide at Risk from Ecosystem Collapse as Biodiversity Declines, Reveals Pioneering Swiss Re Index," Swiss Re, accessed March 14, 2021, https://www.swissre.com/media/news-releases/nr-20200923-biodiversity-and -ecosystems-services.html.

37. "World Economy Set to Lose up to 18% GDP from Climate Change If No Action Taken, Reveals Swiss Re Institute's Stress-Test Analysis," Swiss Re, accessed May 6, 2021, https://www.swissre.com/media/news-releases/nr-20210422-economics-of -climate-change-risks.html.

38. "AT&T Commits to Be Carbon Neutral by 2035," AT&T, accessed March 7, 2021, https://about.att.com/story/2020/att_carbon_neutral.html.

39. Sarah Repucci and Amy Slipowitz, "Democracy under Lockdown," Freedom House, accessed March 9, 2021, https://freedomhouse.org/report/special-report/2020 /democracy-under-lockdown.

40. Vincent Wood, "Britons Enjoying Cleaner Air, Better Food and Stronger Social Bonds Say They Don't Want to Return to 'Normal,'" *Independent*, April 17, 2020, https://www.independent.co.uk/news/uk/home-news/coronavirus-uk-lockdown-end -poll-environment-food-health-fitness-social-community-a9469736.html.

41. Leslie Hook, "World's Top 500 Companies Set to Miss Paris Climate Goals," *Financial Times*, June 17, 2019, https://on.ft.com/2UAlNB3.

42. Sally Uren (Forum for the Future), email communication with authors, March 22, 2021.

43. "About Donella 'Dana' Meadows," *Academy for Systems Change* (blog), accessed March 7, 2021, http://donellameadows.org/donella-meadows-legacy/donella -dana-meadows/.

44. Jim Harter and Annamarie Mann, "The Right Culture: Not Just about Employee Satisfaction," Gallup.com, April 12, 2017, https://www.gallup.com/workplace /231602/right-culture-not-employee-satisfaction.aspx.

45. "Unilever's Purpose-Led Brands Outperform," Unilever global company website, accessed March 7, 2021, https://www.unilever.com/news/press-releases/2019 /unilevers-purpose-led-brands-outperform.html.

46. "Research Highlights," NYU Stern Center for Sustainable Business, accessed March 7, 2021, https://www.stern.nyu.edu/experience-stern/faculty-research/new

-meta-analysis-nyu-stern-center-sustainable-business-and-rockefeller-asset-manage
ment-finds-esg.

47. "Announcing the 2021 Rankings of America's Most JUST Companies,"
JUST Capital (blog), accessed March 7, 2021, https://justcapital.com/reports/
announcing-the-2021-rankings-of-americas-most-just-companies/.

48. Larry Fink, "BlackRock Client Letter—Sustainability," BlackRock, accessed
March 9, 2021, https://www.blackrock.com/corporate/investor-relations/blackrock
-client-letter; Jennifer Thompson, "Companies with Strong ESG Scores Outperform,
Study Finds," *Financial Times*, accessed March 9, 2021, https://www.ft.com/content
/f99b0399-ee67-3497-98ff-eed4b04cfde5.

49. Sophie Baker, "Global ESG-Data Driven Assets Hit $40.5 Trillion," Pensions &
Investments, July 2, 2020, https://www.pionline.com/esg/global-esg-data-driven-assets
-hit-405-trillion.

50. "Sustainable Bond Issuance to Hit a Record $650 Billion in 2021," Moody's, ac-
cessed March 9, 2021, https://www.moodys.com/research/Moodys-Sustainable-bond
-issuance-to-hit-a-record-650-billion--PBC_1263479.

51. "Larry Fink CEO Letter," BlackRock, accessed March 9, 2021, https://www
.blackrock.com/corporate/investor-relations/larry-fink-ceo-letter.

52. Alan Murray, "The 2019 Fortune 500 CEO Survey Results Are In," *Fortune*, accessed March 10, 2021, https://fortune.com/2019/05/16/fortune-500-2019-ceo-survey/.

53. Kathleen McLaughlin (Walmart), conversation with authors, September 20,
2020.

54. "What on Earth Is the Doughnut," accessed March 9, 2021, https://www
.kateraworth.com/doughnut/.

55. "Sustainable Business Could Unlock US$12 Trillion, Creating 380 Million
Jobs," Unilever global company website, accessed March 9, 2021, https://www.unilever
.com/news/news-and-features/Feature-article/2017/Sustainable-business-could-unlock
-12-trillion-dollars-and-380-million-jobs.html.

56. Hanna Ziady, "Climate Change: Net Zero Emissions Could Cost $2 Trillion a
Year, ETC Report Says," CNN Business, September 16, 2020, https://edition.cnn.com
/2020/09/16/business/net-zero-climate-energy-transitions-commission/index.html.

57. "CGR 2021," Circularity Gap Reporting Initiative, accessed March 14, 2021,
https://www.circularity-gap.world/2021.

58. "Record Number of Billion-Dollar Disasters Struck U.S. in 2020," National
Oceanic and Atmospheric Administration," accessed March 9, 2021, https://www.noaa
.gov/stories/record-number-of-billion-dollar-disasters-struck-us-in-2020.

59. "Solar's Future Is Insanely Cheap (2020)," Ramez Naam, May 14, 2020, https://
rameznaam.com/2020/05/14/solars-future-is-insanely-cheap-2020/.

60. Brian Murray, "The Paradox of Declining Renewable Costs and Rising Electricity Prices," *Forbes*, accessed March 9, 2021, https://www.forbes.com/sites/brian
murray1/2019/06/17/the-paradox-of-declining-renewable-costs-and-rising-electricity
-prices/.

61. *Levelized Cost of Energy Analysis*, vol. 14, Lazard, November 2020, https://
www.lazard.com/perspective/levelized-cost-of-energy-and-levelized-cost-of-storage
-2020/.

62. Paul Eisenstein, "GM to Go All-Electric by 2035, Phase Out Gas and Diesel
Engines," NBC News, accessed March 9, 2021, https://www.nbcnews.com/business
/autos/gm-go-all-electric-2035-phase-out-gas-diesel-engines-n1256055; Joshua S. Hill,
"Honda to Phase Out Diesel, Petrol Cars in UK in Favour of EVs by 2022," accessed
March 9, 2021, https://thedriven.io/2020/10/21/honda-to-phase-out-diesel-petrol-cars
-in-uk-in-favour-of-evs-by-2022/.

63. Fred Lambert, "Daimler Stops Developing Internal Combustion Engines to Focus on Electric Cars—Electrek," accessed March 9, 2021, https://electrek.co/2019/09 /19/daimler-stops-developing-internal-combustion-engines-to-focus-on-electric-cars/.

64. Gina McCarthy, "Press Briefing by Press Secretary," White House, January 27, 2021, https://www.whitehouse.gov/briefing-room/press-briefings/2021/01/27/press -briefing-by-press-secretary-jen-psaki-special-presidential-envoy-for-climate-john -kerry-and-national-climate-advisor-gina-mccarthy-january-27-2021/.

65. "Why Corporations Can No Longer Avoid Politics," *Time*, accessed March 9, 2021, https://time.com/5735415/woke-culture-political-companies/.

66. Tracy Francis and Fernanda Hoefel, "Generation Z Characteristics and Its Implications for Companies," McKinsey, accessed March 9, 2021, https://www.mckinsey .com/industries/consumer-packaged-goods/our-insights/true-gen-generation-z-and -its-implications-for-companies.

67. "7 UN Quotes to Get You Inspired for the New Global Goals," unfoundation .org, July 30, 2015, https://unfoundation.org/blog/post/7-un-quotes-to-get-you -inspired-for-the-new-global-goals/.

Chapter 1: You Break the World, You Own It

1. "Decline of Global Extreme Poverty Continues but Has Slowed," World Bank, September 19, 2018, https://www.worldbank.org/en/news/press-release/2018/09/19 /decline-of-global-extreme-poverty-continues-but-has-slowed-world-bank.

2. David Gelles, "Rose Marcario, the Former C.E.O. of Patagonia, Retreats to the Rainforest," *New York Times*, February 18, 2021, https://www.nytimes.com/2021/02 /18/business/rose-marcario-patagonia-corner-office.html.

3. Jasmine Wu, "Wayfair Employees Walk Out, Customers Call for Boycott in Protest over Bed Sales to Texas Border Detention Camp," CNBC, June 26, 2019, https:// www.cnbc.com/2019/06/26/wayfair-draws-backlash-calls-for-boycott-after-employee -protest.html.

4. Kati Najipoor-Schuette and Dick Patton, "Egon Zehnder Survey: CEOs Are Too Unprepared for Leadership," *Fortune*, April 24, 2018, https://fortune.com/2018/04/24 /egon-zehnder-ceos-leadership/.

5. Stéphane Garelli, "Top Reasons Why You Will Probably Live Longer Than Most Big Companies," IMD, December 2016, https://www.imd.org/research-knowledge /articles/why-you-will-probably-live-longer-than-most-big-companies/.

6. Jason M. Thomas, "Where Have All the Public Companies Gone?" *Wall Street Journal*, November 16, 2017, https://www.wsj.com/articles/where-have-all-the-public -companies-gone-1510869125.

7. "The Risk of Rewards: Tailoring Executive Pay for Long-Term Success," FCLT-Global, accessed May 25, 2021, https://www.fcltglobal.org/resource/executive-pay/.

8. *Short termism: Insights from Business Leaders,* CPPIB and McKinsey & Company, 2014, 5, exhibit 3, https://www.fcltglobal.org/wp-content/uploads/20140123-mck -quarterly-survey-results-for-fclt-org_final.pdf.

9. Dominic Barton, James Manyika, and Sarah Keohane Williamson, "Finally, Evidence That Managing for the Long Term Pays Off," *Harvard Business Review*, February 7, 2017, https://hbr.org/2017/02/finally-proof-that-managing-for-the-long-term -pays-off.

10. "Peter Drucker Quote," A–Z Quotes, accessed May 10, 2021, https://www .azquotes.com/quote/863677.

11. David MacLean, "It's Not About Profit," *Whole Hearted Leaders* (blog), October 12, 2016, https://www.wholeheartedleaders.com/its-not-about-profit/; "Henry

Ford Quotes," The Henry Ford, accessed March 11, 2021, https://www.thehenryford
.org/collections-and-research/digital-resources/popular-topics/henry-ford-quotes/.

12. Saikat Chatterjee and Thyagaraju Adinarayan, "Buy, Sell, Repeat! No Room for
'Hold' in Whipsawing Markets," Reuters, August 3, 2020, https://www.reuters.com
/article/us-health-coronavirus-short-termism-anal-idUSKBN24Z0XZ.

13. Bhakti Mirchandani et al., "Predicting Long-Term Success for Corporations
and Investors Worldwide," FCLTGlobal, September 2019, https://www.fcltglobal.org
/resource/predicting-long-term-success-for-corporations-and-investors-worldwide/.

14. "As Jobs Crisis Deepens, ILO Warns of Uncertain and Incomplete Labour Market Recovery," International Labour Organization, June 30, 2020, http://www.ilo.org
/global/about-the-ilo/newsroom/news/WCMS_749398/lang--en/index.htm.

15. Andrew Liveris (Dow), interview by authors, August 27, 2020.

16. *2019 Survey on Shareholder Versus Stakeholder Interests*, Stanford Graduate
School of Business and the Rock Center for Corporate Governance, 2019, 2.

17. "Our Credo," Johnson & Johnson, accessed March 11, 2021, https://www.jnj
.com/credo/.

18. Jessica Shankleman, "Tim Cook Tells Climate Change Sceptics to Ditch Apple
Shares," *Guardian*, March 3, 2014, http://www.theguardian.com/environment/2014
/mar/03/tim-cook-climate-change-sceptics-ditch-apple-shares.

19. "Fact Sheet: Obesity and Overweight," World Health Organization, April 1,
2020, https://www.who.int/news-room/fact-sheets/detail/obesity-and-overweight.

20. "Malnutrition Is a World Health Crisis," World Health Organization, September 26, 2019, https://www.who.int/news/item/26-09-2019-malnutrition-is-a-world
-health-crisis.

21. "The World Bank and Nutrition—Overview," World Bank, October 4, 2019,
https://www.worldbank.org/en/topic/nutrition/overview.

Chapter 2: How Much Do You Care?

1. Adam Smith, *The Theory of Moral Sentiments*, Stewart Ed. (London: Henry G.
Bohn, 1853), https://oll.libertyfund.org/title/smith-the-theory-of-moral-sentiments
-and-on-the-origins-of-languages-stewart-ed#lf1648_label_001.

2. "The Theory of Moral Sentiments," Adam Smith Institute, accessed March 12,
2021, https://www.adamsmith.org/the-theory-of-moral-sentiments.

3. Smith, *The Theory of Moral Sentiments*.

4. Kumi Naidoo, interview by authors, October 6, 2020.

5. Colin Mayer, *Prosperity: Better Business Makes the Greater Good*, 1st ed. (Oxford, United Kingdom: Oxford University Press, 2018).

6. Jenna Martin, "Add Wells Fargo CEO John Stumpf and Ingersoll-Rand CEO
Michael Lamach to List of Executives against North Carolina's House Bill 2," *Char-
lotte Business Journal*, March 31, 2016, https://www.bizjournals.com/charlotte/news
/2016/03/31/add-wells-fargo-ingersoll-rand-ceos-to-list-of.html.

7. Jon Kamp and Cameron McWhirter, "Business Leaders Speak Out against North
Carolina's Transgender Law," *Wall Street Journal*, March 30, 2016, https://www.wsj
.com/articles/business-leaders-speak-out-against-north-carolinas-transgender-law
-1459377292.

8. Josh Rottenberg, "New Oscars Standards Say Best Picture Contenders Must Be
Inclusive to Compete," *Los Angeles Times*, September 8, 2020, https://www.latimes
.com/entertainment-arts/movies/story/2020-09-08/academy-oscars-inclusion
-standards-best-picture.

9. Jeff Beer, "One Year Later, What Did We Learn from Nike's Blockbuster Colin Kaepernick Ad?" *Fast Company*, September 5, 2019, https://www.fastcompany.com/90399316/one-year-later-what-did-we-learn-from-nikes-blockbuster-colin-kaepernick-ad.

10. Ed Stack, *It's How We Play the Game: Build a Business, Take a Stand, Make a Difference* (New York: Scribner, 2019), 2.

11. Yvon Chouinard, *Let My People Go Surfing: The Education of a Reluctant Businessman* (New York: Penguin, 2005), 1.

12. Viktor E. Frankl, *Man's Search for Meaning: An Introduction to Logotherapy*, 3rd ed. (New York: Touchstone, 1984).

13. "State of Workplace Empathy: Executive Summary," Businessolver, 2020, https://info.businessolver.com/en-us/empathy-2020-exec-summary-ty.

14. Jostein Solheim (Unilever), interview by authors, August 28, 2020.

15. Clifton Leaf, "Why Mastercard Isn't a Credit Card Company, According to Its Outgoing CEO Ajay Banga," *Fortune*, December 3, 2020, https://fortune.com/longform/mastercard-ceo-ajay-banga-credit-card-payment-company/.

16. "Wipro Chairman Premji Pledges 34 Percent of Company Shares for Philanthropy," Reuters, March 13, 2019, https://www.reuters.com/article/us-wipro-premji-id USKBN1QU21H; "None Can Take Away Your Humility: Azim Premji," Bengaluru News—*Times of India*, accessed July 15, 2021, https://timesofindia.indiatimes.com/city/bengaluru/none-can-take-away-your-humility-azim-premji/articleshow/60140040.cms.

17. Nimi Princewill, "First Black Woman to Lead WTO Says She Will Prioritize Fair Trade, Access to Covid-19 Vaccines," CNN Business, accessed March 12, 2021, https://www.cnn.com/2021/02/15/business/ngozi-okonjo-iweala-wto-announcement-intl/index.html.

18. Ann McFerran, "'I Keep My Ego in My Handbag,'" *Guardian*, August 1, 2005, https://www.theguardian.com/world/2005/aug/01/gender.uk.

19. "Jesper Brodin," Ingka Group, accessed March 14, 2021, https://www.ingka.com/bios/jesper-brodin/.

20. Adam Bryant, "How to Be a C.E.O., from a Decade's Worth of Them," *New York Times*, October 27, 2017, https://www.nytimes.com/2017/10/27/business/how-to-be-a-ceo.html.

21. "Maya Angelou Quotes: 15 of the Best," *Guardian*, May 29, 2014, http://www.theguardian.com/books/2014/may/28/maya-angelou-in-fifteen-quotes.

22. "Climate Change: The Massive CO_2 Emitter You May Not Know About," BBC News, December 17, 2018, https://www.bbc.com/news/science-environment-46455844.

23. "Sustainability Practices Followed in Dalmia Bharat Group," Dalmia Bharat Group, accessed March 12, 2021, https://www.dalmiabharat.com/sustainability/.

24. We Mean Business Coalition, "Dalmia Cement CEO Mahendra Singhi on Setting Bold Science-Based Targets," YouTube, published September 14, 2018, https://www.youtube.com/watch?v=fgNioqdrSKE.

25. Elizabeth Kolbert, "The Weight of the World: The Woman Who Could Stop Climate Change," *New Yorker*, August 17, 2015, https://www.newyorker.com/magazine/2015/08/24/the-weight-of-the-world.

26. Arun Marsh, "Christiana Figueres on 'Godot Paralysis' and Courage," video, UN Global Compact Speaker Interviews, *Guardian*, October 18, 2013, https://www.theguardian.com/sustainable-business/video/christiana-figueres-godot-paralysis-courage.

27. Stack, *It's How We Play the Game*, 279.

28. Stack, *It's How We Play the Game*, 279.

29. Stack, *It's How We Play the Game*, 286.

30. Stack, *It's How We Play the Game*, 295.

31. Rachel Siegel, "Dick's Sporting Goods Reports Strong Earnings as It Experiments with Reducing Gun Sales," *Washington Post*, August 22, 2019, https://www.washingtonpost.com/business/2019/08/22/dicks-sporting-goods-stock-surges-strong-nd-quarter-earnings/.

32. Steve Denning, "Making Sense of Shareholder Value: 'The World's Dumbest Idea,'" *Forbes*, July 17, 2017, https://www.forbes.com/sites/stevedenning/2017/07/17/making-sense-of-shareholder-value-the-worlds-dumbest-idea/?sh=44bb59142a7c.

33. Bill George, "Courage: The Defining Characteristic of Great Leaders," op-ed, Harvard Business School Working Knowledge, April 24, 2017, http://hbswk.hbs.edu/item/courage-the-defining-characteristic-of-great-leaders.

34. Angie Drobnic Holan, "In Context: Donald Trump's 'Very Fine People on Both Sides' Remarks (Transcript)," PolitiFact, April 26, 2019, https://www.politifact.com/article/2019/apr/26/context-trumps-very-fine-people-both-sides-remarks/.

35. Adam Edelman, "Merck CEO Quits Trump Council over President's Charlottesville Remarks," NBC News, accessed March 11, 2021, https://www.nbcnews.com/politics/donald-trump/merck-ceo-quits-advisory-council-over-trump-s-charlottesville-remarks-n792416.

36. Amelia Lucas, "Merck CEO Kenneth Frazier: George Floyd 'Could Be Me,'" CNBC, June 1, 2020, https://www.cnbc.com/2020/06/01/merck-ceo-george-floyd-could-be-me.html.

37. Jeffrey Sonnenfeld, "CEOs and Racial Inequity," Chief Executive, September 9, 2020, https://chiefexecutive.net/ceos-and-racial-inequity/.

38. K. Bell, "Facebook staff plan 'virtual walkout' over response to Trump posts," Engadget, June 1, 2020, https://www.engadget.com/facebook-employees-virtual-walkout-trump-posts-175020522.html.

39. Nicole Schuman, "Airbnb CEO Delivers Empathetic, Transparent Message Regarding Layoffs," PRNEWS, May 7, 2020, https://www.prnewsonline.com/airbnb-ceo-delivers-empathetic-transparent-message-regarding-layoffs/.

40. Ed Kuffner, "It Was a Relatively Easy Decision: J&J Exec Shares Experience Working in the Frontlines," Yahoo! Finance, June 1, 2020, https://finance.yahoo.com/video/relatively-easy-decision-j-j-170640381.html.

41. Hannah Tan-Gillies, *"The Biggest Challenge Facing Our Generation"—Kering Commits to Net Positive Impact on Biodiversity by 2025*, Moodie Davitt Report, August 4, 2020, https://www.moodiedavittreport.com/the-biggest-challenge-facing-our-generation-kering-commits-to-net-positive-impact-on-biodiversity-by-2025/.

Chapter 3: Unlock the Company's Soul

1. Paul R. Lawrence and Nitin Nohria, *Driven: How Human Nature Shapes Our Choices*, 1st ed. (San Francisco: Jossey-Bass, 2002).

2. Tom Johnson, "Unilever Nabs Bestfoods for $24.3B," CNN Money, June 6, 2000, accessed March 10, 2021, https://money.cnn.com/2000/06/06/deals/bestfoods/.

3. *Short Termism: Insights from Business Leaders*, Focusing Capital on the Long Term, CPPIB and McKinsey & Company, January 2014, p. 5, exhibit 3, https://www.fcltglobal.org/wp-content/uploads/20140123-mck-quarterly-survey-results-for-fclt-org_final.pdf.

4. "Risk Report Reveals Pandemic Forced Companies to Review Strategy," Board Agenda, July 15, 2020, https://boardagenda.com/2020/07/15/risk-report-reveals-pandemic-forced-companies-to-review-strategy/.

5. Sandy Ogg (Unilever), interview by authors, April 4, 2020.

6. "Unilever Issues First Ever Green Sustainability Bond," Unilever global company website, March 19, 2014, https://www.unilever.com/news/press-releases/2014/14 -03-19-Unilever-issues-first-ever-green-sustainability-bond.html.

7. Marc Mathieu (Unilever), interview by authors, August 26, 2020.

8. Keith Weed (Unilever), interview by authors, November 10, 2020.

9. Robert Lofthouse, "Purpose Unlocks Profit," accessed March 15, 2021, https:// www.alumni.ox.ac.uk/quad/article/purpose-unlocks-profit.

10. Lauren Hirsch, "People Thought Hubert Joly Was 'Crazy or Suicidal' for Taking the Job as Best Buy CEO. Then He Ushered in Its Turnaround," CNBC, June 19, 2019, https://www.cnbc.com/2019/06/19/former-best-buy-ceo-hubert-joly-defied -expectations-at-best-buy.html.

11. Adele Peters, "This Food Giant Is Now the Largest B Corp in the World," *Fast Company*, April 12, 2018, https://www.fastcompany.com/40557647/this-food-giant-is -now-the-largest-b-corp-in-the-world.

12. "Danone: Annual General Meeting of June 26, 2020: Shareholders Unanimously Vote for Danone to Become the First Listed 'Entreprise à Mission,'" GlobeNewswire, June 26, 2020, http://www.globenewswire.com/news-release/2020/06/26/2054177/0/en /Danone-Annual-General-Meeting-of-June-26-2020-Shareholders-unanimously-vote -for-Danone-to-become-the-first-listed-Entreprise-%C3%A0-Mission.html.

13. Thomas W. Malnight, Ivy Buche, and Charles Dhanaraj, "Put Purpose at the Core of Your Strategy," *Harvard Business Review*, September 1, 2019, https://hbr.org /2019/09/put-purpose-at-the-core-of-your-strategy.

14. "Announcing the 2021 Rankings of America's Most JUST Companies," JUST Capital, accessed March 7, 2021, https://justcapital.com/reports/announcing-the-2021 -rankings-of-americas-most-just-companies/.

15. "Becoming Irresistible: A New Model for Employee Engagement," *Deloitte Review* 16, January 27, 2015, https://www2.deloitte.com/us/en/insights/deloitte-review /issue-16/employee-engagement-strategies.html.

16. "B Corp Analysis Reveals Purpose-Led Businesses Grow 28 Times Faster Than National Average," Sustainable Brands, March 1, 2018, https://sustainablebrands.com /read/business-case/b-corp-analysis-reveals-purpose-led-businesses-grow-28-times -faster-than-national-average.

17. "2018 Cone/Porter Novelli Purpose Study: How to Build Deeper Bonds, Amplify Your Message and Expand the Consumer Base," Cone Communications, accessed March 14, 2021, https://www.conecomm.com/research-blog/2018-purpose -study; *Meet the 2020 Consumers Driving Change*, IBM and National Retail Federation, 2020, 1.

18. Dr. Wieland Holfelder, in "Chance of a Lifetime? How Governments and Businesses Are Achieving a Green Economic Recovery," Facebook video, The Climate Group: Climate Week NYC, September 22, 2020, https://www.facebook.com/The ClimateGroup/videos/chance-of-a-lifetime-how-governments-and-businesses-are -achieving-a-green-econom/629022581139808/ (see minute 36).

19. "Report Shows a Third of Consumers Prefer Sustainable Brands," Unilever global company website, January 5, 2017, https://www.unilever.com/news/press -releases/2017/report-shows-a-third-of-consumers-prefer-sustainable-brands.html

20. "Our History," Unilever UK & Ireland, accessed March 27, 2021, https://www .unilever.co.uk/about/who-we-are/our-history/.

21. Claire Phillips, "Hubris and Colonial Capitalism in a 'Model' Company Town: The Case of Leverville, 1911–1940—Benoît Henriet," *Comparing the Copperbelt* (blog), October 2, 2017, https://copperbelt.history.ox.ac.uk/2017/10/02/hubris-and

-colonial-capitalism-in-a-model-company-town-the-case-of-leverville-1911-1940
-benoit-henriet/.

22. Thomas W. Malnight, Ivy Buche, and Charles Dhanaraj, "Put Purpose at the Core of Your Strategy," *Harvard Business Review*, September 1, 2019, https://hbr.org /2019/09/put-purpose-at-the-core-of-your-strategy.

23. Gavin Neath, interview by authors, April 10, 2020.

24. Jonathan Donner (Unilever), interview by authors, October 1, 2020.

25. William W. George, Krishna G. Palepu, Carin-Isabel Knoop, and Matthew Preble, "Unilever's Paul Polman: Developing Global Leaders," HBS Case no. N9-413-097 (Boston: Harvard Business School Publishing, 2013), 7, https://www.hbs.edu/faculty /Pages/item.aspx?num=44876.

26. "Mars CEO Speaks on How Gen Z Are Changing the Company's Workplace," *Corporate Citizenship Briefing* (blog), February 28, 2020, https://ccbriefing.corporate -citizenship.com/2020/02/28/mars-ceo-speaks-on-how-gen-z-are-changing-the -companys-workplace/.

27. Jack Kelly, "Millennials Will Become Richest Generation In American History as Baby Boomers Transfer over Their Wealth," *Forbes*, October 26, 2019, https://www .forbes.com/sites/jackkelly/2019/10/26/millennials-will-become-richest-generation -in-american-history-as-baby-boomers-transfer-over-their-wealth/.

28. "The Deloitte Global Millennial Survey 2020," Deloitte, June 2020, https:// www2.deloitte.com/global/en/pages/about-deloitte/articles/millennialsurvey.html.

29. "2016 Cone Communications Millennial Employee Engagement Study," Cone Communications, accessed March 14, 2021, https://www.conecomm.com/research -blog/2016-millennial-employee-engagement-study.

30. Brandon Rigoni and Bailey Nelson, "For Millennials, Is Job-Hopping Inevitable?" Gallup, November 8, 2016, https://news.gallup.com/businessjournal/197234 /millennials-job-hopping-inevitable.aspx.

31. "Engage Your Employees to See High Performance and Innovation," Gallup, accessed March 14, 2021, https://www.gallup.com/workplace/229424/employee -engagement.aspx.

32. "Open Letter to Jeff Bezos and the Amazon Board of Directors," Amazon Employees for Climate Justice, Medium, April 10, 2019, https://amazonemployees4climate justice.medium.com/public-letter-to-jeff-bezos-and-the-amazon-board-of-directors -82a8405f5e38.

33. Jay Greene, "More than 350 Amazon Employees Violate Communications Policy Directed at Climate Activists," *Washington Post*, January 27, 2020, https://www .washingtonpost.com/technology/2020/01/26/amazon-employees-plan-mass-defiance -company-communications-policy-support-colleagues/.

34. "Goldman Sachs to Offer Employees Clean Home Energy," Smart Energy Decisions, February 8, 2021, https://www.smartenergydecisions.com/renewable-energy /2021/02/08/goldman-sachs-to-offer-employees-clean-home-energy.

35. "Members," Time to Vote, accessed March 14, 2021, https://www.maketimeto vote.org/pages/members; Jazmin Goodwin, "Old Navy to Pay Store Employees to Work Election Polls in November," CNN Business, September 1, 2020, https://www.cnn.com /2020/09/01/business/old-navy-employee-pay-election-poll-workers/index.html.

36. "Employers Boosting Efforts to Create Respect and Dignity at Work," Yahoo! Finance, February 5, 2020, https://finance.yahoo.com/news/employers-boosting -efforts-create-respect-155356022.html.

37. Claudine Gartenberg, Andrea Prat, and Georgios Serafeim, "Corporate Purpose and Financial Performance," HBS working paper 17-023 (Boston: Harvard Business School, March 23, 2017), https://dash.harvard.edu/handle/1/30903237.

Chapter 4: Blow Up Boundaries

1. David Causey, "When We Fear the Unknown," Warrior's Journey, accessed March 14, 2021, https://thewarriorsjourney.org/challenges/when-we-fear-the-unknown/.

2. Christiana Figueres, Tom Rivett-Carnac, and Paul Dickinson, "86: The Scientific Case for the Race to Zero with Johan Rockström," January 28, 2021, in *Outrage + Optimism*, podcast, https://outrageandoptimism.libsyn.com/86-the-scientific-case-for-the-race-to-zero-with-johan-rockstrm.

3. Gavin Neath (Unilever), written correspondence with authors, April 10, 2020.

4. "Decarbonising Our Business," Unilever global company website, accessed March 14, 2021, https://www.unilever.com/planet-and-society/climate-action/decarbonising-our-business/.

5. "Unilever Opens \$272m Manufacturing Plant in Dubai," Sustainable Brands, December 27, 2016, https://sustainablebrands.com/read/press-release/unilever-opens-272m-manufacturing-plant-in-dubai.

6. "2019 Sustainability in a Generation Plan," Mars, Incorporated, accessed March 14, 2021, https://www.mars.com/sustainability-plan.

7. "Top 25 Quotes by Azim Premji," A–Z Quotes, accessed March 14, 2021, https://www.azquotes.com/author/11855-Azim_Premji.

8. In situations like optimizing a building's performance, it may be much cheaper than trying to make each component (windows, HVAC, and so on) efficient. The whole thing can be cheaper than the parts. See Paul Hawken, Amory B. Lovins, and L. Hunter Lovins, "Chapter 6: Tunneling Through the Cost Barrier," in *Natural Capitalism: Creating the Next Industrial Revolution*, 1st ed. (Boston: Little, Brown and Co., 1999).

9. Tim Cook (Apple), in keynote speech at Ceres 30th Anniversary event, New York, October 21, 2019.

10. Jemima McEvoy, "Sephora First to Accept '15% Pledge,' Dedicating Shelf-Space to Black-Owned Businesses," *Forbes*, June 10, 2020, https://www.forbes.com/sites/jemimamcevoy/2020/06/10/sephora-first-to-accept-15-pledge-dedicating-shelf-space-to-black-owned-businesses/.

11. Dana Givens, "Sephora Relaunches Business Incubator to Help BIPOC Beauty Entrepreneurs," Black Enterprise, February 10, 2021, https://www.blackenterprise.com/sephora-relaunches-business-incubator-to-help-bipoc-beauty-entrepreneurs/.

12. "Unilever Commits to Help Build a More Inclusive Society," Unilever global company website, January 21, 2021, https://www.unilever.com/news/press-releases/2021/unilever-commits-to-help-build-a-more-inclusive-society.html.

13. "Companies Taking Action," Science Based Targets, accessed March 14, 2021, https://sciencebasedtargets.org/companies-taking-action.

14. "330+ Target-Setting Firms Reduce Emissions by a Quarter in Five Years since Paris Agreement," Science Based Targets, January 26, 2021, https://sciencebasedtargets.org/news/330-target-setting-firms-reduce-emissions-by-a-quarter-in-five-years-since-paris-agreement.

15. "Response Required: How the Fortune Global 500 Is Delivering Climate Action and the Urgent Need for More of It," Natural Capital Partners, October 6, 2020, https://www.naturalcapitalpartners.com/news-resources/response-required.

16. Brad Smith, "Microsoft Will Be Carbon Negative by 2030," *The Official Microsoft Blog* (blog), January 16, 2020, https://blogs.microsoft.com/blog/2020/01/16/microsoft-will-be-carbon-negative-by-2030/.

17. Brad Smith, "One Year Later: The Path to Carbon Negative—A Progress Report on Our Climate 'Moonshot,'" *The Official Microsoft Blog* (blog), January 28, 2021; Chuck Abbott, "Land O'Lakes, Microsoft in Carbon Credit Program,"

Successful Farming, February 5, 2021, https://www.agriculture.com/news/business/land-o-lakes-microsoft-in-carbon-credit-program.

18. Alan Jope, email with authors, March 23, 2021.

19. Sundar Pichai, "Our Third Decade of Climate Action: Realizing a Carbon-Free Future," *Google—The Keyword* (blog), September 14, 2020, https://blog.google/outreach-initiatives/sustainability/our-third-decade-climate-action-realizing-carbon-free-future/.

20. Justine Calma, "IBM Sets New Climate Goal for 2030," The Verge, February 16, 2021, https://www.theverge.com/2021/2/16/22285669/ibm-climate-change-commitment-cut-greenhouse-gas-emissions; IBM is also looking to 2030 for 90 to 100 percent renewables, without offsets or sequestration.

21. Brian Moynihan, Feike Sijbesma, and Klaus Schwab, "World Economic Forum Asks All Davos Participants to Set a Net-Zero Climate Target," World Economic Forum, January 17, 2020, https://www.weforum.org/agenda/2020/01/davos-ceos-to-set-net-zero-target-2050-climate/.

22. "Ingka Group Produces More Renewable Energy than It Consumes—2020 Report," Energy Capital Media (blog), January 28, 2021, https://energycapitalmedia.com/2021/01/28/ingka-group-ikea/.

23. Doug McMillon, "Walmart's Regenerative Approach: Going Beyond Sustainability," Walmart Inc., September 21, 2020, https://corporate.walmart.com/newsroom/2020/09/21/walmarts-regenerative-approach-going-beyond-sustainability.

24. Arjun Kharpal, "Apple pledges to make products like the iPhone from only recycled material and end mining," CNBC, April 20, 2017, https://www.cnbc.com/2017/04/20/apple-mining-end-recycled-material-products.html.

25. "Morgan Stanley Announces Commitment to Reach Net-Zero Financed Emissions by 2050," Morgan Stanley, September 21, 2020, https://www.morganstanley.com/press-releases/morgan-stanley-announces-commitment-to-reach-net-zero-financed-e. ; "Bank of America Announces Actions to Achieve Net Zero Greenhouse Gas Emissions before 2050," Bank of America Newsroom, February 11, 2021, https://newsroom.bankofamerica.com/content/newsroom/press-releases/2021/02/bank-of-america-announces-actions-to-achieve-net-zero-greenhouse.html; "New Citi CEO Jane Fraser Unveils Net-Zero Targets on First Day at the Helm, " Financial News, accessed March 11, 2021, https://www.fnlondon.com/articles/new-citi-ceo-jane-fraser-unveils-net-zero-targets-in-first-day-at-the-helm-20210301.

26. Graham Readfearn, "Insurance Giant Suncorp to End Coverage and Finance for Oil and Gas Industry," *Guardian*, August 21, 2020, http://www.theguardian.com/environment/2020/aug/21/insurance-giant-suncorp-to-end-coverage-and-finance-for-oil-and-gas-industry.

27. "2019 CDP Climate Response," Target Corporation, 2019, https://corporate.target.com/_media/TargetCorp/csr/pdf/2019-CDP-Climate-Response.pdf.

28. "Tesco Set to Become First UK Retailer to Offer Sustainability-Linked Supply Chain Finance," Tesco PLC, accessed May 13, 2021, www.tescoplc.com/news/2021/tesco-set-to-become-first-uk-retailer-to-offer-sustainability-linked-supply-chain-finance/.

29. "Salesforce Suppliers Must Maintain Sustainability Scorecard," *Environment + Energy Leader* (blog), April 30, 2021, https://www.environmentalleader.com/2021/04/salesforce-suppliers-must-maintain-sustainability-scorecard-or-pay-climate-remediation-fee/.

30. "Unilever to Eliminate Fossil Fuels in Cleaning Products by 2030," Unilever global company website, accessed March 15, 2021, https://www.unilever.com/news

/press-releases/2020/unilever-to-invest-1-billion-to-eliminate-fossil-fuels-in-cleaning
-products-by-2030.html.

31. "Tackling Climate Change," Starbucks Coffee Company, accessed March 14,
2021, https://www.starbucks.com/responsibility/environment/climate-change.

32. Lauren Wicks, "Panera Bread Commits to Making Half of Its Menu Plant-
Based," EatingWell, January 10, 2020, https://www.eatingwell.com/article/7561530
/panera-bread-plant-based-menu/.

33. "Zero Hunger, Zero Waste," Kroger Co., accessed March 14, 2021, https://www
.thekrogerco.com/sustainability/zero-hunger-zero-waste/.

34. Hannah Tan-Gillies, *"The Biggest Challenge Facing Our Generation"—Kering
Commits to Net Positive Impact on Biodiversity by 2025*, Moodie Davitt Report, August 4, 2020, https://www.moodiedavittreport.com/the-biggest-challenge-facing-our
-generation-kering-commits-to-net-positive-impact-on-biodiversity-by-2025/.

35. Mandy Oaklander, "Suicide Is Preventable. Hospitals and Doctors Are Finally
Catching Up," *Time*, October 24, 2019, https://time.com/5709368/how-to-solve-suicide/.

36. Jane Fraser, "The Incoming CEO of Citigroup, on How to Smash the Glass
Ceiling," interview by Eben Shapiro, *Time*, October 21, 2020, https://time.com
/collection-post/5900752/jane-fraser-citibank/.

37. "Mastercard Commits to Connect 1 Billion People to the Digital Economy
by 2025," Mastercard Center for Inclusive Growth, April 28, 2020, http://www
.mastercardcenter.org/content/mc-cig/en/homepage/press-releases/mastercard
-commits-to-connect-1billion-by-2025.html.

38. "Ørsted (Company)," *Wikipedia*, accessed March 2, 2021, https://en.wikipedia
.org/w/index.php?title=%C3%98rsted_(company)&oldid=1009848863.

39. "Climate Change Action Plan," Ørsted, accessed March 14, 2021, https://orsted
.com/en/sustainability/climate-action-plan.

40. *BP Annual Report and Form 20-F 2019, 152; Ørsted Annual Report 2020*, 98.
(Note: Ørsted reports in DKK (Danish Kroner); the figure is converted from the exchange rate on March 13, 2021.)

41. "Neste Reports Slump in Oil Sales but Growth in Renewables," Yle Uutiset,
May 2, 2021, https://yle.fi/uutiset/osasto/news/neste_reports_slump_in_oil_sales_but
_growth_in_renewables/11775415.

42. Stephen Jewkes, "Enel to Boost Spending on Clean Energy in Climate Goal
Drive," Reuters, November 26, 2019, https://www.reuters.com/article/uk-enel-plan
-idUKKBN1Y00RL?edition-redirect=uk; "Commitment to the fight against climate
change," Enel Group, accessed March 14; 2021, https://www.enel.com/investors
/sustainability/sustainability-topics-and-performances/greenhouse-gas-emission.

43. Megan Graham, "Unilever Pauses Facebook and Twitter Advertising for Rest of
2020 Due to 'Polarized Atmosphere' in U.S.," CNBC, June 26, 2020, https://www.cnbc
.com/2020/06/26/unilever-pauses-facebook-and-twitter-advertising-for-rest-of-2020
-due-to-polarized-atmosphere-in-us.html.

Chapter 5: Be an Open Book

1. Geoffrey Mohan and Ben Welsh, "Q&A: How Much Pollution Did VW's Emissions Cheating Create?" *Los Angeles Times*, October 9, 2015, https://www.latimes.com
/business/la-fi-vw-pollution-footprint-20151007-htmlstory.html.

2. Alexander C. Kaufman, "Fossil Fuel Air Pollution Linked to 1 In 5 Deaths
Worldwide, New Harvard Study Finds," HuffPost, February 9, 2021, https://www
.huffpost.com/entry/fossil-fuel-air-pollution_n_6022a51dc5b6c56a89a49185.

3. Jack Ewing, "Volkswagen Says 11 Million Cars Worldwide Are Affected in Diesel Deception," *New York Times*, September 22, 2015, https://www.nytimes.com/2015/09/23/business/international/volkswagen-diesel-car-scandal.html.

4. Naomi Kresge and Richard Weiss, "Volkswagen Drops 23% After Admitting Diesel Emissions Cheat," Bloomberg Business, September 21, 2015, https://www.bloomberg.com/news/articles/2015-09-21/volkswagen-drops-15-after-admitting-u-s-diesel-emissions-cheat.

5. Associated Press, "Volkswagen Offers 830 Mln-Euro Diesel Settlement in Germany," *US News and World Report*, February 14, 2020, https://www.usnews.com/news/business/articles/2020-02-14/volkswagen-offers-830-mln-euro-diesel-settlement-in-germany.

6. Jessica Long, Chris Roark, and Bill Theofilou, "The Bottom Line on Trust," Accenture Strategy, 2018, https://www.accenture.com/_acnmedia/Thought-Leadership-Assets/PDF/Accenture-Competitive-Agility-Index.pdf.

7. *2021 Edelman Trust Barometer*, Edelman, 2021, 19, https://www.edelman.com/sites/g/files/aatuss191/files/2021-01/2021-edelman-trust-barometer.pdf.

8. Paul J. Zak, "The Neuroscience of Trust," *Harvard Business Review*, January–February 2017, 84-90, https://hbr.org/2017/01/the-neuroscience-of-trust.

9. *2020 Edelman Trust Barometer*, Edelman, 2020, 2, https://www.edelman.com/trust/2020-trust-barometer.

10. Romesh Ratnesar, "How Microsoft's Brad Smith Is Trying to Restore Your Trust in Big Tech," *Time*, September 9, 2019, https://time.com/5669537/brad-smith-microsoft-big-tech/.

11. Peter Tchir, "What If Buffett Is the One Swimming Naked?" *Forbes*, accessed March 14, 2021, https://www.forbes.com/sites/petertchir/2020/05/04/what-if-buffett-is-the-one-swimming-naked/.

12. "ESG Trends in the 2019 Proxy Season," *FrameworkESG* (blog), July 18, 2019, http://staging.frameworkesg.com/esg-for-cxos-2019-proxy-season-trends/.

13. "S&P Global Makes over 9,000 ESG Scores Publicly Available to Help Increase Transparency of Corporate Sustainability Performance," S&P Global, February 16, 2021, http://press.spglobal.com/2021-02-16-S-P-Global-makes-over-9-000-ESG-Scores-publicly-available-to-help-increase-transparency-of-corporate-sustainability-performance.

14. BlackRock, "Climate Risk and the Transition to a Low-Carbon Economy," Investment Stewardship Commentary. February 2021, https://www.blackrock.com/corporate/literature/publication/blk-commentary-climate-risk-and-energy-transition.pdf.

15. "Intangible Asset Market Value Study," Ocean Tomo, accessed March 15, 2021, https://www.oceantomo.com/intangible-asset-market-value-study/.

16. Jan Kees Vis (Unilever), interview by authors, May 20, 2020.

17. "Larry Fink CEO Letter," BlackRock, accessed March 9, 2021, https://www.blackrock.com/corporate/investor-relations/larry-fink-ceo-letter.

18. "Unilever Completes Landmark Fragrance Disclosure in Industry-Leading Move," Unilever USA, January 22, 2019, https://www.unileverusa.com/news/press-releases/2019/Unilever-completes-landmark-fragrance-disclosure.html.

19. "Unilever Has Raised the Bar for Fragrance Transparency," Environmental Working Group, January 22, 2019, https://www.ewg.org/release/ewg-unilever-has-raised-bar-fragrance-transparency.

20. "The No No List," Panera Bread, April 16, 2018, https://www-beta.panerabread.com/content/dam/panerabread/documents/panera-no-no-list-05-2015.pdf; "Panera

Bread's Food Policy Statement," Panera Bread, June 3, 2014, https://www.panerabread .com/content/dam/panerabread/documents/nutrition/panera-bread-food-policy.pdf.

21. "Unilever Sets out New Actions to Fight Climate Change, and Protect and Re-generate Nature, to Preserve Resources for Future Generations," Unilever global company website, June 15, 2020, https://www.unilever.com/news/press-releases/2020 /unilever-sets-out-new-actions-to-fight-climate-change-and-protect-and-regenerate -nature-to-preserve-resources-for-future-generations.html.

22. "Unilever: How AI Can Help Save Forests—Journal Report," MarketScreener, accessed March 11, 2021, https://www.marketscreener.com/quote/stock/UNILEVER -PLC-9590186/news/Unilever-nbsp-How-AI-Can-Help-Save-Forests-Journal-Report -31682505/.

23. Doina Cocoveanu (Unilever), interview by authors, May 21, 2020.

24. Tim Kleinebenne (Unilever), interview by authors, September 9, 2020.

25. "Unilever Commits to Help Build a More Inclusive Society," Unilever global company website, January 21, 2021, https://www.unilever.com/news/press-releases /2021/unilever-commits-to-help-build-a-more-inclusive-society.html.

26. Sharan Burrow (International Trade Union Confederation), interview by authors, May 18, 2020.

27. James Davey, "UK Food Retailers Hand Back $2.4 Billion in Property Tax Re-lief," Reuters, December 3, 2020, https://www.reuters.com/article/us-sainsbury-s -business-rates/uk-food-retailers-hand-back-2-4-billion-in-property-tax-relief-id USKBN28D1DC.

28. Joshua Franklin and Lawrence Delevingne, "Exclusive: U.S. Companies Got Emergency Government Loans despite Having Months of Cash," Reuters, May 7, 2020, https://www.reuters.com/article/us-health-coronavirus-companies-ppp-excl/exclusive -u-s-companies-got-emergency-government-loans-despite-having-months-of-cash-id USKBN22J2WO.

29. "Ikea Planning to Repay Furlough Payments," BBC News, June 15, 2020, https://www.bbc.com/news/business-53047895.

30. Darrell Etherington, "Medtronic is sharing its portable ventilator design speci-fications and code for free to all," TechCrunch, March 30, 2020, https://tech crunch.com/2020/03/30/medtronic-is-sharing-its-portable-ventilator-design -specifications-and-code-for-free-to-all/.

31. Lauren Hirsch, "IBM Gets Out of Facial Recognition Business, Calls on Con-gress to Advance Policies Tackling Racial Injustice," CNBC, June 8, 2020, https:// www.cnbc.com/2020/06/08/ibm-gets-out-of-facial-recognition-business-calls-on -congress-to-advance-policies-tackling-racial-injustice.html.

32. They were right. In the end, 150 of the 169 SDG targets needed business to succeed.

33. Geoffrey Jones, "Managing Governments: Unilever in India and Turkey, 1950–1980," HBS, working paper 06-061 (Boston: Harvard Business School, 2006), https:// www.hbs.edu/ris/Publication%20Files/06-061.pdf.

34. Shaun Walker, "30 Greenpeace Activists Charged with Piracy in Russia," *Guardian*, October 3, 2013, http://www.theguardian.com/environment/2013/oct/03 /greenpeace-activists-charged-piracy-russia.

35. Kumi Naidoo, interview by authors, October 6, 2020.

Chapter 6: 1+1=11

1. Tony Dunnage (Unilever), interview by authors, June 10, 2020.

2. "Sustainable Business Could Unlock US$12 Trillion, Creating 380 Million Jobs," Unilever global company website, accessed March 9, 2021, https://www.unilever.com /news/news-and-features/Feature-article/2017/Sustainable-business-could-unlock-12 -trillion-dollars-and-380-million-jobs.html.

3. Jonathan Hughes and Jeff Weiss, "Simple Rules for Making Alliances Work," *Harvard Business Review*, November 1, 2007, https://hbr.org/2007/11/simple-rules -for-making-alliances-work.

4. Steve Miles (Unilever), interview by authors, October 7, 2020.

5. Mark Engel (Unilever), interview by author, May 14, 2020.

6. Mark Engel (Unilever), interview by author, July 17, 2020.

7. Marc Benioff, *Trailblazer* (New York: Currency, 2019).

8. Maria Gallucci, "Apple's Low-Carbon Aluminum Is a Climate Game Changer," *Grist* (blog), July 31, 2020, https://grist.org/energy/apples-low-carbon-aluminum-is-an -climate-game-changer/.

9. "What Is ELYSIS?" ELYSIS, January 31, 2019, https://elysis.com/en/what-is -elysis.

10. Stephen Nellis, "Apple Buys First-Ever Carbon-Free Aluminum from Alcoa-Rio Tinto Venture," Reuters, December 5, 2019, https://www.reuters.com/article/us -apple-aluminum/apple-buys-first-ever-carbon-free-aluminum-from-alcoa-rio-tinto -venture-idUSKBN1Y91RQ.

11. Felicia Jackson, "Low Carbon Aluminum Boosted By Audi's Use in Automotive First," *Forbes*, accessed March 26, 2021, https://www.forbes.com/sites/felicia jackson/2021/03/24/low-carbon-aluminum-boosted-by-audis-use-in-automotive-first/.

12. "From Our CEO: We Will Fight This Pandemic Together," Unilever global company website, accessed March 4, 2021, https://www.unilever.com/news/news-and -features/Feature-article/2020/from-our-ceo-we-will-fight-this-pandemic-together .html.

13. Christopher Rowland and Laurie McGinley, "Merck to Help Make Johnson & Johnson Coronavirus Vaccine," *Washington Post*, March 2, 2021, https://www .washingtonpost.com/health/2021/03/02/merck-johnson-and-johnson-covid-vaccine -partnership/.

14. "LCA Study Finds Corrugated Cardboard Pallets as the Most 'Nature-Friendly' Standardized Loading Platform," KraftPal Technologies, August 6, 2020, https://kraftpal.com/news/lca-study-corrugated-cardboard-pallet/.

15. *Leveraging Modular Boxes in a Global Secondary Packaging System of FMCG Supply Chains*, Consumer Goods Forum, 2017, 7.

16. "Agricultural Land (% of Land Area)," World Bank Group, DataBank, accessed March 10, 2021, https://data.worldbank.org/indicator/AG.LND.AGRI.ZS; Tariq Khokhar, "Chart: Globally, 70% of Freshwater Is Used for Agriculture," World Bank Blogs (blog), March 22, 2017, https://blogs.worldbank.org/opendata/chart-globally-70 -freshwater-used-agriculture; Natasha Gilbert, "One-Third of Our Greenhouse Gas Emissions Come from Agriculture," *Nature News*, October 31, 2012, https://doi.org /10.1038/nature.2012.11708.

17. "The Consumer Goods Forum Launches Food Waste Coalition of Action," Consumer Goods Forum, August 17, 2020, https://www.theconsumergoodsforum .com/news_updates/the-consumer-goods-forum-launches-food-waste-coalition-of -action/.

18. *A New Textiles Economy: Redesigning Fashion's Future*, Ellen MacArthur Foundation, 2017, figure 6.

19. "About the RBA," Responsible Business Alliance, accessed March 10, 2021, http://www.responsiblebusiness.org/about/rba/.

20. "ICT Industry Agrees Landmark Science-Based Pathway to Reach Net Zero Emissions," GSMA Association, February 27, 2020, https://www.gsma.com/newsroom /press-release/ict-industry-agrees-landmark-science-based-pathway-to-reach-net-zero -emissions/.

21. *Global Warming Potential (GWP) of Refrigerants: Why Are Particular Values Used?* United Nations Environment Programme; Rob Garner, "NASA Study Shows That Common Coolants Contribute to Ozone Depletion," NASA, October 21, 2015, http://www.nasa.gov/press-release/goddard/nasa-study-shows-that-common-coolants -contribute-to-ozone-depletion.

22. Amy Larkin and Kert Davies, *Natural Refrigerants: The Solutions*, Greenpeace, 2009, https://www.greenpeace.org/usa/wp-content/uploads/legacy/Global/usa/planet3 /PDFs/hfc-solutions-fact-sheet.pdf.

23. "Coca-Cola Installs 1 Millionth HFC-Free Cooler," Coca-Cola Company, January 22, 2014, https://www.coca-colacompany.com/press-releases/coca-cola-installs-1 -millionth-hfc-free-cooler; "Mission Accomplished," Refrigerants, Naturally!, June 25, 2018, https://www.refrigerantsnaturally.com/2018/06/25/mission-accomplished/.

24. Amy Larkin, email communication with authors, October 12, 2020.

25. Lillianna Byington, "Diageo and PepsiCo Will Debut Paper Bottles in 2021," Food Dive, July 14, 2020, https://www.fooddive.com/news/diageo-and-pepsico-will -debut-paper-bottles-in-2021/581512/.

26. Hannah Baker, "Asda, Costa and Morrisons among retailers to sign up to scheme to cut single-use plastic," Business Live, November 12, 2019, https://www .business-live.co.uk/retail-consumer/asda-single-use-plastic-refill-17241796.

27. "Indonesia In-Store Refill Station Launches with 11 Unilever Brands," Unilever global company website, June 3, 2020, https://www.unilever.com/news/news-and -features/Feature-article/2020/indonesia-in-store-refill-station-launches-with-11 -unilever-brands.html.

28. Rebecca Marmot, interview by author, June 22, 2020.

29. Charlie Beevor, interview by author, October 6, 2020. Beevor says that 2.3 billion people live without access to a safe toilet, and 4.5 billion live in places where human waste is not safely managed.

30. Marmot, interview.

31. Sanjiv Mehta, interview by author, October 21, 2020.

32. *Global Market Report: Tea*, International Institute for Sustainable Development, 2019, 1.

33. "The World's Top Tea-Producing Countries," WorldAtlas, September 17, 2020, https://www.worldatlas.com/articles/the-worlds-top-10-tea-producing-nations.html; "Rwandan Tea Sector," Gatsby, accessed March 10, 2021, https://www.gatsby.org.uk /africa/programmes/rwandan-tea-sector.

34. "Unilever Tea Rwanda Project Inaugurated in Nyaruguru District," MINAGRI Government of the Republic of Rwanda, accessed March 10, 2021, https://minagri.prod .risa.rw/updates/news-details/unilever-tea-rwanda-project-inaugurated-in-nyaruguru -district-1.

35. Cheryl Hicks (TBC), email communication with authors, April 1, 2021.

36. Doug Baker (Ecolab), interview by authors, May 12, 2020.

Chapter 7: It Takes Three to Tango

1. Barry Newell and Christopher Doll, "Systems Thinking and the Cobra Effect," United Nations University, *Our World* (blog), September 16, 2015, https://ourworld .unu.edu/en/systems-thinking-and-the-cobra-effect.

2. Adam Mann, "What's Up With That: Building Bigger Roads Actually Makes Traffic Worse," Wired, June 17, 2014, https://www.wired.com/2014/06/wuwt-traffic-induced-demand/.

3. Karl Evers-Hillstrom, "Lobbying Spending Reaches $3.4 Billion in 2018, Highest in 8 Years," OpenSecrets, Center for Responsive Politics, January 25, 2019, https://www.opensecrets.org/news/2019/01/lobbying-spending-reaches-3-4-billion-in-18/.

4. Lynn Grayson, "CERES Confirms Business Supports Climate Change Action," Jenner & Block, *Corporate Environmental Lawyer* (blog), December 2, 2015, https://environblog.jenner.com/corporate_environmental_l/2015/12/ceres-confirms-business-supports-climate-change-action.html.

5. World Bank, "State and Trends of Carbon Pricing 2020" (Washington, DC: World Bank, May 2020), https://openknowledge.worldbank.org/bitstream/handle/10986/33809/9781464815867.pdf?sequence=4.

6. Anne Kelly (Ceres), interview by authors, May 28, 2020.

7. Sharan Burrow (International Trade Union Confederation), interview by authors, May 18, 2020.

8. Gabriela Baczynska and Kate Abnett, "European Politicians, CEOs, Lawmakers Urge Green Coronavirus Recovery," Reuters, April 14, 2020, https://www.reuters.com/article/us-health-coronavirus-climatechange-reco-idUKKCN21W0F2. (These calls for actions could draw on some existing efforts to rethink policy and investment, such as the Club of Rome's "Planetary Emergency Plan" to invest in smart green growth.)

9. "Business for Nature," Business for Nature, https://www.businessfornature.org.

10. "A New Mandate to Lead in An Age of Anxiety," Edelman, accessed May 15, 2021, https://www.edelman.com/trust/2021-trust-barometer/insights/age-of-anxiety.

11. Fiona Harvey, "Industry alliance sets out $1bn to tackle oceans' plastic waste," *Guardian*, January 16, 2019, http://www.theguardian.com/environment/2019/jan/16/industry-alliance-sets-out-1bn-to-tackle-oceans-plastic-waste.

12. Sarah Parsons, "Unilever's Cruelty-Free Beauty Portfolio Now Includes Suave," Cosmetics Business, February 12, 2020, https://cosmeticsbusiness.com/news/article_page/Unilevers_cruelty-free_beauty_portfolio_now_includes_Suave/162313.

13. Tim Kleinebenne, interview by authors, September 9, 2020.

14. Duncan Clark, "Which Nations Are Most Responsible for Climate Change?" *Guardian*, April 21, 2011, http://www.theguardian.com/environment/2011/apr/21/countries-responsible-climate-change.

15. "Deforestation: Solved via Carbon Markets?" Environmental Defense Fund, accessed March 10, 2021, https://www.edf.org/climate/deforestation-solved-carbon-markets.

16. Data calculated from "Oilseeds: World Markets and Trade," Global Market Analysis, Foreign Agricultural Service/USDA, March 2021, https://apps.fas.usda.gov/psdonline/circulars/oilseeds.pdf, table 11.

17. Eoin Bannon, "Cars and Trucks Burn Almost Half of All Palm Oil Used in Europe," Transport & Environment, accessed March 26, 2021, https://www.transportenvironment.org/press/cars-and-trucks-burn-almost-half-all-palm-oil-used-europe.

18. Bhimanto Suwastoyo, "Activists Welcome New Indonesia Oil Palm Plantation Data but Want Follow-Ups," Palm Scribe, January 21, 2020, https://thepalmscribe.id/activists-welcome-new-indonesia-oil-palm-plantation-data-but-want-follow-ups/.

19. Gavin Neath (Unilever), interview by authors, April 10, 2020.

20. Rebecca Henderson, Hann-Shuin Yew, and Monica Baraldi, "Gotong Royong: Toward Sustainable Palm Oil," HBS Case 316-124 (Boston: Harvard Business School, 2016).

21. Henderson, Yew, and Baraldi, "Gotong Royong."

22. John Sauven (Greenpeace), interview by authors, April 27, 2020.

23. David Gilbert, "Unilever, World's Largest Palm Oil Buyer, Shows Leadership. Will Cargill?" Rainforest Action Network, *The Understory* (blog), December 11, 2009, https://www.ran.org/the-understory/unilever_world_s_largest_palm_oil_buyer _shows_leadership_will_cargill/.

24. Sauven, interview.

25. Impacts and Evaluation Division, *RSPO Impact Report 2016*, Kuala Lumpur: Roundtable on Sustainable Palm Oil, 2016, https://rspo.org/library/lib_files/preview/257.

26. Dominic Waughray (World Economic Forum), interview by authors, September 25, 2020.

27. Sauven, interview.

28. A. Muh and Ibnu Aquil, "Indonesia Reduces Deforestation Rate as Researchers Urge Caution," *Jakarta Post*, June 9, 2020, https://www.thejakartapost.com/news /2020/06/08/indonesia-reduces-deforestation-rate-as-researchers-urge-caution.html.

29. Eillie Anzilotti, "This Rwandan Factory Is Revolutionizing How Humanitarian Aid Is Done," *Fast Company*, June 8, 2017, https://www.fastcompany.com/40427006 /this-rwandan-factory-is-revolutionizing-how-humanitarian-aid-is-done.

30. Central Institute of Economic Management, Ministry of Planning and Investment, *Exploring the Links Between International Business and Socio-Economic Development of Vietnam: A Case Study of Unilever Vietnam*, Vietnam, 2009.

Chapter 8: Embrace the Elephants

1. Mindy Lubber (Ceres), interview by author, April 16, 2020.

2. Rupert Neate, "New Study Deems Amazon Worst for 'Aggressive' Tax Avoidance," *Guardian*, December 2, 2019, https://www.theguardian.com/business/2019/dec /02/new-study-deems-amazon-worst-for-aggressive-tax-avoidance.

3. Lorne Cook and Mike Corder, "Starbucks Court Ruling Deals Blow to EU Tax Break Fight," *San Diego Union-Tribune*, September 24, 2019, https://www.sandiego uniontribune.com/business/nation/story/2019-09-24/starbucks-court-ruling-deals -blow-to-eu-tax-break-fight.

4. Tabby Kinder, "Why the UK Tax Authority Is Accusing General Electric of a $1bn Fraud," *Financial Times*, August 4, 2020, https://www.ft.com/content/02a6fa1b -8b62-4e1e-9100-fe620c8ec96c.

5. Jesse Pound, "These 91 Companies Paid No Federal Taxes in 2018," CNBC, December 16, 2019, https://www.cnbc.com/2019/12/16/these-91-fortune-500-companies -didnt-pay-federal-taxes-in-2018.html.

6. Alan Murray and David Meyer, "The Unfinished Business of Stakeholder Capitalism," *Fortune*, January 12, 2021, https://fortune.com/2021/01/12/unfinished -business-of-stakeholder-capitalism-executive-ay-contract-workers-taxes-ceo-daily/.

7. OECD Centre for Tax Policy and Administration, "Revenue Statistics 2020— The United States," https://www.oecd.org/tax/revenue-statistics-united-states.pdf.

8. OECD Centre for Tax Policy and Administration, "Revenue Statistics 2020— Sweden," https://www.oecd.org/ctp/tax-policy/revenue-statistics-sweden.pdf.

9. "Countries Urged to Strengthen Tax Systems to Promote Inclusive Economic Growth," United Nations Department of Economic and Social Affairs, February 14, 2018, https://www.un.org/development/desa/en/news/financing/tax4dev.html.

10. *FACTI Panel Interim Report*, United Nations, September 2020, https://www .factipanel.org/documents/facti-panel-interim-report.

11. Bob Eccles (Saïd Business School at Oxford), email correspondence with author, August 31, 2020.

12. Janine Juggins (Unilever), conversation with author, September 20, 2020.

13. "A Responsible Taxpayer," Unilever, accessed March 8, 2021, https://www
.unilever.com/planet-and-society/responsible-business/responsible-taxpayer/.

14. *The Business Role in Creating a 21st-Century Social Contract*, Business for Social Responsibility, 2020, 28.

15. Janine Juggins (Unilever), conversation with author, September 20, 2020.

16. Sean Fleming, "Corruption Costs Developing Countries $1.26 Trillion Every
Year—Yet Half of EMEA Think It's Acceptable," World Economic Forum, December
9, 2019, https://www.weforum.org/agenda/2019/12/corruption-global-problem
-statistics-cost/.

17. *Ending Anonymous Companies: Tackling Corruption and Promoting Stability
through Beneficial Ownership Transparency*, The B Team, 2015.

18. "Partnering Against Corruption Initiative," World Economic Forum, accessed
March 14, 2021, https://www.weforum.org/communities/partnering-against
-corruption-initiative/.

19. *Ending Anonymous Companies*, 4.

20. David McCabe, "TikTok Bid Highlights Oracle's Public Embrace of Trump,"
New York Times, September 4, 2020, https://www.nytimes.com/2020/09/04
/technology/oracle-tiktok-trump.htm; Kelly Makena, "Oracle Founder Donated
$250,000 to Graham PAC in Final Days of TikTok Deal," The Verge, October 17, 2020,
https://www.theverge.com/2020/10/17/21520356/oracle-tiktok-larry-ellison-lindsey
-graham-super-pac-donation-jaime-harrison.

21. David Montero, "How Managers Should Respond When Bribes Are Business as
Usual," *Harvard Business Review*, November 16, 2018, https://hbr.org/2018/11/how
-managers-should-respond-when-bribes-are-business-as-usual.

22. "Nigeria's Ngozi Okonjo-Iweala's Mother Freed by Kidnappers," BBC, December 14, 2012, https://www.bbc.com/news/world-africa-20725677.

23. "CEO Pay Increased 14% in 2019, and Now Make 320 Times Their Typical
Workers," Economic Policy Institute, August 18, 2020, https://www.epi.org/press/ceo
-pay-increased-14-in-2019-and-now-make-320-times-their-typical-workers/.

24. Drew Desilver, "For Most Americans, Real Wages Have Barely Budged for Decades," August 7, 2018, https://www.pewresearch.org/fact-tank/2018/08/07/for-most
-us-workers-real-wages-have-barely-budged-for-decades/.

25. Theo Francis and Kristin Broughton, "CEO Pay Surged in a Year of Upheaval
and Leadership Challenges," *Wall Street Journal*, April 11, 2021, sec. Business, https://
www.wsj.com/articles/covid-19-brought-the-economy-to-its-knees-but-ceo-pay
-surged-11618142400.

26. "Pay Gap between CEOs and Average Workers, by Country 2018," Statista,
November 26, 2020, https://www.statista.com/statistics/424159/pay-gap-between-ceos
-and-average-workers-in-world-by-country/.

27. David Gelles, "The Mogul in Search of a Kinder, Gentler Capitalism," *New
York Times*, May 15, 2021, sec. Business, https://www.nytimes.com/2021/05/15
/business/lynn-forester-de-rothschild-corner-office.html.

28. Roger Lowenstein, "The (Expensive) Lesson GE Never Learns," *Washington
Post*, October 12, 2018, https://www.washingtonpost.com/business/the-expensive-lesson
-ge-never-learns/2018/10/12/6fb6aafa-ce30-11e8-a360-85875bac0b1f_story.html.

29. Andrew Edgecliffe-Johnson, "GE's Larry Culp Cites Pandemic Sacrifice to Defend $47m Bonus," *Financial Times*, January 26, 2021, https://www.ft.com/content
/2cce969c-80a7-4831-aadf-02c1394ac7ab.

30. Thomas Gryta, Theo Francis, and Drew FitzGerald, "General Electric, AT&T
Investors Reject CEO Pay Plans," *Wall Street Journal*, May 4, 2021, sec. Business,

https://www.wsj.com/articles/general-electric-at-t-investors-reject-ceo-pay-plans
-11620147204.

31. *The Business Role in Creating a 21st-Century Social Contract*, 29.

32. Adele Peters, "Gravity Payments Expands Its $70,000 Minimum Wage to Idaho Office," *Fast Company*, April 28, 2020, https://www.fastcompany.com/90477926 /gravity-payments-is-expanding-its-70000-minimum-wage-from-seattle-to-idaho.

33. William Lazonick et al., "Financialization of the U.S. Pharmaceutical Industry," *Institute for New Economic Thinking* (blog), December 2, 2019, https://www .ineteconomics.org/perspectives/blog/financialization-us-pharma-industry.

34. John R. Graham, Campbell R. Harvey, and Shiva Rajgopal, "The Economic Implications of Corporate Financial Reporting," *Journal of Accounting and Economics* 40 (December 2005): 3–73.

35. William Lazonick, Mustafa Erdem Sakinç, and Matt Hopkins, "Why Stock Buybacks Are Dangerous for the Economy," *Harvard Business Review*, January 7, 2020, https://hbr.org/2020/01/why-stock-buybacks-are-dangerous-for-the-economy.

36. Jonathon Ford, "Boeing and the Siren Call of Share Buybacks," *Financial Times*, August 4, 2019, https://www.ft.com/content/f3e640ee-b537-11e9-8cb2-799a3a8cf37b; "Boeing—Research (R&D) Spending 2006–2018," AeroWeb, http:// www.fi-aeroweb.com/firms/Research/Research-Boeing.html.

37. Rashaan Ayesh, "New Boeing CEO David Calhoun Criticizes Predecessor, Looks to Future," Axios, May 6, 2020, https://www.axios.com/new-boeing-ceo -criticizes-predecessor-looks-future-648df2a3-5973-492e-bb59-5f1cd35f9dc8.html.

38. "Predicting Long-Term Success for Corporations and Investors Worldwide," FCLTGlobal, September 29, 2019, https://www.fcltglobal.org/resource/predicting -long-term-success-for-corporations-and-investors-worldwide/.

39. "S&P 500 Buyback Index," S&P Dow Jones Indices, https://www.spglobal.com /spdji/en/indices/strategy/sp-500-buyback-index/#overview.

40. Saikat Chatterjee and Adinarayan Thyagaraju, "Buy, Sell, Repeat! No Room for 'Hold' in Whipsawing Markets," Reuters, August 3, 2020, https://www.reuters.com /article/us-health-coronavirus-short-termism-anal-idUSKBN24Z0XZ.

41. "Stewardship Code—Sustainable Investing," Robeco, November 16, 2020, https://www.robeco.com/en/key-strengths/sustainable-investing/glossary/stewardship -code.html.

42. Shaimaa Khalil, "Rio Tinto Chief Jean-Sébastien Jacques to Quit over Aboriginal Cave Destruction," BBC News, September 11, 2020, https://www.bbc.com/news /world-australia-54112991.

43. Ben Butler and Calla Wahlquist, "Rio Tinto Investors Welcome Chair's Decision to Step Down after Juukan Gorge Scandal," *Guardian*, March 3, 2021, http:// www.theguardian.com/business/2021/mar/03/rio-tinto-investors-welcome-chairs -decision-to-step-down-after-juukan-gorge-scandal.

44. Tensie Whelan, "U.S. Corporate Boards Suffer from Inadequate Expertise in Financially Material ESG Matters," NYU Stern Center for Sustainable Business, January 1, 2021, https://ssrn.com/abstract=3758584.

45. Tim Quinson, "Corporate Boards Don't Get the Climate Crisis: Green Insight," Bloomberg Green, January 13, 2021, https://www.bloomberg.com/news/articles /2021-01-13/corporate-boards-don-t-get-the-climate-crisis-green-insight.

46. Ceres, *Running the Risk: How Corporate Boards Can Oversee Environmental, Social and Governance (ESG) Issues*, November 2019, 6.

47. J. Yo-Jud Cheng, Boris Groysberg, and Paul Healy, "Your CEO Succession Plan Can't Wait," *Harvard Business Review*, May 4, 2020, https://hbr.org/2020/05/your-ceo -succession-plan-cant-wait; Karlsson Per-Ola, Martha Turner, and Peter Gassman,

"Succeeding the Long-Serving Legend in the Corner Office," *Strategy+Business*, Summer 2019, https://www.strategy-business.com/article/Succeeding-the-long-serving-legend-in-the-corner-office?gko=90171.

48. Deb DeHaas, Linda Akutagawa, and Skip Spriggs, "Missing Pieces Report: The 2018 Board Diversity Census of Women and Minorities on Fortune 500 Boards," *The Harvard Law School Forum on Corporate Governance* (blog), February 5, 2019, https://corpgov.law.harvard.edu/2019/02/05/missing-pieces-report-the-2018-board-diversity-census-of-women-and-minorities-on-fortune-500-boards/.

49. Richard Samans and Jane Nelson, "Integrated Corporate Governance: Six Leadership Priorities for Boards beyond the Crisis," *Forbes*, June 18, 2020, https://www.forbes.com/sites/worldeconomicforum/2020/06/18/integrated-corporate-governance-six-leadership-priorities-for-boards-beyond-the-crisis/.

50. "40 Million in Modern Slavery and 152 Million in Child Labour around the World," International Labour Organization, September 19, 2017, http://www.ilo.org/global/about-the-ilo/newsroom/news/WCMS_574717/lang--en/index.htm.

51. *Global Estimates of Modern Slavery: Forced Labour and Forced Marriage*, International Labour Office, 2017, 25.

52. "Nearly Half of Global Workforce at Risk as Job Losses Increase Due to COVID-19: UN Labour Agency," UN News, April 29, 2020, https://news.un.org/en/story/2020/04/1062792.

53. Rosey Hurst (Impactt), interview by authors, October 1, 2020.

54. *Corporate Human Rights Benchmark, 2019 Key Findings*, World Benchmarking Alliance, 2019, 4.

55. *Corporate Human Rights Benchmark, 2020 Key Findings*, World Benchmarking Alliance, 2020.

56. "Investors BlackRock, NBIM and CalSTRS vote against Top Glove directors after quarter of workforce reportedly contract COVID-19," Business & Human Rights Resource Centre, January 7, 2021, https://www.business-humanrights.org/fr/derni%C3%A8res-actualit%C3%A9s/investors-blackrock-nbim-vote-against-top-glove-directors-after-a-quarter-of-its-workforce-reportedly-contracted-covid-19/.

57. Sharan Burrow (International Trade Union Confederation), interview by authors, May 18, 2020.

58. Jane Moyo, "Gap Inc. Publishes Its Supplier List to Boost Supply Chain Transparency," *Ethical Trading Initiative* (blog), December 2, 2016, https://www.ethicaltrade.org/blog/gap-inc-publishes-its-supplier-list-to-boost-supply-chain-transparency.

59. "Billionaires Got 54% Richer during Pandemic, Sparking Calls for 'Wealth Tax,'" CBS News, accessed May 27, 2021, https://www.cbsnews.com/news/billionaire-wealth-covid-pandemic-12-trillion-jeff-bezos-wealth-tax/.

60. Nichola Groom, "Big Oil Outspends Billionaires in Washington State Carbon Tax Fight," Reuters, October 31, 2018, https://www.reuters.com/article/us-usa-election-carbon/big-oil-outspends-billionaires-in-washington-state-carbon-tax-fight-idUSKCN1N51H7.

61. Center for Responsive Politics, "US Chamber of Commerce Profile," OpenSecrets, https://www.opensecrets.org/orgs/us-chamber-of-commerce/summary?id=D000019798. OpenSecrets tracks 5,500 organizations and their lobbying spending. The Chamber topped them all.

62. Amy Meyer, Kevin Moss, and Eliot Metzger, "Despite Shared Membership, US Chamber of Commerce and Business Roundtable at Odds over Climate Policy," *World Resources Institute* (blog), October 19, 2020, https://www.wri.org/blog/2020/10/us-chamber-commerce-business-roundtable-odds-over-climate-policy.

63. David Roberts, "These Senators Are Going After the Biggest Climate Villains in Washington," Vox, November 18, 2019, https://www.vox.com/energy-and -environment/2019/6/7/18654957/climate-change-lobbying-chamber-of-commerce.

64. "CVS Health Leaves U.S. Chamber of Commerce," *Washington Post*, July 7, 2015, https://www.washingtonpost.com/news/wonk/wp/2015/07/07/cvs-health-leaves -u-s-chamber-of-commerce/.

65. Hal Bernton and Evan Bush, "Energy Politics: Why Oil Giant BP Wants Washington Lawmakers to Put a Price on Carbon Pollution," *Seattle Times*, January 21, 2020, https://www.seattletimes.com/seattle-news/politics/new-bp-ad-campaign-calls -on-washington-legislature-to-put-a-price-on-carbon-pollution-from-fossil-fuels/.

66. Steven Mufson, "French Oil Giant Total Quits American Petroleum Institute," *Washington Post*, January 15, 2021, https://www.washingtonpost.com/climate -environment/2021/01/15/french-oil-giant-total-quits-american-petroleum-institute/.

67. Andrew Berger, "Brandeis and the History of Transparency," *Sunlight Foundation* (blog), May 26, 2009, https://sunlightfoundation.com/2009/05/26/brandeis-and -the-history-of-transparency/.

68. "Financing Democracy: Funding of Political Parties and Election Campaigns and the Risk of Policy Capture" (Paris: Organisation for Economic Co-operation and Development, 2016), https://www.oecd-ilibrary.org/governance/financing-democracy _9789264249455-en, Table 2.6.

69. Alex Blumberg, "Forget Stocks or Bonds, Invest in a Lobbyist," *Morning Edition*, January 6, 2012, https://www.npr.org/sections/money/2012/01/06/144737864 /forget-stocks-or-bonds-invest-in-a-lobbyist.

70. Alan Zibel, "Nearly Two Thirds of Former Members of 115th Congress Working Outside Politics and Government Have Picked Up Lobbying or Strategic Consulting Jobs," Public Citizen, May 30, 2019, https://www.citizen.org/article/revolving -congress/.

71. "Corporate Carbon Policy Footprint—the 50 Most Influential," InfluenceMap, October 2019, https://influencemap.org/report/Corporate-Climate-Policy-Footpint -2019-the-50-Most-Influential-7d09a06d9c4e602a3d2f5c1ae13301b8.

72. Andrew Ross Sorkin, "IBM Doesn't Donate to Politicians. Other Firms Should Take Note," *New York Times*, January 12, 2021, https://www.nytimes.com/2021/01/12 /business/dealbook/political-donations-ibm.html.

73. *Diversity Wins: How Inclusion Matters*," McKinsey & Company, May 2020, 4, https://www.mckinsey.com/~/media/mckinsey/featured%20insights/diversity%20 and%20inclusion/diversity%20wins%20how%20inclusion%20matters/diversity-wins -how-inclusion-matters-vf.pdf.

74. Vijay Eswaran, "The Business Case for Diversity in the Workplace Is Now Overwhelming," World Economic Forum, April 29, 2019, https://www.weforum.org /agenda/2019/04/business-case-for-diversity-in-the-workplace/.

75. Sarah Coury et al., "Women in the Workplace," McKinsey & Company, September 30, 2020, https://www.mckinsey.com/featured-insights/diversity-and-inclusion /women-in-the-workplace#.

76. "The Top Jobs Where Women Are Outnumbered by Men Named John," *New York Times*, The Upshot (blog), April 24, 2018, https://www.nytimes.com/interactive /2018/04/24/upshot/women-and-men-named-john.html?mtrref=undefined&gwh =02D75850C7633B545BCB33CF0AD30264&gwt=regi&assetType=REGIWALL.

77. Ellen McGirt and Aric Jenkins, "Where Are the Black CEOs?" *Fortune*, February 4, 2021, https://fortune.com/2021/02/04/black-ceos-fortune-500/.

78. Lesley Slaton Brown, "HP Unveils Bold Goals to Advance Racial Equality and Social Justice," HP Development Company, L.P., *HP Press Blogs* (blog), January 15,

2021, https://press.hp.com/us/en/blogs/2021/HP-unveils-bold-goals-to-advance-racial-equality.html.

79. Caroline Casey, "Do Your D&I Efforts Include People with Disabilities?" *Harvard Business Review*, March 19, 2020, https://hbr.org/2020/03/do-your-di-efforts-include-people-with-disabilities.

80. "Work and Employment," *World Report on Disability*, World Health Organization, 2011, 242.

81. *Getting to Equal: The Disability Inclusion Advantage*, Accenture, 2018, 4.

82. Silvia Bonaccio et al., "The Participation of People with Disabilities in the Workplace across the Employment Cycle: Employer Concerns and Research Evidence," *Journal of Business and Psychology* 35, no. 2 (2020): 135–158, https://doi.org/10.1007/s10869-018-9602-5; Valentini Kalargyrou, "People with Disabilities: A New Model of Productive Labor," Proceedings of the 2012 Advances in Hospitality and Tourism Marketing and Management Conference, Corfu, Greece, 2012, https://scholars.unh.edu/cgi/viewcontent.cgi?article=1017&context=hospman_facpub.

83. "Disability Inclusion Overview," World Bank, October 1, 2020, https://www.worldbank.org/en/topic/disability; *Design Delight from Disability—Report Summary: The Global Economics of Disability*, Rod-Group, September 1, 2020, 3; calculated from statistic that 52 percent of GDP in the EU is household spending, and GDP is twenty-one trillion: "Household Consumption by Purpose," Eurostat, November 2020, https://ec.europa.eu/eurostat/statistics-explained/index.php/Household_consumption_by_purpose.

84. Tim Cook (Apple), in keynote speech at Ceres 30th Anniversary event, New York, October 21, 2019.

85. "Goldman's Playbook for More Diverse Corporate Boards," *New York Times*, January 24, 2020, https://www.nytimes.com/2020/01/24/business/dealbook/goldman-diversity-boardroom.html.

86. Sarah Coury et al., "Women in the Workplace."

87. "Unilever achieves gender balance across management globally," Unilever global company website, accessed March 14, 2021, https://www.unilever.com/news/press-releases/2020/unilever-achieves-gender-balance-across-management-globally.html.

88. David Bell, Dawn Belt, and Jennifer Hitchcock, "New Law Requires Diversity on Boards of California-Based Companies," *The Harvard Law School Forum on Corporate Governance* (blog), October 10, 2020, https://corpgov.law.harvard.edu/2020/10/10/new-law-requires-diversity-on-boards-of-california-based-companies/.

89. "OneTen," accessed March 9, 2021, https://www.oneten.org/.

Chapter 9: Culture Is the Glue

1. Alan Jope (Unilever), interview by authors, July 8, 2020.

2. Natalie Kitroeff, "Boeing Employees Mocked F.A.A. and 'Clowns' Who Designed 737 Max," *New York Times,* January 10, 2020, https://www.nytimes.com/2020/01/09/business/boeing-737-messages.html.

3. Jim Harter and Kristi Rubenstein, "The 38 Most Engaged Workplaces in the World Put People First," Gallup, accessed March 5, 2021, https://www.gallup.com/workplace/290573/engaged-workplaces-world-put-people-first.aspx.

4. Jeff Hollender (Seventh Generation), interview by authors, August 11, 2020.

5. Jope, interview.

6. Emily Graffeo, "Companies with More Women in Management Have Outperformed Their More Male-Led Peers, According to Goldman Sachs," Markets, Business

Insider, November 11, 2020, https://markets.businessinsider.com/news/stocks
/companies-women-management-leadership-stock-market-outpeformance-goldman
-sachs-female-2020-11-1029793278.

7. "Bloomberg's 2021 Gender-Equality Index Reveals Increased Disclosure as
Companies Reinforce Commitment to Inclusive Workplaces," Bloomberg L.P., press
announcement, accessed March 23, 2021, https://www.bloomberg.com/company/press
/bloombergs-2021-gender-equality-index-reveals-increased-disclosure-as-companies
-reinforce-commitment-to-inclusive-workplaces/; "Bloomberg Opens Data Submis-
sion Period for 2021 Gender-Equality Index," Bloomberg L.P., press announcement,
June 1, 2020, https://www.bloomberg.com/company/press/bloomberg-opens-data
-submission-period-for-2021-gender-equality-index/.

8. James Ledbetter, "The Saga of Sundial: How Richelieu Dennis Escaped War,
Hustled in Harlem, and Created a Top Skin Care Brand," *Inc.*, September 2019, https://
www.inc.com/magazine/201909/james-ledbetter/richelieu-dennis-sundial-shea-butter
-black-skin-care-liberia-refugee.html.

9. Elaine Watson, "Sir Kensington's Joins Unilever: 'This Allows Us to Expand
Distribution While Holding True to Our Values,'" *Food Navigator*, April 20, 2017,
https://www.foodnavigator-usa.com/Article/2017/04/21/Sir-Kensington-s-joins
-Unilever-in-bid-to-scale-more-rapidly.

10. Hollender, interview.

11. John Replogle (Seventh Generation), interview by authors, July 28, 2020.

12. Kees Kruythoff (Unilever), interview by authors, October 5, 2020.

13. "Unilever's Purpose-Led Brands Outperform," Unilever global company website, accessed March 6, 2021, https://www.unilever.com/news/press-releases/2019
/unilevers-purpose-led-brands-outperform.html.

14. *Lifebuoy Way of Life Social Mission Report 2019*, Unilever, 2019. All of the statistics in this section are from this report.

15. "UK Aid and Unilever to Target a Billion People in Global Handwashing
Campaign," UK Government - Department for International Development, March 26,
2020, https://www.gov.uk/government/news/uk-aid-and-unilever-to-target-a-billion
-people-in-global-handwashing-campaign.

16. Shawn Paustian, "Insights from the New Brand Builders, Part 2," *Numerator*
(blog), June 4, 2019, https://www.numerator.com/resources/blog/insights-new-brand
-builders-part-2.

17. Sanjiv Mehta (Unilever), interview by authors, October 21, 2020.

18. Keith Weed (Unilever), interview by authors, November 10, 2020. Weed provided all data on the findings of the Unstereotype Alliance.

19. "Launch of Unstereotype Alliance Set to Eradicate Outdated Stereotypes in
Advertising," Unilever global company website, June 20, 2017, https://www.unilever
.com/news/press-releases/2017/launch-of-unstereotype-alliance-set-to-eradicate
-outdated-stereotypes-in-advertising.html.

20. Weed, interview.

21. Brett Molina, "Unilever Drops 'Normal' from Beauty Products to Support
Inclusivity," accessed March 14, 2021, https://www.usatoday.com/story/money
/2021/03/09/unilever-drops-normal-beauty-products-support-inclusivity/46411
60001/.

22. "Ending the Gun Violence Epidemic in America," Levi Strauss & Co, September 4, 2018, https://www.levistrauss.com/2018/09/04/ending-gun-violence/.

23. Walt Bogdanich and Michael Forsythe. "How McKinsey Has Helped Raise the
Stature of Authoritarian Governments." *New York Times,* December 15, 2018, https://
www.nytimes.com/2018/12/15/world/asia/mckinsey-china-russia.html.

24. Andrew Edgecliffe-Johnson, "McKinsey to Pay Almost $574m to Settle Opioid Claims by US States," *Financial Times*, February 4, 2021, https://www.ft.com/content/85e84e12-6dda-4c91-bde4-8198e29a6767.

25. Tom Peters, "McKinsey's Work on Opioid Sales Represents a New Low," *Financial Times*, February 15, 2021, https://www.ft.com/content/82e98478-f099-44ac-b014-3f9b15fe6bc6.

Chapter 10: Net Positive World

1. "Rate of Deforestation," TheWorldCounts, accessed March 7, 2021, https://www.theworldcounts.com/challenges/planet-earth/forests-and-deserts/rate-of-deforestation/story.

2. "Top 20 Largest California Wildfires," State of California Department of Forestry and Fire Protection, accessed March 10, 2021, https://www.fire.ca.gov/media/4jandlhh/top20_acres.pdf.

3. "Al Gore's Generation Raises $1 Billion for Latest Private Equity Fund," Reuters, May 21, 2019, https://www.reuters.com/article/uk-generation-investment-fund-idUKKCN1SR1LY.

4. "Half of Millennial Employees Have Spoken Out about Employer Actions on Hot-Button Issues," Cision PR Newswire, accessed March 6, 2021, https://www.prnewswire.com/news-releases/half-of-millennial-employees-have-spoken-out-about-employer-actions-on-hot-button-issues-300857881.html.

5. Siobhan Riding, "ESG Funds Forecast to Outnumber Conventional Funds by 2025," *Financial Times*, October 17, 2020, https://www.ft.com/content/5cd6e923-81e0-4557-8cff-a02fb5e01d42.

6. Moody's Investors Service, "Sustainable Bond Issuance to Hit a Record $650 Billion in 2021," February 4, 2021, https://www.moodys.com/research/Moodys-Sustainable-bond-issuance-to-hit-a-record-650-billion--PBC_1263479.

7. Donella Meadows, "Leverage Points: Places to Intervene in a System," *The Academy for Systems Change* (blog), accessed March 26, 2021, http://donellameadows.org/archives/leverage-points-places-to-intervene-in-a-system/.

8. Roc Sandford and Rupert Read, "Breakingviews—Guest View: Let's Gauge Firms' Real CO2 Footprints," Reuters, August 14, 2020, https://www.reuters.com/article/us-global-economy-climatechange-breaking-idUKKCN25A1AO.

9. Solitaire Townsend, "We Urgently Need 'Scope X' Business Leadership for Climate," *Forbes*, June 29, 2020, https://www.forbes.com/sites/solitairetownsend/2020/06/29/we-urgently-need-scope-x-business-leadership-for-climate/.

10. Microsoft News Center, "Microsoft Commits $500 Million to Tackle Affordable Housing Crisis in Puget Sound Region," January 17, 2019, https://news.microsoft.com/2019/01/16/microsoft-commits-500-million-to-tackle-affordable-housing-crisis-in-puget-sound-region/.

11. Isaac Stone Fish, "Opinion: Why Disney's New 'Mulan' Is a Scandal," *Washington Post*, September 7, 2020, https://www.washingtonpost.com/opinions/2020/09/07/why-disneys-new-mulan-is-scandal/.

12. G. Calvo et al., "Decreasing Ore Grades in Global Metallic Mining: A Theoretical Issue or a Global Reality?" 2016, https://doi.org/10.3390/resources504003.

13. "Goal 12: Ensure Sustainable Consumption and Production Patterns," *United Nations Sustainable Development Goals*, accessed March 6, 2021, https://www.un.org/sustainabledevelopment/sustainable-consumption-production/.

14. Hunter Lovins, interview by authors, February 25, 2021.

15. "CGR 2021," accessed March 14, 2021, https://www.circularity-gap.world/2021; Scott Johnson, "Just 20 Percent of E-Waste Is Being Recycled," Ars Technica, December 13, 2017, https://arstechnica.com/science/2017/12/just-20-percent-of-e-waste-is -being-recycled/; Dana Gunders, "Wasted: How America Is Losing Up to 40 Percent of Its Food from Farm to Fork to Landfill," NRDC, August 16, 2017, https://www.nrdc .org/resources/wasted-how-america-losing-40-percent-its-food-farm-fork-landfill.

16. Adele Peters, "How Eileen Fisher Thinks about Sustainable Consumption," *Fast Company*, October 31, 2019, https://www.fastcompany.com/90423555/how-eileen -fisher-thinks-about-sustainable-consumption.

17. Antonia Wilson, "Dutch Airline KLM Calls for People to Fly Less," *Guardian*, July 11, 2019, http://www.theguardian.com/travel/2019/jul/11/dutch-airline-klm-calls -for-people-to-fly-less-carbon-offsetting-scheme.

18. Derrick Bryson Taylor, "Ikea Will Buy Back Some Used Furniture," *New York Times*, October 14, 2020, https://www.nytimes.com/2020/10/14/business/ikea-buy -back-furniture.html.

19. Solitaire Townsend, "Near 80% of People Would Personally Do as Much for Climate as They Have for Coronavirus," *Forbes*, June 1, 2020, https://www.forbes.com /sites/solitairetownsend/2020/06/01/near-80-of-people-would-personally-do-as-much -for-climate-as-they-have-for-coronavirus/.

20. Juliet Schor, "Less Work, More Living," Daily Good, January 12, 2012, https:// www.dailygood.org/story/130/less-work-more-living-juliet-schor/.

21. "'Live Simply So Others May Simply Live,' Gandhi," *Natural Living School* (blog), April 23, 2012, https://naturallivingschool.com/2012/04/22/live-simply-so -others-may-simply-live-gandhi/.

22. Simon Rogers, "Bobby Kennedy on GDP: 'Measures Everything except That Which Is Worthwhile,'" *Guardian*, May 24, 2012, http://www.theguardian.com/news /datablog/2012/may/24/robert-kennedy-gdp.

23. L. Hunter Lovins et al., *A Finer Future: Creating an Economy in Service to Life* (Gabriola Island, BC, Canada: New Society Publishers, 2018), 3.

24. Romina Boarini et al., "What Makes for a Better Life? The Determinants of Subjective Well-Being in OECD Countries—Evidence from the Gallup World Poll," working paper, OECD, May 21, 2012, https://doi.org/10.1787/5k9b9ltjm937-en.

25. Belinda Luscombe, "Do We Need $75,000 a Year to Be Happy?" *Time*, September 6, 2010, http://content.time.com/time/magazine/article/0,9171,2019628,00.html.

26. Sigal Samuel, "Forget GDP—New Zealand Is Prioritizing Gross National Well-Being," Vox, June 8, 2019, https://www.vox.com/future-perfect/2019/6/8 /18656710/new-zealand-wellbeing-budget-bhutan-happiness.

27. David Roberts, "None of the World's Top Industries Would Be Profitable If They Paid for the Natural Capital They Use," *Grist* (blog), April 17, 2013, https://grist .org/business-technology/none-of-the-worlds-top-industries-would-be-profitable-if -they-paid-for-the-natural-capital-they-use/.

28. "Crédit Agricole," Wikipedia, accessed March 1, 2021.

29. "The Business Role in Creating a 21st-Century Social Contract," BSR, June 24, 2020, https://www.bsr.org/en/our-insights/report-view/business-role-creating-a-21st -century-social-contract.

30. "Finance for a Regenerative World," Capital Institute, accessed March 7, 2021, https://capitalinstitute.org/finance-for-a-regenerative-world/.

31. "Coronavirus May Push 150 Million People into Extreme Poverty: World Bank," Reuters, October 7, 2020, https://www.reuters.com/article/us-imf-worldbank -poverty-idUSKBN26S2RV.

32. Sapana Agrawal et al., "To Emerge Stronger from the COVID-19 Crisis, Companies Should Start Reskilling Their Workforces Now," McKinsey & Company, May 7, 2020, https://www.mckinsey.com/business-functions/organization/our-insights /to-emerge-stronger-from-the-covid-19-crisis-companies-should-start-reskilling -their-workforces-now#.

33. International Labour Organization, *Global Employment Trends for Youth 2020: Technology and the Future of Jobs* (Geneva: International Labour Office, 2020), https://www.ilo.org/wcmsp5/groups/public/---dgreports/---dcomm/---publ /documents/publication/wcms_737648.pdf

34. Ronald McQuaid, "Youth Unemployment Produces Multiple Scarring Effects," *London School of Economics* (blog), February 18, 2017, https://blogs.lse.ac.uk/europp blog/2017/02/18/youth-unemployment-scarring-effects/.

35. Sunny Verghese (Olam), interview by authors, June 3, 2020.

36. Melanie Kaplan, "At Greyston Bakery, Open Hiring Changes Lives," *US News and World Report*, June 5, 2019, https://www.usnews.com/news/healthiest-communities /articles/2019-06-05/at-greyston-bakery-open-hiring-changes-lives.

37. United Nations High Commissioner for Refugees, "UNHCR—Refugee Statistics," accessed March 7, 2021, https://www.unhcr.org/refugee-statistics/.

38. Luke Baker, "More Than 1 Billion People Face Displacement by 2050—Report," Reuters, September 9, 2020, https://www.reuters.com/article/ecology-global -risks-idUSKBN2600K4.

39. Ezra Fieser, "Yogurt Billionaire's Solution to World Refugee Crisis: Hire Them," Bloomberg Business, August 28, 2019, https://www.bloomberg.com/news /articles/2019-08-28/yogurt-billionaire-s-solution-to-world-refugee-crisis-hire-them.

40. "Unilever Commits to Help Build a More Inclusive Society," Unilever global company website, January 21, 2021, https://www.unilever.com/news/press-releases /2021/unilever-commits-to-help-build-a-more-inclusive-society.html.

41. Eben Shapiro, "Walmart CEO Doug McMillon: We Need to Reinvent Capitalism," *Time*, October 22, 2020, https://time.com/collection/great-reset/5900765/walmart -ceo-reinventing-capitalism/.

42. "10 Bold Statements on Advancing Stakeholder Capitalism in 2020," *JUST Capital* (blog), accessed March 7, 2021, https://justcapital.com/news/bold-statements-on -advancing-stakeholder-capitalism/.

43. *2020 Edelman Trust Barometer*, Edelman, January 2020, https://www.edelman. com/trust/2020-trust-barometer.

44. "Annual Survey Shows Rise in Support for Socialism, Communism," Victims of Communism Memorial Foundation, October 21, 2020, https://victimsofcommunism .org/annual-survey-shows-rise-in-support-for-socialism-communism/.

45. There's no way to capture all the people doing great work on rethinking capitalism. You could honestly go back to Marx. But in modern times, you can look for work by Gar Alperowitz, Bob Costanza, Michael Dorsey, John Elkington, John Fullerton, Stu Hart, Rebecca Henderson, Jeffrey Hollender, Hunter Lovins, Colin Mayer, Mariana Mazzucato, Njeri Mwagiru, Jonathon Porritt, Kate Raworth, Bob Reich, and Tony Seba, Raj Sisodia, and Pavan Sukhdev. The field is growing fast, so this list is only a sample.

46. "LVMH Carbon Fund Reaches 2018 Objective Two Years after Its Creation with 112 Projects Funded," LVMH, accessed March 12, 2021, https://www.lvmh.com /news-documents/press-releases/lvmh-carbon-fund-reaches-2018-objective-two-years -after-its-creation-with-112-projects-funded/.

47. "Sustainability Information 2020," Munich: Siemens, 2020, https://assets.new

.siemens.com/siemens/assets/api/uuid:13f56263-0d96-421c-a6a4-9c10bb9b9d28
/sustainability2020-en.pdf.

48. Brad Smith, "One Year Later: The Path to Carbon Negative—a Progress Report on Our Climate 'Moonshot,'" *The Official Microsoft Blog* (blog), January 28, 2021, https://blogs.microsoft.com/blog/2021/01/28/one-year-later-the-path-to-carbon -negative-a-progress-report-on-our-climate-moonshot/.

49. Eric Roston and Will Wade, "Top Economists Warn U.S. Against Underestimating Climate Damage," Bloomberg Quint, February 15, 2021, https://www .bloombergquint.com/onweb/top-economists-warn-u-s-against-underestimating -climate-damage.

50. Sean Fleming, "How Much Is Nature Worth? $125 Trillion, According to This Report," World Economic Forum, October 30, 2018, https://www.weforum.org /agenda/2018/10/this-is-why-putting-a-price-on-the-value-of-nature-could-help-the -environment/.

51. "Natural Capital Protocol," Capitals Coalition, accessed March 7, 2021, https:// capitalscoalition.org/capitals-approach/natural-capital-protocol/.

52. "Finance for a Regenerative World," *Capital Institute* (blog), accessed March 7, 2021, https://capitalinstitute.org/finance-for-a-regenerative-world/.

53. Kathleen Madigan, "Like the Phoenix, U.S. Finance Profits Soar," *Wall Street Journal*, March 25, 2011, https://www.wsj.com/articles/BL-REB-13616.

54. Tim Youmans and Robert Eccles, "Why Boards Must Look Beyond Shareholders," *MIT Sloan Management Review*, Leading Sustainable Organizations, September 3, 2015, https://sloanreview.mit.edu/article/why-boards-must-look-beyond -shareholders/.

55. Fiduciary Duty. *Fiduciary Duty in the 21st Century—from a Legal Case to Regulatory Clarification around ESG*, 2019, YouTube, uploaded by PRI, November 22, 2019, https://www.youtube.com/watch?v=t_EK1pPPLBo.

56. Andrew Liveris (FCLTGlobal), interview by authors, August 27, 2020.

57. Hiro Mizuno, interview by authors, April 27, 2020.

58. "The B Team: The Business Case for Protecting Civic Rights," The B Team, accessed May 30, 2021, https://bteam.org/our-thinking/reports/the-business-case-for -protecting-civic-rights.

59. "Country Rating Changes—Civicus Monitor 2020," accessed July 15, 2021, https://findings2020.monitor.civicus.org/rating-changes.html.

60. Henry Foy, "McKinsey's Call for Political Neutrality Only Serves Vladimir Putin," January 27, 2021, *Financial Times*, https://www.ft.com/content/6110fe11-98e4 -42ec-9522-f86d0a458ea2.

61. "How Facebook's Rise Fueled Chaos and Confusion in Myanmar," *Wired*, accessed March 14, 2021, https://www.wired.com/story/how-facebooks-rise-fueled -chaos-and-confusion-in-myanmar/.

62. Daniel Arkin, "U.N. Says Facebook Has 'Turned into a Beast' in Violence-Plagued Myanmar," NBC News, accessed March 14, 2021, https://www.nbcnews.com /news/world/u-n-investigators-blame-facebook-spreading-hate-against-rohingya -myanmar-n856191.

63. Ash Turner, "How Many People Have Smartphones Worldwide," bankmycell (blog), July 10, 2018, accessed March 2021, https://www.bankmycell.com/blog/how -many-phones-are-in-the-world.

64. "The Nobel Peace Prize 2004," NobelPrize.org, accessed March 12, 2021, https://www.nobelprize.org/prizes/peace/2004/maathai/26050-wangari-maathai -nobel-lecture-2004/.

INDEX

ABOUT THE AUTHORS

PAUL POLMAN works to accelerate action by business to achieve the UN Global Goals, which he helped develop. He was the CEO of Unilever from 2009 to 2019 and has been described by the *Financial Times* as "a standout CEO of the past decade."

ANDREW WINSTON is one of the world's leading thinkers on sustainable business strategy. He is a sought-after adviser and speaker on how to build thriving companies that profit by serving the world, and the author of the books *Green to Gold* and *The Big Pivot*.